WILL CATHOLICS BE "LEFT BEHIND"?

MODERN APOLOGETICS LIBRARY

CARL E. OLSON

WILL CATHOLICS BE "LEFT BEHIND"?

*A Catholic Critque of the Rapture
and Today's Prophecy Preachers*

IGNATIUS PRESS   SAN FRANCISCO

Cover design by Roxanne Mei Lum

ISBN 0–89870–950–4
Library of Congress Control Number 2002114409
Printed in the United States of America

To Felicity Rose Olson
who interrupted the writing of this book
and added a beautiful and unexpected
chapter to our lives

CONTENTS

ACKNOWLEDGMENTS

I want to thank Mark Brumley and Fr. Mitch Pacwa for providing encouragement, exhortation, and advice, especially when it seemed as though the world might end before my first draft was finished. I am very appreciative of Catholic Answers and *This Rock*; the idea for this book originated from my article "Waiting for the Rapture in America", featured in the April 1999 issue of *This Rock*.

I am indebted to friends who have helped in ways big and small: Ann Applegarth, Harold Burke-Sivers, Mel Damewood, Ruth Hayes-Barba, Jeff Lang, Deacon Jack Luz, Patrick Madrid, Greg Oatis, Ted Robertson, and Mark Svarverud. A special thanks to Donald Jacob Uitvlugt for carefully reading my first draft and providing a good dose of constructive criticism, to Rick Rencher for graciously sharing his theological acumen and warm hospitality, and to Dr. Paul Thigpen for generously exchanging thoughts and ideas about the topics addressed in this book.

I also wish to express appreciation for numerous permissions to quote various works. These are listed below on page 393.

Finally, I could never repay the debt I owe to my wife Heather. This book would have never come to fruition without her saintly patience and unflagging encouragement.

WILL CATHOLICS BE "LEFT BEHIND"?
AN INTRODUCTION

> The Scripture clearly distinguishes between two different parts of Christ's Second Coming—His return in the air to rapture His saints to heaven and His return to the earth at Armageddon with His saints.... The Rapture must occur without warning at some point in time before the events of the Tribulation period.
>
> —Grant Jeffrey

> In Case of the Rapture, This Car Will Be Unmanned!
>
> —Popular bumper sticker

What is the Rapture?

You have likely heard the word—perhaps you even use it. In Christian circles it comes up in conversation quite often, and a growing number of Catholics are curious about it. More and more Catholics are learning about the Rapture—and believing in it. Other Catholics are wondering "What *is* the Rapture? Does the Catholic Church believe in it?" Other questions lurk just beneath the surface: Is the Rapture just another term for Christ's Second Coming? Is it a secret "snatching away" of Christians to heaven prior to a final tribulation at the end of the world? Doesn't the Bible mention the Rapture in several different places? What does the Catholic Church teach about the end of the world, the Antichrist, and a coming tribulation? What about the mark of the beast and the whore of Babylon? Although Catholics are asking these questions, good answers are often hard to find. In addition, an increasing number of non-Catholic Christians are curious about what the Catholic Church teaches on the same issues, but they cannot find a convenient source that addresses them in a single, accessible volume.

A knowledgeable Catholic friend recently asked me: "Why would a Catholic write a book on the Rapture?" The answer is simple: There is a serious need for a detailed examination of this topic from a Catholic perspective. There is much confusion about the issue, especially among Catholics who are serious about knowing their faith, who spend time explaining it to others, and who defend it against attacks made by anti-Catholic groups and authors. Recently I was talking to a devout and highly intelligent Catholic, Ron, who often goes door to door telling people about the Catholic faith. When I asked him which question, in his experience, was the most difficult to answer, he had a surprising reply: "One day I got into a conversation with a husband and wife who told me they were Bible Christians. They asked me if I had read a book called *Left Behind*, by Tim LaHaye, and I told them I had not. They started talking about the Rapture and their belief that the Bible predicts it will occur in the very near future." Ron told me that he had no idea what they were talking about and went away puzzled. He asked me: "Is there a book about this subject written from the Catholic viewpoint?" I have met other Catholics like Ron, and this book is meant to help them better understand this confusing and complicated issue.

I was raised in an anti-Catholic, Fundamentalist[1] home and believed, into my early adult years, that the secret and silent "snatching" of "true believers" from the earth—the Rapture—would occur in my lifetime. This mysterious event was not to be confused with Christ's Second Coming. Rather, it would occur just before a time of great tribulation and terror, therefore the more specific description was *pretribulation Rapture*. This event would mark the start of the prophetic clock whose hands would wind their way through the cataclysmic events leading up to that glorious and public return of Jesus Christ.

As this book will seek to demonstrate, belief in the Rapture is not an isolated or peripheral point of faith for those who adhere to it. It is the heart of a unique and complex view of the Bible, the world, the Kingdom and Israel, and the end of time. From an early age I learned the principles of this theological system, called *dispensationalism*,[2] developing

[1] Even though the terms Fundamentalism and Evangelicalism are somewhat vague, I attempt to use them, in general, in the same manner that self-described Fundamentalists and Evangelicals use them. For example, Tim LaHaye and Hal Lindsey describe themselves as Fundamentalists, meaning they are conservative Protestants who uphold the inerrancy of Scripture, the divinity of Jesus Christ, the need for salvation through Christ alone, and a belief in the Second Coming. While many Evangelicals, such as Charles Colson, Billy Graham, and Mark Noll, uphold the same beliefs, they are open to a much wider range of scholarship, interact far more with the prevailing culture, and accept Catholicism as being Christian, even while having reservations about certain Catholic doctrines. Many Evangelicals have just as many—or more—reservations about premillennial dispensationalism and the belief in a pretribulation Rapture.

[2] The term *dispensationalism* will be defined more exactly in the chapters to follow. Many Catholics will recognize the term "dispensation" as referring to the "dispensations" of the Old or New Testament. Both Catholics and Protestants recognize that salvation history has divisions, especially that

a keen interest in the signs of the "end times" and those passages of Scripture that I believed unlocked the door to the future.

This perspective was marked by a strange mixture of excitement and fear: excitement, because I believed I knew how the future would unfold; fear, because so much of that future was filled with possible pain and terror. It is one thing to fear properly God and his righteous judgment—it is another to be fearful of computers because they might be instruments used for implementing the mark of the beast,[3] or to fear Christians with different beliefs because they might be deceived by Satan. I discovered that it was often difficult to concentrate on the demands and responsibilities of life when I thought I might not be on the earth within a few years, months, or even days.

I attended an Evangelical Bible college for two years and had the good fortune to take several classes taught by a teacher who specialized in Old Testament studies. I eventually realized that he, unlike his fellow professors, did not hold to dispensationalist beliefs—or at least had serious doubts about them. One day a guest speaker at our daily chapel spoke on the Rapture and its rapid approach; he remarked that it definitely would occur "within our very lifetime". Afterward I ran into my teacher in the hall and asked him, "Do you be-

division marked by the Incarnation. However, in Fundamentalist and Evangelical Protestant circles the word *dispensationalism* is almost universally understood to refer to a particular eschatological system that divides history into seven dispensations, or distinct epochs. A more exact term is *premillennial dispensationalism*.

[3] See Rev 13:16–18. The idea that a computer chip or some other sort of computer device would be used to "mark" people with "666" became very popular in the 1970s among dispensationalist groups. Other suspects include Social Security numbers, UPC codes, and credit cards.

lieve in the Rapture? What do you think is going to happen?" A wry grin crossed his face. "All I know is that Jesus surprised nearly everyone at his first coming," he said, "and I'm sure that will be the case with his second one." Unlike other professors, he would not be drawn into making detailed judgments about future world events.

Around the same time I started noticing that many dispensationalists held beliefs differing in key respects from the beliefs of their fellow dispensationalists. There were also Evangelicals who used the term "Rapture" interchangeably with "The Second Coming", even though the distinction between the two is essential for the entire dispensational system. I needed answers to my questions, but those questions would not be addressed with any satisfaction until I began to study Catholic doctrine.

Fundamentalists and Evangelicals who honestly examine the Catholic Church and develop an interest in her beliefs must wrestle with difficult issues: papal authority, Mary, the sacraments, the priesthood, and a host of others. An often ignored issue is eschatology—what one believes about the end times or "last things".[4] David Currie, a former Fundamentalist whose parents taught at Moody Bible Institute (an influential Fundamentalist, dispensationalist school), knows how significant this issue is because he had to deal with it on

---

[4] *Eschatology* (Greek, *eschatos*, "teachings about the last things") is the study of the "last things" or "end times", including death, resurrection, the *Parousia* (Christ's Second Coming), judgment, heaven, and hell. "The phrase 'last things' refers to a final period of world history when God's majestic plan of salvation is realized as all creation is finally reconciled to Him, reaching the beginning of its fullest possible realization.... This final period of world history begins with the birth of Christ, includes the pilgrim journey of the Church, and will be consummated with the Second Coming of Christ" (*Our Sunday Visitor's Catholic Encyclopedia* [Huntington, Ind.: Our Sunday Visitor, 1991], pp. 364–65).

his journey into the Catholic Church. In his book *Born Fundamentalist, Born Again Catholic*, in a chapter titled "Premillennialism and Eschatology", Currie writes:

> When Colleen [his wife] and I decided that we would become Catholics, we discussed those issues that would be the hardest for certain friends to handle. For many, we knew it would be Mary. For others, it might be the pope. Others would be bothered by the thought of our submission to Catholic morals. She was surprised that I insisted that our departure from premillennialism would be the major stumbling block for certain clergy we knew. She was even more amazed when it turned out that I was correct.[5]

I had a similar experience. I was drawn to the Catholic Church for a number of reasons: theological, philosophical, moral—even political. But what caused me the most anxiety, for quite some time, was the frightening thought that if the Catholic Church were wrong, I could miss the Rapture and would have to endure seven years of tribulation.[6] It did not help that Catholic materials on the subject apparently did not ex-

[5] David Currie, *Born Fundamentalist, Born Again Catholic* (San Francisco: Ignatius Press, 1996), p. 179. Also see Currie's tape series *The Rapture Revealed* (West Covina, Calif.: St. Joseph Communications, 1999).

[6] The belief that true Christians will be raptured prior to the seven years of tribulation is commonly called *pretribulationism*. While this is the majority viewpoint within popular dispensational circles, there are others who believe that Christians will not be raptured until the Tribulation is halfway over (*midtribulationism*), and yet others who believe the Rapture will take place at the end of the Tribulation (*posttribulationism*). Further complicating matters is the *prewrath* view of the Rapture, advocated by Robert Van Kampen in *The Sign* (Wheaton, Ill.: Crossway Books, 1992). Van Kampen teaches that Christians will go through the Tribulation but will be raptured immediately after the Tribulation is cut short by God. The exact time of the Rapture within the Tribulation is not known (although it is likely toward the conclusion of the Tribulation), and therefore the prewrath view falls somewhere outside the realm of the other three views.

ist. While books and articles on the Eucharist, Mary, the pope, and even indulgences were easy to locate, reliable material on the Catholic view of the end times, the Rapture, the Antichrist, and the Tribulation were difficult to find. That is one reason this book has been written—it is the book I wish I could have read when I was an Evangelical Protestant crossing the Tiber on my way to Rome.

Catholics will almost undoubtedly hear or read, at some point and in some form, teaching or conversation about the Rapture and other "end time" issues. While Fundamentalism and dispensationalism are not identical, the overlapping of the two movements is often such that they cannot be separated in the beliefs of a particular denomination or person. Such denominations and individuals are almost always anti-Catholic. At the very least they believe that Catholics are nominal Christians who need assistance in studying the Scripture and "rightly dividing the Word of Truth".[7] It should not surprise serious Catholics that Fundamentalist and Evangelical pews are filled with former Catholics, many of whom are staunch believers in the dispensational version of

---

[7] This popular phrase, which is used often by many Fundamentalists and Evangelicals, is taken from 2 Timothy 2:15. It was also the title of a slim booklet (Neptune, N.J.: Loizeaux Brothers, 1896) written by Cyrus I. Scofield (1842–1921), a key dispensationalist leader and author of the *Scofield Reference Bible* (1909). The subtitle of this influential booklet was "Ten Outline Studies of the More Important Divisions of Scripture". Since dispensationalism emphasizes divisions within Scripture and history, this phrase has become something of a code word among the dispensational faithful. Scofield wrote, "The Word of Truth, then, has right divisions, and it must be evident that, as one cannot be 'a workman that needeth not be ashamed' without observing them, so *any study* of that Word which ignores those divisions must be in large measure profitless and confusing. . . . The purpose of this pamphlet is to indicate the more important divisions of the Word of Truth" (p. 3). Scofield's statement apparently means that all Christian study of the Bible up until the 1830s has been largely "profitless and confusing", a claim that will be examined in more detail later.

the Rapture and are even, in not a few cases, convinced that the Catholic Church is apostate and anti-Christian. Those Catholics who desire to know their faith and defend it will eventually have conversations with a Fundamentalist or Evangelical who will question them about the usual list of suspects: Mary, the pope, the Crusades, and so forth. Even if they never mention the Rapture, it exerts a powerful influence on their understanding of central issues such as the nature of the Church, interpretation of Scripture, and the Christian engagement with culture. The reasons for this influence will become clear as we examine them throughout this book.

The amazing resiliency and continued attraction of the notion of a Rapture can be seen in popular novels, movies, and television programs. In the 1970s the best-selling author of the decade was a youth minister from Southern California named Hal Lindsey, who took a popularized form of dispensationalism and wrote the record-shattering books *The Late Great Planet Earth* and *There's a New World Coming*.[8] Today, despite the fact that many of Lindsey's claims have not come to pass, he still carries on a substantial "ministry" with a weekly television show on the Trinity Broadcasting Network and a fairly steady stream of books, all variations on the same theme as his first best sellers.[9] Meanwhile, one of

---

[8] Hal Lindsey, with C. C. Carlson, *The Late Great Planet Earth* (New York: Bantam Books, 1970). "The nonfiction bestseller of the 1970s, with nine million copies in print by 1978 and twenty-eight million by 1990, was a popularization of [dispensational] pre-millennialism, Hal Lindsey's *Late Great Planet Earth* (1970)" (Paul Boyer, *When Time Shall Be No More* [Cambridge, Mass.: Harvard University Press, 1998], p. 5).

[9] Some of Lindsey's other titles include *Satan Is Alive and Well on Planet Earth* (New York: Bantam Books, 1972), *There's a New World Coming* (Santa Ana, Calif.: Vision House Publishers, 1973), *The 1980's: Countdown to Arma-*

the biggest publishing stories of the last several years has been a group of books entitled the *Left Behind* series,[10] novels about life on earth during the Tribulation following the Rapture. As of this writing ten books have been published, totaling close to forty million copies sold. The last three books have topped the *New York Times, Wall Street Journal, USA Today,* and *Publishers Weekly* best-seller lists, new territory for works of Christian fiction. Coauthored by Tim LaHaye, a retired pastor from Southern California, and Jerry B. Jenkins, former editor of *Moody Magazine*, these apocalyptic novels have been a publishing sensation rivaled by few other works of recent fiction. If they provide a reliable gauge, popular interest in the Rapture and the end of the world has not waned in recent years; rather, it appears to be growing.

The *Left Behind* novels and similar books, combined with the aggressive proselytizing common to Fundamentalist and

---

geddon (New York: Bantam Books, 1980), and *The Rapture* (New York: Bantam Books, 1983). Lindsey hosts a weekly half-hour television program, *International Intelligence Briefing*, that airs on Trinity Broadcasting Network (TBN), which claims to be the largest Christian television network in the world.

[10] The only modern publishing story larger than the *Left Behind* series is that of the controversial Harry Potter books. The *Left Behind* series is published by Tyndale House Publishers (Wheaton, Ill.; 1995–). The books published so far in the series include:

1. *Left Behind: A Novel of the Earth's Last Days* (1995)
2. *Tribulation Force: The Continuing Drama of Those Left Behind* (1996)
3. *Nicolae: The Rise of the Antichrist* (1997)
4. *Soul Harvest: The World Takes Sides* (1998)
5. *Apollyon: The Destroyer Is Unleashed* (1999)
6. *Assassins: Assignment—Jerusalem, Target—Antichrist* (1999)
7. *The Indwelling: The Beast Takes Possession* (2000)
8. *The Mark: The Beast Rules the World* (2000)
9. *Desecration: Antichrist Takes the Throne* (2001)
10. *The Remnant: On the Brink of Armageddon* (2002)

Evangelical groups, continue to puzzle and confuse Catholics who come into contact with them. Bob, a life-long Catholic, told me that he and his wife have been attending a Protestant Bible study (their parish did not offer any studies of Scripture) and that they have been learning about the Rapture. When I told him that the Rapture, as it is taught by such groups, is a theological fiction invented less than two centuries ago, his brow furrowed in puzzlement. "But it's right in the Bible!" he exclaimed. I have also talked with Catholics who have been bewildered by my concern and exasperation with the *Left Behind* books. One Catholic told me the books were the "best" he had ever read and claimed they had changed his life for the better. Another said it was "paranoid" of me to think that these books are in any way contrary to the Catholic faith. "They spread the gospel," he said, "and isn't that something Catholics should support?" On the surface this might seem reasonable. But as we shall see, there are a host of problems with the *Left Behind* version of the gospel, ranging from its presentation of God to its view of the Church and to its antagonism toward Catholicism.

The Catholic Church has much to offer when it comes to the issue of the "end times", especially since the nature of the Church and the reality of the Kingdom are central issues. And there is no greater teacher about the Church than the Church herself, the Mystical Body of Christ, "the pillar and bulwark of truth" (1 Tim 3:15). Many insightful books have been written by Reformed Protestants and other Evangelical scholars about these controversial and complex issues. I have profited immensely from their study and labor, and I gratefully acknowledge my debt to them. But these works occasionally miss, or leave undeveloped, important points about the mystery of the Church and the culmination of history, topics that the Magisterium and faithful Catholic theologians have addressed with great profundity.[11]

This book is not meant to be polemical, but the subject itself guarantees that disagreements cannot be avoided. However, the goal is not to anger or insult non-Catholic Christians, or even to help Catholics "win" arguments. This book is meant to be a resource and guide for Catholics and non-Catholics alike. It is intended to aid the reader in understanding the inner workings of the dispensationalist view of the Rapture and end times, the flaws of that position as seen from the Catholic perspective, and also the Catholic stance on the same issues. To those ends it has been written in a style that seeks to be popular without being breezy, with a tone that is serious but hopefully not overbearing. The main body is meant to be accessible to the reader with little or no familiarity with the topic, while the footnotes offer detail for the reader looking for additional insights and sources, often scholarly in nature.

There are two main parts to this book. The first part—"The Story of the Rapture . . . and So Much More"—is meant to provide a theological and historical context while offering some evaluations along the way. It begins with a look at the "big picture": What are the "end times", the "last days", the "Second Coming", and the "Rapture"? The second

[11] Official Catholic documents on the nature of the Church include two documents from the Second Vatican Council (1962–1965): the Dogmatic Constitution on the Church, *Lumen Gentium* (hereafter abbreviated *LG*), and the Pastoral Constitution on the Church in the Modern World, *Gaudium et Spes* (hereafter abbreviated *GS*). Also relevant are two papal documents: Pope Paul VI's encyclical *Ecclesiam Suam* ("On the Church", 1964) and Pope John Paul II's encyclical *Redemptoris Missio* ("Mission of the Redeemer",1990). Other important works of Catholic ecclesiology are listed in the bibliography.

chapter examines the *Left Behind* phenomenon and what Catholics should know about it and the men behind it. This is followed by a chapter about the book of Revelation—perhaps the most misunderstood and misused book in the Bible. We then look into the "millennium", a serious point of contention and division among Christians. Chapters 5 and 6 focus on the history of "end times" beliefs within Christendom, with special attention to the origins and history of dispensationalism and the "Rapture".

The second part, "A Catholic Critique of Dispensationalism", consists of three chapters focused on the central areas of disagreement between Catholics and dispensationalists: the relationship between Old Testament Israel, the Church, and the Kingdom; "Bible prophecy" and the interpretation of Scripture; and the Rapture. The third chapter of this part—"Unwrapping the Rapture"—explores the theological, practical, and historical flaws of this central dispensationalist tenet. The concluding chapter, "The Catholic Vision", steps away from the fray and presents what the Catholic Church teaches about the culmination of time and history. Also included is a glossary of terms and a list of persons, as well as a selected bibliography of key works consulted and cited.

In writing about this important and difficult topic, my prayer is that of St. John: "Amen. Come, Lord Jesus" (Rev 22:20). As we wait in joyful expectation for the glorious Second Coming of our Lord, may we always seek the will of him who is "the Alpha and the Omega".

PART ONE

THE STORY OF THE RAPTURE
... AND SO MUCH MORE

THE PAROUSIA, THE RAPTURE,
AND THE END TIMES

Turning and turning in the widening gyre
The falcon cannot hear the falconer;
Things fall apart; the centre cannot hold;
Mere anarchy is loosed upon the world,
The blood-dimmed tide is loosed, and everywhere
The ceremony of innocence is drowned;

The best lack all conviction, while the worst
Are full of passionate intensity.

Surely some revelation is at hand;
Surely the Second Coming is at hand.

— William Butler Yeats, "The Second Coming"

Virtually all Christians who take the Bible literally expect
to be raptured before the Lord comes in power to this
earth.

— Tim LaHaye

"Do Catholics believe in the Second Coming of Jesus Christ?"
The question was asked in good faith by a Protestant friend.
Apparently he had heard that Catholics do not expect Christ's
return, or perhaps he had surmised as much from what another Catholic had told him.

"We certainly do believe in the Second Coming", I told him.

"But you don't believe in the Rapture", he objected.

"No," I said, "at least not in the way that the term is understood today in America by certain non-Catholic Christians."

Similar discussions leave two impressions. First, there is much confusion regarding what Catholics believe about the Second Coming and just as much confusion over what the Church teaches about the end times. Secondly, the belief in the Rapture, as it is commonly taught among Fundamentalists and Evangelicals, is not only bewildering to Catholics, it can even be rather puzzling for those who believe in it and teach it.

Are We Living in the "End Times"?

Over the last three decades there has been an explosion of books and tapes produced by self-proclaimed "Bible prophecy experts" announcing that the Rapture and the end of the world are just around the corner. Fundamentalist and Evangelical pastors, televangelists, and teachers are warning of economic collapse, societal anarchy, global warfare, an apostate "one world religion", and the rise of the Antichrist. According to these experts, the "end times" and the "last days" have finally arrived, two thousand years after Jesus Christ walked the planet. Hal Lindsey, the biggest-selling prognosticator among these prophetic experts, has been warning of impending doom for over thirty years. In *Planet Earth— 2000 A.D.*, written in 1994, he admits, "No, I am not a prophet." Yet he then continues: "But I have studied the prophets. And I am certain that all that they predict for mankind up to and including the Second Advent will occur in the next few years—probably in your lifetime." [1] Although Lindsey is certainly no prophet, it appears that he wants to be one. Tim LaHaye is not about to be outdone. His aptly titled *Are We Living in the End Times?*, written with *Left Behind* co-author Jerry B. Jenkins, states that the " 'times of the signs' indicate rather startlingly that the 'end of the age' is upon us; the time for Christ to return to set up His kingdom appears to be drawing near." Elsewhere he scoffingly writes: "Only the biblical illiterate is unable to see that these are the last days." [2]

Are we, as these men teach and many Christians believe, living in the end times? Are we currently witnessing the last days? If so, how long before the Second Coming occurs, and what exactly will transpire when Christ "will appear a second time" (Heb 9:28)? In order to gain some necessary context on these issues, we must step back and look at the larger picture. For the Catholic, adequate answers to these questions start with the understanding that the terms "end times" and "last days" refer not only to the end of time at some future date, but equally—even especially—to the last two thousand years. Scripture teaches that it was the Incarnation, the entrance of God into time and space, in the person of Jesus Christ, that marked the start of the end times and the last days. The epistle to the Hebrews declares, "In many and various ways God spoke of old to our fathers by the prophets; but in these last days he has spoken to us by a Son, whom he appointed the heir of all things, through whom also he created

---

[1] Hal Lindsey, *Planet Earth—2000 A.D.* (Palos Verdes, Calif.: Western Front, 1994), p. 3. Beginning in 1970 with the publication of his megaseller *The Late Great Planet Earth*, Lindsey has consistently claimed that the "end" would come within a few years. Many of Lindsey's remarks will be examined in detail in later chapters.

[2] Tim LaHaye and Jerry B. Jenkins, *Are We Living in the End Times?* (Wheaton, Ill.: Tyndale House Publishers, 1999), p. 24, and Tim LaHaye, *Revelation Unveiled* (Grand Rapids, Mich.: Zondervan Publishing House, 1999), p. 10.

the world" (Heb 1:1–2). Jesus Christ, the incarnate Word of God, ushered in the last days when he was born. He then declared during his public ministry that he was establishing the Kingdom of God (Mt 12:28; Mk 4:11; Lk 8:1–10). This establishment was realized through his death, his Resurrection, and his Ascension into heaven. Christ himself is the Kingdom, and he calls all men to enter into his life, which here on earth is found in the Church, his Mystical Body. *Lumen Gentium*, the Second Vatican Council's Dogmatic Constitution on the Church, states:

> The Son, therefore, came, sent by the Father. It was in Him, before the foundation of the world, that the Father chose us and predestined us to become adopted sons, for in Him it pleased the Father to re-establish all things. To carry out the will of the Father, Christ inaugurated the Kingdom of heaven on earth and revealed to us the mystery of that kingdom. By His obedience He brought about redemption. The Church, or, in other words, the kingdom of Christ now present in mystery, grows visibly through the power of God in the world.... All men are called to this union with Christ, who is the light of the world, from whom we go forth, through whom we live, and toward whom our whole life strains.[3]

---

[3] *LG* 3. Also, "The mystery of the holy Church is already brought to light in the way it was founded. For the Lord Jesus inaugurated his Church by preaching the Good News, that is, the coming of the kingdom of God, promised over the ages in the scriptures: 'The time is fulfilled, and the kingdom of God is at hand' (Mk. 1:15; Matt. 4:17)." *LG* 5. Joseph Cardinal Ratzinger writes, "In [Christ] the future is present, God's Kingdom is at hand, but in such a way that a mere observer, concerned with recording symptoms or plotting the movement of the stars, might well overlook the fact.... Jesus is the Kingdom, not simply by virtue of his physical presence but through the Holy Spirit's radiant power flowing forth from him. In his Spirit-filled activity, smashing the demonic enslavement of man, the Kingdom of God becomes reality, God taking the government of this world into his own hands. Let us remember that God's Kingdom is an event, not a sphere.... Jesus *is* that Kingdom since through him the Spirit of God acts in the world" (Joseph Ratzinger,

What does this mean? The last days involve a new creation and a new people, the Church, formed and chosen by Jesus Christ and now mysteriously growing in history. This new creation was established by the New Covenant. This new and everlasting covenant was ratified by the body and blood of Christ, and it transcended *and* completed the Old Covenant.[4] The "last days" is the time of the New Covenant, the gathering together of God's people in the Church, which

---

Eschatology, Death and Eternal Life [Washington, D.C.: Catholic University of America Press, 1988], pp. 34–35).

[4] "But as it is, Christ has obtained a ministry which is as much more excellent than the old as the covenant he mediates is better, since it is enacted on better promises. For if that first covenant had been faultless, there would have been no occasion for a second.

For he finds fault with them when he says:

" 'The days will come, says the Lord,
when I will establish a new covenant with the house of Israel
and with the house of Judah;
not like the covenant that I made with their fathers
on the day when I took them by the hand
to lead them out of the land of Egypt;
for they did not continue in my covenant,
and so I paid no heed to them, says the Lord.
This is the covenant that I will make with the house of Israel
after those days, says the Lord:
I will put my laws into their minds,
and write them on their hearts,
and I will be their God,
and they shall be my people.
And they shall not teach every one his fellow
or every one his brother, saying, "Know the Lord,"
for all shall know me,
from the least of them to the greatest.
For I will be merciful toward their iniquities,
and I will remember their sins no more.'

In speaking of a new covenant he treats the first as obsolete. And what is becoming obsolete and growing old is ready to vanish away" (Heb 8:6–13; see Jer 31:31–34).

"becomes on earth the initial budding forth of that king-dom".[5] Therefore Christ's first coming established the King-dom of God on earth, and Christians are now living in that Kingdom—in the Church—which is still growing and be-ing established throughout the world. The full revelation and manifestation of the Kingdom will occur at the end of time when Christ returns in glory.

The last days are not just ahead of us—we live in them today. God's judgment of man has already begun, is on-going, and will be finalized at the end of time at the Last Judgment.[6] This means Christians live in a state of tension because the Kingdom of God has been inaugurated and re-

[5] LG 5.

[6] "First of all, it [the Incarnation] means that the Last Things have already begun. The resurrection of Christ is presented as the first and decisive act of the last day. The Word of God took humanity to himself in the Incarnation, and cleansed it through his precious blood, and brought it into his Father's house for ever at his ascension. The work of salvation has been substantially done, everything essential has been secured already.... On the other hand, this work of Judgment which Christ has substantially completed has not yet pro-duced its due consequences throughout mankind and throughout creation.... We are still waiting for that Judgment that will destroy the world of corruption and establish the kingdom of saints. This twofold relationship to something achieved and to something awaited specifies the current phase of time, which is the epoch of the Church. It is the period of grace allowed to mankind for the acceptation of the judgment which Christ has substantially won, and so escape the Judgment to come. The Church's preaching is eschatological in character, consisting in an announcement of the danger that threatens the hu-man race, with notice of the way of salvation, the Ark of the Church, afford-ing the only safe passage through the deep waters of the Judgment" (Jean Daniélou, *The Lord of History* [London: Longmans, Green, 1958], pp. 274–75). Orthodox bishop and theologian Kallistos Ware writes: "Yet the Second Com-ing is not simply an event in the future, for in the life of the Church, the Age to Come has already begun to break through into this present age. For mem-bers of God's Church, the 'Last Things' are already inaugurated, since here and now Christians enjoy the firstfruits of God's Kingdom. *Even so, come, Lord*

vealed but has not yet been fully disclosed and realized.[7] Christ, by his death and Resurrection, has conquered sin and destroyed the power of Satan, if only men will recognize and enter into this salvific reality.

After the Ascension, the disciples in the Upper Room were filled with the Holy Spirit on the Day of Pentecost (Acts 2:1–4). This was the "counselor" whom Christ had promised to send to the disciples in order to teach them "all things" (Jn 14:26) and to give them power and authority (Acts 1:8). Immediately afterward, Peter, the leader of the apostles, preached that the last days had arrived, in fulfillment of the words of the prophet Joel:

Jesus. He comes already—in the Holy Liturgy and the worship of the Church" (Timothy Ware, *The Orthodox Church*, rev. ed. [London: Penguin Books, 1964], p. 268).

[7] "In one sense, the Kingdom of God has already come—in the form of the Church, or the Mystical body of Christ, which is, as we have seen, the Kingdom in the state of pilgrimage and crucifixion. In another sense, the Kingdom of God is to come, namely, as to its fulfillment in the Jerusalem of glory—the Church triumphant—and in the world of the resurrection" (Jacques Maritain, *On the Philosophy of History* [New York: Charles Scribner's Sons, 1957], p. 150). "The paradoxical extension of time between two dialectically related moments will be eliminated only at the parousia when Christ 'delivers the kingdom to God the Father ... that God may be everything to every one' (1 Cor 15:24, 28). Meanwhile, it constitutes the mystery of the time of the Church, during which the Lord is at once present and absent: so intimately present that he acts directly in the sacraments, which are instrumental prolongations of the action of his sacred humanity, and yet also absent, for he is seated at the right hand of the Father, whence he shall come again to judge the living and the dead. The time of the Church is therefore *eschatological time*, because no radical innovation is still to come, since the work of creation and revelation is complete; but it is also *historical time*, during which the whole work of creation is progressively recapitulated and revelation is continually remembered" (I. H. Dalmais, "Theology of the Liturgical Celebration", in A. G. Martimort, ed., *The Church at Prayer*, vol. 1: *Principles of the Liturgy* [Collegeville, Minn.: Liturgical Press, 1987], p. 261).

"For these men are not drunk, as you suppose, since it is only the third hour of the day; but this is what was spoken by the prophet Joel:

'And in the last days it shall be, God declares,
that I will pour out my Spirit upon all flesh,
and your sons and your daughters shall prophesy,
and your young men shall see visions,
and your old men shall dream dreams.' " (Acts 2:15–17;
see Joel 2:28–32)[8]

The Holy Spirit, the soul of the Church, has been—and is being—poured out because of the redemptive work of Jesus Christ. Man enters into union with Christ and communion with the Father through the power of the Holy Spirit, "the Lord, the giver of life". The Holy Spirit, with the Father and Son, continually works to bring about the salvation of mankind in these last days.[9]

The Catholic understanding of the end times is quite different from that of many other Christians, especially those who believe in the Rapture. The basic tenets held by dispensationalists and those who believe in a pretribulational Rapture are radically opposed to the Catholic vision of the Church and the Kingdom. *The essential disagreement has to do*

---

[8] "We know that at Pentecost the Apostles were to use this text [Joel 2:28–32] to show in the Church of Christ the final coming into being of the people of God. . . . The gift of the Spirit, therefore, represents the inauguration of the eschatological times. This is what the Apostles, in the Acts, state on Pentecost, in applying to what is happening under their eyes the prophecy of Joel concerning the Spirit which, at the last times, is to be poured out over all flesh" (Louis Bouyer, *The Meaning of Sacred Scripture* [Notre Dame, Ind.: University of Notre Dame Press, 1958], pp. 148, 222).

[9] See *Catechism of the Catholic Church* (CCC), 2d ed. (United States Catholic Conference—Libreria Editrice Vaticana, 1997), nos. 686, 2819, and 732. All references to "*Catechism*" or CCC refer to this work.

with the nature of the Kingdom. The Catholic Church teaches that Jesus Christ established his Kingdom, the Church, at his first coming. Dispensationalists such as Lindsey and LaHaye claim that he offered the Kingdom—an earthly, political reign—to the Jewish people, but they refused.[10] This forced Christ to form a "mystery" people, the Church—something completely different from the Kingdom. Catholic doctrine teaches that at Christ's Second Coming time will end, all men will be judged, and the Kingdom will be consummated. At that time Christ will hand over the Kingdom to his Father:

> Christ, made obedient unto death and because of this exalted by the Father, has entered into the glory of his kingdom. All things are subjected to him until he subjects himself and all created things to the Father, so that God may be all in all.[11]

Dispensationalists essentially teach what amounts to the belief that Christ will return twice—once secretly for the Church (the Rapture) and then in glory to conquer evil (the Second Coming) with his Church—followed by an earthly reign of

---

[10] For example, here is a representative quote from Charles C. Ryrie, a leading dispensational theologian: "Throughout his earthly ministry Jesus' Davidic kingship was offered to Israel (Matt. 2:2; 27:11; John 12:13), but He was rejected.... Because the King was rejected, the messianic, Davidic kingdom was (from a human viewpoint) postponed. Though He never ceases to be King and, of course, is King today as always, Christ is never designated as King of the Church.... Though Christ is a King today, He does not rule as King. This awaits His second coming. Then the Davidic kingdom will be realized (Matt. 25:31; Rev 19:15, 20)" (Charles C. Ryrie, *Basic Theology* [Wheaton, Ill.: Victor Books, 1986], p. 259). Ryrie, long-time professor of theology at Dallas Theological Seminary, has written many works on the topic, and *Basic Theology* has been used as a textbook in many Bible colleges in the United States and Canada.

[11] LG 36.

a thousand years, a rebellion by Satan, and then, finally, eternity. The differences between Catholic doctrine and these dispensationalist beliefs cannot be reconciled since they are based on widely divergent views of the Church, Old Testament Israel, the Kingdom, and the interpretation of Scripture.

While the Catholic Church teaches that there will be a definite "end of time" and that history as we know it will cease, she emphasizes that every human being will face the end of his time on earth and that this should be of more urgent concern than the end of the world.[12] As one Catholic scholar has written:

> "Mankind is now face to face with the Son of Man at every moment of existence: the judgment is now".... Judgment does indeed consist now from moment to moment in the relation of man to God; but that is because mankind is historically going through the time of judgment. And this process has only begun; it looks forward to the Last Judgment for the final ratification.[13]

Catholics Believe in the Second Coming!

Every Sunday and Holy Day at Mass, Catholics proclaim that Jesus Christ will "come again in glory to judge the living and the dead". The Catholic Church believes and affirms that on that "last day" the "Lord himself will descend from heaven with a cry of command, with the archangel's call,

---

[12] See CCC 1002, 1011.

[13] Jean Daniélou quoting, and then commenting upon, Fr. Donatien Mollat, in *Lord of History*, pp. 272–73.

and with the sound of the trumpet of God. And the dead in Christ will rise first" (1 Thess 4:16).[14]

This is not symbolic language or wishful thinking, but a concrete belief in the actual, bodily return of the Savior. This Second Coming is often called the *Parousia*, a Greek word that literally means "presence" or "arrival" (e.g., Mt 24:27, 37, 39; 1 Cor 15:23; 1 Thess 2:19; 3:13; 4:15; 5:23; 2 Thess 2:1, 8; 2 Pet 3:4; 1 Jn 2:28). It is used throughout the New Testament to describe Christ's coming in victorious glory. Jesus himself stated that "then will appear the sign of the Son of man in heaven, and then all the tribes of the earth will mourn, and they will see the Son of man coming on the clouds of heaven with power and great glory" (Mt 24:30). St. Paul assures his readers that Christ's appearance will put an end to the work of Satan: "And then the lawless one will be revealed, and the Lord Jesus will slay him with the breath of his mouth and destroy him by his appearing and his coming" (2 Thess 2:8). The Parousia will be realized fully at the end of time but is already a reality initiated by the Incarnation, which revealed the glory of God among men: "And the Word became flesh and dwelt among us, full of grace

---

[14] See CCC 1001. *Lumen Gentium* states: "Before we reign with Christ in glory we must all appear 'before the judgment seat of Christ, so that each one may receive good or evil, according to what he has done in the body' (2 Cor. 5:10), and at the end of the world 'they will come forth, those who have done good, to the resurrection of life, and those who have done evil, to the resurrection of judgment' (Jn. 5:29; cf. Matt. 25:46). We reckon then that 'the sufferings of this present time are not worth comparing with the glory that is to be revealed to us' (Rom. 8:18; cf. 2 Tim. 2:11–12), and strong in faith we look for 'the blessed hope, the appearing of the glory of our great God and Savior Jesus Christ' (Tit. 2:13) 'who will change our lowly body to be like his glorious body' (Phil. 3:21) and who will come 'to be glorified in his saints, and to be marveled at in all who have believed' (2 Thess. 1:10)" (*LG* 48).

and truth; we have beheld his glory, glory as of the only Son from the Father" (Jn 1:14). So the Parousia, God's presence among men, began when the Son became a man and continues with the presence of the Holy Spirit. Cardinal Ratzinger states, "By gazing on the risen Christ, Christianity knew that a most significant coming had already taken place. It no longer proclaimed a pure theology of hope, living from mere expectation of the future, but pointed to a 'now' in which the promise had already become present. Such a present was, of course, itself hope, for it bears the future within itself." [15] For Catholics, this presence is most fully experienced in the Eucharist, in the partaking of the actual Body and Blood of the risen Lord.

Of course, recent history has witnessed tremendous speculation about the timing of Christ's return and a fascination with the "signs of the times". This has been especially true in the United States, where attempts by some Christians to figure out exactly when the Second Coming will transpire have sometimes gotten out of hand, resulting in embarrassment, confusion, and even loss of faith. Catholics, for the most part, have been immune to these more extreme movements. But the serenity demonstrated by some Catholics might be as much from apathy as from a refusal to be drawn into an irresponsible game of date setting. Certainly date setting is not an option; Jesus said, "But of that day or that hour no one knows, not even the angels in heaven, nor the Son, but only the Father" (Mk 13:32). On the other hand, Jesus warned his disciples always to be prepared for his return: "Take heed, watch and pray; for you do not know when the time will come" (Mk 13:33). Reiterating this tension between not

---

[15] Ratzinger, *Eschatology*, pp. 44–45.

knowing and yet always being ready, the *Catechism of the Catholic Church* teaches that Christ's return "has been imminent [cf. Rev 22:20]" even while there has been a delay in his Second Coming.[16]

When the *Catechism* refers to the Parousia being "delayed", it emphasizes that God is merciful and desires all men to receive his freely offered salvation: "The Lord is not slow about his promise as some count slowness, but is forbearing toward you, not wishing that any should perish, but that all should reach repentance" (2 Pet 3:9). It could be many more centuries or millennia before Christ comes again—or it could be in the near future. But there are also at least three events that must take place before the Second Coming: an unparalleled period of tribulation and apostasy, the spread of the gospel to all the world, and the recognition of Jesus as the Christ by "all Israel".

Of the first event, the *Catechism* states, "Before Christ's second coming the Church must pass through a final trial that will shake the faith of many believers [cf. Lk 18:8; Mt 24:12]." [17] There will be religious deception, apostasy, and the rise of the Antichrist, a movement that will deify man while denying God and Jesus Christ. Considering the fact that more Christians were killed in the twentieth century than in all other centuries combined, it could be that this time of trial is already in progress. The abandonment of Christianity by numerous nations during the past couple of centuries, combined with the rise of communism, secular humanism, and neo-paganism, points to disbelief on a scale perhaps never witnessed before. Or could a future era be even worse? It is, of course, impossible to know. However,

---

[16] CCC 673.
[17] CCC 675.

not all Christians accept this teaching that the Church will go through a time of great persecution and apostasy, commonly called "the Tribulation". Dispensationalists believe that there already exists widespread apostasy within Christendom but reject the belief that "true believers" will have to go through the Tribulation.[18]

In the Olivet Discourse Jesus spoke of the second event with his disciples: "And this gospel of the kingdom will be preached throughout the whole world, as a testimony to all nations; and then the end will come" (Mt 24:14). Has this occurred? Arguments can be made either way. As Ralph Martin has noted, "It is difficult to know whether this universal proclamation has taken place. Certain nations have had the gospel preached to them in the past but not in the present." [19] The one certainty is that the gospel must be continually preached to as many people as possible.

Of the third event, the Church teaches that Israel's recognition of Jesus as the Messiah will take place prior to the

---

[18] Many dispensationalists, such as LaHaye, see the Catholic Church as an apostate institution. The National Council of Churches and the ecumenical movement are also understood to be apostate. LaHaye writes: "We are living in a day of ecumenical propaganda calling on the churches of the world to amalgamate.... This unity movement should not, however, be limited to apostate Christianity. We can expect it to move toward amalgamating all the religions of the world under Rome's headship because our text states that the religious system at the end time will be a one-world religion: 'Where the prostitute sits, are peoples, multitudes, nations and languages' (Rev 17:15). This can only mean a one-world religious system" (LaHaye, *Revelation Unveiled*, pp. 271–72).

[19] Ralph Martin, *Is Jesus Coming Soon? A Catholic Perspective on the Second Coming* (San Francisco: Ignatius Press, 1997), p. 63. Martin's book is an excellent overview of the topic of the Second Coming that is balanced in tone and thoroughly scriptural in approach. Also see his book *The Catholic Church at the End of an Age* (San Francisco: Ignatius Press, 1994).

Parousia.[20] This is based on Romans 9–11 and Paul's teaching that "a hardening has come upon part of Israel, until the full number of the Gentiles comes in" (Rom 11:25). How this "full inclusion" of ethnic Israel into the Church, the "people of God", will be realized is unclear. It would seem that it has not yet taken place; perhaps it has already begun in ways not yet understood or recognized.[21] What is known for certain is that Catholics have an obligation to be prepared, to evangelize, and to advance the Kingdom in every way possible.

What Is the "Rapture"?

During the 1970s, the little Fundamentalist group my family was a part of kept close watch as the Cold War raged, the energy crisis escalated, and the European Common Market came together just as the book of Revelation said it would—at least according to the preachers we listened to and the books we read. While in junior high school I read Hal Lindsey's *The Late Great Planet Earth*, the biggest-selling nonfiction book of the decade, with over thirty million copies sold since appearing in 1970. I marveled that so many people, among them Catholics, were oblivious to the approach of the pretribulation Rapture, even though students of Bible prophecy, such as Lindsey, were warning of its rapid approach:

[20] See CCC 674.

[21] While allowing that the restoration of the nation of Israel in 1948 is significant, Ralph Martin cautions against seeing this as a fulfillment of prophecy, although he states that it could be that "the time of the Gentiles may be coming to an end, and that God has also begun to set the scene for a significant dealing with Israel" (*Is Jesus Coming Soon?* p. 62).

The word "rapture" means to snatch away or take away. But whether we call this event "the Rapture" or the "translation" makes no difference—the important thing is that it will happen. It will happen! Someday, a day that God only knows, Jesus Christ is coming to take away all those who believe in Him. He is coming to meet all true believers in the air.[22]

What exactly is this "rapture" event? Is this return of Christ to take away those who believe in him the same event as the Second Coming, the Parousia? No, according to Lindsey and other dispensationalists, it is not. Lindsey explains in his 1983 best seller, *The Rapture*, that this secret coming of Christ in the clouds must not be confused with the Second Coming: "All who interpret the Bible in a literal sense believe in the *fact* of the Rapture and that it is distinct from the second coming of Christ."[23]

Many people, both Christian and non-Christian, believe in a "rapture" of some sort. The word has been used to refer to a broad range of spiritual experiences within a number of religious contexts, including spiritual ecstasy and mystical visions. *Even Catholics believe in a form of the "rapture", properly defined and understood.* However, unless otherwise noted, I will use the term "the Rapture" in referring to the unique belief held by many Fundamentalist and Evangelical Christians. This specific belief has existed for less than two centuries; it was most clearly defined by the Englishman John Nelson Darby, who placed it within the theological system known as dispensationalism in the 1830s.

---

[22] Hal Lindsey with C. C. Carlson, *The Late Great Planet Earth* (New York: Bantam Books, 1970), p. 126.

[23] Hal Lindsey, *The Rapture* (New York: Bantam Books, 1983), p. 29.

For Darby, as for modern-day Fundamentalist and Evangelical denominations and groups, the Rapture is the "snatching up" of true believers from the earth to be taken to heaven prior to and separate from the Second Coming. This event will be silent and secret and is "imminent"—it could happen at any time. Only those being raptured will see Christ; he will not come to earth but will meet the raptured in the air and then take them to heaven. Most of those who believe in this stealth event also believe it will happen within their lifetime. The majority of dispensationalists believe that this mysterious disappearance of Christians will occur immediately before seven years of tribulation; this view is called *pretribulationalism*. A far smaller number hold that believers will be raptured halfway through the seven years of tribulation (*midtribulationalism*), and another relatively small group of dispensationalists believes that the Rapture will occur at the very end of the Tribulation (*posttribulationalism*).

The term "rapture" is taken from 1 Thessalonians 4:16–17:

> For the Lord himself will descend from heaven with a cry of command, with the archangel's call, and with the sound of the trumpet of God. And the dead in Christ will rise first; then we who are alive, who are left, shall be caught up together with them in the clouds to meet the Lord in the air; and so we shall always be with the Lord.

The Greek root (harpázō) of the term "caught up" literally means "to seize upon" or "snatch away".[24] LaHaye explains that the "familiar word *rapture* does not appear in the Greek New Testament, for it is a Latin word. Those who translated

[24] Spiros Zodhiates, *The Complete Word Study Dictionary: New Testament* (Chattanooga, Tenn.: AMG Publishers, 1992), p. 257; *Vine's Expository Dictionary of Biblical Words* (Nashville: Thomas Nelson, 1985), p. 92.

the Greek New Testament into Latin used *rapture* to describe 'snatched up'. Somehow that word caught on as the unofficial title of the event."[25] Who translated the Bible from Greek to Latin? St. Jerome (ca. 340–420), a Catholic, a priest, and monk, a Church Father who was encouraged by Pope Damasus to work on the translation known as the Vulgate. St. Jerome translated the Greek word *harpazo* into the Latin word *rapiemur*, from which *rapture* was derived. This is rather ironic since not only are many defenders of the Rapture opposed to Catholicism; many claim that the use of Latin by the Catholic Church was meant to keep the Scriptures from the ordinary, uneducated people during the "Dark Ages" and even now to maintain control over modern-day Catholics who cannot read the language![26]

While the belief in the Rapture is largely based on 1 Thessalonians 4, dispensationalists also appeal to other verses from Scripture, including sections from 1 Corinthians 15, Revelation 3, and Matthew 24. These various texts are placed

[25] Tim LaHaye, *Rapture under Attack* (Sisters, Ore.: Multnomah Publishers, 1998), p. 32.

[26] Perhaps the most influential anti-Catholic of the past fifty years was Loraine Boettner (d. 1990), a Presbyterian theologian whose *Roman Catholicism* (Phillipsburg, N.J.: Presbyterian and Reformed Publishing House, 1962) can be aptly described as the "Bible" of anti-Catholicism. See Karl Keating, *Catholicism and Fundamentalism* (San Francisco: Ignatius Press, 1988), pp. 28–50. Boettner produced an infamous list of "Some Roman Catholic Heresies and Inventions", which included such puzzling things as "wax candles", "worship of St. Joseph", and, of course, "Latin language, used in prayer and worship ..." (Boettner, *Roman Catholicism*, pp. 7–8). This list, with some variations, is reproduced by LaHaye in his commentary *Revelation Unveiled*, p. 66. In describing a tour of the Shrine of Guadalupe in Mexico City, LaHaye remarks on the similarities between the Catholic practices witnessed there and "pagan rituals", stating that the "mysterious nature of the service could be seen in the fact that individuals could not understand the Latin being spoken during the Mass, and no message was given in a language they recognized" (pp. 67–68).

into an elaborate chronology of "end time" events based in the broader context of "dispensations", or eras of time, usually seven in number. This system of historical division is broadly known as *dispensationalism*,[27] or, more precisely, *premillennial dispensationalism*, because most people who adhere to this system believe that Christ's Second Coming will be prior to the millennium, which they understand to be the literal one-thousand-year reign of Christ on earth. The Rapture is also known as the "day of the Lord", which will come like "a thief in the night" (1 Thess 5:2). Most dispensationalists believe that following the Rapture will be the unveiling of the New World Order, the rise of the Antichrist, and the implementation of the "mark of the beast"—all during a seven-year period of tribulation. At the conclusion of those seven years will be the Second Coming of Christ. He will meet and conquer the forces of evil in the great battle of Armageddon, subdue Satan and his allies, and bind them for the duration of the millennial Kingdom. During this reign there will likely be a reinstitution of animal sacrifices at the Temple in Jerusalem since the earthly Kingdom will be for

[27] "There is a method of interpretation which is absolutely essential for determining which view concerning the Rapture is correct. This method is called dispensationalism. Dispensationalism (which is the Divine ordering of worldly affairs) not only helps answer the Rapture question, but helps harmonize many Scripture passages that on first observation seem contradictory.... The theological system that most adheres to a consistent, literal, grammatical and historical interpretation of the Bible is dispensationalism" (Lindsey, *Rapture*, pp. 51, 57). "A concise definition of a dispensation is this: A dispensation is a distinguishable economy in the outworking of God's purpose.... Dispensationalism views the world as a household run by God. His household-world God is dispensing or administrating its affairs according to His own will and in various stages of revelation in the passage of time. These various stages mark off the distinguishably different economies in the outworking of His total purpose, and these different economies constitute the dispensations" (Charles C. Ryrie, *Dispensationalism* [Chicago: Moody Press, 1995], pp. 28, 29).

God's earthly people (the Jews), not for his heavenly people
(the Church). At the end of that idyllic earthly reign, God
will loose Satan for a short while, then finally toss the Prince
of Darkness into the Lake of Fire for eternity.

Does Any of This Really Matter?

Most Catholics find such beliefs about the future to be foreign and bizarre. Most people, regardless of denomination
or church affiliation, are unfamiliar with the term *dispensationalism* and have no knowledge of the movement's roots,
history, or influence. Those who believe in the pretribulation (and midtribulation) Rapture and other assorted dispensational tenets think they come directly from the Bible.
Most other Christians have little interest in the matter. Why
should they? Is this not just another esoteric strain of Christianity, hardly worth noting among all the other fringe groups,
movements, theologies, and fads? Thinking this seriously un-
derestimates the profound influence that dispensational beliefs and theology have on American thinking and attitudes—
even foreign policy and pop culture. In the preface to his
seminal study of prophecy beliefs in America, *When Time
Shall Be No More*, Paul Boyer notes that this particular brand
of millenarianism[28] has been a powerful force within American culture for many decades and needs to be taken more
seriously:

---

[28] Millenarianism is, generally speaking, the belief in a thousand-year-long
era of peace and justice on earth. A wide range of people believe in some sort
of millenarianism, including Nazis, certain Orthodox Jews, New Age groups,
Fundamentalist Christians, and certain cults. More specifically it refers to the
belief of different Christian groups in a thousand-year earthly reign by Christ.

I advance two related arguments: first, that prophecy belief is far more central in American thought than intellectual and cultural historians have recognized, and second, that in the years since World War II the popularizers of a specific belief system—dispensational premillennialism—have played an important role in shaping public attitudes on a wide range of topics from the Soviet Union, the Common Market, and the Mideast to the computer and the environmental crisis.[29]

There are additional reasons why Catholics should have at least a general understanding of the dispensational system and its unique features. The most pressing is that the dispensationalist system has historically been antagonistic to Catholicism in both content and tone and holds many beliefs that are contrary to Catholic doctrine. Therefore it is not surprising that many of the most well-known popularizers of this belief system—authors such as Hal Lindsey, Dave Hunt, Tim LaHaye, Salem Kirban, Chuck Smith, Jack Chick, John

[29] Paul Boyer, *When Time Shall Be No More: Prophecy Belief in Modern American Culture* (Cambridge, Mass.: Harvard University Press, 1998), p. ix. Boyer's book is an excellent sociological and historical examination of the influence of various millenarianist movements, especially premillennial dispensationalism, within America. The prologue, titled "The Hidden World of Prophecy Belief" (pp. 1–18), concisely demonstrates how influential are the beliefs of dispensationalism and other end-time movements in America. Citing Dwight Wilson, Boyer conservatively estimates that in 1977 there were at least eight million "firmly committed premillennialists" in the U.S. (p. 2), and the number is—according to Evangelical scholar Richard Kyle—double that today (see Kyle, *The Last Days Are Here Again: A History of the End Times* [Grand Rapids, Mich.: Baker Books, 1998], p. 100). Boyer writes, "My claim on the reader's attention, and my justification for devoting so many pages to a belief system seemingly so marginal and fantastic, is, first, that these beliefs are in fact far more pervasive than many realize and, second, that if one examines them attentively, themes emerge that tell us much more about the larger worldview of those who embrace and promulgate them" (*When Time Shall Be No More*, p. 17).

Hagee, and Grant Jeffrey—are critics of the Catholic Church either explicitly or in a more subtle fashion.[30] It is fair to say that most Fundamentalist or Evangelical Protestants who are opposed to the Catholic Church and who would label her as an "apostate" or "false" religion usually hold to some form of dispensational thinking, with the notable exception of many from the Reformed tradition.[31]

Dispensationalism, like so many theological and cultural movements, is not seamless but is full of rifts, divisions, and competing groups who disagree with one another, sometimes viciously. In fact, the term *dispensationalism* is rather misleading, since all Christians believe that there exist various dispensations, if that term is taken to mean that God deals with men in a certain way in specific epochs of his-

---

[30] A couple of major exceptions are Billy Graham and Jack Van Impe. However, it is rare to find a work of overt dispensationalism with any kind words about Catholics. Either there is silence or open attacks on the Catholic Church and her teachings.

[31] Many of the best refutations of dispensationalism have been written by theologians from different corners of the Reformed tradition who see dispensationalism as a rival system of interpretation. A short list of those works could include Oswald T. Allis, *Prophecy and the Church* (Nutley, N.J.: Presbyterian and Reformed Publishing Co., 1974); Greg L. Bahnsen and Kenneth L. Gentry, Jr., *House Divided: The Break-up of Dispensational Theology* (Tyler, Tex.: Institute for Christian Economics, 1989); Loraine Boettner, *The Millennium* (Philadelphia: Presbyterian and Reformed Publishing, 1957); John H. Gerstner, *Wrongly Dividing the Word of Truth: A Critique of Dispensationalism* (Brentwood, Tenn.: Wolgemuth and Hyatt Publishers, 1991); Keith A. Mathison, *Dispensationalism: Rightly Dividing the People of God?* (Phillipsburg, N.J.: P and R Publishing, 1995); Philip Mauro, *The Gospel of the Kingdom: With an Examination of Modern Dispensationalism* (Swengel, Pa.: Reiner Publications, 1966); Gary North, *Rapture Fever: Why Dispensationalism Is Paralyzed* (Tyler, Tex.: Institute for Christian Economics, 1993); Gary DeMar, *Last Days Madness: Obsession of the Modern Church* (Atlanta: American Vision Press, 1999); and Vern S. Poythress, *Understanding Dispensationalists* (Phillipsburg, N.J.: P and R Publishing, 1994).

tory.[32] The most obvious dispensations, agreed upon by all Christians, are those of the Old and New Covenants, the division between the two being the Incarnation, the entrance of the Divine Word into history. However, dispensationalism has come to mean a specific belief system about current and future events and will be used in that way throughout this book. Although dispensationalism has only existed as a formal system for less than two hundred years, it has gone through a series of developments, as most dispensationalists admit. Craig A. Blaising and Darrell L. Bock, two of the foremost "progressive dispensationalists" writing today,[33] note that there are at least "four discernible phases of the dispensational tradition [that] can be identified" in America alone.[34] When considering both its British and American forms, I think there are at least five major phases, or stages, of dispensationalism worth noting:

1. John Darby and the Plymouth Brethren (1830–1870s)
2. The Niagara Conferences (1870s–1890s)
3. Cyrus I. Scofield and "Scofieldism" (1900s–present)
4. Popular dispensationalism, or "Lindseyism" (1970s–present)
5. Progressive dispensationalism (1980s–present)[35]

---

[32] "However, the word 'dispensationalist' is not really apt.... Virtually all ages of the church and all branches of the church have believed that there are distinctive dispensations in God's government of the world, though sometimes the consciousness of such distinctions has grown dim" (Poythress, *Understanding Dispensationalists*, pp. 9–10).

[33] See Craig A. Blaising and Darrell L. Bock, *Progressive Dispensationalism* (Wheaton, Ill.: Victor Books, 1993), and Craig A. Blaising and Darrell L. Bock, eds., *Dispensationalism, Israel and the Church: The Search for Definition* (Grand Rapids, Mich.: Zondervan Publishing House, 1992).

[34] Blaising and Bock, *Dispensationalism, Israel and the Church*, p. 379.

[35] Ibid.

The differences between these five phases are in emphasis and terminology; the essentials of the dispensationalist system exist in all of them. A possible exception is progressive dispensationalism, which is mostly academic in influence and moving steadily toward views that were once considered contrary to dispensationalism.[36]

---

[36] It appears that progressive dispensationalists are willing to compromise to some degree on key dispensational beliefs, putting their status as "dispensationalists" in question within some quarters. In fact, some progressive dispensationalists seem to be moving toward a more Reformed or historical premillennialist stance. Progressive dispensationalists claim that dispensationalism has always been a "developing" system and that it should not be criticized today for the beliefs of early leaders like Darby, Scofield, and Chafer (see Craig A. Blaising, "Doctrinal Development in Orthodoxy", *Bibliotheca Sacra*, April–June 1998, and its follow-up, "Development of Dispensationalism by Contemporary Dispensationalists", *Bibliotheca Sacra*, July–September 1998). Stanley N. Gundry, in his foreword to Blaising and Bock's *Dispensationalism, Israel and the Church*, writes, "Critics of dispensationalism have always found it easier to identify the simplistic approaches of Scofield, to criticize the excesses of Lewis Sperry Chafer, and to poke fun at the charts of Clarence Larkin than to understand and appreciate the self-critical and self-corrective drive that has characterized dispensationalism at a deeper level. But such critiques are superficial and generally at least fifty years out of date. They have failed to understand that dispensationalism and its proponents have been and continue to be in process" (p. 12). There are a couple of problems, however, with progressive dispensationalists and their plea for "understanding". First, people in the pew do not embrace progressive dispensationalism or buy its books in large numbers. They instead embrace the popular dispensationalist writings of Lindsey, LaHaye, and other men who proudly claim to be followers of Darby, Scofield, and Chafer. Secondly, one of the great appeals of dispensationalism historically (albeit a short history) has been its absolute and definite character. To depict dispensationalism now as a "process" is, it seems, a way of avoiding any specific opinions or beliefs.

For a comparison between the "traditional" and "progressive" views within dispensationalism, see Herbert W. Bateman IV, ed., *Three Central Issues in Contemporary Dispensationalism: A Comparison of Traditional and Progressive Views* (Grand Rapids, Mich.: Kregel Publications, 1999). The three central issues discussed are hermeneutics, the covenants, and Israel and the Church.

The focus of this book is on those essential beliefs that have been held within dispensationalism since the movement was founded, but especially those taught by popular dispensationalists in the last several decades. Although the average reader may know little or nothing about progressive dispensationalism, he may be familiar with some of the distinctive beliefs presented in the writings of popular dispensationalists Hal Lindsey, Dave Hunt, Grant Jeffrey, John Hagee, Tim LaHaye, and others. These are the authors whose works are selling thousands of copies and shaping the attitudes of Christians throughout America. While the more scholarly and academic dispensationalists toil away in obscure books and journals, the Lindseys, Hagees, and LaHayes light up the air waves, climb the best-seller lists, and wield considerable influence in various Fundamentalist and Evangelical circles. It is these popularizers whose beliefs and teachings are the central focus of this book for the simple reason that they are, for the person in the pew, the faces and mouthpieces of dispensationalism today. As Paul Boyer astutely notes, this form of dispensationalism is not going to disappear any time soon:

> So long as premillennial dispensationalism continues to meet the emotional and psychological needs of a great many Americans and so long as the popularizers of Bible prophecy continue to weave our deepest collective anxieties into their endtime scenarios, [premillennial dispensationalism], with its infinite adaptability and its imaginative, drama-filled vision of history, will remain a significant shaping force in our politics and culture. To fail to understand the enduring power of these ancient apocalyptic texts is to fail to understand contemporary America.[37]

---

[37] Paul Boyer, "The Apocalyptic in the Twentieth Century", in *Fearful Hope: Approaching the New Millennium*, Christopher Kleinhenz and Fannie J. LeMoine, eds. (Madison, Wis.: University of Wisconsin Press, 1999), p. 164.

2

CATHOLICS AND THE
LEFT BEHIND PHENOMENON

The main features of this story are not fiction. Those not prepared will be left behind. This book describes the dramatic days ahead. Here is a book that demands to be read.

—Dr. John F. Walvoord

The Church of Rome denies the finished work of Christ but believes in the continuing sacrifice that produces such things as sacraments and praying for the dead, burning candles, and so forth. All of these were borrowed from mystery Babylon, the mother of all pagan customs and idolatry, none of which is taught in the New Testament.

—Tim LaHaye

The first exposure to "the Rapture" for many people was when they picked up a copy of *Left Behind*, a slickly produced, attractively packaged novel about "the earth's last days". Perhaps a co-worker, friend, or neighbor mentioned the book and its central premise: millions of people—Christians— have disappeared from the planet, and chaos has spread throughout the world. While popularized dispensationalism has sold well in Protestant bookstores for many decades, it appeared that Hal Lindsey's amazing success in the 1970s within the non-Christian marketplace would not be repeated any time soon, if ever. But those who scoffed at Lindsey and his imitators and said that only right-wing Christian fanatics would read such books were in for surprise.

In 1995 Tyndale House Publishers published *Left Behind: A Novel of the Earth's Last Days*, co-authored by Tim LaHaye and Jerry B. Jenkins. The series has become a full-blown industry,[1] with a *Left Behind* series for kids, books on tape, clothing, calendars, and related books by LaHaye, including *Are We Living in the End Times?* and the *Tim LaHaye Prophecy Study Bible*.[2] *Left Behind: The Movie* was released on video in

---

[1] "In addition to the movie, the series has also spawned a successful kid's series that has already sold 4.5 million copies; a top-selling dramatic audio series broadcast on more than 500 radio stations nationwide; a *Have You Been Left Behind?* video by Reverend Bernon Billings and the New Hope Village Church; the Reunion Records soundtrack for *Left Behind: The Movie*, including songs from Bob Carlisle, Michael W. Smith, Avalon, Kathy Troccoli, Clay Crosse and others; a compilation that serves as a companion to the book series, ForeFront Records' *People Get Ready*; web-based 'Readers Groups,' where *Left Behind* addicts can discuss storylines, characters and end-time events (even Jenkins admits to visiting some of the groups and 'chatting' with readers); and there's talk of a comic book series. There is also 'The Underground', a web-community for kids. The nifty membership kit, which 'equips today's Young Trib Force and teaches them how to share Christ,' includes: a watch; a mousepad; a keychain; a pocket-sized New Testament; an Army-style dog tag; a copy of *The Vanishing*, the first book in the kids series; an interactive CD ROM; and a sixteen-page manual on sharing Christ along with a daily journal" (Nicki Reno, "Ripe Harvest: The Left Behind Phenomenon", *Profile*, December 2000/January 2001). Also see Dinitia Smith, "Apocalyptic Potboiler Is Publisher's Dream", *New York Times*, June 8, 2000. Regarding earlier success of the series, see Jay Grelen, "The Revelation of LaHaye and Jenkins", *Christian Reader*, November/December 1999.

[2] Tim LaHaye and Jerry B. Jenkins, *Are We Living in the End Times?* (Wheaton, Ill.: Tyndale House Publishers, 1999). This book was written as a direct tie-in to the *Left Behind* books and is dedicated to "the millions of readers of the *Left Behind* series". The *Tim LaHaye Prophecy Study Bible King James Version* is published by AMG Publishers (Chattanooga, Tenn., 2000) and features the work of several members of the Pre-Trib Research Center, a dispensationalist group founded by LaHaye "for the purpose of encouraging the research, teaching, propagation, and defense of the pretribulational rapture and related Bible prophecy doctrines".

November 2000 and then, in an unusual move, appeared in theaters in early February 2001. It boasted a reported budget of $17 million, the largest ever for a movie produced by a Christian production company,[3] and a known, if not noted, actor, Kirk Cameron, himself a professed "born again" Christian. A sequel followed in 2002. Not only does the *Left Behind* phenomenon have staying power, it has influenced how thousands of readers view the world, God, and the end of time—which is exactly what the authors intended.

The Men behind the *Left Behind* Books

While Hal Lindsey was an unknown youth minister in Southern California at the start of his rapid rise to publishing

---

[3] Cloud Ten Pictures is a Canadian production company operated by brothers Paul and Peter Lalonde. The Lalondes have written popular dispensational articles and books and have produced several "end time" films, including *Revelation, Judgement*, and *Tribulation*. *Left Behind: The Movie* has sold close to three million units on video and was 2000's best-selling independent video (Lorenza Munoz, "Christian Movie Gains a Firm Toehold on Mainstream Circuit", *Los Angeles Times*, February 2, 2001). A detailed look at the making of current apocalyptic Christian movies can be found in Jim Nelson's "God Is on Line One", *GQ*, March 2001. Also see Denyse O'Leary, "Cameras Rolling", *Christianity Today*, July 10, 2000.

Cloud Ten Pictures was also a key player in the surprisingly successful *The Omega Code*, which was financed by Trinity Broadcasting Network (TBN) with a reported budget of $7 million. Marked by sketchy special effects, anti-Catholic overtones (the Antichrist is a former Catholic priest), and pseudo-dispensational theology, *The Omega Code* benefited from a strong grass-roots effort, aided by around-the-clock plugs by TBN, and grossed nearly $13 million. Although such movies are usually contained within the Fundamentalist subculture, apocalyptic elements do occasionally surface in more secular projects. A notable example was *The Rapture*, a 1991 big-budget picture starring Mimi Rogers (the former Mrs. Tom Cruise), loosely depicting the dispensationalist world view in an inaccurate and highly Hollywoodized fashion.

stardom in 1970, neither LaHaye nor Jenkins is a stranger to success in the Fundamentalist publishing world and beyond. Jenkins' accomplishments include an impressive list of some 120 books that he has authored or co-authored; he lent literary assistance to best-selling autobiographies by Billy Graham, Hank Aaron, Walter Payton, and a host of other (mostly Christian) celebrities. He was also the editor of *Moody Magazine*, a publication of Moody Bible Institute (MBI), one of the most venerable Fundamentalist Bible colleges in the United States and a dispensationalist stronghold.[4] True to the school's tradition, *Moody Magazine* is consistently dispensationalist and is often critical of Catholicism.

LaHaye, a graduate of Bob Jones University,[5] has been a well-known Fundamentalist pastor, author, and speaker since the 1970s, pastoring a megachurch in San Diego, founding FamilyLife Seminars and the Pre-Trib Research Center, and active in forming Christian schools. He has also authored nonfiction books on marriage, sexuality, and personal growth, many co-authored with his wife, Beverly. Some of these titles include *How to Win over Depression*, *The Act of Marriage*, *Spirit Controlled Living*, *How to be Happy though Married*, and *Anger Is a Choice*. LaHaye published his first work of "Bible prophecy" in 1972, *The Beginning of the End: Amazing Fulfillment of Prophecy Tells Earth's Future*, which was essentially an imitation

---

[4] Originally called Chicago Evangelization Society, MBI was founded in 1886 by Dwight L. Moody, a noted preacher and evangelist who supported dispensationalist teaching. For many decades it was considered to be one of the two or three more important educational centers for dispensationalists, the others being Dallas Theological Institute (Texas) and Bible Institute of Los Angeles (BIOLA).

[5] Bob Jones University, located in Greenville, South Carolina, is one of the more infamous anti-Catholic Fundamentalist schools in the United States.

of Hal Lindsey's early works.[6] A year later he published *Revelation: Illustrated and Made Simple*, a popular-level commentary filled with dramatic graphics and charts and a heavy dose of anti-Catholic rhetoric; it has since been republished as *Revelation Unveiled*.[7] In 2001 he founded the Tim LaHaye School of Prophecy in conjunction with Liberty University, an "independent, fundamentalist Baptist university" located in Lynchburg, Virginia. Liberty University is a premillennialist Bible school[8] founded by Jerry Falwell, the well-known Fundamentalist leader who has stated that he believes the Antichrist, a Jew, is alive today and will likely come to power within a few years. Without a doubt, LaHaye's reputation as a Fundamentalist leader, premillennial dispensationalist teacher, and opponent of Catholicism is well deserved.

Behind the Scenes of the *Left Behind* Books

Fictional portrayals of the end times and the Rapture, both in cinematic and literary form, have been regular and popular fare within Fundamentalist and Evangelical circles since the early 1970s, and in many ways the *Left Behind* books are par for the course. One unique feature is the arrangement

[6] Tim LaHaye, *The Beginning of the End* (Wheaton, Ill.: Tyndale House Publishers, 1972, 1991).

[7] Tim LaHaye, *Revelation: Illustrated and Made Plain* (Grand Rapids, Mich.: Zondervan Publishing House, 1973, 1975) and *Revelation Unveiled* (Grand Rapids, Mich.: Zondervan Publishing House, 1999).

[8] The Liberty University doctrinal statement includes: "We affirm that the return of Christ for all believers is imminent. It will be followed by seven years of great tribulation, and then the coming of Christ to establish His earthly kingdom for a thousand years. The unsaved will then be raised and judged according to their works and separated forever from God in hell. The saved, having been raised, will live forever in heaven in fellowship with God."

between LaHaye and Jenkins: the former provides the theological structure and general story line; the latter does the actual writing.[9] The books attempt to render the events of the book of Revelation in a fictional narrative, following the lives of several characters caught in the aftermath of the Rapture. These characters discover that they have been "left behind", come to accept the biblical "truth" of the Rapture, have "born again" experiences, and begin working to save as many souls as they can from impending destruction and the emerging Antichrist. All of this is in keeping with the traditional premillennial dispensationalist view of the end of the world.

From a literary perspective the *Left Behind* books are less than impressive.[10] The writing is mediocre, saturated with cliches and filled with wooden dialogue between two-dimensional characters. But the average writing and paper-thin

[9] In an interview with Larry King on June 19, 2000, both LaHaye and Jenkins talked candidly about how the books are written and for what purpose. LaHaye, the prophecy expert, provides Jenkins, the storyteller, with a notebook outlining the future "biblical events". LaHaye, Jenkins stated, "gives me a fairly ambitious workup before each book. I get a notebook from him that shows the chronology of the Biblical events and any character plot ideas, that type of thing. But mostly I get his commentary.... And I really immerse myself in those notebooks...." He later adds that "But when we cover the Biblical events, we try to tell those exactly the way we see them coming down if they're literal, and putting these fictitious characters in the way."

[10] Remarking in general on the quality of writing found in such popular prophecy books, whether fiction or otherwise, Paul Boyer writes that "[t]he genre of prophecy interpretation is an example of a collective discourse at the mass level. Individually, most of the authors lack stylistic or intellectual distinction. The writing is generally pedestrian and formulaic, the ideas for the most part banal and derivative. Yet viewed more broadly, and from a perspective of decades and even centuries, the genre is an engrossing one" (*When Time Shall Be No More: Prophecy Belief in Modern American Culture* [Cambridge, Mass.: Harvard University Press, 1998], p. xi).

characters hardly matter since the point of the series is to propagate dispensational beliefs about the end of the world, as evidenced by the numerous pages filled with sermons, lectures, and explanations about the Rapture, impending doom, and the coming Antichrist. In essence, the books are "tract novels", stories wrapped around huge chunks of blatant proselytizing. This is not lost on many readers of the series, as a perusal of their reviews on the Internet indicates. Some readers express annoyance at the "religious jargon", but many others are enthusiastic, making comments such as "I just finished this book and must say that it's the best novel I ever read" and "Upon stumbling upon Tim LaHaye and Jerry Jenkins' novel, *Left Behind*, I could finally get a grasp of Revelation through the glimpse of modern-day and real people I could relate to [sic]." One reader launched this revealing defense of the books:

> I have a hard time understanding those who berate this or any of the books in the series. Except the fact that their [sic] blind to the truths revealed. You have to remember that this is Biblically based fiction. And the authors are trying to get a message out. Will you hear it?[11]

What about Those Catholics?

After reading one of my articles criticizing the *Left Behind* series, a Catholic fan of the books told me that my concerns had no basis in reality. "You know," he said, "they actually have the Pope raptured. So they cannot be anti-Catholic." I encouraged him to read the books more closely since the

---

[11] All quotes from reader's reviews located on www.amazon.com.

passage he was referring to, found in the second book of the series, *Tribulation Force*, is actually an example of how the Catholic faith is subtly attacked in the *Left Behind* books. It depicts deep confusion among Catholics, as some have been raptured and others have been left behind. Among those Catholic who have disappeared is the newly installed pope, presented as a controversial figure who had taught "new doctrine" that was more in keeping with the teachings of Martin Luther than with official Catholic doctrine.[12]

The intent of this passage is clear: the new pope is secretly raptured *despite* being Catholic because he embraces the views of Martin Luther and has, by virtue of this fact, renounced Catholic teaching. So those Catholics who *reject* the Catholic faith can be "saved" and raptured, leading to the logical conclusion that Catholics who are loyal to Church are not "saved", are not true Christians, and will not be raptured.

This point is also made by depicting the leading Catholic character, the American Cardinal Mathews, as a greedy, power-hungry, biblically illiterate egomaniac whose devious actions apparently are the result of his adherence to "normal" Catholic beliefs and practices.[13] He later becomes the new pope and then the head of Enigma One World Faith, an evil, one-world religion. Taking the title *Pontifex Maximus Peter*, he declares war on anyone believing in the Bible. His anger is especially directed toward true Christians who meet in small house churches in suburbs across America. The

---

[12] See Tim LaHaye and Jerry B. Jenkins, *Tribulation Force: The Continuing Drama of Those Left Behind* (Wheaton, Ill.: Tyndale House Publishers, 1996), p. 53. Passages from *Tribulation Force* are not quoted here because Tyndale House denied me permission to reproduce them, apparently concerned with the critical stance of this book toward the *Left Behind* series.

[13] Ibid., pp. 271–78.

evil pope makes it clear that these believers and their attach-
ment to biblical truth will not be tolerated. He forms alliances with major world religions and preaches a message of
"tolerance" and "unity" devoid of any orthodox Christian
beliefs. The only people who stand up and denounce these
actions are, of course, Fundamentalists and Evangelicals who
hold fast to their belief in Jesus Christ. Pontifex Maximus
Peter persecutes those Christians for their "heretical" belief
that the Bible is the final authority for Christian doctrine
and practice. In other words, true Christians embrace *sola
scriptura* (no authority except the Bible).[14] Those familiar
with Fundamentalist culture and language will recognize this
as a way of saying that non-denominational "Bible churches"
are full of true Christians, with the strong implication that
the Catholic Church is evil, anti-Christian, and fully corrupt. It also wrongly equates affirming the Bible as the final
authority for faith and practice with affirming that salvation
comes only through Christ. Catholics affirm the latter, but
not the former.

Early in *Tribulation Force*, Cameron "Buck" Williams, the
senior staff writer for the *Global Weekly*, an international news
magazine[15] presses Cardinal Mathews for an explanation of
the disappearance of millions of people from earth. The shifty
cardinal makes some inane comments about the "days of
Noah" and the "Apocrypha" after which Buck asks him about
various passages of Scripture, especially Ephesians 2:8–9: "For
by grace you have been saved through faith, and that not of
yourselves; it is the gift of God, not of works, lest anyone
should boast." The cardinal dismisses Buck's questions by

[14] Ibid., pp. 401–2.
[15] Ibid., p. ix.

insisting that such passages are always being taken out of context.[16]

After his conversation with the cardinal, Buck writes an article in which the cardinal's evasion of "the doctrine of grace" brought to light. The implications of this fictional passage are evident: Catholicism is a false religion based on works, not grace, and the Catholics who were raptured were those who went against official Church teaching. This reflects LaHaye's Fundamentalist beliefs in *sola fide* (salvation by "faith alone") and *sola scriptura*. As LaHaye writes elsewhere, "Rome's false religion too often gives a false security that keeps people from seeking salvation by faith. Rome is also dangerous because some of her doctrines are pseudo-Christian. For example, she believes properly about the personal deity of Christ but errs in adding Babylonian mysticism in many forms and salvation by works."[17] Anyone familiar with the early ecumenical councils will find this amusing, but for those dispensationalists and Fundamentalists who are unfamiliar with Church history LaHaye's depiction of the Catholic Church is the Gospel truth.

Despite these jabs at Catholicism, the *Left Behind* novels are relatively subtle in their attacks on the Catholic faith; other dispensationalist works—as we will see—are more openly antagonistic to Catholicism. A contributing factor to this more mellow approach may be that LaHaye and Jenkins

---

[16] Ibid., pp. 54–55. Ephesians 2:8–9 is a favorite text for Fundamentalists to use in confronting what they believe to be "works righteousness" in Catholic doctrine. Most Fundamentalists insist that Catholics believe they can "earn" their way to heaven by being good and following Church law. A refutation of this claim and a presentation of the Catholic doctrine of salvation can be found in James Akin's *The Salvation Controversy* (San Diego: Catholic Answers, 2001).

[17] LaHaye, *Revelation Unveiled*, p. 269.

recognize that Catholics make up a substantial part of the Christian fiction market and might respond positively to the "soft sell". Ignorant or nominal Catholics make up a large number of "converts" to Fundamentalist groups, and LaHaye—who has written of his Catholic father's "conversion" experience[18]—undoubtedly wants to reel them in. When a reader complained online that one of the books— *Tribulation Force*—depicted most Catholics as being "left behind", Jenkins vehemently insisted that the books are "not anti-Catholic" and that "[a]lmost every person in the book who was left behind was Protestant. Astute readers will understand where we're coming from. True believers in Christ, regardless of their church 'brand' will be raptured."[19] Although that is debatable, Jenkins' remark about "church brands" is just as significant as his denial of anti-Catholic bias. The *Left Behind* books ignore, for the most part, denominational differences within the Protestant world. This is not altogether surprising since the dispensationalist system stresses that the "true Church" is invisible and that "true Christians" come from every sort of denomination, making

[18] "My own father was a Roman Catholic for the first twenty-six years of his life. He considered himself 'a good Catholic,' for he was baptized and confirmed in the church, went to Catholic schools, sang in the boys' choir, was an altar boy, and even had me baptized as an infant lest I die prematurely and go to hell or purgatory. When he heard the gospel at twenty-six and was personally 'born again' by faith in Jesus Christ, it totally changed his life. Often I heard him complain, 'No one in the church had ever told me I needed to be born again, by faith, not of works, but by God's grace. The sisters never told me; neither did the priest, the bishops, the cardinal, or even the pope.' ... Failing to bring him to God, my father's church had clouded the way of truth with all their Babylonian pagan innovations brought up through the centuries" (Ibid., pp. 269–70).

[19] From www.amazon.com, August 26, 1999.

such distinctions meaningless.[20] Of course, what constitutes a "true Christian" usually involves adhering to substantial portions of the dispensational perspective. Another, more practical reason is the authors' desire to attract a wide audience, which means playing down denominational differences within conservative Protestantism.

Far more overt attacks on Catholicism can be found in La-Haye's "nonfiction" books on Bible prophecy. Two of these—*Rapture under Attack* and *Revelation Unveiled*—are recently revised and reprinted editions of earlier books. A third, *Understanding the Last Days*, is a study guide for those interested in "Bible prophecy", and a fourth, *Are We Living in the End Times?*, was co-authored with Jenkins.[21] *Rapture under Attack* is a combative defense of the pretribulational Rapture. It includes the ironic claim that both "amillennialism and postmillennialism" use methods of Scripture interpretation similar to that of Christian Science, the Jehovah's Witnesses, Armstrong's World Church of Tomorrow "and most of the cults"[22]—a remark that betrays a polemical bent and questionable scholarship.[23]

---

[20] See chapter 7, "The Church, the Kingdom and Israel", for more on this concept of an "invisible church".

[21] LaHaye and Jenkins, *Are We Living in the End Times?*; Tim LaHaye, *Rapture under Attack* (Sisters, Ore.: Multnomah Publishers, 1998); *Revelation Unveiled*; and *Understanding the Last Days: The Keys to Unlocking Bible Prophecy* (Eugene, Ore.: Harvest House Publishers, 1998).

[22] LaHaye, *Rapture under Attack*, p. 223.

[23] These attempts to discredit amillennialism and postmillennialism using a "guilt by resemblance" tactic are toothless, since the eschatological views of the Watchtower Society and Armstrong's World Church of Tomorrow bear a far closer—even striking—resemblance to LaHaye's premillennial dispensationalist views. For more information on both groups, see Walter Martin's *The Kingdom of the Cults* (Minneapolis, Minn.: Bethany House Publishers, 1985).

Are We Living in the End Times? and *Revelation Unveiled* are both packaged to tie in with the *Left Behind* books.[24] Both contain lengthy and blatant attacks on the Catholic faith that would make Jack Chick, Loraine Boettner, and Dave Hunt[25] proud, especially since much of the material used is directly or indirectly taken from those authors. In *Revelation Unveiled*, LaHaye uses the traditional Fundamentalist tactic of correlating the church of Thyatira (Rev 2:18–29) with "the Pagan Church" of Rome. According to LaHaye, this apostate Church mixed paganism with Christianity, resulting in the Dark Ages and the existence of "Babylonian mysticism", a term he uses repeatedly in describing Catholicism. Boettner's infamous list of "doctrines" is provided,[26] including the practices of using holy water and singing the *Ave Maria*. LaHaye later praises "the greatest book ever written on [Babylon] ... the masterpiece *The Two Babylons*, by Rev. Alexander Hislop", and states that "to my knowledge" the book has never been refuted.[27] Unfortunately, he is apparently ignorant of the works of Catholic apologetics and historical scholarship that soundly refute the claims of Hislop and oth-

---

[24] "Now twenty-five years later [after the first publication] there is an even greater need for this book, particularly among the millions who are reading the *Left Behind* novels and becoming acquainted with the field of Bible prophecy for the first time" (LaHaye, *Revelation Unveiled*, p. 11).

[25] Chick, Boettner, and Hunt are three of the most infamous anti-Catholics of the last forty years. Jack Chick specializes in creating comic books and tracts with titles such as *The Death Cookie, Why Is Mary Crying?*, and *Are Roman Catholics Christian?* Loraine Boettner was the author of the anti-Catholic "Bible", *Roman Catholicism* (Phillipsburg, N.J.: Presbyterian and Reformed Publishing House, 1962). Dave Hunt is the author of *A Woman Rides the Beast: The Roman Catholic Church and the Last Days* (Eugene, Ore.: Harvest House Publishers, 1994), a work that seeks to prove that the Catholic Church is the whore of Babylon and the epitome of apostate, paganized Christianity.

[26] LaHaye, *Revelation Unveiled*, p. 66. See Boettner, *Roman Catholicism*, pp. 7–9.

[27] LaHaye, *Revelation Unveiled*, pp. 266–67.

ers like him.[28] After quoting several paragraphs of Hislop's book, LaHaye proclaims that "[a]fter reading the above quotations, you may be inclined to think me anti-Catholic, but that isn't exactly true; I am anti-false religion."[29] Not surprisingly, he does not directly quote from any official Catholic documents, but continually relies on standard anti-Catholic authors and works, all of which have been refuted in numerous ways and venues.

Are We Living in the End Times?, co-authored with Jenkins and laced with excerpts from the *Left Behind* series, is cut from the same cloth. Writing about the "Mystery Babylon religion", the authors make the remarkable and unsubstantiated claim that "Every false religion in the world can be traced back to Babylon." Babylon "is the mother of all false religions and Jerusalem is the mother of true faith", while Rome "is the mother of an unholy mixture of the two."[30]

---

[28] Perhaps the most damning indictment of Hislop's *The Two Babylons: The Papal Worship Proved to Be the Worship of Nimrod and His Wife* (originally written in 1853–1858) is Ralph Woodrow's *The Babylon Connection?* (Ralph Woodrow Evangelistic Association, 1997). In 1966 Woodrow wrote *Babylon Mystery Religion: Ancient and Modern* (Riverside, Calif.: Ralph Woodrow Evangelistic Association, 1966), a reworking of Hislop's book. After some time passed, Woodrow did further study and saw that Hislop's book was seriously flawed and historically untenable. "As I [studied]," Woodrow admits, "it became clear—Hislop's 'history' was often only mythology. Even though myths may sometimes reflect events that actually happened, an arbitrary piecing together of ancient myths can not provide a sound basis for history. Take enough tribes, enough tales, enough time, jump from one time to another, from one country to another, pick and choose similarities—why anything could be 'proved'!" (from www.amazon.com). Woodrow then wrote *The Babylon Connection?* and admitted the errors of his first book. For a Catholic critique of both Hislop and Woodrow, see Karl Keating, *Catholicism and Fundamentalism* (San Francisco: Ignatius Press, 1988), pp. 68–69, 159–63, 219–24.

[29] LaHaye, *Revelation Unveiled*, p. 269.

[30] *Are We Living in the End Times?*, p. 172.

The history of Christianity's slide into pagan practices such as "prayers for the dead, making the sign of the cross, worship of saints and angels, instituting the mass, and worship of Mary" are presented in somber fashion.[31] The "spiritualizing of Scripture" instituted by Augustine is pinpointed as the key moment in the decline in "scriptural authority",[32] while the "disappearance" of the Scriptures for 1,100 years is fully explained: they "were kept locked up in monasteries and museums" while "the Dark Ages prevailed."[33] When LaHaye and Jenkins solemnly note "that as many as 40 million persons were killed during that period when Babylonian mysticism controlled the church",[34] one can only conclude that the authors' Fundamentalist and dispensationalist beliefs have shaped their seriously flawed views of the Catholic Church, Church history, and historical theology. In turn, LaHaye and Jenkins are shaping the opinions of millions of readers who either knowingly or unconsciously are absorbing their faulty belief system.

In *Revelation Unveiled* LaHaye dedicates a chapter to the "Babylonian idolatrous religion"—the Catholic faith.[35] He also makes the unsubstantiated charge that nearly every distinctively Catholic doctrine or practice is based on the pagan activities of "Hindus, Buddhists, Confucianists, Taoists, Mohammedans, and primitive religionists".[36] In fact, LaHaye claims, "In India we find that Hinduism is so parallel to the practices of Romanism that many of the Hindus can become

[31] Ibid., pp. 173–74.

[32] Ibid., p. 174.

[33] Ibid.

[34] Ibid., p. 175. No footnote is given by the author, and for good reason: the claim is completely spurious. See Keating's *Catholicism and Fundamentalism*, pp. 290–300.

[35] *Revelation Unveiled*, pp. 260–77.

[36] Ibid., p. 264.

Roman Catholics and need not give up Hinduism." [37] The Catholic Church, is "not the only form of Babylonian Religion, but merely the one that has infiltrated Christianity".[38] Catholicism, LaHaye insists, is at the heart of the "plan of the devil"—ecumenical unity and "a one-world religious system".[39]

Not surprisingly, LaHaye has never retreated from these sorts of erroneous statements. This makes the success of the *Left Behind* books all the more bothersome, especially considering how popular they appear to be among so many Catholics. LaHaye and Jenkins' apocalyptic potboilers have been written for one main purpose, and it has nothing to do with leaving a literary heritage: it is to spread and encourage LaHaye's Fundamentalist, dispensationalist, anti-Catholic beliefs. The novels are simply fictionalized narratives based on his previous works of "Bible prophecy"; they are also largely dependent on the works and ideas of other dispensationalists, especially Hal Lindsey. As one Evangelical critic flatly states: *"Left Behind is a rehash of Hal Lindsey's Late Great Planet Earth."* [40]

What Has Been Done Has Been Done . . . Before

In an interview with *Pentecostal Evangel* magazine, LaHaye boasts that *"Left Behind* is the first fictional portrayal of events that are true to the literal interpretation of Bible prophecy. It

[37] Ibid., p. 275. See Keating, *Catholicism and Fundamentalism*, pp. 154–63.

[38] *Revelation Unveiled*, p. 271. Again, no explanation or documentation is given. Anyone familiar, even modestly, with Hinduism and Catholicism knows that the two beliefs and practices are very different in many essential regards, most significantly with respect to the Catholic doctrines of one God, the Trinity, and the Incarnation.

[39] Ibid., pp. 271–72.

[40] Gary DeMar, *Biblical Worldview Magazine*, vol. 17, no. 3 (March 2001).

was written for anyone who loves gripping fiction featuring believable characters, a dynamic plot that also weaves prophetic events in a fascinating story." [41] Setting aside the question of whether or not the books are actually "gripping" or "dynamic", LaHaye's claim of fictional originality is simply false. Not only have other novels based on dispensational premises been written prior to 1995, LaHaye and Jenkins' initial novel was not even the first dispensational-driven book to be published using the title *Left Behind*!

In July 1995 Harvest House Publishers, a prominent Fundamentalist publishing house located in Eugene, Oregon, released husband and wife team Peter and Patti Lalonde's endtime book *Left Behind* [42] (LaHaye's *Left Behind* was first published in September of the same year). Though not a novel, the Lalondes' book describes life on earth after the Rapture and warns readers to be prepared for that imminent event. Although its cover claims that there are "over 200,000" copies in print, the Lalondes' book was dwarfed by LaHaye and Jenkins' work of the same name, published just a couple of months later. Ironically, the names of Lalonde and LaHaye would be linked together when LaHaye and Jenkins sold the movie rights to their books to the Lalondes' movie production company, Cloud Ten Pictures. [43]

[41] "Conversation with Tim LaHaye: Prophecy-Based Fiction", *Pentecostal Evangel*, March 28, 2000. *Pentecostal Evangel* claims to be "the world's largest Pentecostal magazine".

[42] Peter and Patti Lalonde, *Left Behind* (Eugene, Ore.: Harvest House Publishers, 1995).

[43] LaHaye has subsequently sued Cloud Ten Pictures for breach of contract. He claims that the production company did not deliver on its promises to spend at least $40 million in making the movie and to have it in theaters by January 1, 2000. See John Lippman, "Christianity at the Cineplex", *The Wall Street Journal*, February 1, 2001.

End-time novels in the premillennial dispensationalist mold actually date back to the 1930s, when a book titled *Be Thou Prepared, for Jesus Is Coming* was published, depicting "the impact of the Rapture on a typical American city, where the righteous have suddenly vanished, leaving the ungodly behind".[44] The novel describes in graphic detail the bloodthirsty actions of the Antichrist, including scenes of people receiving the infamous mark of the beast. The same events and story line surfaced in 1970 in Salem Kirban's *666*, a book described by the author as "a novel" and "fiction", with the additional remark that "it is important to note that very much of it is also FACT."[45] The plot and characters are remarkably similar to those found in LaHaye's "original" *Left Behind* novel. Kirban's novel opens as a non-believing reporter experiences the Rapture (as an observer, not participant) while on an airplane flight. Upon returning home he finds that his Christian wife is (of course) missing; he finds her Bible, reads 1 Corinthians 15:52–53, and comes to believe in Jesus Christ. Soon he discovers that the Antichrist is a rogue Catholic leader. After managing to infiltrate the Antichrist's inner circle, he witnesses the forces of Russia and China descending upon Israel, only to see them destroyed by the returning Christ at the battle of Armageddon. The publisher of Kirban's novel was Tyndale House Publishers, LaHaye and Jenkins' publishing house. Not only are the best-selling *Left Behind* books *not* the "first fictional portrayal" of dispensational end-times events, they bear a close resemblance to the earlier, admittedly less sophisticated, apocalyptic novel by Kirban.

---

[44] Boyer, *When Time Shall Be No More*, pp. 106, 370.

[45] Salem Kirban, *666* (Wheaton, Ill.: Tyndale House Publishers, 1970), p. 10; emphasis in original. Kirban would go on to write dozens of books on the end times during the 1970s, 1980s, and 1990s.

Since LaHaye has been in the Bible prophecy business for over thirty years, it is difficult to believe he had no knowledge of the books by Kirban and the Lalondes. Regardless, it goes to show that much of today's "Bible prophecy" is not nearly as current as is sometimes claimed but is often of a recycled, reworked variety. While "Bible prophecy" experts like LaHaye may miss the mark about the future, perhaps the *Left Behind* books have, in a certain way, fulfilled *these* words of Scripture: "What has been is what will be, and what has been done is what will be done; and there is nothing new under the sun" (Eccles 1:9).

3

A BOOK OF CONFUSION
OR REVELATION?

Many rush from their first profession of faith to the last book in the Bible, treating it as little more than a book of hallucinations, hastily disdaining a sober-minded attempt to allow the Bible to interpret itself—and finding, ultimately, only a reflection of their own prejudices.

—David Chilton

The book of Revelation is easily the most fascinating book in the Bible, for it gives a detailed description of the future.

—Tim LaHaye

You might be a dispensationalist ... if you've only been a Christian for one year and your pastor has preached through the book of Revelation more than two times.

— *The Door Magazine*

The book of Revelation, the Apocalypse, is arguably the most cryptic, difficult, mysterious, and disputed book in the New Testament—or in the entire Bible, for that matter. As Catholic theologian Scott Hahn notes, "In all of its parts, the book seems to defy common sense and good taste." [1] Historian

---

[1] Scott Hahn, *The Lamb's Supper: The Mass as Heaven on Earth* (New York: Doubleday, 1999), p. 61.

Paul Boyer writes, "For centuries Revelation has challenged believers and unbelievers alike. Jerome concluded that it contains 'as many mysteries as it does words'; George Bernard Shaw flippantly dismissed it as the product of a drug addict's fevered brain." [2] While Shaw spoke from ignorance and anti-Christian bias, his remark does capture the bewilderment common to many readers. Even some of the early Church Fathers were disturbed by the book and were reluctant to place it in the New Testament canon. Throughout Church history opinions about the book's value and meaning have been numerous and varied, with the Eastern Churches expressing reservations about it for several centuries. [3]

While the Apocalypse sometimes repulsed readers over the centuries, it attracted and mesmerized others. Joachim of Fiore (ca. 1135–1202), a Catholic monk and Scripture scholar whose influence on the study of the book of Revelation is still felt today, wrote that the book is "the key of things past, the knowledge of things to come; the opening of what is sealed, the uncovering of what is hidden". [4] As we will see, Joachim's

---

[2] Paul Boyer, *When Time Shall Be No More: Prophecy Belief in Modern American Culture* (Cambridge, Mass.: Harvard University Press, 1998), p. 42. Boyer's book contains a chapter entitled "Origins of the Apocalypse" (pp. 21–45) that provides an overview of key texts, including the book of Revelation, written from a non-Christian, scholarly perspective.

[3] "So at the close of the first decade of the fifth century the entire Western Church was in possession of the full Canon of the New Testament. In the East ... opinions were still somewhat divided on the Apocalypse. But for the Catholic Church as a whole the content of the New Testament was definitely fixed, and the discussion closed" (George J. Reid, "Canon of the New Testament", *The Catholic Encyclopedia*, vol. 3 [Robert Appleton Company, 1908; online edition, 1999]).

[4] *Expositio in Apocalypsim* (Venice, 1527; reprint, Frankfurt on the Main, 1964), fol. 3r. Quoted in Richard K. Emmerson and Bernard McGinn, eds. *The Apocalypse in the Middle Ages* (Ithaca, N.Y.: Cornell University Press, 1992), p. 19.

controversial opinions have not been viewed favorably by the Church. Even men like Martin Luther and John Calvin, neither known for being silent about controversial matters, initially shied away from the work. Calvin, in fact, never did say or write much about it. Eventually Luther would teach that the book of Revelation prophesied and outlined the gradual unfolding of history since the time it was written. He was, Evangelical scholar Steve Gregg notes, "one of the first commentators to see Revelation from chapter 4 onwards as a prophetic survey of church history.... Luther's general approach to Revelation was followed by virtually all the Reformers and by Protestants well into the 19th century." [5] Luther's teaching shaped the popular Protestant belief that the Catholic Church and the papacy were, respectively, the whore of Babylon and the Antichrist written of in the

---

[5] Steve Gregg, ed., *Revelation, Four Views—A Parallel Commentary* (Nashville: Thomas Nelson Publishers, 1997), p. 31. "Luther alone among the magisterial reformers displayed a healthy interest in things apocalyptic, and even he only gradually overcame his disdain for the book of Revelation. In a 1522 preface, he condemned the text as 'neither apostolic nor prophetic,' and suggested that Jerome, who had taken an interest in it, should have devoted his attention to more worthy areas of scripture. He concluded a three-paragraph introduction with the decidedly uninspired opinion, 'My spirit cannot fit itself into this book. There is one sufficient reason for me not to think highly of it,—Christ is not taught or known in it.' In his revised preface to the Apocalypse in 1530, however, he abandoned the traditional Augustinian interpretation for a more literal stance.... Despite his increased interest in Revelation, in 1530 (as compared to 1522) Luther made only a few cautious attempts to identify its various vials, trumpets, and seals with events from church history. He stated at the outset that the Revelation fell under the most obscure sort of prophecy, which foretold the future 'without either words or interpretations,' but with dreams, visions, and symbols" (Benjamin A. Ehlers, "Luther and English Apocalypticism: The Role of Luther in Three Seventeenth-Century Commentaries on the book of Revelation", *Essays in History*, vol. 34 [Corcoran Department of History at the University of Virginia, 1992]; accessed online).

Apocalypse.[6] In an attempt to counter this interpretation, some sixteenth-century Jesuits spread the notion that the book referred to only two periods of time: the early Church and the very end of time.[7] And so, ironically, the basis for modern futurism—the belief that the book of Revelation is primarily about the end of time—was born, a creation of Catholic minds.

Over the last couple of centuries many Christians, including most Catholics, have avoided the final book of the Bible, confounded by its imagery and uncertain as to whether or not it offered any meaning useful for their lives. Others have viewed it as a cosmic puzzle begging for the right key to unlock its mysteries, a blueprint of the future for those careful enough to decipher its markings. Premillennial dispensationalists, of course, see in the book of Revelation "the key to the mystery", a mystery that has "for eighteen centuries ... remained largely unexplored".[8]

"Book" to the Future

The basic dispensationalist approach to the book of Revelation begins with the premise that it had little or no meaning for the early Christians. It was a book meant to be "locked",

---

[6] The belief that the Catholic Church was evil and somehow related to the whore of Babylon and the Antichrist was not new with the Protestant Reformers. John Henry Newman, in *The Development of Christian Doctrine*, notes that many of the early heretical groups taught similar beliefs: "In one point alone the heresies seem universally to have agreed,—in hatred to the Church.... Catholics were called ... by Donatists, 'the traitors,' and 'the sinners,' and 'servants of Antichrist'" (*The Development of Christian Doctrine* [New York: Longmans, Green, 1949], pp. 234–35).

[7] Gregg, ed. *Revelation*, pp. 31–32.

[8] Hal Lindsey, *There's a New World Coming* (Santa Ana, Calif.: Vision House Publishers, 1973), pp. 21, 15.

or "sealed" until the time of its fulfillment approached.[9] Hal Lindsey, quoting C. I. Scofield, the editor of the dispensational Bible, the *Scofield Reference Bible*, explains:

> "The book is so written that as the actual time of these events approach, the current events will unlock the meaning of the book." He [Scofield] pointed out that the book of Revelation didn't have too much meaning to people a few centuries ago, and that for this reason very few people were willing to study its message. Revelation is written in such a way that its meaning becomes clear with the unfolding of current world events.[10]

In the popular dispensationalist reading of the book of Revelation, current events reveal, and even interpret, its meaning. While Christians of past centuries had occasionally aligned images and symbols within it to events and persons of their own times, this method of interpreting its meaning is largely a recent approach. It is also one filled with problems, including the possibility—long realized now—of an endless stream of highly subjective interpretations of "Bible prophecy" in light of current events. Lindsey claims the recent "great revival of interest in prophecy is actually one of the important signs of the end times",[11] providing a perfectly ironic example of a "self-fulfilled prophecy". Yet it logically follows that once people accepted the dispensational method of interpreting the book of Revelation there would be a flood of interpretations connecting it to events as varied as the French Revolution, the Civil War, the Holocaust, the assassination

[9] These are references to Daniel 12:9 and Revelation 10:4. See Lindsey, *There's a New World Coming*, pp. 21–22.

[10] Lindsey, *There's a New World Coming*, p. 21.

[11] Ibid.

of John Kennedy, and the creation of the European Common Market.

The latest and most popular dispensational take on the book of Revelation can be found, of course, in the *Left Behind* novels. As Tim LaHaye acknowledges, the novels are simply an interpretation of the book of Revelation in which the characters are fictional, while the global events described in the books reflect the "definitive" teachings of the last book of the Bible:

> For that entire series is based on the future events found in the book of Revelation. Modern men and women want answers to the future and Revelation provides them. Thousands of readers of the *Left Behind* series have written or e-mailed us to say our prophetic novels have inspired them to read the book of Revelation for the first time (some several times) and found it thrilling. That should not be surprising, particularly in light of the fact that it is the only source we have for definitive answers for those events of the future that intrigue us all.[12]

Thus, according to LaHaye, the point of John's vision is to foretell the future for twenty-first century Americans. Oddly enough, prognosticators like LaHaye always seem to locate the date of the end times no more than a few years ahead in time, conveniently within their life span. This was usually the case with millenarians two centuries ago and is still the case with dispensationalists today. Christ may have said, "But of that day and hour no one knows, not even the angels of heaven, nor the Son, but the Father only" (Mt 24:36), but

---

[12] Tim LaHaye, *Revelation Unveiled* (Grand Rapids, Mich.: Zondervan Publishing House, 1999), p. 9.

his words have not restrained popular dispensationalists from creeping as close to the date-setting line as they can without actually crossing over it. LaHaye writes, "A study of the 'signs' of the end of the age or the return of Christ should always be undertaken with a degree of restraint. Date-setters are to be ignored or, even better, rebuked as false teachers." [13] Yet a bit later he pens another passage filled with the strained mixture of temerity and ambiguity often found in popular dispensational writings:

> We really do have some powerful reasons for supposing that our generation has more reason than any before us to believe He could come in our lifetime! Still, although there are several signs of the end in existence today, we refuse to set limits on the season. But we will point out that some of these signs did not exist even a half generation ago. At the outset, however, we wish to state categorically that we refuse to predict that Christ *will* come in our lifetime, for He may delay His coming another fifty years or more. Still, we believe the evidence is to the contrary. [14]

This tension between not knowing and knowing creates some of the high-wire appeal of the dispensationalist method, since it seemingly bridges the gap between the present and the future with a string of ingeniously knotted together Bible verses. Unlike the Millerites or the Watchtower Society— nineteenth-century American millenarians who set exact dates for the Second Coming—dispensationalists will rarely state a

[13] Tim LaHaye and Jerry B. Jenkins, *Are We Living in the End Times?* (Wheaton, Ill.: Tyndale House Publishers, 1999), pp. 22–23.
[14] Ibid., pp. 23–24.

definitive date for the pretribulational Rapture.[15] Instead they speak of the "signs" of Christ's coming, pointing to a variety of current events that come and go with dizzying rapidity. Adherents of this method rarely have a chance to ponder why last week's events, which offered remarkable proof that the Rapture could occur within days, are now forgotten and replaced with new events, which in turn will also disappear in short order.[16] Inevitably an overly eager and confident prognosticator sets a firm date. Sometimes the date comes and goes and no one notices; occasionally it ruins the date-setter's reputation. But for those who master the tightrope, it stretches on into the future with no real end in sight.

[15] The Millerites were a millenarian group in the American Midwest, led by a Baptist farmer, William Miller, who predicted that Christ's Second Coming would occur in March 1844. When that date came and went, Miller recalculated that Christ would return in October of the same year. The failure of Millerism "discredited historicist premillennialism, causing it to fade out almost entirely after 1844; and the Millerite fiasco demonstrated the perils of setting definite dates for Christ's return" (Richard Kyle, *The Last Days Are Here Again: A History of the End Times* [Grand Rapids, Mich.: Baker Books, 1998], p. 91). The Jehovah's Witnesses, Kyle notes, "may be the most persistent date-setters in history. Most such groups make one or perhaps two failed predictions. But the Jehovah's Witnesses won't quit. Their leaders have earmarked the years 1874, 1878, 1881, 1910, 1914, 1918, 1925, 1975, and 1984 as times of eschatological significance" (p. 93).

[16] An example—just one of many possible—is a small book written by Jack Van Impe titled *Bible Headlines* (Royal Oak, Mich.: Jack Van Impe Ministries, 1980). On the inside flap, Van Impe writes, "These are exciting days for Christians—and fearful ones for unbelievers. Never have we witnessed so many of the signs predicted by the Lord Jesus Christ to be in effect immediately prior to His return." The book is filled with dozens of newspaper headlines and the opening paragraphs of news stories, all dated from late 1979 and early 1980. Each of these is compared to biblical passages that, Van Impe claims, show that the time is short: "No longer is it intelligent to scoff God's Word. By doing so, one only shows his ignorance of current events" (p. 12).

Four Approaches to the Four Horsemen

There are four generally recognized methods of interpreting the book of Revelation: the *idealist*, the *futurist*, the *historicist*, and the *preterist*.[17]

The *idealist* believes the book to be mostly or entirely symbolic, containing little or no real reference to actual historical events whether past or future. For him, the book is meant to portray the spiritual conflict between good and evil that each Christian endures within the circumstances of his life or that transpires within reality on a cosmic scale: "The symbols or events [the book of Revelation] describes will not come to pass at some specific point in history, but represent and present some 'timeless truths,' truths about the nature of reality or human existence that either are continuously present or continually recur. One does not ask of them 'When?' but rather 'What?' "[18] Also called the *spiritual* form of interpretation, the roots of this approach can be found in the early

---

[17] Gregg's "parallel commentary", *Revelation*, is a unique and helpful resource that parallels these four views using texts from adherents of each respective position and also provides a helpful introduction to the book of Revelation and a history of the four interpretive methods. Other views, not as well known or utilized, do exist. Catholic scholar Patrick Fannon, S.M.M., in his essay "The Apocalypse", lists "seven different approaches to the interpretation of the Apocalypse": (1) millenarianism, (2) recapitulations—"successive cycles of visions" that repeat the same events in different ways, (3) the method of universal history, or historicism, (4) the method of contemporary history, or preterism, (5) the eschatological interpretation, or futurism, (6) the method of literary analysis, which claims the book is a complex mix of disparate sources, and (7) the comparative method, which compares the book to non-Christian religions and sources (Patrick Fannon, "The Apocalypse", in M. Rosalie Ryan, C. S. J., ed., *Contemporary New Testament Studies* [Collegeville, Minn.: Liturgical Press, 1965], pp. 443–52).

[18] Millard J. Erickson, *A Basic Guide to Eschatology: Making Sense of the Millennium* (1977; Grand Rapids, Mich.: Baker Book House, 1998), p. 30.

Alexandrian Fathers, especially in the writings of Origen (ca. 185–254). Intent on repudiating *chiliasts*[19]—those who believed in a literal thousand-year reign of Christ—Origen, Clement of Alexandria, and others interpreted the symbols and events in the book of Revelation without reference to historical events, but saw them as guides to spiritual truths:[20]

> According to this view, the great themes of the triumph of good over evil, of Christ over Satan, of the vindication of the martyrs and the sovereignty of God are played out throughout Revelation without necessary reference to single historical events. The battles in Revelation may be seen as referring to spiritual warfare, to the persecution of Christians, or to natural warfare in general throughout history.[21]

Variations of this view are held by some Catholic theologians and can also be found in many mainstream Protestant churches. While this method has sometimes been labeled a "liberal" approach, this statement is a simplistic understanding of a view with an ancient and rich heritage.[22]

The *futurist*, as the name indicates, believes that the book of Revelation outlines events that are going to occur primarily in the future, at the end of time. Dispensationalists and others who believe in some sort of Rapture are futurists.

---

[19] From the Greek word *chilioi*, meaning "one thousand".

[20] "The Alexandrian Fathers rejected millennialism. These Fathers introduced a more spiritualizing approach to Revelation. Origen (ca. 185–254) repudiated the literal interpretation of the chiliasts as 'Jewish'" (Gregg, *Revelation*, p. 30). While Origen's method of interpretation was occasionally extreme, a more modified form of idealism—as applied to the book of Revelation—was used by Augustine in *City of God*.

[21] Gregg, *Revelation*, p. 43.

[22] Although it ignores Catholic scholarship, an introduction to the idealist, or spiritual, approach can be found on pages 30–33 and 43–46 of Gregg's *Revelation*.

Not all futurists are dispensationalists; others who can be classified as futurists would include historical premillennialists (Protestants who believe in an earthly millennium but not in a pretribulational Rapture) and sects such the Church of the Latter-Day Saints, the Watchtower Society, radical right-wing political groups, and pseudo-Christian neo-Gnostic cults.[23] This approach apparently originated with a Jesuit, Francisco Ribiera, who used it in the late 1600s to refute the historicist claim that the papacy was the "beast" found in the book of Revelation.[24] For at least two centuries afterward Protestants avoided the futurist view. But in the early 1800s it was accepted by certain British millenarians, including John Nelson Darby, and today it is the most well-known of the four views, especially as developed in the form of dispensational premillennialism.

Historicists contend that the events described by John take place over the whole of Christian history, beginning with the early Church and continuing on into the present age. This view dates back about a thousand years, with the most important of the early historicists, Joachim of Fiore, being a Catholic monk and scholar. Martin Luther popularized the historicist view, which was accepted by nearly all the Protestant Reformers and leaders of the next two hundred years, including John Calvin, John Wesley, Jonathan Edwards, Charles Finney, and Matthew Henry.[25] In this view, the one "non-negotiable feature ... is the assertion that the papacy is

---

[23] A fine book about such groups is Richard Kyle's *The Religious Fringe: A History of Alternative Religions in America* (Downers Grove, Ill.: InterVarsity Press, 1993).

[24] Gregg, *Revelation*, p. 42.

[25] Ibid., p. 34.

'Antichrist'".[26] Since the early 1800s its popularity has waned dramatically, corresponding to the rise of futurism. Today, adherents to this interpretive method would include Seventh-Day Adventists, for whom equating the whore of Babylon with the Catholic Church is a key premise within their entire eschatological system.[27] Many Seventh-Day Adventists propose that the futurist and preterist views were created by Jesuits for the purpose of undermining the truth of the historicist method. As we will see, when it comes to the first three chapters of the book of Revelation many dispensationalists follow the historicist interpretation in one form or another.

The *preterist* believes that the book of Revelation describes events that have already occurred in the life of the

---

[26] Ibid., p. 35.

[27] An excellent example are the writings of the Seventh-Day Adventist "prophetess" Ellen G. White. Her book *The Great Controversy* (1888) is a lengthy history of Christianity, based on the central premise that the Catholic Church is satanic and pagan in nature, while the Seventh-Day Adventists have restored truth and pure Christianity. Chapters include subheadings such as "The Rites of Heathenism Adopted", "Establishment of Romanism", "Pagan and Papal Errors", and so forth. Seventh-Day Adventists believe that the "mark of the beast" revealed in Revelation 13 refers to worship on Sunday. White writes, "The spirit of concession to paganism opened the way for a still further disregard of Heaven's authority. Satan tampered with the fourth commandment also, and essayed to set aside the ancient Sabbath, the day which God had blessed and sanctified, and in its stead to exalt the festival observed by the heathen as 'the venerable day of the sun'.... The great apostate [Satan] had succeeded in exalting himself 'above all that is called God, or that is worshiped.' He had dared to change the only precept of the divine law that unmistakably points all mankind to the true and living God" (*The Great Controversy* [Phoenix, Ariz.: Inspiration Books, 1973], pp. 49, 50–51). A critique and summary of Seventh-Day Adventist beliefs can be found in Walter Martin's *The Kingdom of the Cults* (Minneapolis, Minn.: Bethany House Publishers, 1985), pp. 409–500. Martin does not label Seventh-Day Adventism as a cult, but points out the many serious problems with the group's unique beliefs.

early Church, usually understood as the persecution of Christians by the Jewish leaders and the Roman emperors (especially Nero) and the fall of Jerusalem in A.D. 70. While early Church writings, such as Eusebius' *Ecclesiastical History*,[28] contain elements of preterism, the modern preterist system was created by the Jesuit Luis de Alcazar (1554–1613) in another attempt to refute the historicist view held by most of the early Protestants.[29] Today, many Christians of the Reformed Protestant tradition are preterists. Although some of these preterists believe that parts of the book of Revelation may apply to the future, they are especially opposed to dispensationalist beliefs. Some of the best critiques of dispensationalism have been written by preterist theologians. An increasing number of Catholic scholars adhere to preterism, at least in a modified form.

As If It Wasn't Messy Enough Already!

Within each interpretative camp there exists an often bewildering range of opinions about a large number of factors. Often the lines are blurred between any number of the four groups. For example, as mentioned, many futurists will interpret the first three chapters of the book of Revelation

---

[28] Eusebius, after quoting some of Christ's words from the Olivet Discourse (Mt 24:19–21), talks about the destruction of Jerusalem: "In computing the whole number of those who lost their lives, the historian says that famine and the sword destroyed 1,100,000 persons.... These things happened in the second year of Vespasian's reign [A.D. 70], in exact accordance with the prophetic predictions of our Lord and Saviour Jesus Christ, who by divine power had foreseen them as though already present, and wept and mourned over them, as we learn from the holy evangelists ..." (Eusebius, *The History of the Church*, bk. 3, chap. 7 [London: Penguin Books, 1965], p. 117).

[29] Gregg, *Revelation*, p. 39.

using a method best described as historicist. Pointing to Revelation 4:1, where John is told by a voice from heaven, "Come up hither, and I will show you what must take place after this", dispensationalists claim this verse is an implicit reference to the Rapture[30] and the dividing line between those events that John had seen in his own day and those events that were yet to come in the future.[31] Therefore, what is described in the first three chapters of Revelation pertains to John's time—but also, on another level, to the whole of Church history. Thus the messages to the seven churches, found in the second and third chapters of the book of Revelation, are believed to have more than one "application", meaning that each church and its particular qualities relates to a specific era of Church history. LaHaye, in his commentary *Revelation Unveiled*, follows this fairly common practice, stating that while this belief in the "seven stages of

[30] "Inasmuch as John was the last remaining apostle and a member of the universal Church, his elevation to heaven is a picture of the Rapture of the Church just before the Tribulation begins.... The Rapture of the Church is not explicitly taught in Revelation 4 but definitely appears here chronologically at the end of the Church Age and before the Tribulation" (LaHaye, *Revelation Unveiled*, pp. 99, 100).

[31] This method of dividing the book is based upon Revelation 1:19: "Now write what you see, what is and what is to take place hereafter." LaHaye writes of this verse that it "is the key verse that unlocks the door to the entire outline of the book. It is further evidence of the threefold division of this great Revelation. John was told expressly by Christ to write—

1.   'what you have seen
2.   what is now ...
3.   what will take place later'

"From this it seems evident that the book is made up primarily of future events. It includes some things that existed in John's day (chaps. 2–3), all based on the things he saw. From this, we see that the futurist interpretation of the book is the valid one" (ibid., p. 21).

church history has never been unanimous, it is held by most premillennialists".[32] He outlines the supposed correlation between the churches and particular eras of history, using a method of labeling that has an obvious bias against the Catholic Church:

1. Ephesus—Apostolic church (A.D. 30–100)
2. Smyrna—Persecuted church (A.D. 100–313)
3. Pergamos—State church (A.D. 313–590)
4. Thyatira—Papal church (A.D. 590–1517)
5. Sardis—Reformed church (A.D. 1517–1790)
6. Philadelphia—Missionary church (A.D. 1730–1900)
7. Laodicea—Apostate church (A.D. 1900–)[33]

LaHaye admits that characteristics of each of these seven churches can be found in churches or among Christians

---

[32] Ibid., p. 100. This method of interpreting the seven churches of Revelation goes back to at least Cyrus I. Scofield, whose *Scofield Reference Bible* (1909; New York: Oxford University Press, 1945) exerted tremendous influence within Fundamentalist and Evangelical circles during the twentieth century. His reference Bible outlines the "fourfold application" that should be used in understanding the messages to the churches (pp. 1331–32). His notes within the text refer to "The message of Thyatira. A.D. 500–1500: the triumph of Balaamism and Nicolaitianism; a believing remnant".

Hal Lindsey popularized this method in his best-selling book *There's a New World Coming*. In chapters titled "Panorama of Church History—I" and "Panorama of Church History—II", Lindsey writes that the church of Thyatira fits "the church era [that] spanned the Middle Ages. During this time the dominant church fabricated a system, that, like Jezebel, bound the people to image-worship, superstition, and priestcraft. These Scripture verses indicate this church will still have some adherents and some power into the 'great tribulation' (verse 22). But the believing remnant from this prostituted form of Christianity is promised it will be present at the Rapture and will be delivered from the clutches of the 'mother' church by Christ's return (verse 25)" (p. 58).

[33] LaHaye, *Revelation Unveiled*, 36. Hal Lindsey essentially follows the same structure and alignment in *There's a New World Coming*, pp. 38–73.

today. In devoting a chapter to each church, LaHaye first
focuses on the historical church in question (according to
his chronological system) and then on the positive and negative qualities of each church that he believes still exist in
present-day churches.

Within anti-Catholic Fundamentalist denominations, a sermon on the church of Thyatira (Rev 2:18–30) is guaranteed
to be an "exposé" of the Catholic Church, her "pagan" practices, and her many "man-made" traditions. For example, I
was recently given a tape of a sermon—presented within a
large Baptist church—that followed this script perfectly. The
title of the sermon was "The Church of Thyatira—Jezebel
Lives".[34] After reading Revelation 2:18–30, the pastor provided some historical background, emphasizing Thyatira's
idolatry, immorality, and blindness to truth. He then launched
into a rapid tour of the "pagan practices" that he claimed
evolved out of Thyatira's sin: worship of saints, the idolatry
of the Mass, and purgatory. This led to the assertion that
"millions and millions of people went to their graves without Jesus Christ because they trusted the Church instead of
the Bible." [35] In all of this the pastor nimbly avoided using
the word "Catholic" even one time, but no doubt existed as
to the subject of the sermon. When I contacted the pastor
by telephone and questioned his claims and methods, he
matter-of-factly explained that he was not anti-Catholic but
believed that only the Catholic Church possesses the size
and influence necessary to establish the "One World Religion" prophesied in the book of Revelation. Not surprisingly, the fear of an apostate, global religion and a belief in

[34] Pastor Kimball Hodge, "Jezebel Lives: The Church of Thyatira", audio
tape (First Baptist Church, Eugene, Ore., February 28, 1999).
[35] Ibid.

its connection to the Catholic Church are central features of almost all popular dispensationalist teachers.[36]

Another example of tension within the interpretive approaches to the book of Revelation is found in the preterist school of interpretation. As noted, many Protestants of the Reformed tradition are preterist, but not all of them are of the same mold. "Full" or "radical preterists" believe that the Parousia, the resurrection, the Day of the Lord, and the Judgment *all* took place in A.D. 70 with the fall of Jerusalem. "Partial" or "moderate preterists" believe that Christ's statements about these events either have more than one fulfillment or need to be carefully distinguished and rightly applied to events occurring around A.D. 70 or to events at the end of time. Noted Reformed pastor and theologian R. C. Sproul states in his study of preterism and eschatology, *The Last Days according to Jesus*, "We may distinguish between two distinct forms of preterism, which I call radical preterism and moderate preterism. Radical preterism sees all future prophecies of the New Testament as having already taken place, while moderate preterism still looks to the future for crucial events to occur."[37]

Which Interpretive Method Is Catholic?

While the liturgy and tradition of the Catholic Church draw deeply from the liturgical and theological elements of the book of Revelation, there is no official Catholic choice among

[36] Those institutions or groups under suspicion of being potential members or catalysts of the New World Order or One World Government include the United Nations, the European Common Market, the Vatican and Catholic Church, and the United States.

[37] R.C. Sproul, *The Last Days according to Jesus: When Did Jesus Say He Would Return?* (Grand Rapids, Mich.: Baker Books, 1998), p. 24.

the four interpretive methods. And for good reason. While these interpretations are helpful—providing foundations and structures for more detailed study—they all have certain limitations and flaws. None offers a completely satisfying explanation of the book of Revelation—nor does it need to. The Catholic need not succumb to an "either/or" dilemma. Catholics can embrace a "both/and"—in this case "all/and"—approach, recognizing in each method a solid core of truth and insight that does not contradict the others. In *The Lamb's Supper*, Scott Hahn describes how as a Protestant he embraced each of the four methods at different points of his Christian life, choosing one while spurning the others. "Which view do I follow [now]?" Hahn writes, "Well, all of them. There's no reason they can't all be true simultaneously." [38] In other words, a Catholic is quite free to believe that the book of Revelation describes the conflict of good and evil as experienced on a cosmic, transhistorical scale (idealism) *and* makes certain prophetic utterances about events that have yet to occur (futurism) *and* also refers both explicitly or indirectly to events that have already occurred, either in the early Church or farther along in the history of the Church (preterism and historicism).

Such flexibility is due, not to any lack of decisiveness on the part of the Catholic, but to a recognition that Scripture, inspired by God, can be multivalent and full of overlapping, yet complementary, meanings. [39] This does not mean that

[38] Hahn, *The Lamb's Supper*, p. 73.

[39] This understanding of Scripture as having different meanings on different "levels" is based in the ancient Catholic recognition of the four senses of Scripture. The *Catechism of the Catholic Church* distinguishes between two senses of Scripture: the *literal* and the *spiritual* (see CCC 112–19). A helpful popular introduction to the four senses of Scripture is Mark P. Shea's *Making Senses out of Scripture: Reading the Bible as the First Christians Did* (San Diego, Calif.: Basilica Press, 1999), pp. 161–245.

just any interpretation can be placed onto the Apocalypse or that every element of each interpretive method can be embraced equally or completely by the Catholic. For example, full preterism, which insists that all of the events depicted, including the Second Coming, occurred in A.D. 70 is contrary to the Catholic Church's clear belief that the Second Coming will be visible and has not yet occurred.[40] But a form of "partial preterism", which holds that the beast of Revelation 13 is first-century Rome *and* also any system of belief that is opposed to God is a valid position for a Catholic. One of the finest Catholic commentaries, *The Navarre Bible*, largely follows an idealist interpretation, but writes that "John is describing the situation of the Church in his own time *and* he is also surveying the panorama of the last times."[41] There is a vital tension in the book of Revelation between the immediacy of the end times—we live in them *now*—and the fact that the End has yet to be reached and realized. "The Parousia of the Lamb, slain but triumphant, is not, in the Apocalypse, something still to be achieved in the far future: it is here and now, within us.... Standing as [the Apocalypse] does between the two comings of Christ, its message is one of consolation and hope to a Church that will reach its glory through suffering."[42]

---

[40] See CCC 673–74, 1001, 1038.

[41] *The Navarre Bible. Revelation: Texts and Commentaries* (Dublin: Four Courts Press, 1992), p. 19. Also: "The Apocalypse is a theological vision of the entire panorama of history, a vision which underlines its transcendental and religious dimension.... The book does depict the cosmic struggle between good and evil, but it takes for granted Christ's ultimate triumph. This is, in our view, the most valid interpretation of the book and therefore it is the one we follow in the commentary provided" (ibid., p. 19).

[42] Dom Celestin Charlier, *The Christian Approach to the Bible* (Westminster, Md.: Newman Press, 1965), p. 201.

Handle with Caution!

Presbyterian scholar David Chilton offers these words of wisdom regarding the study of the final book of the Bible:

> From the outset, two problems confront us when we attempt to study the book of Revelation. First is the question of ensuring that our interpretation is correct—placing checks on our imagination, so that we do not force God's holy Word into a mold of our own inventions. We must let the book of Revelation say what God intended it to say. The second problem is the issue of ethics—what to do with what we've learned.[43]

The ease with which either of these two points can be violated or ignored should not be underestimated. The first problem—the temptation to interpret the book of Revelation based on subjective or unsubstantiated grounds—is rampant, especially among popular dispensationalists. Once this temptation is embraced, the second problem—what do I *do* with my interpretation?—logically follows. Since dispensationalists insist that the book of Revelation is a blueprint of the immediate future, their natural instinct is to warn the world of this impending doom. Or, just as often, attempt to scare people into believing in a God who apparently desires little more than the annihilation of most of humanity.

Newcomers to the book of Revelation should doubt anyone claiming that it is primarily about rapidly approaching events and that *he* has (finally!) correctly interpreted its meaning. Such claims are spurious and almost completely subjective. They rest on the flawed assumption that John's vision

---

[43] David Chilton, *Paradise Restored: A Biblical Theology of Dominion* (Tyler, Tex.: Dominion Press, 1994), p. 151.

was written exclusively for our day and therefore can be accurately understood in light of current global events. This leads to an obsessive search of newspapers and television footage for the key that will unlock the door to the book of Revelation, instead of letting Scripture interpret Scripture.[44]

A good example of the search for current events that will interpret the Apocalypse is afforded by the infamous "mark of the beast", referred to several times by John (Rev 13:15–18; 14:9–11; 16:2; 19:20; 20:4), but most famously in Revelation 13: "This calls for wisdom: let him who has understanding reckon the number of the beast, for it is a human number, its number is six hundred and sixty-six" (Rev 13:18). The dispensationalist interpretations of this infamous number's meaning range from curious (entertainment park validation stamps on the hand) to common (credit cards and social security numbers) to hi-tech (computer chips under the skin). However much they disagree about how the mark will be applied, dispensationalists insist this is a "literal" mark. Yet they are largely silent when it comes to passages that describe people with "his Father's name written on their foreheads" (Rev 14:1; 7:3; 9:4; 22:4). Why has there not been much, if any, attention given to these passages, especially since they pertain directly to Christians? As Chilton notes, the astute reader of Scripture will not go to modern computer technology in order to interpret the mark of the beast or God's name on the forehead of his servants, but to Scripture:

---

[44] Both Hal Lindsey and Jack Van Impe provide classic examples of interpreting Scripture through newspaper clippings. In their respective television programs they are continually pulling up headlines and showing footage from the Middle East, explaining how this event and that nonevent have been foretold in Scripture. And then, the following week, new headlines and fresh footage are shown, fulfilling the same prophecies. And on and on it goes....

The symbols would have made them think immediately of several Biblical references: the "mark" of sweat on Adam's forehead, signifying God's Curse on his disobedience (Gen. 3:19); the forehead of the High Priest, marked with gold letters proclaiming that he was now HOLY TO THE LORD (Ex. 28:36); Deuteronomy 6:6–8 and Ezekiel 9:4–6, in which the servants of God are "marked" on the hand and forehead with the law of God, and thus receive blessing and protection in His name. The followers of the Beast, on the other hand, receive his mark of ownership: submission to ungodly, statist, antichristian law.[45]

While the mark of the beast may point to a specific person, such as Nero,[46] the scriptural approach still holds true—the mark indicates obedience and loyalty either to Christ or to the Antichrist, for "he who is not with me is against me" (Mt 12:30).

The key to the book of Revelation is not found in some technological or political event, but in The Event—the Incarnation, the entrance of God into time and space. As the

---

[45] David Chilton, *Days of Vengeance: An Exposition of the Book of Revelation* (Fort Worth, Tex.: Dominion Press, 1987), p. 31.

[46] Chilton writes: "For example, the symbolic number 666 (Rev 13:18) clearly refers to Nero Caesar; but if John had merely intended that his readers should understand 'Nero Caesar,' he would have written 'Nero Caesar', not '666.' He used the number 666 because of an already established system of Biblical imagery that allowed him to say a great many things about Nero simply by using that number" (ibid., p. 35). Also see pp. 344–52 for a detailed examination of "666". Remarking on Revelation 13:18, the *Navarre Bible, Revelation* commentary states: "The author of the Apocalypse here uses a method (called *gematria* in Greek) to reveal the name of the beast in a numerical form. In both Hebrew and Latin letters of the alphabet were also used as numbers. The figure 666 fits with the name Caesar Nero in Hebrew. Some manuscripts gave the number as 616, which fits Caesar Nero in Greek. However, Tradition does not provide an exact interpretation and various other names have in fact been suggested" (p. 108).

Dominican scholar H. M. Féret observes, "The Christian vision that comes to us from Patmos is primarily this: a vision of Christ, and a delineation of the invisible but positive part he plays in history."[47] Although the book of Revelation *is* about history, it is history as seen from the throne room of God (Rev 4:1–2).[48] It is true that John's vision culminates with an end of temporal history, the "new heaven and new earth" and the full realization of the Kingdom, the New Jerusalem (Rev 21:1–2). To that end the book *is* about the future. It is also about the future to the degree that it describes the sort of persecution, difficulties, and troubles the Church will endure throughout time. But to insist that it is concerned with placing names and dates on approaching earthly events such as battles and treaties and nuclear wars is a serious mistake. Such a slavish futurism not only makes the book meaningless for the vast majority of Christians, it misses the apostle's continually developing theme of the eternal entering into the temporal, first at the Incarnation, and ever since then through the working of the Holy Spirit in building up the Church, "the seed and the beginning" of the Kingdom. Of this central idea another Dominican, Celestin Charlier, states:

[47] H. M. Féret, O. P., *The Apocalypse Explained* (Fort Collins, Colo.: Roman Catholic Books, 1958), p. 59. Féret also remarks, "In reality [the Apocalypse] presents the elements of a genuine Christological synthesis, sometimes by inference, sometimes explicitly formulated. One may even go so far as to say that, of all the writings of the New Testament previous to the fourth gospel, it presents Christology in its most developed form" (p. 59).

[48] "Confusion has been caused by John the Seer being told, in Revelation 4, 'Come up here, and you will be shown what must happen hereafter.' Revelation 4 itself is not a picture of the future. It is a symbolic picture of the heavenly throne room *within which* the secrets of the future are revealed" (N. T. Wright, "The Future of Jesus", in Marcus J. Borg and N. T. Wright, *The Meaning of Jesus: Two Visions* [San Francisco: HarperCollins, 2000], p. 198).

It is a pity that the Apocalypse has so often been regarded as a secret code containing details of the whole of Church history. In fact the only prophecy that it makes is that there will always be persecution until the final triumph. It is much more than a cipher—it is a prolongation throughout time of that rhythm of God's plan which was conceived in eternity and gradually woven into the very material of this world through the double incarnation, verbal and personal, of the Son of God. The entire history of all ages is the framework of the Father's plan—that is the theme of the Apocalypse. The Father's merciful design has not been cut short, nor is his love in any way exclusive. Christ is infinitely more than the climax of God's plans—his is the beginning of a new cycle of redemption which penetrates heaven itself.[49]

The Catholic belief that the Kingdom has been established and is growing even now, until the end, is at complete odds with the futurist, dispensationalist belief that the Kingdom has not yet come and that the King is not even ruling the world![50] These opposing visions form the backdrop against which essential disagreements over the Apocalypse's main themes, context, and meaning for Christians today come into bold relief.

Apocalypse and Prophecy

The book of Revelation opens with the words "The Apocalypse of Jesus Christ...." The Greek word *apokalupsis* means

---

[49] Charlier, *Christian Approach to the Bible*, p. 201.

[50] "Had the people received Him, He would have fulfilled the kingly prophecies in their day in addition to the ones regarding the suffering Messiah. But when the Jewish nation as a whole rejected Christ, the fulfillment of His kingship was postponed until the final culmination of world history" (Lindsey, *There's a New World Coming*, p. 30).

"an uncovering" or "unveiling".[51] The *apocalypse* was a popular form of Jewish religious literature in the two centuries immediately prior to Christ. While the prophets had written mostly about the need of the people to repent and return to God, the authors of apocalyptic works turned their attention to the end of time and the hope that God would soon destroy Israel's enemies and establish an earthly kingdom.[52] These works were "characterized by the presence of vision, symbolism, a human seer and an otherworldly mediator, an otherworldly journey, and emphasis on events in the cosmic rather than human realm, an increased interest in

---

[51] "The word 'apocalypse' means a 'revelation' or 'unveiling', so that an apocalyptic book claims to reveal things which are normally hidden and to unveil the future" (F. L. Cross and E. A. Livingstone, eds., *The Oxford Dictionary of the Christian Church*, 3d ed. [Oxford: Oxford University Press, 1997], p. 82). "The very word apocalyptic denotes the unveiling by which for the seer the veil that covers the supernal or infernal realities is drawn aside, and he is enabled to contemplate the secrets of the cosmos and of history. This feature appears again and again in Jewish Christian apocalyptic, which is likewise composed of ascensions or heavenly visions" (Jean Daniélou, S.J., *The Theology of Jewish Christianity*, The Development of Christian Doctrine before the Council of Nicaea, vol. I [London: Darton, Longman and Todd, 1964], p. 173).

[52] "Whereas the Israelite Prophets were primarily teachers, concerned with current problems of their own generation and nation, the Apocalyptists were pre-eminently writers, directing their attention towards the end of things and to the destiny of the world in general. The origins and growth of this literature reflect the history of Israel's conflicts with other nations and the conviction that trust in military power was useless. As the nation continued to be subjected to foreign domination, it despaired of ever attaining political supremacy, and the conclusion was drawn that God would eventually intervene, destroy Israel's enemies, and set up His Kingdom on earth" (Cross and Livingstone, *Oxford Dictionary*, pp. 82–83). "These books all had two basic features: (a) they dealt with the subject of the last age of the world, when good would triumph and evil would be annihilated; (b) they made much use of symbolism taken from the animal kingdom, astrology, numbers, and so forth, to depict past and present history and to prophesy the future" (*Navarre Bible, Revelation*, p. 17).

angels and demons, the notion of the transcendence of God, and pseudonymity".[53] Because John's book describes itself as "the apocalypse of Jesus Christ", it has unfortunately, but conveniently, been labeled a "Christian apocalypse", as though it were simply a christianized version of the Jewish works. This is misleading, for whatever obvious similarities exist between the book of Revelation and Jewish apocalyptic literature,[54] they are not as striking or as significant as the differences.

Some traits often found in many Jewish apocalyptic writings that are not found in the book of Revelation include an inconsistent use of symbolism that is understandable to only a select few and an overwhelming sense of pessimism and despair. Apocalyptists believed that God would have little or

---

[53] David Noel Freedman, ed., *Eerdmans Dictionary of the Bible* (Grand Rapids, Mich.: W.B. Eerdmans, 2000), p. 72. Also, "Jewish apocalyptic featured a marked dualism of the ages, with the present age, as it drew to a close, hopelessly given over to the powers of evil. The future age was about to commence through divine intervention. Soon God would put down evil once and for all, so that he might inaugurate a new age of blessedness. It was frequently declared that the old earth would be replaced by a new one. As the old age was in its death throes, there would be marked activity by angels and demons.... In apocalyptic, cosmic disturbances are prominent, including the shaking of the earth's foundations, the opening of the doors of the underworld, the roaring of the oceans, and a host of natural disasters. Even the heavenly bodies are disturbed, and there are universal calamity and woe. Some of the apocalypses describe a messiah-like figure called the Son of man. The Son of man stands in opposition to the champion of evil, and antichrist sometimes depicted as a human and other times as a mythological character or the incarnation of a demon" (Daniel J. Lewis, *3 Crucial Questions about the Last Days* [Grand Rapids, Mich.: Baker Books, 1998], p. 70).

[54] Obvious similarities include a cosmic vision conveyed with intense and complex symbolism; they are written both to console and encourage readers experiencing crisis and persecution; and they look forward to God's righteous judgment of evil-doers.

nothing to do with history until he ended it.[55] These elements bear a remarkable similarity to the popular dispensationalist perspective, which asserts that only dispensationalists can understand the book of Revelation, that life on earth is mostly pessimistic, and that there is little reason for working within history to better the earth and the state of humanity. The saying, "Too heavenly minded for any earthly good" can safely be applied to many popular dispensationalists and their attitudes toward culture, society, and history.[56] In

[55] "The book of Revelation is often treated as an example of the 'apocalyptic' genre of writings which flourished among the Jews between 200 B.C. and A.D. 100. There is no basis for this opinion whatsoever, and it is unfortunate that the word *apocalyptic* is used at all to describe this literature.... There are, in fact, many major differences between the 'apocalyptic' writings and the book of Revelation. The 'apocalyptists' expressed themselves in unexplained and unintelligible symbols, and generally had no intention of making themselves really understood. Their writings abound in pessimism: no real progress is possible, nor will there be any victory for God and His people in history. All we know is that the world is getting worse and worse. The best we can do is hope for the End—soon" (Chilton, *Days of Vengeance*, p. 25). "Compared with the Prophets, authors of apocalypses have distinct features of their own: a) they write under pseudonyms, using the names of celebrated figures who might have received divine revelations—men like Enoch who Genesis 5:24 tells us was taken to heaven at the end of his life; b) in general, they conceive this world as being in the power of Satan and incapable of regeneration, and therefore they place their hopes in a new world to be created by God: the most that man can contribute is prayer; c) they exhibit a marked tendency towards determinism: everything that has to be said is contained in these books, and very little room is left for freedom and personal conversion" *(Navarre Bible, Revelation*, p. 17).

[56] "Dispensationalism promoted a kind of supernaturalism that, for all of its virtues in defending the faith, failed to give proper attention to the world. The supernaturalism of dispensationalism, especially in the extreme forms that were easiest to promote among the populace at large, lacked a sufficient place for the natural realm and tended toward a kind of gnosticism in its communication of truth. Adherents were instructed *about* nature, world events, ethics, and other dimensions of human existence, but almost always without studying these matters head-on. Bible verses were quoted to explain conditions and

direct contrast to Jewish apocalyptic works, the book of Revelation has a consistent and thoroughly biblical symbolism; it
is marked by a strong sense of triumph and peace; and it
clearly depicts the ongoing work of God on earth, first and
foremost in the person of Jesus Christ and his Body, the
Church, but also through the activity of angels and even the
forces of nature. Chilton writes: "The apocalyptists said:
The world is coming to an end: Give up! The Biblical prophets
said: *The world is coming to a beginning: Get to work!*"[57]

The book of Revelation has much more in common with
the Old Testament prophets than with Jewish apocalyptic writings.[58] John refers to his work as "prophecy" several times, as
in his opening passage, where he writes, "Blessed is he who

---

events in the world, but with very little systematic analysis of the events and
conditions themselves" (Mark Noll, *Scandal of the Evangelical Mind* [Grand
Rapids, Mich.: W. B. Eerdmans, 1994], p. 132). Noll, a prominent Evangelical
scholar and professor of history at Wheaton College, provides an insightful
and occasionally scathing critique of dispensationalism in his acclaimed (and
controversial) book.

[57] Chilton, *Days of Vengeance*, p. 26.

[58] "While employing the style, imagery, and procedure of Jewish apocalyptic, [the New Testament Apocalypse] remains faithful to the great tradition of
the ancient prophets. Like the prophets, the author has a passion for the salvation of souls (as the seven opening letters show) and wishes to reply to the
most vexatious problems of his time. The prophetic core in the Apocalypse
has always been recognized in tradition, but an oblique view of the nature of
prophecy had the unfortunate effect of seeing the contents of the Apocalypse
as a detailed blueprint of events to be pursued during the history of the
Church.... But not only is the Apocalypse firmly embedded in the prophetic
tradition; it has no hesitations in borrowing from Ezekiel, Zechariah and Daniel to an extent which is nothing short of plagiarizing. We can go further. John
has exploited the Old Testament in such a way that no less than five hundred
Old Testament allusions decorate his work" (Fannon, "Apocalypse", pp. 446–
47). Chilton notes that the book of Revelation draws deeply upon the prophet
Ezekiel, with "no less than 130 separate references to Ezekiel" occurring in
John's work (*Days of Vengeance*, p. 20). He provides a detailed list of parallels
between the two works (*Days of Vengeance*, p. 21).

reads aloud the words of the prophecy, and blessed are those who hear, and who keep what is written therein; for the time is near" (Rev 1:3). As the *Navarre* commentary notes, "Although St John's work is entitled Apocalypse (Revelation), its key features are more akin to the books of the Prophets than to those of 'apocalyptic writers.' He in fact describes his book as 'prophecy' (1:3; cf. 22:7, 10, 18, 19; 22:9), and although for the most part he uses language and symbolism akin to Jewish apocalyptic writing, his historical perspective is quite different." [59] This raises the issue of the nature and purpose of biblical prophecy, another source of disagreement between dispensationalists and many other Christians, including Catholics.

For dispensationalists, biblical prophecy is "history written in advance" [60] by God. It is the exact and detailed foretelling of events—some already in the past, some yet to come—meaning that "Bible prophecy can become a sure foundation upon which your faith can grow—and there is no need to shelve your intellect while finding this faith." [61] For most Fundamentalists and some Evangelicals, the fulfilled prophecies of Scripture are primary evidence that the Bible is truly God's Word. Best-selling dispensationalist author Grant Jeffrey writes, "One of the strongest evidences of the divine inspiration of Scripture is the phenomenon of fulfilled prophecy." [62] While there is nothing wrong with

[59] *Navarre Bible, Revelation*, p. 18.

[60] This popular phrase, used by many dispensationalists, is apparently the creation of Herbert W. Armstrong (1892–1986), founder of the apocalyptic cult the Worldwide Church of God.

[61] Hal Lindsey with C. C. Carlson, *The Late Great Planet Earth* (New York: Bantam Books, 1970), p. 7.

[62] Grant R. Jeffrey, *Armageddon: Appointment with Destiny* (Toronto: Frontier Research Publications, 1997), p. 67.

noting fulfilled prophecy—a practice used often within the New Testament—popular dispensationalists either implicitly or explicitly make Bible prophecy a central feature of belief and practice, tacitly making Christianity into a matter of statistics and probability.

Jeffrey, a former accountant, is especially fond of number-crunching when it comes to demonstrating the veracity of biblical prophecy. In "The Precision of Prophecy", a chapter from his book *Armageddon: Appointment with Destiny*, Jeffrey compares the predictions of modern psychics with the prophecies in the Bible, in which "we encounter a different phenomenon of staggering mathematical proportions. The Bible contains hundreds of incredibly accurate predictions of events ... that defy mathematical probability." [63] After several pages of evaluating eleven fulfilled biblical prophecies according to the "Laws of Probability", Jeffrey concludes that "the odds of the prophets of the Bible correctly guessing all eleven prophecies is 1 chance in 10 to the 19th power. That is only one chance in 10 billion times 1 billion." [64] This approach emulates and reflects the influence of Hal Lindsey in its predictions of the future and elaborate interpretations of end-time events, [65] a practice also followed by LaHaye, John Walvoord, and numerous others. [66]

[63] Ibid., p. 15.

[64] Ibid., p. 22.

[65] Lindsey's megaselling *The Late Great Planet Earth* (1970) was all about "Bible prophecy" and current-day events. Early chapters—such as "When Is a Prophet a Prophet?"—use statistics and probabilities to show the accuracy of Bible prophecy, while the remainder of the book features Lindsey relating prophecies (many from the book of Revelation) to global events in the late sixties and early seventies.

[66] In addition to titles and authors already mentioned, other popular dispensational best sellers have included Dave Hunt, *Global Peace and the Rise of Antichrist* (Eugene, Ore.: Harvest House Publishers, 1990); Grant R. Jeffrey, *Apocalypse: The Coming Judgment of the Nations* (New York: Bantam Books, 1992), and *Arma-*

Although many passages in Scripture are predictive in nature, the intention of such prophecy is not to provide a detailed blueprint of the future. It is meant to change the lives of the recipients by calling them to repentance and exhorting them to live in accordance with God's law. Chilton emphasizes that

> if there was one major concern among the Biblical prophets, it was ethical conduct. No Biblical writer ever revealed the future merely for the sake of satisfying curiosity: The goal was always to direct God's people toward right action in the present. The overwhelming majority of Biblical prophecy had nothing to do with the common misconception of "prophecy" as foretelling the future. The prophets told of the future only in order to stimulate godly living.[67]

This call to obedience is evident in the book of Revelation, as when John writes, "Blessed is he who reads aloud the words of the prophecy, and blessed are those who hear, and who *keep* what is written therein; for the time is near" (Rev 1:3; emphasis added). For Christians, the life of holiness comes by being united with Christ, who is the Prophet (Jn 6:14; 7:40), the source of prophecy (Rev 22:6–7), and the subject of all prophecy: "For the testimony of Jesus is the spirit of

---

geddon; Peter and Patti Lalonde, *Left Behind* (Eugene, Ore.: Harvest House Publishers, 1995); John Walvoord, *Armageddon, Oil and the Middle East Crisis* (Grand Rapids, Mich.: Zondervan Publishing House, 1990), and *Major Bible Prophecies: 37 Crucial Prophecies that Affect You Today* (New York: HarperCollins, 1991).

[67] Chilton, *Days of Vengeance*, p. 27. Old Testament scholar Gerhard von Rad writes, "The characteristic feature of the prophet's message is its actuality, its expectation of something soon to happen. This should be the touchstone of the use of the term 'eschatological'.... Their concern was not the faith, not even the 'message': it was to deliver a specific message from Yahweh to particular men and women who, without themselves being aware of it, stood in a special situation before God" (*The Message of the Prophets* [New York: Harper and Row, 1965], pp. 91, 100).

prophecy" (Rev 19:10). Sadly, the constant focus on Jesus Christ within the book of Revelation is often missed or downplayed by modern readers, a testimony to the attraction of "knowing" the future instead of following the call to "die in the Lord" (Rev 14:13), whether it be physically or by taking up our cross daily.

Prophecy and Covenant in the Apocalypse

John the Revelator's prophetic work, like that of the Old Testament prophets, centers on the covenant relationship between God and his people and emphasizes the blessings and curses that come with the covenant. Many Christians are ignorant of the vital place of the covenant in the book of Revelation since they are largely illiterate when it comes to the Old Testament. This lack of knowledge is perhaps the biggest obstacle to understanding and appreciating the book, since it "depends on the Old Testament much more than does any other New Testament book.... The symbolism of the Revelation is saturated with Biblical allusions that were commonly understood by the early Church." [68] Oftentimes the Old Testament is viewed as a collection of fine stories

---

[68] Chilton, *Days of Vengeance*, p. 30. "The book of Revelation thus tells us from the outset that its standard of interpretation is the Bible itself. The book is crammed with allusions to the Old Testament. Merrill Tenney says: 'It is filled with references to events and characters of the Old Testament, and a great deal of its phraseology is taken directly from the Old Testament books. Oddly enough, there is not one direct citation in Revelation from the Old Testament with a statement that it is quoted from a given passage; but a count of the significant allusions which are traceable both by verbal resemblance and by contextual connection to the Hebrew canon number three hundred and forty-eight. Of these approximately ninety-five are repeated, so that the actual number of different Old Testament passages that are mentioned are nearly two hundred and fifty, or an average of more than ten for each chapter in Revelation.' Tenney's count of 348 clear Old Testament references breaks down as

meant for teaching lessons in morality and ethics. It is, how-ever, much more—the history of God's relationship with hu-manity, formed through a series of covenants made with Abraham, Moses, and David.[69] These covenants followed the structure of peace treaties among ancient Near Eastern peo-ples and included a preamble, a historical prologue, ethical stipulations, sanctions (blessings and curses), and arrange-ments for succession.[70] Ken Guenter, an Evangelical profes-sor of Old Testament, provides this analogy explaining the covenantal relationship between God, the people, and the prophets:

> It is helpful to compare reading the prophets with listening to a game on the radio. The players are the Israelites and they were in the last quarter of their history when the proph-ets wrote. The rules which governed their play were the Laws of Moses. God was the referee. He penalized the guilty and rewarded those who followed the rules, the Law. The whole system of penalties and rewards had been clearly spelled out from the beginning in their covenants. We know about the game through two sources, the O.T. Historical Books and the Prophets.[71]

---

follows: 57 from the Pentateuch, 235 from the Prophets, and 56 more from the historical and poetical books" (Chilton, *Days of Vengeance*, pp. 29–30).

[69] See CCC 56–64.

[70] "Unless we see the book of Revelation as a Covenant document—i.e., if we insist on reading it primarily as either a prediction of twentieth-century nuclear weapons or a polemic against first-century Rome—its continuity with the rest of the Bible will be lost. It becomes an eschatological appendix, a view of 'last things' that ultimately has little to do with the message, purpose, and concerns of the Bible. Once we understand Revelation's character as a Cov-enant Lawsuit, however, it ceases to be a 'strange,' 'weird,' book; it is no longer incomprehensible, or decipherable only with the complete New York Times Index. In its major themes at least, it becomes as accessible to us as Isaiah and Amos" (Chilton, *Days of Vengeance*, p. 30).

[71] Ken Guenter, *The Prophets in Israel: A Biblical Anthology* (Caronport, Sask.: Briercrest Bible College, 1990), p. iii. Also, "For a variety of reasons most Old

The indictments of the Old Testament prophets, who acted as "prosecuting attorneys" sent by God,[72] were always given within the context of the covenants, first outlining the sins of Israel and Judah and then announcing the judgments that would fall on them. These judgments were patterned after the original covenantal structure found in the Pentateuch.[73] The book of Revelation is concerned with the relationship between two covenants: the Old Covenant, established with the people of Israel, and the New Covenant, established with the New Israel through the blood of the Lamb who had been slain (Rev 5:6).

Although John only uses the word "covenant" one time (Rev 11:19), covenantal elements are abundant; according to some scholars John followed the same covenant structure as did the Old Testament prophets.[74] The book of Revelation begins with the declaration that the Church is the New Israel, "a kingdom" (Rev 1:6), ruled by Christ, the "son of

---

Testament scholars are aware of most of the covenants but they do not necessarily emphasize them. Over the years my students and I have found over 1600 fairly clear quotations from the covenants or uses of distinct covenant concepts in the prophets" (p. 67). Guenter teaches Old Testament at Briercrest Bible College in Saskatchewan, Canada.

[72] Chilton, *Days of Vengeance*, p. 15.

[73] "In other words, just as the Biblical covenants themselves follow the standard five-part treaty structure, the Biblical prophecies follow the treaty form as well" (ibid., p. 15). Chilton compares the prophecy of Hosea to the covenantal structure of Deuteronomy.

[74] Ibid., pp. 13–20. In relation to the covenant structure found in the Old Testament, especially Deuteronomy, Chilton outlines the book of Revelation as follows (p. 17):

1. Preamble: Vision of the Son of Man (1)
2. Historical Prologue: The Seven Letters (2–3)
3. Ethical Stipulations: The Seven Seals (4–7)
4. Sanctions: The Seven Trumpets (8–14)
5. Succession Arrangements: The Seven Chalices (15–22)

man" (Rev 1:13), who comes as the eternal High Priest (Rev
1:12–20). This is followed by a historical prologue (chapters
2 to 3), in which a history of the covenant among the seven
churches is given. This includes a series of exhortations to
repent, patterned after the prophet Ezekiel (Ezek 14:6; 18:30).
At the start of the fifth chapter John writes of the One on
the Throne: "And I saw in the right hand of him who was
seated on the throne a scroll written within and on the back,
sealed with seven seals" (Rev 5:1). This is a reference to the
Ten Commandments, the heart of the Mosaic covenant, consisting of "tables that were written on both sides; on the one
side and on the other were they written" (Ex 32:15). The
only one found worthy to open the scroll is Jesus Christ, the
Mediator and Author of the New Covenant, who by his
death and Resurrection has formed a new people, the New
Israel:

> and they sang a new song, saying, "Worthy art thou to take
> the scroll and to open its seals, for thou wast slain and by thy
> blood didst ransom men for God from every tribe and tongue
> and people and nation, and hast made them a kingdom and
> priests to our God, and they shall reign on earth" (Rev
> 5:9–10).[75]

The New Covenant, rooted in Christ's person and work,
reaches fulfillment at the end of the book of Revelation when
the holy city, the New Jerusalem, comes "down out of heaven
from God, prepared as a bride adorned for her husband"

---

[75] Compare to Peter's first epistle: "But you are a chosen race, a royal priesthood, a holy nation, God's own people, that you may declare the wonderful
deeds of him who called you out of darkness into his marvelous light. Once
you were no people but now you are God's people; once you had not received
mercy but now you have received mercy" (1 Pet 2:9–10).

(Rev 21:2). Here, in the final book of the Bible, the imagery of the Old Testament (e.g., Is 54:5) and that of the New Testament (e.g., Eph 5:23–33) unite to describe the Church, "destined to descend all glorious from heaven at the end of time, [and] now building itself up on earth in the history which is unfolding today".[76] Those who have kept the commandments (Rev 12:17; 14:12) will enter into the presence of God: "And I heard a great voice from the throne saying, 'Behold, the dwelling of God is with men. He will dwell with them, and they shall be his people, and God himself will be with them'" (Rev 21:3). This fulfills the covenant made with Moses and the people of Israel at Mt. Sinai, where they were promised, "If you walk in my statutes and observe my commandments and do them" (Lev 26:3), they would be God's people:

> "And I will have regard for you and make you fruitful and multiply you, and will confirm my covenant with you. And you shall eat old store long kept, and you shall clear out the old to make way for the new. And I will make my abode among you, and my soul shall not abhor you. And I will walk among you, and will be your God, and you shall be my people" (Lev 26:9–12).

---

[76] Louis Bouyer, *The Meaning of Sacred Scripture* (Notre Dame, Ind.: University of Notre Dame Press, 1958), p. 195. "When in Revelation 21:9–21 John describes the dimensions and adornments of the New Jerusalem, he describes the heaven enjoyed by the saints at the end of time, the ultimate fulfillment of the New Covenant. We will enter into the fullness of the New Covenant, but only in eternity" (Scott Hahn, *A Father Who Keeps His Promises: God's Covenant Love in Scripture* [Ann Arbor, Mich.: Charis, 1998], p. 258). Hahn's chapter "Here Comes the Bride", (pp. 245–62) examines this theme, especially in regards to the liturgy, a relationship he explores further in the popular work *The Lamb's Supper*.

Major Themes of the Apocalypse

Since there are an abundance of books about the book of Revelation—many of them written from a dispensationalist position—emphasizing a sensationalized and unsubstantiated study of "Bible prophecy", a brief overview of the book's major themes will be useful for readers who are new to its intricate and symbol-laden tapestry. *The Navarre Bible* commentary summarizes the book in this way:

> The Apocalypse is a theological vision of the entire panorama of history, a vision which underlines its transcendental and religious dimension. According to this interpretation (favoured by most Fathers of the Church) John is describing the situation of the Church in his own time and is also surveying the panorama of the last times; but for him these last times have already begun: they began with the entry into the world of Jesus Christ, the Son of God made man.[77]

With this "panorama of history" in mind, here are the central themes and ideas of the book of Revelation:

- *God, the Alpha and Omega, the beginning and the end.* The Lord God refers to himself as the Alpha and Omega, "who is and who was and who is to come, the Almighty". This description, playing on the first and last letters in the Greek alphabet, is used to bookend the Apocalypse (Rev 1:8; 21:6; 22:13), indicating God's complete providential control over creation, history, and the activities of man.[78]

---

[77] *Navarre Bible, Revelation*, p. 19.

[78] Bouyer writes, "It is always by the Cross that we come to glory. This is clarified by an idea of divine providence which is contained in the oldest Apocalypses, at least in seed, but which shines out brilliantly in the Apocalypse of John. If the present world is ruled by the 'powers' in revolt against

■ *Jesus Christ, the slain and triumphant Lamb.* The connections between John's Revelation and his Gospel are evident in his description of Christ as the Lamb. He is seen "standing, as though it had been slain" (Rev 5:6), he is worshipped (Rev 5:8–12); he renders judgment upon mankind (Rev 6:16); he saves his people (Rev 7:9–17); he is the Bridegroom of the Church (Rev 21:9); he is the new Temple (Rev 21:22); and he is the everlasting ruler (Rev 22:3). Christ is also revealed as the "Word of God" (Rev 19:13), perhaps the most well-known Johannine description of the Son (Jn 1). The divinity of Christ is continually emphasized throughout the book.[79]

■ *The witness and consolation of the martyrs.* Those who are a witness (*marturia*) to Christ are described as "the souls of those who had been slain for the word of God and for the witness they had borne" (Rev 6:9).

> The martyr is so important to John because, by the martyr, we can say that the heavenly Jerusalem, destined to descend all glorious from heaven at the end of time, is now building itself up on earth in the history which is unfolding today....

God, this does not in the least mean that the present world escapes from God. Even in revolt, the 'powers' remain in His hands, and the raising of their revolt can accomplish nothing other than His plans" (*Meaning of Sacred Scripture*, p. 195).

[79] "Jesus Christ is also given the title 'Son of man', destined to receive power and dominion over all nations and tongues (cf. Dan 7:13–14; Rev 1:13–16). He is 'Lord of lords and King of kings' (cf. 17:14; 19:12–16); he is above the angels, who are his emissaries, and unlike them he is rendered the worship due to God alone (cf. 1:1; 22:6; 19:10; 22:8–9). In other passages Christ is given divine titles and attributes (cf. 1:18; 3:7; 5:13; 22:1–3). He is also depicted as the Word of God: this is in line with the Fourth Gospel and clearly teaches that he is divine (cf. 19:13; Jn 1:1–14; 1 Jn 1:1)" (*Navarre Bible, Revelation*, p. 24).

In John, it appears that it is not only the Word as announced by the Apostles which builds up the temple of God, but also the Word as received and bearing fruit in our hearts. Only this is always a crucified fruit. It is always by the Cross that we come to glory.[80]

■ *The Church and the New Covenant.* The Church, the people formed by the New Covenant with the Lamb, is depicted in many ways, but most often as martyrs for the faith. There are the seven local churches in Asia (Rev 1:4; 2–3), and the universal Church, "a kingdom, priests to his God and Father" (Rev 1:6; see 1 Pet 2:9). She is also described as the "bride" (Rev 21:2) and "the wife of the Lamb" (Rev 21:9), and as the holy city, the New Jerusalem, where God dwells with his people (Rev 21:2, 10; 22:19).[81]

■ *Heavenly liturgy and earthly worship.* A theme ignored by dispensationalist writers is that of the relationship between the heavenly throne room (see Rev 4) and the worship of God's people on earth. John's vision occurs while he "was in the Spirit on the Lord's day" (Rev 1:10). "Following the tradition of Isaias, the heavenly world [in the book of Revelation] appears as a liturgical world."[82] There is speculation that John wrote passages in the book of Revelation as

---

[80] Bouyer, *Meaning of Sacred Scripture*, p. 195.

[81] Rudolph Schnackenburg writes: "This is the other aspect of Christ's eschatological victory: the bringing home of his bride, the Church, its reception into the perfect kingdom, the heavenly city of God [Rev 21:9ff]. The prophet foresees the close of the ecclesiological series. The Church, seen to begin with in its form at once of earth and heaven, passes now after all its trials and sufferings on earth wholly into eschatological fulfilment" (*God's Rule and Kingdom* [New York: Herder and Herder, 1963], pp. 336–37).

[82] Bouyer, *Meaning of Sacred Scripture*, p. 194.

lectionary or liturgical texts for the seven churches.[83] References to the Eucharist include the gift of the "hidden manna" (Rev 2:17), "Behold, I stand at the door and knock; if any one hears my voice and opens the door, I will come in to him and eat with him, and he with me" (Rev 3:20), and "Blessed are those who are invited to the marriage supper of the Lamb" (Rev 19:9).[84]

■ *The conflict between the followers of Christ and the forces of darkness.* While the victory has been already won by the "Lamb who was slain, to receive power and wealth and wisdom and might and honor and glory and blessing" (Rev 5:12), there is still an ongoing battle. It is between those who are clothed in white (Rev 6:11; 7:9–14) and those who worship the beast and make war against the saints (Rev 13).

The basic structure of the Apocalypse of the struggle of the sons of darkness against the sons of light (a theme common

[83] Chilton notes that "both [John's] Gospel and the Revelation 'give their testimony from the vantage point of experience of the Paschal liturgy of the Asian churches.' The lectionary nature of Revelation helps explain the wealth of liturgical material in the prophecy. Revelation is not, of course, a manual about how to 'do' a worship service; rather, it *is* a worship service, a liturgy conducted in heaven as a model for those on earth" (*Days of Vengeance*, p. 24). Chilton quotes Orthodox theologian Thomas Hopko, who states: "The worship of the Church has traditionally, quite consciously, been patterned after the divine and eternal qualities revealed in [Revelation]. The prayers of the Church and its mystical celebration are one with the prayer and celebration of the kingdom of heaven. Thus, in Church, with the angels and saints, through Christ the Word and the Lamb, inspired by the Holy Spirit, the faithful believers of the assembly of the saved offer perpetual adoration to God the Father Almighty" (Hopko, "The Orthodox Faith", in vol. 4: *The Bible and Church History* [Orthodox Church of America, 1973], pp. 64f., cited in *Days of Vengeance*, p. 24).

[84] See Hahn, *Lamb's Supper*, pp. 9–10.

to the Fourth Gospel) transcends any particular phase of history, but behind that struggle lies the permanent vision of faith recorded in chapters four and five of the Apocalypse: God maintains a controlling interest over earthly catastrophes, subordinating them to His divine plan.[85]

■ *Mary, the Mother of the Church.* There are several parallels between Genesis and the book of Revelation (e.g., the tree of life [Gen 2:8–9; Rev 2:7; 22:19]), including the depiction of Mary as the New Eve: "And a great portent appeared in heaven, a woman clothed with the sun, with the moon under her feet, and on her head a crown of twelve stars; she was with child and she cried out in her pangs of birth, in anguish for delivery" (Rev 12:1–2). Although the "woman" may also refer to either the Church or Israel, it certainly represents Mary as well, as popes such as Pius X and John Paul II have noted.[86]

■ *The Parousia and the end of time.* The presence of God is finally and fully realized at the end of time when the

---

[85] Fannon, "Apocalypse", p. 451. Bouyer states: "The two associated images of the 'light' and the 'life' are as it were the keys to the whole thought of John. They reveal to us at once what the content of the Kingdom of God is for John, and in what consists the glory of the Messias" (*Meaning of Sacred Scripture*, p. 197).

[86] "More than once, the Church's Magisterium has given [this passage] a Marian interpretation. For example, Pius X says: 'Everyone knows that this woman was the image of the Virgin Mary, who, in giving birth to our head, remained inviolate.... It was the birth of all of us who, while being exiles here below, are not yet brought forth into the perfect love of God and eternal happiness.' ... John Paul II [states]: 'Mary ... carries the features of that woman whom the Apocalypse describes.... She it is with whom the apocalyptic dragon makes war, for being the mother of the redeemed, she is the image of the Church whom we likewise call mother" (*Navarre Bible, Revelation*, pp. 26–27).

new heaven and new earth are revealed and the New Jerusalem comes down from heaven (Rev 21:1–2): "And I heard a great voice from the throne saying, 'Behold, the dwelling of God is with men. He will dwell with them, and they shall be his people, and God himself will be with them'" (Rev 21:3).

In addition to these themes, the reader should be aware of the significant use of numbers by John. The number *seven* occurs numerous times; it represents completeness and quality and is rooted in the seven days of creation (Gen 1). *Twelve* and multiples of twelve (twenty-four, and 144,000) have special reference to the people of God, as in the twelve tribes of Israel and the twelve apostles, who represent the Church (Mt 19:28; Jas 1:1). *One thousand*, as in the millennium (Rev 20:1–7), indicates both fullness and quantity, not an exact number of years. For example, "the cattle on a thousand hills" (Ps 50:10) refers to all cattle, not just a limited number. Numbers in the book of Revelation always signify something far more important than a simple quantity or amount—they point the way to the spiritual significance of the events and persons described.

Conclusion: The Catholic View

Dispensationalism teaches that "The book of Revelation is our key to understanding the cataclysmic events unfolding in the closing decades of this millennium." [87] These events,

---

[87] Jeffrey, *Apocalypse*, p. 1.

it is claimed, have yet to transpire; most of the Apocalypse has had little meaning for Christians until now.[88] The Catholic reply is that this is a limited and narrow understanding of this great book, for John the Revelator is not interested in describing the movements of Chinese armies or the attacks of Cobra helicopters or the implanting of computer chips in human hands. He has been caught up into the throne room of God on the Lord's Day, and gazing over the vista of human history he sees that God has already transformed it, is now united with humanity through the Incarnation, and is destroying sin and Satan through Christ's death and Resurrection. The Kingdom is here and is growing and will one day be revealed for all to see:

> It is essential, indeed, to the faith of the Bible and equally to the faith of the Apocalypses [the Book of Daniel and the Book of Revelation], that the world which is coming be not only a world "to come": it exists already, and it is even the only "true" world, in a sense of the word which is very peculiar to John and which signifies the absolute reality of that which the divine Word affirms to faith.... The heavenly world of John has already begun to invade the earthly world, and, reciprocally, the earthly world has already begun to have access to it. It is in fact this double process, of the descent of the Shekinah to earth and of the ascension of humanity

[88] For example, Lindsey writes: "I believe that down through the centuries since John wrote these incredible revelations from God, men have received a blessing from reading them even if they understood very little of what they read. But today we live in a unique era. Now the promise of blessing carries an unprecedented comfort and practical fulfillment for every person who lets the Holy Spirit illuminate the words he reads" (*There's a New World Coming*, p. 22).

following the Merkabah, which makes up the whole history proclaimed to us by the Apocalypse.[89]

---

[89] Bouyer, *Meaning of Sacred Scripture*, pp. 193–94. "The *Shekinah*, His Presence, transitory in the Old Testament, is here to stay. God has taken up a permanent dwelling with His people, the Church. One great hope of the Old Dispensation has been fulfilled. But the figure of the Son of Man in the midst of the vision of heaven tells us that still another ancient expectation is being realized—the ascent of humanity to God. The closing chapters of the Apocalypse show that state finally attained: the Church is clothed at last in the glory that was hers from the beginning. The Bride is sharing in the privileges of the Bridegroom, Paradise has been regained" (Fannon, "Apocalypse", p. 451). "As a whole, the book of Revelation is a prophecy of the end of the old order and the establishment of the new order. It is a message to the church that the terrifying convulsions coursing throughout the world in every sphere comprised the final 'shaking of heaven and earth', ending once and for all the Old Covenant system, announcing that the kingdom of God had come to earth and broken Satan's hold on the nations. In the destruction of Jerusalem, the old kingdom, and the Temple, God revealed that they had been merely the scaffolding for His eternal City, His Holy Nation, and the most glorious Temple of all [quoting Heb 12:25–29]" (Chilton, *Paradise Restored*, p. 169).

4

THE MILLENNIUM:
HOW LONG IS A THOUSAND YEARS?

Then I saw an angel coming down from heaven, holding in his hand the key of the bottomless pit and a great chain. And he seized the dragon, that ancient serpent, who is the Devil and Satan, and bound him for a thousand years, and threw him into the pit, and shut it and sealed it over him, that he should deceive the nations no more, till the thousand years were ended. After that he must be loosed for a little while.

—Revelation 20:1–3

The only place in the Bible that speaks of an actual millennium is the passage in Revelation 20:1–6. Any millennial doctrine must be based upon the most natural exegesis of this passage.

—George E. Ladd

We will be able to become invisible and move across the universe at the speed of thought. Our primary home will be the heavenly Jerusalem that apparently hovers in juxtaposition over the earthly Jerusalem during the millennial era. Meanwhile, there will be people down below—on Earth—living in their mortal human bodies under the personal rule of the Lord Jesus, the King on David's throne.

—Hal Lindsey

If the book of Revelation is the most important book for those trying to figure out the "signs of the times", the most important portion of that book is the twentieth chapter. It is there that the one and only description of the millennium occurs in the New Testament. The term "millennium" is Latin in origin and means "thousand years" (*mille* meaning a "thousand", and *annus* a "year"). How the reader interprets the book of Revelation as a whole will shape how he understands these "thousand years". Is Revelation 20:1–6 to be read literally, symbolically, metaphorically, allegorically, or in a combination of two or more of these possible methods? Are the thousand years meant to be an actual period of time only? Or do they refer to something else, using a form of language that John's readers would understand but modern readers struggle to fathom? As we have seen, the apocalyptic elements of John's prophetic writing in the book of Revelation are difficult and mysterious, contributing to many of the disagreements regarding the book's meaning and message. However, while dispensationalists may disagree over the identity of the locusts (Rev 9:1–11) or the two witnesses (11:3), about how the mark of the beast (13:15–18) will be administered or over a number of other images and phrases in the Apocalypse, they are unanimous in their interpretation of Revelation 20:1–6: it refers to a future, earthly reign of Jesus Christ.

The nature of the millennium is central to three key, intertwining issues: the character of the Church, the nature of the Kingdom, and the place of the people of Israel in future events. Of these, the timing and the purpose of the Kingdom that Christ preached is the most important, as Presbyterian David Chilton has noted: "In essence, the question of the Millennium centers on the mediatorial

Kingdom of Christ: When did (or will) Christ's Kingdom begin?"[1] Has the Kingdom already come, or does Christ need to return to earth to usher in the Kingdom in the form of an earthly, thousand-year reign? Will the millennium be primarily for "Church age" Christians or for Jews who turned to Christ and became Christian while suffering in the Tribulation after the pretribulational Rapture? Is the Kingdom different from the Church? How will the Old Testament promises to Israel be fulfilled? Or have those promises already been fulfilled in and by the Church?

There are three basic approaches to interpreting the "thousand years" found in Revelation 20: *premillennialism*, *amillennialism*, and *postmillennialism*. Although these terms are used to refer to ancient as well as modern Christian beliefs, they should be handled with caution. As Evangelical scholar Richard Kyle explains, "Pre-, post-, and amillennialism are relatively modern terms. Thus one must be careful not to impose them on earlier ages. Nevertheless, many of the millennial positions expressed through the course of Western history roughly approximate the outlines of pre-, post-, and amillennialism."[2] Because these are the terms commonly used and accepted in discussing this issue, they are necessary and helpful. But since there are disagreements among Christians about the exact meaning of each term, they can also cause further misunderstandings, especially—as we will see—when they are misrepresented by those holding contrary positions.

[1] David Chilton, *The Days of Vengeance: An Exposition of the Book of Revelation* (Fort Worth, Tex.: Dominion Press, 1987), p. 493.

[2] Richard Kyle, *The Last Days Are Here Again: A History of the End Times* (Grand Rapids, Mich.: Baker Books, 1998), p. 20.

Premillennialism

There are two forms of premillennialism: *historical* and *dispensational*. Both teach that Christ's Second Coming will occur *prior* to his visible and earthly millennial rule from the city of Jerusalem. This millennial Kingdom will come about through Christ's conquering of the forces of evil in a dramatic and decisive victory at the battle of Armageddon. In this way God's power will be manifested on earth through Christ's righteous and perfect reign over humanity: "This reign means that there will be complete peace, righteousness, and justice among men. Some premillennialists would make this a literal period of exactly one thousands years. Others would be less literal, making it simply an extended period of time. The essential point, however, is that this reign will be on earth and Jesus Christ will be bodily present."[3] George Eldon Ladd, the leading contemporary historical premillennialist, writes, "Premillennialism is the doctrine stating that after the Second Coming of Christ, he will reign for a thousand years over the earth before the final consummation of God's redemptive purpose in the new heavens and the new earth of the Age to come."[4] Premillennialists believe that during the millennial reign Satan and his followers

[3] Millard J. Erickson, *A Basic Guide to Eschatology: Making Sense of the Millennium* (Grand Rapids, Mich.: Baker Book House, 1998), pp. 91–92. Renald E. Showers, a dispensationalist scholar, writes that "Premillennialists believe that Christ *will* fulfill these promises [to King David] in the *future* when He returns to earth in His Second Coming and then establishes and reigns over a *literal, earthly, political kingdom* for 1,000 years *on this present earth* and for eternity *on the new eternal earth*" (Renald E. Showers, *There Really Is a Difference! A Comparison of Covenant and Dispensational Theology* [Bellmawr, N.J.: Friends of Israel Gospel Ministry, 1990], p. 88; emphasis in original).

[4] Ladd, "Historic Premillennialism", in Robert G. Clouse, ed., *The Meaning of the Millennium: Four Views* (Downers Grove, Ill.: InterVarsity Press, 1977), p. 17.

will be bound, then loosed for a short time at its conclusion and allowed to lead people into rebellion and apostasy one final time. "Then will come a second or postmillennial advent [coming], which will be followed by the last judgment and the final state." [5]

The timing of the Last Judgment is dependant on another key feature of premillennialism: the belief in two distinct bodily resurrections. First there will be a resurrection of the righteous prior to the earthly millennial reign, then a second resurrection of the unrighteous at the end of that same reign. This is based, in part, on Revelation 20:4b–5: "They came to life, and reigned with Christ a thousand years. The rest of the dead did not come to life until the thousand years were ended. This is the first resurrection." In contrast, both postmillennialists and amillennialists believe there is just one bodily resurrection of all the dead, good or evil, which will take place at Christ's Second Coming. They commonly interpret these verses as a reference to a first resurrection that is spiritual, that is, baptism. This was the understanding of Augustine, who explained his reasoning in *City of God*:

> As, then, there are two regenerations, of which I have already made mention,—the one according to faith, and which takes place in the present life by means of baptism; the other according to the flesh, and which shall be accomplished in its incorruption and immortality by means of the great and final judgment—so are there also two resurrections,—the one the first and spiritual resurrection, which has place in this life, and preserves us from coming into the second death; the other the second, which does not occur now, but in the end of the world, and which is of the body, not of the soul,

[5] Oswald T. Allis, *Prophecy and the Church* (Nutley, N.J.: Presbyterian and Reformed Publishing, 1974), p. 7.

and which by the last judgment shall dismiss some into the second death, others into that life which has no death.[6]

Despite their shared beliefs, there are several differences between historical premillennialism and dispensational premillennialism. These differences are crucial since dispensationalists argue that many of the early Church Fathers adhered to a form of dispensational premillennialism,[7] a claim that non-dispensationalists—including historical premillennialists—insist is without basis. It is true that several of the early Christian writers—notably Papias, Justin Martyr, Irenaeus, Tertullian, Hippolytus, Methodius, Commodianus, and Lactantius[8]—were premillennialists who believed that Christ's

---

[6] Augustine, *City of God*, bk. 20, chap. 6, trans. Marcus Deds, in *Nicene and Post-Nicene Fathers*, 1st series, ed. Philip Schaff (Peabody, Mass.: Hendrickson Publishers, 1994) (hereafter abbreviated *NPNF1*), 2:426.

[7] The common practice of popular dispensationalists is to note that the early Christians were premillennialists, thereby implying that they were dispensationalists—which does not logically follow at all. For instance, LaHaye—after explaining that the "Kingdom" is the same as the "Millennium"—writes, "The early Christians were almost unquestionably premillennialists" (Tim LaHaye, *Revelation Unveiled* [Grand Rapids, Mich.: Zondervan Publishing House, 1999], p. 331). He then goes on, a few sentences later, to claim that "Many of the detractors of the premillennial position suggest that it [premillennialism] is a relatively new theory, having come on the scene during the days of John Darby and others [in the early 1800s]" (p. 332). But this is misleading since no one denies that many early Church Fathers were premillennialists. What is denied is that they were premillennial dispensationalists who believed in a pretribulational Rapture and the radical distinction between Israel and the Church—central tenets of dispensationalism.

[8] The patristic scholar J. N. D. Kelly, writing about millenarianism in the second century, notes, "The Gnostic tendency to dissolve Christian eschatology into the myth of the soul's upward ascent and return to God had to be resisted. On the other hand millenarianism, or the theory that the returned Christ would reign on earth for a thousand years, came to find increasing support among Christian teachers. We can observe these tendencies at work in the Apologists. Justin [Martyr], as we have suggested, ransacks the Old

Second Coming would lead to a visible, earthly reign. But, as we shall see, the premillennialism they embraced was quite different from that taught by modern dispensationalists. Prominent dispensationalist theologian Charles Ryrie argues in his seminal works *The Basis of the Premillennial Faith* and *Dispensationalism*[9] that the distinction between the two forms of premillennialism is of no real concern. This distinction, Ryrie insists, is simply a ploy used by those who wish to deny the future reign of Christ:

> Others, attempting to confuse the issue and to take the eyes of the premillennialist off the historicity of his faith, enumerate as many distinctions as possible between so-called historic premillennialism and modern premillennialism, which they sometimes call pretribulationism or dispensationalism.[10]

Ryrie goes on to make two arguments: the early Church and the Church Fathers were truly premillennialists, and the "discovery and refinement of doctrine does not mean at all that

Testament for proof, as against Jewish critics, that the Messiah must have a twofold coming.... The former coming was enacted at the incarnation, but the latter still lies in the future. It will take place, he suggests, at Jerusalem, where Christ will be recognized by the Jews who dishonoured Him as the sacrifice which avails for all penitent sinners, and where He will eat and drink with His disciples; and He will reign there a thousand years. This millenarian, or 'chiliastic', doctrine was widely popular at this time" (*Early Christian Doctrines*, 5th ed. [New York: Harper and Row, 1978], p. 465). Kelly goes on to mention Barnabas, Papias, and Hippolytus. Also see Erickson, *Basic Guide to Eschatology*, pp. 94–97, and mention of Justin Martyr, Irenaeus, Hippolytus, and Lactantius.

[9] Charles C. Ryrie, *The Basis of the Premillennial Faith* (Neptune, N.J.: Loizeaux Brothers, 1981) and *Dispensationalism* (Chicago: Moody Press, 1995).

[10] Ryrie, *Basis of the Premillennial Faith*, p. 17. Of course, the terms "pretribulationism" and "dispensationalism" are not pejorative or misleading in any way and are commonly—almost exclusively—used by adherents to modern premillennialism.

such doctrine is extra-Biblical".[11] In his later work *Dispensationalism*, considered to be one of the best apologetics for dispensationalism, Ryrie again takes up this argument, remarking that

> [a]nother typical example of the use of a straw man is this line of argument: pretribulationism is not apostolic; pretribulationism is dispensationalism; therefore, dispensationalism is not apostolic. But dispensationalists do not claim that the system was developed in the first century; nor is it necessary that they be able to do so.... Doctrinal development is a perfectly normal process in the course of church history. This straw man leads to a second fallacy—the wrong use of history. The fact that something was taught in the first century does not make it right (unless taught in the canonical Scriptures), and the fact that something was not taught until the nineteenth century does not make it wrong unless, of course, it is unscriptural.[12]

This startling remark reveals an irony fatal to the dispensationalist argument. In attempting to prove the validity of their beliefs by appealing to early Church Fathers, dispensationalists always ignore the Church Fathers' *unanimous* teachings about the nature of the Eucharist, the authority and nature of the Church, and a host of other distinctively Catholic beliefs.[13] Catholic scholars acknowledge that some of the

---

[11] Ibid., p. 18.

[12] Ryrie, *Dispensationalism*, p. 62.

[13] For detailed examinations of passages by the early Church Fathers teaching that the Eucharist is the actual Body and Blood of Jesus Christ, see James O'Connor, *The Hidden Manna* (San Francisco: Ignatius Press, 1988), pp. 1–93, and Kelly, *Early Christian Doctrines*, pp. 196–98, 440–55. Grant Jeffrey is quite fond of referring to early Church Fathers in support of his premillennial, pretribulational beliefs while ignoring their writings supporting doctrinal beliefs contrary to his own. In his book *Apocalypse: The Coming Judgment of the Nations*

Fathers were influenced by the Jewish belief in an earthly Messianic Kingdom, while others embraced millenarianism as a reaction to the Gnostic antagonism toward the material realm.[14] But the Catholic Church does not look to individual Church Fathers in isolation, or even a select group of Fathers, and claim that their teachings are infallible or definitive. Rather, the Church views them as invaluable guides and witnesses to tradition who provide insights and perspectives that assist the Magisterium—the teaching office of the Church—in defining, clarifying, and defending Church doctrine.[15]

Ryrie's protests notwithstanding, those early premillennialists did not hold to distinctively modern and dispensationalist beliefs, especially not the belief in a pretribulational Rapture and the radical distinction between an earthly and a heavenly people of God. The early Church Fathers, whether premillennialist or otherwise, believed that the Church was the New Israel and that she—consisting of both Jews and Gentiles (Rom 10:12)—had Israel as God's chosen people.

(New York: Bantam Books, 1992), Jeffrey cites extensively from works by early Church Fathers such as Barnabas, Hippolytus, Justin Martyr, and especially Lactantius (see pp. 296–316 and 383–402). However, all he proves is what everyone admits: These Church Fathers believed in an earthly reign of Christ, yet never taught a pretribulational Rapture or a severe dichotomy between Israel and the Church.

[14] See Jean Daniélou, *The Theology of Jewish Christianity*, The Development of Christian Doctrine before the Council of Nicaea, vol. 1 (London: Darton, Longman and Todd, 1964), pp. 377–408, for a scholarly treatment of this subject. Also see Kelly, *Early Christian Doctrines*, pp. 464–69. There appears to be a strong parallel between the early Christian apologists, who were millenarian because of their conflicts with Gnosticism, and modern millenarians, who see their position as a necessary defense of the veracity and "literal" nature of Scripture over against liberal Protestantism and modernism, which deny the supernatural character of the Bible.

[15] See, e.g., CCC 250. Also see CCC 11, 78, and 100.

For example, in his *Dialogue with Trypho the Jew*, Justin Martyr (d. ca. 165) remarks:

> And He has called all of us by that voice, and we have left already the way of living in which we used to spend our days, passing our time in evil after the fashions of the other inhabitants of the earth; and along with Abraham we shall inherit the holy land, when we shall receive the inheritance for an endless eternity, being children of Abraham through the like faith. For as he believed the voice of God, and it was imputed to him for righteousness, in like manner we, having believed God's voice spoken by the apostles of Christ, and promulgated to us by the prophets, have renounced even to death all the things of the world. Accordingly, He promises to him a nation of similar faith, God-fearing, righteous, and delighting the Father; but it is not you, 'in whom is no faith'.... As, therefore, Christ is the Israel and the Jacob, even so we, who have been quarried out from the bowels of Christ, are the true Israelitic race.[16]

---

[16] Justin Martyr, *Dialogue with Trypho the Jew*, chaps. 119 and 135, trans. Alexander Roberts and James Donaldson, ed. A. Cleveland Coxe, in *Ante-Nicene Fathers* (Peabody, Mass.: Hendrickson Publishers, 1994) (hereafter abbreviated as *ANF*), 1:259 and 267. Alan Patrick Boyd, a graduate student (and also a dispensationalist) at Dallas Theological Seminary exposed Ryrie's (and other dispensationalists') misrepresentation of patristic beliefs. In his master's thesis Boyd provided clear evidence that the early Church Fathers were in no way premillennial dispensationalists, writing, "It is the conclusion of this thesis that Dr. Ryrie's statement is historically invalid within the chronological framework of this thesis. The reasons for this conclusion are as follows: 1). the writers' writings surveyed did not generally adopt a consistently applied literal interpretation; 2). they did not generally distinguish between the Church and Israel; 3). there is no evidence that they generally held to a dispensational view of revealed history; 4). although Papias and Justin Martyr did believe in a Millennial kingdom, the 1,000 years is the only basic similarity with the modern system (in fact, they and dispensational premillennialism radically differ on the basis for the Millennium); 5). they had no concept of imminency or a pretribulational rapture of the Church; 6). in general, their eschatological

An Earthly, Jewish Millennium?

Early Church Fathers of the premillennialist persuasion believed that the Church would go through a time of tribulation and experience great turmoil. There would be no pretribulational Rapture—no "snatching away" of true believers prior to this time of unrest.[17] It was also understood that the earthly millennial reign of Christ would involve the

---

chronology is not synonymous with that of the modern system. Indeed, this thesis would conclude that the eschatological beliefs of the period studied would be generally inimical to those of the modern system (perhaps, seminal amillennialism, and not nascent dispensational premillennialism ought to be seen in the eschatology of the period)" (Alan Patrick Boyd, *A Dispensational Premillennial Analysis of the Eschatology of the Post-Apostolic Fathers [until the Death of Justin Martyr]* [Th.M. thesis, Dallas Theological Seminary, 1977], pp. 90–91). Quoted in Gary DeMar's *The Debate over Christian Reconstruction* (Atlanta: American Vision Press, 1988), p. 96.

[17] For example, Irenaeus (ca. 130–202), in his famous apologetic against Gnostic heretics, *Adversus haereses*, writes: "But when this Antichrist shall have devastated all things in this world, he will reign for three years and six months, and sit in the temple at Jerusalem; and then the Lord will come from heaven in the clouds, in the glory of the Father, sending this man and those who follow him into the lake of fire; but bringing in for the righteous the times of the kingdom, that is, the rest, the hallowed seventh day; and restoring to Abraham the promised inheritance, in which kingdom the Lord declared, that 'many coming from the east and from the west should sit down with Abraham, Isaac, and Jacob'" (*Adversus haereses*, bk. 5, chap. 30, no. 4, in *ANF* 1:560). And later, in the midst of describing the wonders of the earthly millennial Kingdom, he remarks: "For all these and other words were unquestionably spoken in reference to the resurrection of the just, which takes place after the coming of Antichrist, and the destruction of all nations under his rule; in [the times of] which [resurrection] the righteous shall reign in the earth, waxing stronger by the sight of the Lord: and through Him they shall become accustomed to partake in the glory of God the Father, and shall enjoy in the kingdom intercourse and communion with the holy angels, and union with spiritual beings; and [with respect to] those whom the Lord shall find in the flesh, awaiting Him from heaven, and who have suffered tribulation, as well as escaped the hands of the Wicked one" (*Adversus haereses*, bk. 5, chap. 35, no. 1, in *ANF* 1:565).

New Israel, the Church. This is in direct contrast to the dispensationalist belief that the millennial reign will be thoroughly Jewish in nature and orientation, right down to the reinstitution of animal sacrifices in the Temple:

> According to dispensational premillennialists, the primary purpose of the millennium will be the restoration of Israel. During the millennium God will fulfill all of the covenant promises he made to national Israel. Jesus will reign from David's throne in the city of Jerusalem. The temple will be rebuilt, and animal sacrifices will be reinstituted. Jerusalem and the nation of Israel will once again be given a place of prominence.[18]

This would have repulsed the early Church Fathers,[19] yet Ryrie acknowledges that the millennial reign will be Jewish, not Christian, in nature, stating "that Christian ordinances will be terminated at the beginning of the millennium"; the Lord's Supper "will not be observed during the millennium"; and animal sacrifices will be offered once again in the Temple. Quoting John L. Mitchell, Ryrie writes,

---

[18] Keith A. Mathison, *Dispensationalism: Rightly Dividing the People of God?* (Phillipsburg, N.J.: P and R Publishing, 1995), p. 123. Millard Erickson, another Reformed theologian, summarizes the dispensationalist belief about the millennium and Israel: "[D]ispensational premillennialists hold that there will be a virtual restoration of the Old Testament economy. According to this view God has only temporarily turned from His prime dealings with national Israel to the church, or spiritual Israel. When God has accomplished His purpose in connection with the church, however, He will resume His relations with Israel. In the millennium Israel will be restored to the land of Palestine. Jesus will sit upon the literal throne of David and rule the world from Jerusalem. The Old Testament temple worship and priestly order will be restored, including the sacrificial system. Into the millennium is placed the fulfilment of virtually all Old Testament prophecies not fulfilled by the time of Christ, or at least by Pentecost" (Erickson, *Basic Guide to Eschatology*, p. 103).

[19] For example, the second chapter of the *Epistle of Barnabas* is emphatic about the abolition of the old Jewish sacrifices.

The Church will be taken out of the earth at the rapture at which time God's program for the Jew will be resumed and continue from where it was at the time of Christ's death.... [The millennium] will simply be a continuation of the old order, this time with Christ accepted as and reigning as King. The Jews will continue their animal sacrifices in worship as they did before Christ died. It is true that these sacrifices will be types and symbols of their faith in Christ's death, but that does not make them nonetheless real.[20]

This statement simply cannot be squared with the entire book of Hebrews, whose author writes that "In speaking of a new covenant he treats the first as obsolete. And what is becoming obsolete and growing old is ready to vanish away" (Heb 8:13), and, "For it is impossible for the blood of bulls and goats [to] take away sins" (Heb 10:4). Yet this belief is made necessary by the dispensational understanding of the Kingdom and its particular method of biblical interpretation. No historical premillennialist would agree with this view of the millennial reign. No historical premillennialist spoke of the millennium being a period only for the Jews, or of Israel and the Church being radically distinct "peoples of God", or of the Church being some sort of parenthetical insert into history—perhaps the most distinctive and important claim of the dispensational system.[21]

---

[20] Ryrie, *Basis of the Premillennial Faith*, pp. 150, 153. This is a common teaching among popular dispensationalists. For instance, LaHaye states: "Ezekiel goes into great detail [in chapters 40–48] regarding the matter of worshiping in the Temple, even pointing out that the sacrificial systems will be reestablished. These sacrifices during the millennial Kingdom will be to the nation of Israel what the Lord's Supper is to the Church today: a reminder of what they have been saved from" (*Revelation Unveiled*, p. 341).

[21] John F. Walvoord, perhaps the most important dispensational theologian of the last fifty years and former president of Dallas Theological Seminary, a

What happened to historical premillennialism? As time passed, the early Christians realized that Christ's return might not be quite as soon as they anticipated. They also had a chance to reflect on the nature of the Incarnation, the Paschal Mystery, and the "great mystery" of the Church. All of this would lead, by the fourth century, to refinements in the teachings of the Church Fathers about the end of time and Christ's Second Coming. Opposition to premillennialism, or *chiliasm* (from the Greek word meaning "a thousand"; here a thousand years is implied), came early, especially from the theological school in Alexandria led by Origen.[22] Chiliasm— the belief in a visible, earthly millennial reign of Christ— disappeared for several centuries, but today it is alive and

---

leading dispensational school, states: "Any answer to the rapture question must therefore be based on a careful study of the doctrine of the church as it is revealed in the New Testament. To a large extent premillennialism, as well as pretribulationism [the belief the church will be raptured prior to the Tribulation], is dependent on the definition of the church, and premillenarians who fail to distinguish between Israel and the church erect their structure of premillennial doctrine on a weak foundation" (*The Rapture Question*, rev. ed. [Grand Rapids, Mich.: Academie Books, 1979], p. 20).

[22] "Opposition to this chiliasm arose rather early, particularly in the East. The excesses of Montanism helped to discredit it and to stamp it as Jewish in origin and character rather than Christian. This rejection was due, at least in part, to the chiliasts' ideas of the millennium being so realistic (materialistic) and crass. This certainly helped repulse the more intellectually inclined Christians like the Alexandrian school—Clement, Origen, and Dionysius—which led the opposition to chiliasm. Origen, who had a tendency to spiritualize conceptions, opposed the chiliasts vigorously. At times the controversy was severe; the Egyptian church nearly split over the issue. What finally prevailed in the East was a moderately spiritualistic view, not as extreme as Origen's but allowing no room for chiliasm. In the West, chiliasm was quite strong for a considerable period. While never universally accepted, it was a potent force up to Augustine and later. . . . The reinterpretation of Revelation by Augustine . . . proved to be the major factor in the decline of chiliasm in the West" (Erickson, *Basic Guide to Eschatology*, p. 96). See Augustine's criticism of chiliasm in *City of God* (bk. 20, chap. 7).

quite well in the new and "updated" form of dispensational premillennialism. But the Catholic Church has clearly rejected any and all beliefs in a future millennial era—whether religious or secular in nature. In specifically condemning the secular millenarianism of communism, the Church has also renounced, in general, all types of millenarianism: "The Church has rejected even modified forms of this falsification of the kingdom to come under the name of millenarianism [cf. DS 3839]."[23] So the Catholic Church condemns the idea that earthly perfection can or will occur within human history. In the words of Cardinal Ratzinger,

> The Christian hope knows no idea of an inner fulfilment of history. On the contrary, it affirms the impossibility of an inner fulfilment of the world. . . . The biblical representation of the End rejects the expectation of a definitive state of salvation within history. This position is also rationally correct, since the idea of a definitive intra-historical fulfilment fails to take into account the permanent openness of history and of human freedom, for which failure is always a possibility.[24]

In other words, as long as history and time exist as we know them, man will be free to sin, meaning that a future, historical era of messianic peace and perfection—whether religious or secular—is impossible. True peace will come at the Second Coming, when the risen, glorious Messiah will "judge the living and the dead", separate the sheep and the goats (Mt 25:31–46), and reveal the "new heavens and a new earth" (2 Pet 3:10–13; Rev 21:1). The Second Coming and the

---

[23] CCC 676.
[24] Joseph Ratzinger, *Eschatology, Death and Eternal Life* (Washington, D.C.: Catholic University of America Press, 1988), p. 213.

new heaven and new earth bring history as we know it to completion.

The premillennial understanding of Revelation 20 is incorrect because the Bible simply never speaks about a literal, thousand-year earthly reign. The proof text—Revelation 20—is a highly symbolic, difficult passage found in a highly symbolic, difficult book. It is best understood as symbolic language expressing a literal truth. David Chilton writes that just "as the number seven connotes a fullness of quality in Biblical imagery, the number ten contains the idea of a fullness of quantity; in other words, it stands for manyness. A thousand multiplies and intensifies this (10 × 10 × 10), in order to express great vastness (cf. 5:11; 7:4–8; 9:16; 11:3, 13; 12:6; 14:1, 3, 20)." [25] Besides, if the millennium is supposed to be a fulfillment of promises to Israel, why does Revelation 20:1–10 never mention Israel, the Jewish race, Jerusalem, or the Temple? [26]

There is also a serious discrepancy between the dispensational understanding of the millennium and the description given in Revelation 20. Dispensationalists believe that at

---

[25] Chilton, *Days of Vengeance*, pp. 506–7. For an excellent discussion of the millennium, Revelation 20, and the differences between postmillennialism and amillennialism, see *Days of Vengeance*, pp. 493–534.

[26] Hoekema notes that for the dispensationalist "the purpose of the millennium is to set up the earthly kingdom which was promised to David, in which Christ, David's seed, will rule from an earthly throne in Jerusalem over a converted Israelite nation. If this is the purpose of the millennium, is it not passing strange that Revelation 20:4–6 says not a word about the Jews, the nation of Israel, the land of Palestine, or Jerusalem? This would not be so serious if the idea of the restoration of Israel were only an incidental aspect of the millennium. But, according to dispensational teaching, the restoration of Israel is the *central purpose* of the millennium!" (Anthony A. Hoekema, *The Bible and the Future* [Grand Rapids, Mich.: W. B. Eerdmans, 1979, 1994], p. 222, emphasis in original).

the start of the millennium the earth will be populated by people, both Jewish and Gentile, who had passed through the Tribulation and turned to God during that perilous time. "The millennial period therefore begins with a society in which both Jews and Gentiles are saved", writes John Walvoord.[27] In other words, these are non-resurrected people with natural bodies—not glorified, resurrected ones. But Revelation 20:6 states: "Blessed and holy is he who shares in the first resurrection! Over such the second death has no power, but they shall be priests of God and of Christ, and they shall reign with him a thousand years." Those who are not resurrected, John has already made clear, "did not come to life until the thousand years were ended" (Rev 20:5). Dispensationalists identify the resurrected "priests of God" who "reign with him" as Christians who have been resurrected and who reign from the "heavenly Jerusalem" over those "who are still in their natural bodies".[28] And so *the* New Testament passage that supposedly proves the dispensational concept of the millennial kingdom makes *no* mention of those people—the natural, non-resurrected, earthly believers—who are, we are told, the focus of this material Kingdom. As Anthony A. Hoekema, a Reformed Protestant and amillennialist theologian, concludes:

[27] John F. Walvoord, *The Millennial Kingdom* (Grand Rapids, Mich.: Zondervan Publishing House, 1959), p. 317. Walvoord's book is arguably *the* premillennial dispensational text on the subject of the millennium.

[28] Walvoord, *Millennial Kingdom*, p. 329. Joe Jordan writes, "Although the redeemed will go into Messiah's kingdom, the living saints from the tribulation will enter into that kingdom in their natural bodies with the power of procreation. Those born to them during the millennium will be in need of salvation, and this salvation will be brought to them through Israel" ("The Marvelous Millennium", in Charles C. Ryrie, Joe Jordan, and Tom Davis, eds., *Countdown to Armageddon: The Final Battle and Beyond* [Eugene, Ore.: Harvest House Publishers, 1999], p. 231).

Dispensationalists also teach that the millennial age will concern unresurrected people, people who are still living in their natural bodies. But about such people, this passage *does not breathe a word*! We conclude that Revelation 20:4–6 does not describe the millennium of the dispensationalists, even when it is understood as dispensationalists want us to understand it. The dispensationalist understanding of the millennium, in other words, is not based on a literal interpretation of this most important passage.[29]

Postmillennialism

While premillennialism in its dispensational form currently dominates the popular eschatological landscape in America, one hears little about postmillennialism. At one time this millennial viewpoint overshadowed premillennialism in Protestant America and was king of the eschatological hill from the time of the Civil War until the 1920s. Currently it is experiencing a resurgence, mostly within the Reformed Protestant tradition. Like both premillennialism and amillennialism, postmillennialism teaches that Christ will return literally and visibly to earth. This personal return of the Lord will be *after* the millennium (hence the term *post*millennialism), but the millennium is usually understood to be, not a literal thousand years, but rather a period of time of unknown length.[30]

---

[29] Hoekema, *Bible and the Future*, p. 221, emphasis in original.

[30] "It should be noted that the postmillennialist is not literalistic about the length of the millennium: the millennium is a long period of time, not necessarily one thousand calendar years. Its length would be difficult to reckon anyway because the millennium has no clear point of beginning. There will not one day be a condition of peace that was completely absent the previous day; the kingdom will arrive by degrees" (Erickson, *Basic Guide to Eschatology*, p. 56).

In addition, this millennium has a particular quality that distinguishes it from the premillennialist view. While the millennium for the premillennialist is an entirely transformed, even different, world,[31] for the postmillennialist it is the same world as exists currently, but perfected and made nearly sinless. Loraine Boettner, a leading Presbyterian theologian and a postmillennialist explained that the millennium

> to which the postmillennialist looks forward is thus a golden age of spiritual prosperity during this present dispensation, that is, during the Church Age. This is to be brought about through forces now active in the world. It is to last an indefinitely long period of time, perhaps much longer than a literal one thousand years. The changed character of individuals will be reflected in an uplifted social, economic, political and cultural life of mankind. The world at large will then enjoy a state of righteousness which up until now has been seen in relatively small and isolated groups. . . . This does not mean that there will be a time on this earth when every person will be a Christian or that all sin will be abolished. But it does mean that evil in all its many forms eventually will be reduced to negligible proportions, that Christian principles will be the rule, not the exception, and that Christ will return to a truly Christianized world.[32]

[31] For one of many possible examples, see Hal Lindsey and C. C. Carlson, *There's a New World Coming* (Santa Ana, Calif.: Vision House Publishers, 1973), chapter 21, titled "The Coming New World" (pp. 283–98). Lindsey states that the earth "will be restored as it was in the Garden of Eden, so that it will be quite a spot. It will be much different than what we're used to now, since there will be no oceans or seas, yet everything will be lush and green. . . . The new earth as a whole will not be the principal residence of the believers, though they will have free access to it" (p. 288).

[32] Loraine Boettner, *The Millennium* (Philadelphia: Presbyterian and Reformed Publishing, 1957), p. 14.

Accompanying this understanding of the millennium is the belief that "the kingdom of God is primarily a present reality.... It is ... the rule of Christ in the hearts of men."[33] The postmillennialist expects all nations and the majority of peoples to convert to Christianity prior to Christ's return,[34] accomplished by the power of the Holy Spirit working through faithful, evangelizing Christians.[35] As the gospel spreads throughout the world over a lengthy period of time— "like the coming of summer"[36]—the Kingdom of God will be slowly realized in time and history on earth. Immediately prior to the end of this idyllic millennial period there will be a time of great tribulation and apostasy as Satan is allowed to sow evil upon the earth. Christ's return in glory will put an end to this outbreak of rebellion, and it will be immediately followed by the judgment of both the living and the dead, the good and the evil.

Because postmillennialism emphasizes the slow and steady growth of the Kingdom, the apocalyptic rhetoric and end-time visions common among premillennialists are usually avoided. The postmillennialist emphasis on a progression toward a time of peace and goodness became popular in the early 1700s in America, where the influence of Enlightenment-era rationalism and a strong sense of the United States as being God's chosen nation existed hand in hand. Jonathan Edwards, the great eighteenth-century New England preacher and a postmillennialist, believed that the Great Awakening—a period of Christian revival in the

---

[33] Erickson, *Basic Guide to Eschatology*, p. 55.

[34] See Boettner, "Redeemed World or Race?", *Millennium*, pp. 22–29.

[35] Erickson, *Basic Guide to Eschatology*, p. 56.

[36] Clouse, *Meaning of the Millennium*, p. 133.

1740s—was "a prelude to the millennium".[37] At first there was intense evangelical fervor at the heart of this postmillennialism, rooted in the belief that America would lead the way into the millennial era. But this began to change in the nineteenth century, when postmillennialism increasingly took on a political and secular tone and people "began to equate the kingdom of God with the political and moral destiny of America.... Eventually it developed into a more secular millennialism largely devoid of religious impulse."[38] The optimism of the postmillennial view was dampened by the two World Wars, the rise of communism, and the proliferation of nuclear weapons. However, in the midst of these events, Loraine Boettner published *The Millennium*, an apologetic for postmillennialism that unabashedly proclaimed that the world was slowly, if sometimes unevenly, moving toward becoming fully christianized.

A more recent form of postmillennialism is Christian reconstructionism, or *theonomy*. Theonomy (literally "rule by the law of God") teaches that the Kingdom of God will involve the complete transformation of culture, political systems, and institutions through "the application of biblical law".[39] David Chilton was a theonomist and summed up the movement's belief in this way: "Our goal is world dominion under Christ's lordship, a 'world takeover' if you will; but our strategy begins with the reformation and reconstruction of the Church. From that will flow social and political reconstruction, indeed a flowering of Christian

[37] Kyle, *Last Days Are Here Again*, p. 80.

[38] Ibid., p. 81.

[39] R. C. Sproul, *The Last Days according to Jesus: When Did Jesus Say He Would Return?* (Grand Rapids, Mich.: Baker Books, 1998), p. 201.

civilization." [40] He also stated that "As the gospel progresses throughout the world it will win, and win, and win, until all kingdoms become the kingdoms of our Lord, and of His Christ; and He will reign forever and ever." [41] While not all postmillennialists would completely agree with this statement, it does capture the heart of the postmillennialist vision.

There is much about postmillennialism that Catholics can accept and agree with, such as the once-only return of Christ at the end of time, the belief that the Church is (at the very least) the Kingdom in "seed" form, and the belief that the Kingdom began with the Incarnation and the Resurrection of Jesus Christ. Catholics would also join postmillennialists in rejecting the dispensationalist teaching about a pretribulational Rapture. On the other hand, the Catholic Church rejects the idea of a progressive growth of goodness and peace that would eventually result in the fullness of the Kingdom being realized on earth prior to Christ's Second Coming. [42]

Amillennialism

Of the three general perspectives, amillennialism is likely the most misunderstood and confusing, partially because the term itself is flawed. Because the prefix "a" means "without" or "not", amillennialism is commonly misinterpreted by dispensationalists to mean that there will not be a millennial reign. Grant Jeffrey writes that "Augustine adopted an amillennial view which rejected any literal period of thousand

---

[40] David Chilton, *Paradise Restored: A Biblical Theology of Dominion* (Tyler, Tex.: Dominion Press, 1994), p. 214.

[41] Ibid., p. 192.

[42] See CCC 677.

years before or after Christ's return."[43] The implication—often expressed more explicitly—is that Augustine (and therefore the Catholic Church) rejected any notion of the millennium. Yet Augustine clearly taught that not only is there a "literal" millennial period, but that Christians are currently living in it.[44] He did not accept that the "thousand years" was an exact number, but he believed it conveyed truths about the spiritual nature of a millennial period whose actual length is unknown. The millennium is the time of the Kingdom on earth, the Church age, which will last an indefinite time—a period of time that will be full and complete at the time of Christ's return.

Unfortunately, such misunderstandings are not easily set right. Perhaps the term itself was flawed from the start, as amillennialist and Reformed theologian Anthony A. Hoekema points out:

> The term amillennialism is not a happy one. It suggests that amillennialists either do not believe in any millennium or that they simply ignore the first six verses of Revelation 20, which speak of a millennial reign. Neither of these two statements is true. Though it is true that amillennialists do not believe in a literal thousand-year earthly reign which will follow the return of Christ, the term amillennialism is not an accurate description of their view.[45]

Admitting that it is clumsy, Hoekema suggests that the term *realized millennialism* is more accurate, "since 'amillennialists' believe that the millennium of Revelation 20 is not exclusively

[43] Jeffrey, *Apocalypse*, p. 18. A dislike for Augustine is obvious in the works of Jeffrey, LaHaye, Lindsey, and other popular dispensationalists.

[44] See *City of God*, bk. 20, chap. 9.

[45] Anthony A. Hoekema, "Amillennialism", in Clouse, *Meaning of the Millennium*, p. 155.

future but is now in process of realization".[46] This is very similar to Catholic doctrine, which teaches that the Church is the Kingdom, but that here on earth she exists in a state of expectancy.[47]

Another problem is that amillennialism "has frequently been stated in a primarily negative fashion, and consequently its positive features have not always emerged clearly".[48] In addition, many of the explanations of what amillennialism is conflict with one another, leading one to wonder if "one is dealing with sub-types of a single basic view or with different views".[49] Finally, since amillennialists have often focused on refuting premillennialism, they are sometimes unclear about their agreements and disagreements with postmillennialists. In fact the two views have much in common—including their claims that both Augustine and John Calvin were proponents of their respective positions. This is understandable since there are many similarities between the two views and because discussions about eschatological positions are often ambiguous. It is easy to judge inaccurately by labels, and, in the case of postmillennialism and amillennialism, care must be taken to assess each position fairly on its own terms rather than on convenient labels.

One area of agreement between the two views is that Christ's Second Coming will mark the end of time and the advent of the final judgment. There will be no earthly, millennial reign by Christ from Jerusalem, nor does the millennium of Revelation 20 refer to an actual one-thousand-year period of time. The number "one thousand" is used in a figurative way throughout Scripture to speak of perfection

---

[46] Ibid., pp. 155–56.
[47] Cf. CCC 669.
[48] Erickson, *Basic Guide to Eschatology*, p. 73.
[49] Ibid.

and fullness (see Deut 7:9; Ps 50:10). In Revelation 20 it likely comes from the idea of $10 \times 10 \times 10 = 1000$, since 10 is the number of completion in Scripture.[50] It is similar to Christ's command that the disciples forgive others "seventy times seven", another use of a number that the Jewish people believed represented fullness and perfection (based on the seven days of creation). Therefore, it can be said that the Catholic Church's position most closely aligns with amillennialism and agrees with postmillennialism on specific points, including the rejection of distinctively premillennial beliefs.

Despite these important agreements with postmillennialists,[51] amillennialists (including Catholics) agree with premillennialists that history will not result in the worldwide

---

[50] Augustine writes: "He used the thousand years as an equivalent for the whole duration of this world, employing the number of perfection to mark the fullness of time. For a thousand is the cube of ten. For ten times ten makes a hundred, that is, the square on a plane superficies. But to give this superficies height, and make it a cube, the hundred is again multiplied by ten, which gives a thousand. Besides, if a hundred is sometimes used for totality, as when the Lord said by way of promise to him that left all and followed Him, 'He shall receive in this world an hundredfold'; of which the apostle gives, as it were, an explanation when he says, 'As having nothing, yet possessing all things,'—for even of old it had been said, The whole world is the wealth of a believer,—with how much greater reason is a thousand put for totality since it is the cube, while the other is only the square? And for the same reason we cannot better interpret the words of the psalm, 'He hath been mindful of His covenant for ever, the word which He commanded to a thousand generations,' than by understanding it to mean 'to all generations'" (*City of God*, bk. 20, chap. 7 in *NPNFI* 2:427).

[51] While acknowledging differences between postmillennialism and amillennialism, Chilton writes: "[The millennium] ... is simply the Kingdom of Christ. It was inaugurated at Christ's First Advent, has been in existence for almost two thousand years, and will go on until Christ's Second Advent at the Last Day. In 'millennial' terminology, this will take place *after* 'the Millennium.' In this objective sense, therefore, *orthodox Christianity has always been postmillennialist....* At the same time, orthodox Christianity has always been amillennialist (i.e., non-millenarian). The historic Church has always rejected the heresy of Millenarianism" (Chilton, *Days of Vengeance*, p. 493).

growth of perfect peace and righteousness. They also agree that Christ's Second Coming could occur in the near future. But while this expectancy produces intense interest in biblical prophecy and end-time events among premillennialists, it rarely has such an effect among amillennialists—their eschatological perspective is far less pessimistic than that of premillennialists. Indeed, the whole subject of eschatology receives far less attention from amillennial theologians than from premillennial theologians.[52]

Augustine and the Millennium

Augustine's thought has exerted a strong influence on the Catholic understanding of the nature and meaning of the millennium. Over the course of many years he modified his view of Revelation 20 and related passages. Early in his life he held a postmillennial interpretation of Revelation 20: "The millennium, for the early Augustine, is still not eternity but a part of history, 'the seventh and last period of this age'."[53] At that time, Augustine adhered to the common patristic idea of history being broken into seven periods of a thousand years, each period corresponding to a day of the week, with the seventh period being a culmination corresponding

[52] "Thus, the amillennialist seldom bemoans the deterioration of world conditions or condemns the prevalent culture. He has noticeably less preoccupation with the details and sequence of the last things and less curiosity about 'signs of the times.' Indeed, the whole subject of eschatology seems to receive less attention from amillennial theologians than from premillennialist theologians, particularly those who are dispensational" (Erickson, *Basic Guide to Eschatology*, p. 75).

[53] Brian E. Daley, S.J., *The Hope of the Early Church: A Handbook of Patristic Eschatology* (Cambridge: Cambridge University Press, 1991), p. 133.

to the Sabbath—" 'a day of rest' that will have no end".[54] However, when he wrote his masterpiece, *City of God*, just a few years before his death, he presented a view more in accord with amillennialism. This "ecclesiological interpretation"[55] interprets the thousand years of Revelation 20 as being "all the years of the Christian era",[56] with the Church identified as the Kingdom:

> But while the devil is bound, the saints reign with Christ during the same thousand years, understood in the same way, that is, of the time of His first coming. For, leaving out of account that kingdom concerning which He shall say in the end, "Come, ye blessed of my Father, take possession of the kingdom prepared for you," the Church could not now be called His kingdom or the kingdom of heaven unless His saints were even now reigning with Him, though in another and far different way; for to His saints He says, "Lo, I am with you always, even to the end of the world." Certainly it is in this present time that the scribe well instructed in the kingdom of God, and of whom we have already spoken, brings forth from his treasure things new and old.[57]

[54] Ibid.

[55] Ibid., p. 134. Jean Daniélou, S.J., provides a helpful analysis of the development of Augustine's view of the millennium. See *The Bible and the Liturgy* (Notre Dame, Ind.: University of Notre Dame Press, 1956), pp. 281–86.

[56] Daley, *Hope of the Early Church*, p. 134.

[57] *City of God*, bk. 20, chap. 9 in *NPNFI* 2:429–30. Also: "Therefore the Church even now is the kingdom of Christ, and the kingdom of heaven. Accordingly, even now His saints reign with Him, though otherwise than as they shall reign hereafter; and yet, though the tares grow in the Church along with the wheat, they do not reign with Him. For they reign with Him who do what the apostle says, 'If ye be risen with Christ, mind the things which are above, where Christ sitteth at the right hand of God. Seek those things which are above, not the things which are on the earth.' Of such persons he also says that their conversation is in heaven. In fine, they reign with Him who are so in His kingdom that they themselves are His kingdom" (ibid., in *NPNFI* 2:430).

While the Catholic Church has never officially interpreted Revelation 20:1–6 and the meaning of the "thousand years", this recognition of the Church as the Kingdom *is* official Catholic teaching, reiterated at the Second Vatican Council in the Dogmatic Constitution on the Church, *Lumen Gentium*:

> To carry out the will of the Father Christ inaugurated the kingdom of heaven on earth and revealed to us his mystery; by his obedience he brought about our redemption. The Church—that is, the kingdom of Christ—already present in mystery, grows visibly through the power of God in the world.[58]

As we will soon see in more detail, ecclesiology is the cornerstone for eschatology. Throughout history, the ramifications of faulty ecclesiologies have often resulted in distorted views of the end times and in beliefs that range from humorous to tragic.

[58] *LG* 3.

5

MILLENARIANISM: EARLY CHURCH TO JOHN NELSON DARBY

The last days are here. So let us abase ourselves and stand in awe of God's patience, lest it turn out to be our condemnation. Either let us fear the wrath to come or let us value the grace we have: one or the other. Only let our lot be genuine life in Jesus Christ.

—Ignatius of Antioch

He who loves the coming of the Lord is not he who affirms it is far off, nor is it he who says it is near. It is he who, whether it be far or near, awaits it with sincere faith, steadfast hope, and fervent love.

—Augustine of Hippo

[T]he Church is ruined; and though much may be enjoyed of what belongs to the Church, I believe from Scripture that the ruin is without remedy, that the professing church will be cut off.

—John Nelson Darby

Someone has always been claiming that the end of the world is near. In *The Last Days Are Here Again*, his study of beliefs about the end times, Richard Kyle writes, "Through much of human history there have been the Chicken Littles who have dashed about proclaiming that the sky was falling or that some other catastrophe would soon follow. There have also been many people willing to follow these prophets of doom." [1] Even prior to Christianity some of these groups were millenarianist, anticipating a soon-to-be-realized time of unprecedented peace on earth. Many early Christians believed that the return of Jesus Christ was imminent, and some of them looked for an earthly reign resembling the Golden Age expected by many Jews. [2] This millenarianist strand stretches down to our own day and manifests itself in many forms, including dispensational premillennialism. How did dispensationalism—a unique brand of millenarianist theology and eschatology—come into existence? What does it have in common with other, older forms of millenarianism, and how is it different? To answer these questions, it is necessary to go back two thousand years and trace the

---

[1] Richard Kyle, *The Last Days Are Here Again: A History of the End Times* (Grand Rapids, Mich.: Baker Books, 1998), p. 15.

[2] Norman Cohn writes: "More than any other religion, Jewish religion centers on the expectation of a future Golden Age; and Christianity, developing out of Judaism, inherited that expectation. Moreover, in the time of Jesus the Jews were much given to millenarian movements; and for many of its early adherents Christianity was just such a movement. Whatever Jesus himself may have meant when he talked of the imminence of the kingdom of God, it is certain that many Christians from the first to the fourth centuries, including such eminent Fathers of the Church as Papias, Irenaeus and Lactantius, expected a dispensation in which the earth would without cultivation produce unheard-of abundance of wine and corn and milk and in which the heathen would be handed over to servitude under the faithful. Such fantasies are indistinguishable from those in the Jewish apocalypses; even the very notion that the age of bliss will occupy the last thousand years before the End is of Jewish origin" ("Medieval Millenarism: Its Bearing on the Comparative Study of Millenarian Movements", in *Millennial Dreams in Action: Essays in Comparative Study*, Sylvia L. Thrupp, ed. [The Hague: Mouton, 1962], p. 33).

millenarianist strand that weaves its way throughout Church history.[3]

Early Millenarianism and Augustine

Apparently many early Christians expected Christ's Second Coming within their lifetime. Some of the early Church Fathers were chiliasts and expected Jesus Christ to return to earth, set up an earthly kingdom, and reign for a thousand years. As it became clear that this would not happen as quickly as they originally hoped, some Christian sects began claiming that they had special knowledge about the Second Coming, including details about its timing and how it would transpire. The most well-known and important of these early Christian millenarianist were the Montanists, formed by the self-proclaimed prophet Montanus in the 170s. Adhering to a strict, ascetic life-style, the Montanists based their beliefs on ecstatic gifts of the Holy Spirit that they claimed to receive on an exclusive basis. They expected Jesus Christ to return to Phrygia, in Asia Minor, and establish the New Jerusalem. Eventually the Montanists faded away, although many of their defining traits endured.[4] Later individuals, such as Hippolytus (170–236) and Sextus Julius Africanus (ca. 160–240), calculated the year of the Second Coming by using the

---

[3] Recent popular works that provide histories of millennialism and apocalyptic movements are Richard Kyle's *Last Days Are Here Again*, pp. 15–137; Paul Boyer's *When Time Shall Be No More: Prophecy Belief in Modern American Culture* (Cambridge, Mass.: Harvard University Press, 1998), pp. 21–151; and Frederic J. Baumgartner's *Longing for the End: A History of Millennialism in Western Civilization* (New York: St. Martin's Press, 1999).

[4] See Ronald Knox's chapter "The Montanist Challenge", in his *Enthusiasm: A Chapter in the History of Religion* (1950; Notre Dame, Ind.: University of Notre Dame Press, 1994), pp. 25–49.

supposed date of creation and adding six thousand years to it. This was based on 2 Peter 3:8 ("with the Lord one day is as a thousand years, and a thousand years as one day") and the belief that each of the seven days of creation corresponded to a thousand-year period, with the seventh "day" marking the end of time.[5]

Origen (ca. 185–254), a Scripture scholar from Alexandria, was a strong opponent of chiliasm. Famous for his allegorical interpretations of Scripture, Origen located types and foreshadowings of Christ in nearly every nook and cranny of the Old Testament. He taught that the book of Revelation is highly symbolic and should not be interpreted literally. While Origen's writings were influential, the most powerful opponent of chiliasm was Augustine. In *City of God*, Augustine firmly rejected millenarianism, offering instead "a subtle interpretation of history shaped by biblical eschatol-

---

[5] "[T]his symbolism of the eighth day took a preeminent place and this is why we must dwell on it. The seven days, figure of time, followed by the eighth day, figure of eternity, appeared to the Fathers of the fourth century as being the symbol of the Christian vision of history. This symbolism, however, was developed along two different lines. The Alexandrians, more inclined to allegory, conceived the seven days as a pure symbol of the whole epoch of the world in contrast to the eighth day, the figure of life everlasting, and did not concern themselves with trying to make each of these seven days coincide with a special period in history. But the westerners, continuing the speculations of the apocalypses, and thinking more realistically, tried, on the contrary, to make the seven days into precise historical epochs and to use them as the basis for calculations which enable them to foretell the date of the Parousia. These two currents of thought, freed from their immediate associations of Alexandrine allegorism or millenarianism, were expressed in the fourth century by the Cappadocians and by St. Augustine in two theologies of history" (Jean Daniélou, *The Bible and the Liturgy* [Notre Dame, Ind.: University of Notre Dame Press, 1956] p. 262). See Daniélou's entire chapter "The Eighth Day" (pp. 262–86) for a detailed explanation of this belief among the early Fathers.

ogy but free of end time speculation or predictions of a literal, earthly Kingdom of God".[6] Throughout time and history, Augustine taught, the City of God and the city of Satan war with one another, with the outcome already decided but not yet realized. At the end of time, at the Last Judgment, the citizens of these two cities would finally be separated—the sheep from the goats (Mt 25:32–46). Augustine saw God orchestrating time and history like an "unchanging conductor",[7] ordering events according to his providential will. Of Augustine's writings on eschatology, Paul Boyer writes:

> The recurrent musical imagery is noteworthy. Twentieth-century prophecy popularizers often portray God as a cosmic playwright stage-managing a vast melodrama, shifting about a huge cast of puzzled and unwitting actors. Augustine offered a different metaphor: God as composer and conductor, history as an indescribably lovely musical work, unfolding for the sheer pleasure of its human listeners.[8]

Augustine's teachings would be the mostly undisputed view of the millennium and end times within the Church for several centuries to follow. Belief in a literal thousand-year reign of Christ on earth waned. There were periods of anxiety and anticipation when dates of the Second Coming set by some Christians (notably the years 500, 800, and 1000) came and went. But apocalyptic fever began to increase dramatically during the late Middle Ages (1100–1500), a time of increasing social and religious instability in the West.

---

[6] Boyer, *When Time Shall Be No More*, p. 48.
[7] Augustine, *Letter* 38, 1.
[8] Boyer, *When Time Shall Be No More*, p. 49.

Joachim of Fiore: History and the New Age

The growth of Islam, the steady development of national-
ism, and the Crusades contributed to the unraveling of a
unified Western civilization during the late Middle Ages. The
Crusades, focused on Jerusalem and the heresy of Islam, fu-
eled apocalyptic thinking, which only increased when the
Black Death wiped out about a third of Europe's population
in the mid-1300s. But perhaps the most important element
behind a rebirth of millenarianism was the establishment of
reform movements inside the Catholic Church, including
several within the monastic tradition.

The Cistercian abbot Joachim of Fiore (ca. 1135–1202)
produced the Middle Age's most influential and original view
of the end times. A biblical scholar, he spent a tremendous
amount of time studying the book of Revelation. Claiming
to have received visions about the end of time, Joachim wrote
a major work titled *Exposition on the Apocalypse*. He based his
view of history on the Trinity,[9] dividing time into three major sections, each one corresponding to one of the Divine
Persons:

> The age of the Father was the age of the Old Testament, and
> law, marriage, and water were among its characteristics. The
> age of the Son, the present one but rapidly coming to an
> end, is the age of the New Testament and of faith, the clergy,

---

[9] "Although the chiliastic viewpoint had practically disappeared by the fifth
century, Joachim revived it as a systematic doctrine of God. It was even made
into something of a program of practical action, in that one could work toward the awaited third age by founding suitable religious Orders. The hope
aroused by Joachim's teaching ... subsequently underwent increasing secular-
ization until eventually it was turned into political utopia" (Joseph Ratzinger,
Eschatology, Death and Eternal Life [Washington, D.C.: Catholic University of
America Press, 1988], p. 13).

and the wine. The age of the Holy Spirit will be the age of perfection, love, monks, and oil.[10]

This tripartite view of history would prove to be quite influential, having an impact on philosophers of history such as Hegel and Marx.[11] It also filtered down into grass-roots movements, including modern-day syncretistic religions mixing Eastern mysticism and apocalyptic beliefs. As Richard Kyle notes, "Even the modern New Age movement claims Joachim as [its] predecessor. New Agers believe that the coming new age will share characteristics with Joachim's third stage."[12]

Joachim was convinced that he was witnessing end-times events in his own day and that the Antichrist—who he believed was an apostate Christian—was already alive in the world. He saw the Church's struggle against Islam to be a further sign of the end of the second age of his schematic. He calculated that the move from the second age to the third would transpire between 1200 and 1260. However, before the third and final stage could come about there would need to be a three-and-a-half-year-long reign by the Antichrist.

[10] Baumgartner, *Longing for the End*, p. 64.

[11] "Joachim was convinced that God's plan for his human creatures could triumph only if it also succeeded on earth. It seemed to follow, then, that the time of the Church, as men have experienced it since the apostles, cannot be the definitive form of salvation.... The mingling of rational planning with suprarational goals, already observable in the Old Testament and in Judaism, now receives [with Joachim's tripartite structure] systematic form. It will soon slough off the spiritual dreams of Abbot Joachim and emerge into the political history of Europe, where it will take the form of messianism through planning.... Hegel's logic of history and Marx's historical scheme are the end products of these beginnings. Those messianic goals in which Marxism's fascination lies rest upon a faulty underlying synthesis of religion and reason" (Ratzinger, *Eschatology*, pp. 211–12).

[12] Kyle, *Last Days Are Here Again*, p. 48.

In 1191 Joachim told Richard the Lion-Hearted that the Antichrist was already in the world, preparing for his rule.

Joachim promoted a sort of evolutionary progression that he believed would culminate in a utopian age in which the Holy Spirit would communicate directly to humanity without need of a Church. He also interpreted the book of Revelation literalistically, ignoring the allegorical interpretation of Augustine that had been accepted for so many centuries. He taught that the Antichrist, Gog and Magog, the beast, and other puzzling elements should not be understood metaphorically but as real people, institutions, and places. Without intending to do anything more than explain the steady progression of history toward a state of perfection, Joachim unleashed a view of the end times that would have consequences for centuries to come. "His tripartite scheme of history", writes Boyer, "anticipates in rudimentary form the dispensationalism popularized by British and American prophecy writers in the nineteenth and early twentieth centuries, which similarly segments history into a series of divinely ordained stages, or 'dispensations.' " [13]

The Protestant Revolution and
the Whore of Babylon

In 1215 the Fourth Lateran Council condemned some aspects of Joachim of Fiore's writings, including his teachings

[13] Boyer, *When Time Shall Be No More*, p. 52. Boyer adds, "Joachim of Fiore had an enormous impact on late medieval thought, reinforcing an already strong eschatological bent. Joachim manuscripts both authentic and spurious, complete with illustrations and elaborate charts (a staple of later prophecy writers as well), circulated through Europe and England stimulating apocalyptic speculation" (p. 53).

about the Trinity, but to little avail. His writings influenced the Spirituals, one of the two Franciscan groups. The Spirituals were radical chiliasts who claimed that anyone who opposed them—including the popes—were of the Antichrist. One of these Spiritual Franciscans, Peter Olivi (ca. 1248–1298), elaborated on Joachim's view of history and divided time into seven epochs, another precursor to the dispensationalist system.

During the late 1300s and early 1400s an outbreak of apocalyptic fever in Bohemia produced a deadly movement headed by the Taborites. Angry at the corruption and wealth of the German clerics who led the Church in Bohemia, Czech preachers began stirring up the people. John Hus (1371–1415), a professor at the University of Prague, was the most famous of these preachers. Declaring the pope to be the Antichrist, Hus was eventually condemned by the Council of Constance and burned to death for his anti-papal views and other doctrinal positions. The Taborites began killing those they judged to be sinners—nearly anyone who was not a part of their movement—convinced such violence was necessary in order to bring about the Second Coming. Eventually, in 1434, the Taborites were destroyed in battle by the more moderate Hussites. Similar events and movements became common in Europe during the fourteenth and fifteenth centuries.

The era of the Protestant Reformation (ca. 1517–1550s) was a time of intense apocalyptic speculation and anticipation. Martin Luther believed that the end of the world would take place within a hundred years of his lifetime.[14] Such an expectation was normal for the time. Revolutionary changes

---

[14] Kyle, *Last Days Are Here Again*, p. 55.

in culture, economics, politics, and religion were occurring at a rapid pace:

> As a result, the years from about 1500 to 1650 were charged with apocalyptic expectation. Europeans believed that they were living in the perilous last times.... The sixteenth century had many "calendarizers"—people who make end-time calculations. They saw the events of their time in the light of Daniel, Revelation, and even astrological predictions. Many Europeans concluded that they were standing on the extreme edge of time.[15]

Luther, Calvin, and most of the other Reformation leaders accepted much of the Augustinian, Catholic view of the end times, but with one major difference: they identified the papacy as *the* Antichrist.[16] The Turks, often seen as the Antichrist by earlier generations, were identified as Gog and Magog, the two mysterious countries found in the book of Revelation (Rev 20:8).

Although there were no specific Catholic millenarianist groups, there was a strong millenarian fervor among some Catholics of the time. In response to Luther's attacks on the papacy, many Catholics took to calling the German Reformer

---

[15] Ibid., p. 57.

[16] "When Martin Luther and early Protestants used the term Antichrist to refer to the pope, as he did in one of his earliest printed works, *Against the Execrable Bull of Antichrist* (1520), it meant they were convinced that they were living in the last days because the papacy was responsible for the great apostasy before the Parousia. For them, the signs of the coming end time included the papacy's nonbiblical authority in the Church, proof of the manifest corruption of their era. Another sign was the success of the Ottoman Turks, obviously the hordes of Gog and Magog, in taking Constantinople in 1453 and most of the Balkans over the next decades" (Baumgartner, *Longing for the End*, p. 83). Kyle notes that John Wyclif (ca. 1329–1384) believed that the papacy was the Antichrist, a belief that had a strong influence on Luther (*Last Days Are Here Again*, p. 61).

the Antichrist. Some Catholic theologians, however, insisted that most of the events of the book of Revelation were meant for the far future and had nothing to do with current events or the papacy. This view was perpetuated by Jesuits such as the Spaniard Franciscus Ribeira, whose literal futuristic interpretation of sections of the book of Revelation foreshadowed the premillennialism movement—including dispensationalism—that would follow some three hundred years later.[17]

British Millenarianism and the Emergence of Darby

The origins of dispensational premillennialism are complex, but certain influential factors stand out. They include British millenarianism, the French Revolution, the reaction against theological liberalism, and an interest in restoring Jews to a Palestinian homeland. In his seminal study *The Roots of Fundamentalism*, Ernest R. Sandeen states, "[The] French Revolution was directly responsible for the revival of prophetic concern. To live through the decade of the 1790s in itself constituted an experience in apocalypticism for many of the British. The violent uprooting of European political and social institutions forced many to the conclusion that the end of the world was near."[18] This strong sense of an

---

[17] Kyle, *Last Days Are Here Again*, p. 62. Also see Steve Gregg, ed. *Revelation, Four Views: A Parallel Commentary* (Nashville: Thomas Nelson Publishers, 1997), p. 42.

[18] Ernest R. Sandeen, *The Roots of Fundamentalism: British and American Millenarianism, 1800–1930* (Chicago: University of Chicago Press, 1970), p. 5. Kyle writes, "In particular, the French Revolution fostered an interest in prophecy. The turbulence of the revolution created an apocalyptic mood, causing many to believe that the end was near. The demolition of papal power in France was of special interest to Bible scholars in both Britain and America

approaching end was further heightened when some students of "Bible prophecy" calculated that the papacy would last 1,260 years and that it was, at last, coming to an end in the late 1700s. This calculation was based on Daniel 7:25 ("a time, two times, and a half a time") and Revelation 12:6 ("one thousand two hundred and sixty days"), combined with the belief that whenever a passage of Bible prophecy referred to a "day" it really meant a "year" [19]—a premise still common in contemporary dispensationalism. When Catholic power in France was destroyed during the Revolution and French troops marched on Rome in 1798, many interpreted those events to be the "deadly wound" of Revelation 13. A simple computation revealed that the papacy had first emerged in A.D. 538, a date still used by groups such as the Seventh-Day Adventists. Anti-Catholicism was not a secondary issue but was at the heart of British and American millenarianism. "Millenarians without exception were stoutly

---

who believed that the papacy had to be destroyed before the millennium could come" (*Last Days Are Here Again*, p. 87). Baumgartner writes of this same era: "The profound social and economic changes wrought by the Industrial Revolution created a deep need for security, a need that millennialism answered for some by offering certainty in a world that had lost its stability. The French Revolution was also a source of uncertainty, sowing confusion in the minds of English millennialists" (*Longing for the End*, p. 155).

[19] Sandeen, *Roots of Fundamentalism*, p. 6. Sandeen explains that the 1260 years result "by substituting 'year' wherever 'day' was mentioned in prophetic chronology", based, of course, on 2 Peter 3:8. "When weeks were described (as in Daniel 9), they were interpreted as periods of seven years, and when months were mentioned, as periods of thirty years.... Forty-two months (Rev 13:5) was quite easily figured out at 1,260 years (when the month was calculated to be worth thirty years), and only a little more ingenuity was necessary to correlate 'time, times, and a half' (Dan. 12:7) with three and one-half years or forty-two months. The influential commentator Joseph Mede had come to that conclusion as early as 1631, and many others had followed him" (*Roots of Fundamentalism*, p. 6, fn. 5).

anti-Catholic", notes Sandeen, "and viewed every agitation [for emancipation] by English and Irish Catholics as confirmation of the increasing corruption of the world and thus of the increasing likelihood of the second advent." [20]

During the early 1800s, numerous sects in Britain split off from the Church of England; most were devoting themselves to the study of biblical prophecy, anticipating the imminent return of Christ to establish his millennial Kingdom. Connections between prophetic passages of Scripture and the apparent demise of the papacy in 1798 were accepted as keys to understanding other passages of Scripture, especially the apparently unfulfilled Old Testament promises of an earthly kingdom for the Jews. Interest in restoring the nation of Israel eventually resulted in strong support of the Zionist movement, which in turn influenced British and American policies toward the Jews and the nation of Israel. [21]

The most eccentric and influential of the early British millenarians was the Scottish preacher Edward Irving, who founded the Catholic Apostolic church in the early 1830s. During the mid-1820s the prophetically obsessed Irving taught himself Spanish in order to translate an obscure book written by Manuel Lacunza, a renegade Chilean Jesuit, under the alias of Juan Ben-Ezra and titled *The Coming of Messiah in Glory and Majesty*. Lacunza's work, written around 1791, stated that believers would be caught up to meet Christ in the air, where they would somehow remain for forty-five days, after which they would return with him in triumph at the

[20] Ibid., p. 17.

[21] Ibid., p. 6. For a detailed examination of the premillennial obsession with Israel, see Dwight Wilson's *Armageddon Now! The Premillenarian Response to Russia and Israel since 1917* (Tyler, Tex.: Institute for Christian Economics, 1991).

Second Coming. Lacunza advocated a form of premillennialism, declared that the Catholic priesthood would form the Antichrist, and believed a new Jewish temple would be built and used in the millennial Kingdom.[22] Irving believed that the correlation between the heretical priest's book and his own premillennial views was providential. Inspired by his study of Lacunza's book, Irving organized a prophetic conference in 1827, the first of many such conferences in both Britain and America. Later conferences organized by Irving focused on the inevitable judgment coming upon apostate Christendom, the restoration of the Jews to Palestine, the millennial Kingdom, and the 1,260 years of Daniel 7 and Revelation 12–13.[23] Irving appeared destined to be a major leader among British millenarians, but he quickly fell out of favor (even within the church he founded) around 1830 when he began teaching that Jesus' earthly nature was sinful.[24] Destitute and shunned, Irving wasted away and died in 1834.

As Irving rapidly faded away, John Nelson Darby (1800–1882), a former lawyer and a priest in the Church of Ireland, began to assert himself among British millenarians. A charismatic and keenly intelligent man, Darby was frustrated with the apparent corruption and spiritual laxity within the Irish church. Tireless, driven, and anxious to save souls, Darby exerted much effort at his first parish working among Catholics, claiming that because of his work they "were becoming Protestants at the rate of 600 to 800 a

---

[22] Manuel Lacunza, *The Coming of Messiah in Glory and Majesty*, by Juan Ben-Ezra, a Converted Jew, trans. Rev. Edward Irving (London: L. B. Seeley and Son, 1827). New edition published by J. G. Tillin (England).

[23] Ibid., p. 21.

[24] Boyer, *When Time Shall Be No More*, p. 87.

week".[25] Increasingly disgusted by the ties of the Anglican Church to the English throne, Darby began to frequent millenarian circles. By 1828 he had left the Church of Ireland and become a leader in what would soon be known as the Plymouth Brethren movement, named after the city containing its largest group of adherents.

In many ways Darby resembled a more famous "reformer" of Christianity, Martin Luther. Opinionated, harsh, and absolutely convinced of his ability to interpret Scripture authoritatively, Darby allowed no dissent or disagreement. Those who dared question his teachings were immediately excommunicated, making fragmentation and discord an almost normal state of affairs among the Brethren. Whatever his personal flaws, it was Darby's system of eschatology that polarized support for him—and opposition against him—among British millenarians.

Darby, Divisions, and Dispensations

Dividing salvation history into dispensations, or different eras, was not unique to Darby. In fact, his use of dispensations was a by-product of a Baconian view of secular history, which believed that history can be more perfectly understood through analysis and categorization.[26] Darby taught that

---

[25] Clarence B. Bass, *Backgrounds to Dispensationalism: Its Historical Genesis and Ecclesiastical Implications* (1960; Grand Rapids, Mich.: Baker Book House, 1977), p. 50.

[26] "In addition to a common interest in prophecy and a common dedication to literalism in biblical interpretation, Darby also shared with other millenarians, and indeed with many nonmillenarian nineteenth-century thinkers, a philosophy of history which divided the past into a number of distinct eras in each of which the mode of God's operations, if not nature's, was unique. The eras were called dispensations" (Sandeen, *Roots of Fundamentalism*, p. 68).

dispensations are periods of time in which certain conditions are placed on mankind by God in order for salvation to be realized. Each of these dispensations, usually seven in number, ends with mankind's failure and God's righteous judgment. Following Darby's lead, the American Cyrus I. Scofield later defined these seven dispensations as Innocence (Adam), Conscience (post-Adam to the Flood), Human Government (Gentiles after the Flood), Promise (Abraham to Moses), Law (Moses to Christ), Grace (Church age), and future Kingdom (the millennium). In his 1896 work, *Rightly Dividing the Word of Truth*, Scofield explained the significance of these different time periods:

> The Scriptures divide time ... into seven unequal periods, usually called "Dispensations" (Eph 3:2), although these periods are also called "ages" (Eph 2:7) and "days"—as, "day of the Lord", etc. These periods are marked off in Scripture by some change in God's method of dealing with mankind, in respect of two questions: of sin, and of man's responsibility. Each of the dispensations may be regarded as a new test of the natural man, and each ends in judgment-marking his utter failure in every dispensation. Five of these dispensations, or periods of time, have been fulfilled; we are living in the sixth, probably towards its close, and have before us the seventh, and last—the millennium.[27]

In creating his historical schematic, Scofield was simply repeating Darby, who wrote that

> the dispensations themselves all declare some leading principles or interference of God, some condition in which He

---

[27] C. I. Scofield, *Rightly Dividing the Word of Truth: Ten Outline Studies of the More Important Divisions of Scripture* (Neptune, N.J.: Loizeaux Brothers, 1896), p. 12.

has placed man.... It is not my intention to enter into any great detail, but to show simply how, in every instance, there was a total and immediate failure as regarded man, however the patience of God might tolerate and carry on by grace the dispensation in which man thus failed in the outset; further, that there is no instance of the restoration of a dispensation afforded us, though there might be partial revivals of it through faith.[28]

These dispensations were periods of testing meant to show man his sinfulness and his inability to achieve any good without God's grace. Each dispensation begins with man having a certain position, then given responsibility by God, and then failing to meet the demands placed upon him. It is not difficult to see the pessimism inherent in this system of belief. This pessimism meant that most Christians were viewed as apostate and that a future tribulation would destroy the majority of humanity.

The use of dispensations reflected a particular understanding of how Scripture is to be read and interpreted. Evangelical scholar and historian George M. Marsden notes that Darby and his followers believed that "all they were doing was taking the hard facts of Scripture, carefully arranging and classifying them, and thus discovering the clear patterns which Scripture revealed. The unusual firmness of the facts of Scripture was believed guaranteed by its supernatural inspiration." [29] This desire to "divide and classify everything is one

---

[28] J. N. Darby, *The Apostasy of the Successive Dispensations*, in *Collected Writings, Ecclesiastical*, 1:193. Quoted in Bass, *Backgrounds to Dispensationalism*, p. 20.

[29] George M. Marsden, *Fundamentalism and American Culture: The Shaping of Twentieth Century Evangelicalism, 1870–1925* (New York: Oxford University Press, 1980), p. 56.

of the most striking and characteristic traits of dispensation-alism".[30] The attempt to classify Scripture "scientifically" was spurred on by increasing attacks on the historicity and va-lidity of the Bible, a growing tendency within many main-line churches. This intensifying skepticism was another indication to Darby of the inevitable corruption of Chris-tendom and the need for "true believers" to remove them-selves from communion with mainline churches.

The Church and Israel: Two Peoples of One God

The unique features of Darby's teachings were twofold: "the doctrine of the secret rapture and the subsequent necessity to divide the New Testament into Jewish and churchly texts".[31] These two distinguishing marks were the logical conclusions of Darby's guiding principle: a radical distinc-tion and dichotomy between Israel, the earthly people of God, and the Church, the heavenly people of God. Con-vinced that Christendom was failing and was mostly apos-tate, and believing that many Old Testament promises had yet to be fulfilled, Darby concluded that God had two peo-ple, not one. He pronounced "The Church is in ruins"[32]—it was, he claimed, being destroyed by hierarchy, institutional-ization, structure, ritual, ceremony, and the ordained clergy. So pessimistic was Darby that he declared:

[30] Ibid., p. 59.

[31] Sandeen, *Roots of Fundamentalism*, pp. 69–70.

[32] Darby, *On the Formation of Churches: Further Developments*, in *Collected Writings, Ecclesiastical*, 1:303. Quoted in Bass, *Backgrounds to Dispensationalism*, p. 100. Bass, in his footnote on the same page, writes, "This statement is one of the most often asserted in [Darby's] volumes on Ecclesiology, and one to which he repeatedly turns to answer any argument relative to the church as it exists in governmental form."

I fully recognize that there was an organization in apostolic and scriptural times, but affirm that what now exists is not the scriptural organization at all, but mere human invention, each sect arranging itself according to its own convenience, so that as an external body, the Church is ruined; and though much may be enjoyed of what belongs to the Church, I believe from Scripture that the ruin is without remedy, that the professing church will be cut off.[33]

Such pessimism meant that only a "remnant"—a few faithful and true Christians—existed in the world. Not surprisingly, this remnant consisted mostly of those who followed Darby and were under his leadership, the Plymouth Brethren.[34] In

[33] Darby, *What the Christian Has Amid the Ruins of the Church, Collected Writings, Ecclesiastical*, 3:417. Quoted in Bass, *Backgrounds to Dispensationalism*, p. 103. The "professing church" mentioned by Darby would have included the Church of England and the Catholic Church, along with any other mainline Protestant church. Of Darby's separatist mentality, Bass writes: "Two ideas, the individual *heavenly* relation to Christ as constituting the church, and the distrust of ecclesiastical systems, combined to establish a spirit of separatism in Darby's movement. All who did not agree with Darby's interpretation were characterized as 'not having the truth' or as 'not understanding the divine plan of the ages,' and therefore as somewhat 'apostate'" (p. 47).

[34] "[God] has told us when the church was become utterly corrupt, as He declared it would, we were to turn away from all this corruption and those who were in it, and turn to the scriptures which 'are able to make the man of God wise unto salvation'" (Darby, *God, Not the Church, the Teacher of His Word*, in *Collected Writings, Ecclesiastical*, 4:366. Quoted in Bass, *Backgrounds to Dispensationalism*, p. 106). Bass writes that "Darby rejects with utter disregard all claims of others to be the true representatives of Christ's body on earth, and makes for the Brethren a sole claim of this distinction. Only the Brethren gather in His name. Others gather as Baptist, Congregationalist, etc., not as 'His body.' Only the Assembly (Brethren) is the church of God on earth.... Darby consigns the entire professing church in visible form to the judgment of a dispensation of failure and enumerates the principle of believer-assembly which has characterized the Brethren movement. Precisely these same beliefs about apostate Christendom and separate assembly are held by contemporary dispensationalists" (pp. 107–8).

this regard Darby was like so many others who vainly sought to reform Christianity by separating themselves from historical Christianity as found in the Catholic Church and setting themselves up as final arbiters of truth and orthodoxy.

Darby believed that the remnant—the "true church"—consisted of those who joined themselves to Christ as individuals. The Church was not the Body of Christ as a community or people, but as individuals having a direct relation to Christ, regardless of any denominational affiliation. In this way Darby was the father of "nondenominational" groups. Although he insisted that people join the Brethren, his ecclesiology led to a radical individualism that discarded denominations, positing an opposition between having a personal relationship with Christ and belonging to the visible Church: "It then became clear to me that the church of God, as He considers it, was composed only of those who were so united to Christ [Eph 2:6], whereas Christendom, as seen externally, was really the world, and could not be considered as the 'church.' " [35] The Church, severed from Christ, is effectively rendered meaningless for the Christian—only an individual, "personal" relationship with Christ is of any value.

Darby believed that the *true* Church's spiritual character meant she should have little or no involvement in earthly affairs. He wrote that "the Church is properly heavenly, in its calling and relationship with Christ, forming no part of the course of events on earth." [36] Because the Church—the spiritual remnant—is heavenly and cannot be aligned with earthly realities, she will need to be removed from the world

---

[35] Darby, *Letters*, 3:298; quoted by Vern S. Poythress, *Understanding Dispensationalists* (Phillipsburg, N.J.: P and R Publishing, 1994), p. 15.

[36] Darby, "The Rapture of the Saints", in *Collected Writings, Prophetic*, 4:237. Quoted in Bass, *Backgrounds to Dispensationalism*, p. 39.

and taken to her rightful place before God can continue his work with the earthly people, the Jews. Thus, the need for the pretribulational Rapture, a secret and silent removal of the remnant out of the world. The great Tribulation following the Rapture will not affect the heavenly people since it will be concerned with earthly things; it will be a testing of the Jewish people meant to bring them to a recognition of Jesus as the true Messiah.

The absolute distinction made by Darby and subsequent dispensationalists between Old Testament Israel and the Church resulted in a division of the New Testament into parts, some meant for Jews (most of the Gospels), and some meant for Christians (most of Paul's writings). Lewis Sperry Chafer, a leading American dispensationalist of the early to mid-twentieth century, wrote, "Only those portions of the Scriptures which are directly addressed to the child of God under grace are to be given a personal or primary application.... It is obvious that, apart from the knowledge of dispensational truth, the believer will not be intelligently adjusted to the present purpose and will of God in the world." [37] In other words, the Bible was incomprehensible to humanity until the 1830s, when the dispensational system finally made sense of it!

---

[37] Lewis Sperry Chafer, *Major Bible Themes* (Chicago: Moody Press, 1944), pp. 97–98. Quoted in Bass, *Backgrounds to Dispensationalism*, p. 37. Bass comments: "The implications here are apparent—certain parts of the Bible may be restricted to certain people, and entire groups may be exempt from others. If, as dispensationalism avows, the church was not instituted until Pentecost, none of the Gospels apply directly to the Christian: the sermon on the mount, the Lord's Prayer, the ethical teaching of Jesus—these are 'kingdom truths'" (pp. 37–38). Here Bass is referring to the common dispensationalist belief that most of the Gospels have no direct relation to the Church but are meant for the future, earthly Jewish Kingdom during the millennium.

The Jews, according to dispensationalism, were meant to accept Jesus as the Christ and enter into the Kingdom when he first came. When they rejected him, they did not lose their right to the Kingdom, but it was postponed until a later time. The rejection of Jesus by the Jewish people meant that another people had to become his Body and Bride— the Church. Darby wrote, "The Lord, having been rejected by the Jewish people, is become wholly a heavenly person. This is the doctrine which we peculiarly find in the writings of the apostle Paul. It is no longer the Messiah of the Jews, but a Christ exalted, glorified; and it is for want of taking hold of this exhilarating truth, that the church has become so weak." [38] Here the dualism of dispensationalism is further crystallized: heavenly versus earthly, Jewish versus Christian, and material Messiah versus heavenly Person.

The Church is therefore a back-up plan, a "parenthetical" insert into history. Salvation history has been detoured into the Church age until the Jewish people are ready to return to God. The prophetic clock is paused until the spiritual remnant, the Church, is removed from earth by the Rapture. Clarence Bass correctly summarizes this belief by stating, "Whatever evaluation history may make of [dispensationalism], it will attest that dispensationalism is rooted in Darby's concept of the church—a concept that sharply distinguishes the church from Israel, assigns an exclusivist role to the church in an apostate Christendom, [and] gives the church a heavenly title and futuristic character." [39]

---

[38] Darby, *Writings*, 2:376. Quoted in Poythress, *Understanding Dispensationalists*, p. 18.

[39] Bass, *Backgrounds to Dispensationalism*, p. 127.

The Rapture: The Necessary Escape

The pretribulational Rapture, or the "any-moment coming of the Lord" prior to a time of great tribulation, is the most widely recognized teaching of Darby. However, it existed in different, more ambiguous forms prior to the 1830s. Darby saw the pretribulational Rapture as a necessary and logical centerpiece of premillennial dispensationalism. But it was not accepted by many of his fellow millenarians, who thought that what amounted to the belief in "two second comings" was both unbiblical and illogical. But Darby was convinced the Rapture was the proper conclusion of his distinction between Israel and the Church:

> It is this conviction, that the church is properly heavenly, in its calling and relationship with Christ, forming no part of the course of events of the earth, which makes its rapture so simple and clear; and on the other hand, it shews how the denial of its rapture brings down the church to an earthly position, and destroys its whole spiritual character and position. Our calling is on high. Events are on earth. Prophecy does not relate to heaven. The Christian's hope is not a prophetic subject at all.[40]

This secret Rapture, Darby taught, could come at any time. There was nothing yet to be fulfilled to keep Christ from suddenly removing his heavenly people from earth. This

---

[40] Darby, *Collected Writings*, 11:156. Quoted in Sandeen, *Roots of Fundamentalism*, p. 63. Sandeen documents the controversy among British millenarians over Darby's teachings about the pretribulational Rapture in "John Nelson Darby and Dispensationalism", the third chapter of *Roots of Fundamentalism* (pp. 59–80).

was contrary to the expectations of some millenarians, who believed that specific events had yet to take place before Christ's Second Coming. By inserting an additional coming of Christ, Darby could insist that the Rapture was imminent—it could occur right now, right here, without warning: "To me, the Lord's coming is not a question of prophecy, but of my present hope. Events before His judging the quick are the subject of prophecy; His coming to receive the church is our present hope. There is no event between me and heaven."[41]

While the main source of Darby's belief in the Rapture was his ecclesiology and his interpretation of Old Testament prophecies relating to Israel, many have speculated about other influences. Sandeen notes, "As late as 1843 or possibly even 1845, Darby was expressing doubts about the secret rapture. In later years he seems to have felt that he was convinced about the doctrine as early as 1827."[42] Some claim that Darby learned of the belief from Edward Irving in the early 1830s.[43] A more recent charge is that the Rapture originated in 1830 from the visions of a young Scottish girl, Margaret McDonald, whose family was associated with Irv-

---

[41] Darby, *Letters*, 1:329–30. Quoted in Sandeen, *Roots of Fundamentalism*, p. 64.

[42] Sandeen, *Roots of Fundamentalism*, p. 64.

[43] "Darby's opponents claimed that the doctrine originated in one of the outbursts of tongues in Edward Irving's church about 1832. This seems to be a groundless and pernicious charge. Neither Irving nor any member of the Albury group advocated any doctrine resembling the secret rapture" (Sandeen, *Roots of Fundamentalism*, p. 64). For an opposing viewpoint, see Dave MacPherson's *The Rapture Plot*, 2d ed. (Simpsonville, S.C.: Millennium III Publishers, 2000).

ing's Catholic Apostolic church.[44] While these assertions may have some legitimacy and should be seriously considered, Darby's teachings about the Rapture, the Church, and Old Testament Israel need to be addressed on their own merits. Continuing our critique of premillennial dispensationalism will require following its spread to the United States and its growth in popularity among American Fundamentalists and Evangelicals.

---

[44] In 1973 and 1974 Dave MacPherson, a Christian journalist, wrote, respectively, *The Unbelievable Pre-Trib Origin* and *The Late Great Pre-Trib Rapture*. These would eventually be published in one volume as *The Incredible Cover-Up: Exposing the Origins of Rapture Theories* (Medford, Ore.: Omega Publications, 1999). A later book, *The Rapture Plot*, is an even more thorough treatment of MacPherson's central thesis that Darby was not the originator of the pretribulational Rapture. MacPherson provides compelling evidence that Darby based his pretribulational Rapture on the vision of a young Scottish invalid, Margaret McDonald. MacPherson also documents what he alleges are repeated instances of plagiarism in the works of Tim LaHaye, Hal Lindsey, Jerry Falwell, and Charles C. Ryrie.

6

DISPENSATIONALISM AND
THE RAPTURE IN AMERICA

Whatever the future holds for American evangelical religion, one of its most noticeable elements is the interest in, even obsession with, biblical prophecy. Once considered the preoccupation of relatively few fanatics, eschatology (the doctrine of "final things") has come close to reaching cult status in American society, or at least in a significant part of it.

—Timothy P. Weber

We are the generation the Prophets were talking about! We have witnessed Biblical prophecies come true.... We are the generation that will see the end times ... and the return of Jesus.

—Hal Lindsey

First of all you must understand this, that no prophecy of scripture is a matter of one's own interpretation, because no prophecy ever came by the impulse of man, but men moved by the Holy Spirit spoke from God.

—2 Peter 1:20–21

Premillennial dispensationalism has flourished in the United States since the late 1800s, and the United States is today the world's primary producer of dispensationalist books, tapes, and "prophecy experts".[1] Even before the United States were formed, the New World was the home of prophetic aspirations. Colonized by Christians such as the Puritans, North America was thought to be a Promised Land where millennial dreams would be realized.[2] "Over the centuries prophecy belief has remained a bedrock of American popular religion", Paul Boyer observes. "Through decades of social change, technological innovation, and world upheaval, millions of Americans have clung to the conviction that the Bible offers a key to history and its final end."[3] The history of dispensationalism in America, especially in the twentieth century, is not only fascinating, it provides an essential context for understanding the continuing popularity of this eschatological system.

Apocalypse Then: The 1700s and 1800s

Many Americans in the 1600s and 1700s had an apocalyptic outlook, expecting God to bless their "chosen nation" by bringing the millennium to pass in the near future. The Puritans were mostly millenarian, and some, like the well-known preachers Increase Mather (1639–1723) and his son

[1] Today, almost every well-known dispensationalist author or teacher is from the U.S., with the exception of Grant Jeffrey, who is Canadian. The leading publishers of dispensationalist books are nearly all American as well.

[2] "From the first, Puritans showed that they thought of America as the place where they would serve as God's chosen instruments to establish the New Kingdom. It was the wilderness to which the godly were required to flee to escape the dragon" (Frederic J. Baumgartner, *Longing for the End: A History of Millennialism in Western Civilization* [New York: St. Martin's Press, 1999], p. 124).

[3] Paul Boyer, *When Time Shall Be No More: Prophecy Belief in Modern American Culture* (Cambridge, Mass.: Harvard University Press, 1998), p. 293.

Cotton (1663–1728), believed Christ was returning soon.[4] Cotton Mather was prone to setting dates and expected the New Jerusalem to be located in New England. His father, Increase, taught a form of the second advent that "foreshadowed that of the dispensationalists—a rapture in which believers are taken into the air".[5]

The famed preacher Jonathan Edwards (1703–1758) was a postmillennialist who taught that a golden age was approaching and that America would be at the center of it. Following classical Protestant teachings, Edwards believed that the papacy was the Antichrist; he also taught the millennium would begin in America by about the year 2000. Americans increasingly saw their nation as being closely tied to the Kingdom of God—perhaps even being that very Kingdom. When the Revolutionary War broke out, many viewed the English monarchy and the Church of England as the Antichrist.

The early 1800s witnessed an explosion of sects, fringe groups, and millenarian movements, including the Shakers and the Church of the Latter-Day Saints, or Mormons. The most famous American "prophet" and millenarianist of the time was the Baptist layman William Miller (1782–1849), who predicted that Christ would return in March 1844. After that

---

[4] "The early Puritans were fervent millennialists, insisting that the millennium was coming. Like the English millennialists, they often blurred the distinctions between pre- and postmillennialism. Most Puritans looked for the apocalyptic events surrounding the defeat of the Antichrist and the inauguration of Christ's kingdom. Whether Christ would come before or after the millennium was disputed and unclear. Some Puritans, however, can best be seen as chiliasts or premillennialists. Increase and Cotton Matthew, for example, held Christ's return to be imminent. Believers would be caught up into the air, and then the disasters and persecutions would begin, followed by the millennium" (Richard Kyle, *The Last Days Are Here Again: A History of the End Times* [Grand Rapids, Mich.: Baker Books, 1998], p. 78).

[5] Ibid., p. 79.

date passed, Miller recalculated and arrived at a new date in October 1844. Miller's beliefs resembled those of British millenarians, but he denied any significant role to Israel. After the "Great Disappointment" of Miller's failed prophecies, the Millerites split into several factions, the largest and best-known being the Seventh-Day Adventists. A group that would eventually become the Jehovah's Witnesses later split from the Adventists in the 1870s.[6] A significant result of the Millerite movement was that it "discredited historicist premillennialism" and "demonstrated the perils of setting definite dates for Christ's return".[7] The stage was set for the growth of dispensationalism, imported to America from England by Darby and other British dispensationalists.

The Plymouth Brethren movement in England was marked by serious conflict and division. Despite these problems, the Brethren's belief in the pretribulational Rapture and its opposition to "apostasy" in the Church of England attracted followers. The movement could have become a more powerful group in England if Darby had put effort into it, but he was more interested in travelling to Europe and America, proclaiming his unique eschatological views. Darby visited the United States and Canada seven times between 1862 and 1877, but he did not have immediate or notable success. After visiting North America he declared, "The church is more worldly in America than anywhere you would find it, that is, the professing bodies, the world—professedly

---

[6] Seventh-Day Adventism was founded shortly after Miller's failed prophecies in the mid-1840s, with the name being formally adopted in 1861. Charles Russell, initially a Seventh-Day Adventist, formed his own brand of millenarianism in the early 1870s, calling his group the Watchtower Bible Society, better known as Jehovah's Witnesses since adopting that name in 1931.

[7] Kyle, *Last Days Are Here Again*, p. 91.

such—inordinately wicked." [8] He discovered Americans were reluctant to leave their denominations, even though they were open to his teachings about the Rapture, the Church, and the restoration of Jews to Palestine. Among the most open were Baptists and Presbyterians; Darby was particularly impressed by the Calvinists' position on grace and works. By the time Darby made his last trip to America in 1877 at the age of seventy-seven, there were nearly ninety small Brethren meetings in existence.

A key supporter of premillennialism and dispensationalism was the evangelist Dwight L. Moody (1837–1899). The greatest American evangelist of his time, Moody founded Moody Bible College in Chicago; it would become one of the best-known centers of dispensational thought in America. Moody rarely spoke directly about dispensationalist beliefs—it is not even clear that he believed in the pretribulation Rapture. But the schools, groups, and publishing houses that he founded and influenced would eventually reflect a solid dispensationalist character. At Moody's funeral in 1899, famed dispensationalist leader C. I. Scofield—then pastor of the Congregational Church of East Northfield, Massachusetts—led the service.[9] Other famous evangelists and evangelical leaders would also either embrace or support dispensationalism, including Billy Sunday, Reuben A. Torrey, and A. B. Simpson, founder of the Christian and Missionary Alliance.

---

[8] Darby, *Letters*, 1:351. Quoted in Ernest R. Sandeen, *The Roots of Fundamentalism: British and American Millenarianism, 1800–1930* (Chicago: University of Chicago Press, 1970), p. 71.

[9] See *Christian History*, vol. 9, no. 1 (1990). The entire issue, titled "The Unconventional Dwight L. Moody", is devoted to the life and work of Moody.

During the last quarter of the nineteenth century the popularity of prophecy and Bible conferences grew tremen-
dously, and several Bible schools were founded, all of which
proclaimed the dispensationalist message. A series of Bible
studies developed in New York state and eventually gave birth
to the Niagara Conferences, which convened between 1883
and 1897.[10] These conferences were attended by people from
many different denominations, who came to study the Scripture, particularly biblical prophecy. American and British leaders of the loosely knit dispensationalist viewpoint presented
their respective views about biblical prophecy, the dispensations, and the gospel, creating a "protodenominational movement" within American Protestantism—a movement uniting
a number of different denominations into an organized en-
tity.[11] A seminal event was the publication in 1878 of an
influential work, *Jesus Is Coming*, written by William E. Blackstone, a prominent Chicago businessman and avid dispensationalist. Blackstone organized meetings between Christians
and Jews and actively advocated the return of the Jews to
a Palestinian homeland. He garnered strong support for
his Zionist cause from leading politicians (including U.S.
presidents), journalists, and business leaders, influencing

[10] "These conferences furnished an opportunity for the broader dissemination of the millenarian message, but also provided occasions at which friend-
ships could be formed and personal leadership could develop. Millenarianism,
though not for a moment forgetting the need to proclaim the imminent second advent of Christ, became something more after 1875. At its center, among
the true initiates, it became a spiritual home, a community.... The Niagara
Bible Conference was the mother of them all—the Monte Cassino and Port
Royal of the movement" (Sandeen, *Roots of Fundamentalism*, p. 132).
[11] Kyle, *Last Days Are Here Again*, p. 105. See Sandeen, *Roots of Fundamentalism*, pp. 132–43.

American policy toward Palestine and Zionism for decades to come.[12]

The prevalent attitude at the prophetic conferences was one of pessimism in the face of what attendees and supporters believed were the two major problems in American Christianity: Catholicism and liberalism. Much of the rabid anti-Catholic literature of the late nineteenth century was produced by dispensationalists and Plymouth Brethren groups. The pope was identified as the "Man of Sin"—the Antichrist—and Catholicism was considered a serious threat to true Christianity. These beliefs are evident in this dispensationalist article, written in 1878:

> Two-thirds of nominal Christendom is one vast overshadowing hierarchy, a system of Mariolatry, if not of idolatry, with a false ritualism, and a grossly materialistic sacramentarianism, while the remaining third of the professed church is sadly compromised by rationalism in its theology, and humanitarianism in its Christology. Outside the church and within, spiritualism enrolls its millions; annihilationism and second probationism, a kind of "incipient, theological dry rot," boast their thousands, hundreds of whom stand in so-called orthodox pulpits, and openly proclaim these false doctrines, or secretly entertain them.... Nearly the whole church, Catholic and Protestant, in the United States has drifted away

---

[12] "Some premillennialists were not satisfied to be mere observers of the Zionist movement. A few became strong supporters and actually gained recognition within the movement for their aggressive advocacy. No American premillennialist earned more acclaim among Zionists than W. E. Blackstone, the author of *Jesus Is Coming*, probably the most widely read premillennialist book of its time" (Timothy P. Weber, *Living in the Shadow of the Second Coming: American Premillennialism 1875–1925* [New York: Oxford University Press, 1979], p. 137). For the story of relations between Jews and dispensationalists in the late 1800s and early 1900s, see pp. 128–57.

from the apostolic doctrine of Christ's premillennial advent.
... Wanted, a man in all our religious schools to teach the
entire system of prophetic and dispensational truth![13]

At the end of the nineteenth century dispensationalism had
a growing but still modest influence in the United States.
That would change dramatically with the publication of the
"dispensational Bible".

Scofield and the Dispensational Bible

American dispensationalism at the end of the nineteenth
century was still sorting through competing viewpoints, with
many key issues heavily debated and without consensus.
Cyrus I. Scofield (1843–1921), a Kansas City lawyer with a
tainted past,[14] solidified the way dispensationalism would be

[13] A. J. Frost, "Condition of the Church and World at Christ's Second Advent", *Prophetic Studies*, pp. 174–75. Quoted in C. Norman Kraus, *Dispensationalism in America: Its Rise and Development* (Richmond, Va.: John Knox Press, 1958), pp. 96–97. Speaking of the general sense of gloom among dispensationalists of the late 1800s, Marsden writes, "The area where dispensationalists were perhaps most out of step with the rest of nineteenth-century thinking was in their view of contemporary history, which had little or no room for social or political progress. When they spoke on this question, dispensational premillennialists were characteristically pessimistic.... Clearly the dispensationalists were not much interested in social or political questions as such, except as they bore on spiritual history.... The idea of a 'Christian civilization' was often a particular target of their scorn. The Pope of Rome was the preeminent example of this pretense and always fair game for Protestant Americans" (George M. Marsden, *Fundamentalism and American Culture: The Shaping of Twentieth Century Evangelicalism, 1870–1925* [New York: Oxford University Press, 1980], pp. 66–67).

[14] "A Tennessean dogged by scandal, heavy drinking, and marital problems in his early years, Scofield fought as a Confederate in the Civil War, practiced law in Kansas, and hastily left that state in 1877 (abandoning a wife and two children) amid accusations that he had stolen political contributions to Senator John Ingalls, a former partner.... Jailed in St. Louis in 1879 on forgery

understood for the next several decades. Having gained a reputation as a speaker and leader during the Niagara Conferences, Scofield (who had no formal theological training) decided he would create a "study Bible" containing extensive notes, cross references, and commentary so that the "scientific" nature of biblical prophecy would be evident to the average layman. After several years of labor and with the assistance of a group of editors, the *Scofield Reference Bible* (King James Version) was published in 1909. Presented in a neatly organized and systematic manner, its dispensationalist premises regarding key passages of Scripture—especially books like Daniel and Revelation—entered into the mainstream of conservative American Protestantism. In the sixty years following publication, Scofield's *Reference Bible* sold at least five million copies—and perhaps up to ten million.[15] It is "perhaps the most influential single publication in millenarian and Fundamentalist historiography.... The book has ... been subtly but powerfully influential in spreading [dispensational] views among hundreds of thousands who have regularly read that Bible and who often have been unaware of the distinction between ancient text and the Scofield interpretation."[16] A popular witticism, sung to a favorite hymn, declared: "My hope is built on nothing less/Than Scofield's

---

charges, Scofield experienced religious conversion in prison and fell under the influence of James Brookes, the Darbyite dispensationalist" (Boyer, *When Time Shall Be No More*, p. 97).

[15] Ibid., p. 98.

[16] Sandeen, *Roots of Fundamentalism*, p. 222. Kraus writes, in 1958, "Probably no other one man has been more influential in spreading dispensational teachings than C. I. Scofield. Through his Bible study course, participation in Bible conferences, numerous magazine articles and pamphlets, and most of all through the Scofield Reference Bible, he popularized the doctrine throughout the United States and Canada. He did not claim originality for his work, and in this disclaimer he was correct. He clarified and standardized the work

Notes and Moody." [17] The updated version, the *New Scofield Reference Bible*, printed in 1967, is still used today in many Fundamentalist circles.

Scofield's *Reference Bible* was "uncompromisingly Darbyite dispensationalist in doctrine and taught the any-moment coming and the secret rapture of the church".[18] Scofield also taught that Scripture contains passages meant for each respective time period and that many passages are not meant—at least primarily—for Christians in the "Church age". This was based on Darby's radical distinction between the Church and Old Testament Israel and meant that most of Christ's teachings, including the Sermon on the Mount, were for the future Jewish Kingdom age, not for the Church. William M. Pettingill, dean of the Philadelphia School of the Bible and an editor of *The Scofield Reference Bible*, claimed, "The Sermon on the Mount, then, is not the way of salvation for the sinner. Neither is it the rule of life for the Christian. . . . He [Christ] has not neglected to give to His church ample directions for her guidance, but these directions are not to be found in the Sermon on the Mount. The Sermon on the Mount is pure law." [19] This was a radical break from 1900 years of Christian teaching, which had always placed great emphasis on the centrality and primacy of the Gospels and the importance of the Beatitudes, considered normative for growth in the Christian faith. But for dispensationalists

---

of others. . . . His unique contribution is his organization of the data into a popular system" (Kraus, *Dispensationalism in America*, pp. 111, 114).

[17] Boyer, *When Time Shall Be No More*, p. 98.

[18] Sandeen, *Roots of Fundamentalism*, p. 224. Many of the main supporters of Scofield's project were Plymouth Brethren, including the initial publisher of the *Reference Bible*, Francis Fitch.

[19] William L. Pettingill, *The Gospel of the Kingdom: Simple Studies in Matthew* (Findley, Ohio: Durham Publishing, n.d.) pp. 57–58.

the writings of Paul became central for the "Church age", while the Gospels were relegated to a peripheral position. In this regard Scofield's teachings strongly resembled those of Marcion, the third-century heretic who made an absolute break between the Old and New Testaments and who placed Paul's writings at the heart of Christian doctrine.

The strength of Scofield's *Bible* lies in its orderly structure, the appearance of scientific accuracy in its commentary on Scripture, and its direct appeal to the average reader. Scofield took pride in having little formal education and no theological training; " 'This is a layman's age' Scofield wrote—and the observation is the key to his popularity.... He believed that anyone could interpret prophecy; book learning and theological training were unnecessary and probably a hindrance." [20] Scofield's lack of training did not hurt sales or hinder the influence of his reference work. One Protestant critic laments, "From my own experience I would say that in many conservative evangelical student groups, as they were in the early 1950s, perhaps a half, and among those who had been brought up in conservative evangelical homes a larger proportion, were well accustomed to the Scofield Bible and regarded its interpretations as normal, often being surprised to discover that any other interpretation is possible." [21] Another Evangelical writes that "for many evangelicals the Scofield notes possessed what amounted to *de facto* canonicity." [22] There is little doubt that without the *Scofield Reference Bible* the theological and eschatological landscape of the United States would look quite different today.

[20] Boyer, *When Time Shall Be No More*, p. 99.

[21] James Barr, *Fundamentalism* (Philadelphia: Westminster Press, 1978), p. 191.

[22] Robert G. Clouse, Robert N. Hosack, and Richard V. Pierard, *The New Millennium Manual: A Once and Future Guide* (Grand Rapids, Mich.: Baker Books, 1999), p. 99.

Lewis Sperry Chafer: The Systematizer

The many small Bible institutes and colleges that sprang up across the United States beginning in the late 1800s were major avenues of dissemination for Scofield's synthesis of dispensationalist thinking. A leading figure in that educational movement was Lewis Sperry Chafer (1871–1952), a Presbyterian pastor and a pupil and colleague of Scofield who took up the dispensational torch after Scofield's death in 1921. Chafer, like Scofield, had no formal theological training, a fact in which he took apparent pride. Like his mentor, he was also a popular speaker, tireless in his efforts to spread dispensationalist beliefs throughout America. In 1924 he helped found the school in Dallas, Texas, that would become Dallas Theological Seminary; along with Moody Bible Institute in Chicago it developed into a major center of dispensational teaching in America. Building upon Scofield's work, Chafer further systematized dispensational theology, writing numerous books and articles. Chafer's debt to Scofield, with whom he had a sonlike relationship, was immense. "Without a doubt," dispensationalist author Jeffrey J. Richards acknowledges, "the man who had the most significant influence and impact upon the theological and, more specifically, the eschatological thinking of Lewis Sperry Chafer was C. I. Scofield." [23]

Another of Chafer's contributions to dispensationalism was his systematic, theological exposition of the movement's

[23] Jeffrey J. Richards, *The Promise of Dawn: The Eschatology of Lewis Sperry Chafer* (Lanham, Md.: University Press of America, 1991), p. 66. After a detailed comparison of Chafer's eschatological beliefs to those of Scofield, Richards states: "As one views Chafer's eschatology, it is readily apparent there are only minor differences from the eschatology of C. I. Scofield.... Chafer was the successor of Scofield's eschatology" (p. 80).

beliefs. His *Systematic Theology* (1947), an ambitious eight-volume work, was a dispensationalist *Summa*, an attempt to relate every area of theology to the movement's understanding of the distinction between Israel and the Church. Chafer reiterated this absolute dichotomy in his book titled *Dispensationalism*: "The dispensationalist believes that through the ages God is pursuing two distinct purposes: one related to the earth with earthly people and earthly objectives involved, which is Judaism; while the other is related to heaven with heavenly people and heavenly objectives involved, which is Christianity." [24] For Chafer this schema was imperative if the gospel was going to be preached correctly. He insisted that unless a person held dispensationalist beliefs he was doomed to teach a false gospel: "How many even sincere men can preach an uncomplicated gospel sermon? No man can be trusted to do this until he is dispensationally instructed.... The great expositors of this and past generations are such because they are thoroughly established in these essential distinctions." [25] As with Scofield, such distinctions led to a Marcion-like view of the New Testament: "Chafer taught that the Scriptures addressed specifically to the Church are the Gospel of John (especially the Upper Room discourses), the Acts, and the Epistles." [26]

Although Chafer's writings have faded in popularity and his name does not appear as often as that of Scofield in the writings of popular dispensationalists, his influence as a systematizer, theologian, educator, and tireless champion of dis-

---

[24] Lewis Sperry Chafer, *Dispensationalism* (Dallas, Tex.: Dallas Theological Seminary, 1936), p. 107.

[25] Lewis Sperry Chafer, "Gospel Preaching", *Bibliotheca Sacra* 95 (July 1938): 343.

[26] Kraus, *Dispensationalism in America*, p. 122.

pensationalist teaching cannot be underestimated. His *Systematic Theology* provided American dispensationalists with an apparently comprehensive and sophisticated theology addressing nearly every aspect of Christian thought and doctrine. Dallas Theological Seminary, which he founded and was president of for many years, has educated thousands of pastors and laypeople schooled in dispensationalist thinking—including a young man named Hal Lindsey, who attended Dallas Theological Seminary in the late 1950s and early 1960s.

The Jews Return to the Promised Land

Shortly before Chafer's death in 1952, an event took place that was, for dispensationalists, *the event* of the century: the creation of a Palestinian homeland for Israel in 1948. As one dispensationalist author excitedly wrote shortly after the declaration of Israel's establishment as a nation in Palestine: "There isn't the slightest doubt that the emergence of the Nation Israel among the family of nations is the greatest piece of prophetic news that we have had in the twentieth century." [27]

The relationship between American dispensationalism and the nation of Israel is a complicated and occasionally odd story filled with political, historical, and theological ramifications. Boyer writes:

> Israel and the Jews loom large in post-World War II American prophecy popularizations. Complex and deeply paradoxical, the treatment of these interwoven topics merits careful

[27] From William W. Orr, *The New Nation of Israel and the Word of God!*, 1948; quoted in Dwight Wilson's *Armageddon Now! The Premillenarian Response to Russia and Israel since 1917* (Tyler, Tex.: Institute for Christian Economics, 1991), p. 123. Wilson's book provides a detailed examination of the relationship between premillennialists and Zionism during the twentieth century.

exploration. What writers have had to say on these subjects has influenced millions of Americans' perceptions of events in the Middle East—and of their Jewish fellow citizens. In the premillennial system the Jews enjoy a privileged niche. But they also face future horrors worse than anything yet encountered in millennia of suffering and persecution.[28]

For centuries many Christians have believed that the Jews would either be restored to the Promised Land or would finally recognize Christ as the true Messiah. As noted earlier, the *Catechism of the Catholic Church* teaches that there will be, at some point in time, a "full inclusion" of the Jews in the New Covenant.[29] While the Catholic Church says nothing about how this might take place, other groups, especially dispensationalists, have formed detailed and often elaborate scenarios about Israel in the "last days". Although Catholic teaching emphasizes the future reality of repentance and spiritual renewal on the part of "all Israel", it states nothing about the necessity of Israel returning to the Promised Land—the restoration of Israel as a nation is not the central issue in Catholic theology. In direct contrast, dispensationalists have insisted for nearly two centuries that Israel, God's "earthly people", must return to Palestine before the prophetic clock could once again start ticking. Dispensationalist writers and the numerous American prophetic conferences in the late 1800s and early 1900s focused intently upon the return of the Jews to Palestine,[30] and dispensationalist

---

[28] Boyer, *When Time Shall Be No More*, p. 181.

[29] CCC 674, quoting Rom 11:12.

[30] "Darby and the dispensationalists turned the prophetic spotlight on the Jews, where hundreds of subsequent expositors kept it tightly focused. The promised restoration to Palestine loomed large in the U.S. prophecy conferences held between 1878 and 1918, and in the influential books of Robert

leaders and groups actively sought to aid the rebirth of the nation of Israel.

The door of dispensationalist eschatology hinges upon Israel's role and restoration as a nation. In his history of American premillennialism, *Living in the Shadow of the Second Coming*, Timothy Weber provides an excellent summary of the dispensationalist end-time scenario involving Israel:

> At the end of the age, God would again make Israel the center of his concern. Daniel's seventieth week would begin, leading up to the coming of Messiah and the setting up of the long-promised kingdom. But those who would reign with Messiah Jesus in the coming kingdom must first be purged by suffering for past sins. After the partial re-gathering of the Jews in Palestine and the re-establishment of the state of Israel would come the ill-fated pact with the Antichrist, betrayal at his hands, immense suffering for those Jews who accepted Jesus as Messiah before his coming, and the final invasion by hordes of Gentile armies.
>
> Though intense, the suffering would be brief. When the Gentile powers had the Jews close to total annihilation, Jesus Christ would return to earth, slaughter Antichrist's armies, and finally establish the kingdom that he had originally offered to the Jews at his first advent. After witnessing his majestic display of power, the Jews would acknowledge Messiah Jesus and once again bask in the blessings of God.[31]

Anderson of Scotland Yard and the Reverend James Brookes of St. Louis.... Cyrus Scofield followed the well-worn path. 'Israel regathered from all nations, restored to her own land and converted,' he declared in his 1909 Reference Bible, 'is yet to have her greatest earthly exaltation and glory.' In another work he proclaimed, 'Upon the sacred soil of Palestine God has decreed the reconstitution of the nation of Israel'" (Boyer, *When Time Shall Be No More*, p. 185).

[31] Weber, *Living in the Shadow of the Second Coming*, pp. 130–31.

As Weber observes, for dispensationalists "the entire redemptive plan of God hinged on the restoration of the Jews. Without a restored Jewish state in Palestine, God's cosmic program would not succeed." [32]

With such expectations, it is easy to see why the Balfour Declaration in 1917 and the restoration of Israel to Palestine in 1948 were greeted with such excitement by dispensationalist leaders. In late 1917 the British foreign secretary, Arthur Balfour, expressed the British government's desire that "a national home for the Jewish people" be established in Palestine; that goal would be realized three decades later when the Jewish National Council proclaimed on May 14, 1948, that Israel was a nation. For dispensationalists these events were powerful validations of their views as well as indications that they were indeed living in the final days of history, with only the Rapture standing between them and the restart of the biblical prophetic clock. [33] As Jerry Falwell, a staunch dispensationalist and one of the most prominent American Fundamentalist leaders of the past thirty years, has stated, the return of Israel to Palestine is "the single greatest sign

[32] Ibid., p. 131.

[33] This theme is a central one for Hal Lindsey, whose Zionism approaches fanaticism. He has gone so far as to imply that Christians who are not dispensationalist are anti-Semitic. In *The Rapture*, after stating that amillennialism and Augustine's thought were the "philosophical basis for anti-Semitism", Lindsey declares the belief that "the Church has been given the promises made to the Israelites" is "demonic and heretical". He continues: "I am thankful to say that no person who believes in the premillennial view can be anti-Semitic. In fact, the premillennialists are probably the truest non-Israelite friends the Israelites have in the world today, for they believe God will keep His promises to the Israelites, including punishing all who persecute them" (Hal Lindsey, *The Rapture* [New York: Bantam Books, 1983], p. 35). For a response to Lindsey's charges of anti-Semitism, see Gary DeMar and Peter Leithart, *The Legacy of Hatred Continues: A Response to Hal Lindsey's* The Road to Holocaust (Tyler, Tex.: Institute for Christian Economics, 1989).

indicating the imminent return of Jesus Christ", and "the most important date we should remember is May 14, 1948." [34]

Charles Ryrie and Dispensationalism
Today, Yesterday, and Tomorrow

After Lewis Sperry Chafer's death in 1952, the most influential and visible dispensationalist theologian was Charles C. Ryrie. One of Chafer's prize students, Ryrie would later be the chairman of the theology department and professor of systematic theology at Dallas Theological Seminary from 1962 to 1983. Ryrie has written books on a variety of topics but has largely focused on eschatology and defending dispensationalist teachings. Most important was his 1965 apologetic for dispensationalism, *Dispensationalism Today* (revised and expanded as *Dispensationalism* in 1995)—the last scholarly defense of dispensationalism to appear to this day. Written as a response to attacks made by leading Protestant postmillennialists and historical premillennialists, the book marked a shift from Scofieldian dispensationalism to what has commonly been termed "revised dispensationalism". [35] While

[34] Boyer, *When Time Shall Be No More*, p. 189.

[35] Dispensationalist theologian Herbert W. Bateman IV describes revised (or "normative") dispensationalism in this way: "During the 1950s, 1960s, and 1970s, the offspring of previous dispensationalists made clarifications, and, when necessary, changed their predecessors' dispensational interpretations of the text.... Two significant changes, in my mind, concern (1) the lack of distinction between the kingdom of God and the kingdom of heaven, and (2) the emphasis on one new covenant" (Bateman, "Dispensationalism Yesterday and Today", in *Three Issues in Contemporary Dispensationalism: A Comparison of Traditional and Progressive Views*, Herbert W. Bateman IV, gen. ed. [Grand Rapids, Mich.: Kregel Publications, 1999], p. 23). He notes that the term "revised", used to describe dispensationalism during the 1950s to 1970s, "is due primarily to [the] 1967 revision of the *Scofield Reference Bible*" (p. 25). The main

Ryrie still adhered to the essential teachings of Darby and Scofield, his work did reflect a more nuanced understanding of the relationship between the Kingdom of heaven and the Kingdom of God, as well as between the Church and both Kingdoms.[36]

Ryrie's first book was *The Basis of the Premillennial Faith* (1953), a revised version of his doctoral thesis. Its main argument is that since some of the early Church Fathers were premillennialists, it follows that premillennial dispensationalism is the ancient belief of the Church. Ryrie attempts to downplay the importance of Darby, barely mentioning him except to deny his central role in assembling the distinctive beliefs of dispensationalism into a theological system. Ryrie argues, "Certain refinements [in premillennialism] may be of recent origin, but premillennialism was certainly the faith of the Church centuries before the Brethren and Darby. The assertion that premillennialism is a new thing is not at all warranted in the light of historical evidence."[37] This is misleading since Ryrie was replying to criticisms that *premillennial dispensationalism* is modern in origins—all scholars acknowledge that an ancient form of premillennialism (often called "historical premillennialism") existed in the early centuries of Christianity.

In *Dispensationalism Today* Ryrie does acknowledge that dispensationalism is not the same as historical premillenni-

---

revision to *Scofield's Reference Bible*, Bateman adds, is that Scofield's "explicit dichotomy between the kingdom of God and the kingdom of heaven" has been changed, that is, softened and blurred.

[36] See Bateman, "Dispensationalism Yesterday and Today", pp. 25–34. Catholics, like most other Christians, believe that the terms "Kingdom of heaven" and "Kingdom of God" are synonymous.

[37] Charles C. Ryrie, *The Basis of the Premillennial Faith* (Neptune, N.J.: Loizeaux Brothers, 1981), p. 33.

alism, stating that "there are those who are premillennial who definitely are not dispensational." [38] He also points out that dispensations are not, in fact, the essence of dispensationalism. Instead, Ryrie highlights the "*sine qua non* of dispensationalism" as being threefold in nature:

1. The distinction between Israel and the Church;
2. A system of hermeneutics described as "literal interpretation";
3. The belief that all of God's activities are for the purpose of glorifying himself.[39]

In explaining the first point, Ryrie quotes Chafer, who wrote of the "two distinct purposes" pursued by God—one having to do with "earthly people", the other with "heavenly people".[40] Ryrie then flatly states that this distinction between the earthly and heavenly people is "probably the most basic theological test of whether or not a person is a dispensationalist, and it is undoubtedly the most practical and conclusive. The one who fails to distinguish Israel and the church consistently will inevitably not hold to dispensational distinctions; and one who does will." [41] It is here, first and foremost, that the Catholic parts ways with the dispensationalist—all other differences flow from this foundational tenet. In Catholic doctrine the Old Covenant *concludes* with the New Covenant and is *included* in it. [42] The Church is the New Israel; whether or not Israel reorganizes as a nation has no

[38] Charles C. Ryrie, *Dispensationalism* (Chicago: Moody Press, 1965), p. 38.
[39] Ibid., pp. 38–41.
[40] Chafer, *Dispensationalism*, p. 107.
[41] Ryrie, *Dispensationalism*, p. 39.
[42] This key idea will be examined in detail in chapter 7, "The Church, the Kingdom, and Israel".

necessary bearing on the New Covenant since its source is Jesus Christ and its goal is the trinitarian life, not a future earthly millennial Kingdom. For the Catholic the Kingdom is a living reality—the Church is the Kingdom, even though not yet fully revealed and realized. But for Ryrie and all dispensationalists, the Kingdom is earthly and Jewish in character—even though "the Church will share in the rule of that kingdom." [43]

While the foundation of the dispensationalist system is the dichotomy between Israel and the Church, the instrument that builds the foundation is the dispensationalist method of interpreting Scripture. Of his second point of the *sine qua non* Ryrie writes:

> This distinction between Israel and the church is born out of a system of hermeneutics that is usually called literal interpretation. Therefore, the second aspect of the *sine qua non* of dispensationalism is the matter of historical-grammatical hermeneutics. The word *literal* is perhaps not as good as either the word *normal* or *plain*, but in any case it is interpretation that does not spiritualize or allegorize as nondispensational interpretation often does.... Consistently literal, or plain, interpretation indicates a dispensational approach to the interpretation of the Scriptures. And it is this very consistency— the strength of dispensational interpretation—that seems to

---

[43] Ryrie, *Dispensationalism*, p. 135. Ryrie writes that "if our concept of the kingdom were as broad as it appears to be in the Scriptures and our definition of the Church as strict as it is in the Scriptures, perhaps nondispensationalists would cease trying to equate the Church with the kingdom and dispensationalists would speak more of the relationship between the two" (*Dispensationalism*, pp. 136). The short answer (presented more thoroughly in chapters to come) to this statement is that (1) Christ and the apostles clearly equated the Church and the Kingdom, and (2) the dispensationalist view of "church" is far too limited and anemic and does not begin to do justice to the Scriptures.

irk the nondispensationalist and becomes the object of his ridicule.[44]

The problem with Ryrie's contention (to be taken up in more detail later) is that the dispensationalist method of interpretation is not consistent at all, nor are the grounds for labeling one's interpretation as "plain", stable, or clear. What Ryrie does establish is a pattern of dispensationalist apologetics that other authors have taken to even further extremes, such as implying or claiming that opposition to their position is evidence of an unorthodox, unbiblical doctrine. This "damning the origin" approach is a favorite tactic for authors of popular works of "Bible prophecy". The best-known and best-selling of these authors is Hal Lindsey.

The Birth of *The Late Great Planet Earth*

The story of Hal Lindsey is unique in its scale and influence. In terms of impact and popularity, Lindsey is to "Bible prophecy" what the Rolling Stones were to rock music—he set the standard, however dubious, for an audacious brand of dispensationalism that has had an impact on millions of people, many of whom are not even professing Christians. How exactly did he do it, and what are his contributions to the dispensationalist movement?

Born in Houston, Texas, in 1929, Lindsey attended the University of Houston, served in the Korean War, and then spent several years working as a tugboat captain on the Mississippi. When his first marriage fell apart he considered suicide. Instead, he found a Gideon New Testament and became

---

[44] Ibid., p. 40.

a Christian.[45] In 1958 he entered Dallas Theological Seminary, graduating four years later with a degree in theology. Throughout the 1960s, he and his second wife, Jan, worked as domestic missionaries for Campus Crusade, speaking to college students throughout the United States, often lecturing on Bible prophecy and the signs of the end times. It was at this time that he developed his lean, contemporary vocabulary, avoiding technical and theological language that might confuse or alienate listeners. In the late 1960s he began compiling his Dallas Theological Seminary and Campus Crusade notes into a book, and the resulting work, co-authored with C. C. Carlson, was published in 1970. It was titled *The Late Great Planet Earth* and was one of the best-selling books of the decade, translated into over fifty languages and eventually selling over thirty-five million copies worldwide.

Lindsey's experience with college students in the 1960s and his awareness of the anti-establishment subculture helped shape his combative, brash style. He uses a canny mix of pessimism, current global events, selective use of Scripture, and science fiction[46] to convey his vision of impending doom

---

[45] Clouse, Hosack, and Pierard, *New Millennium Manual*, pp. 124–29.

[46] James Barr, a hard-nosed critic of dispensationalism, writes of Lindsey's best-selling *The Late Great Planet Earth*: "On the one hand the racy journalese in which it is written should not conceal the fact that this farrago of nonsense is in essence little different from traditional premillennial dispensationalism. On the other hand it is obvious from title, style and presentation how close a work like this has moved towards the genre and interest of science fiction, how consciously it relates itself to astrology and the occult. The addition of some three pages of traditional Christian sermonizing at the end cannot disguise the fact that the work as a whole attracts (if it does attract) as a secular science fiction fantasy, which contributes nothing to the Christian faith and has no intention of doing so" (Barr, *Fundamentalism*, pp. 206–7).

and gloom. Lindsey's favorite theme is that Old and New Testament prophecies are being fulfilled right before our eyes: the restoration of Israel as a nation, the "apostasy" of main-line churches, the complete collapse of morality in Western culture, and the frightening realities of the Cold War:

> We are the generation the prophets were talking about! We have witnessed Biblical prophecies come true: The rebirth of Israel. The decline of American power and morality. The rise of Russian and Chinese might. The threat of war in the Middle East. The increase of earthquakes, volcanoes, famine and drought. . . . The decade of the 1980s could very well be the last decade of history as we know it.[47]

While Lindsey broke no new theological ground, his confident linking of obscure and difficult passages of Scripture to modern-day events and global situations endeared him to millions of readers. He played to the pessimism that had enveloped many Americans in the late 1960s and 1970s and promised them that if they believed in Jesus Christ they would be spared terrible future events that were imminent—at least according to his calculations. The means of salvation? The "Ultimate Trip", the Rapture:

> God's Word tells us that there will be one generation of believers who will never know death. These believers will be removed from the earth before the Great Tribulation—before that period of the most ghastly pestilence, bloodshed, and starvation the world has ever known. Examine the prophecies of this mysterious happening—of the "Rapture." Here

[47] Back cover and inside page of Hal Lindsey's *The 1980's: Countdown to Armageddon* (New York: Bantam Books, 1981).

is the real hope for the Christian, the "blessed hope" for true believers (Titus 2:13–15).[48]

Astute readers who examine the passage cited from the epistle to Titus will notice there is no mention of a Rapture, let alone one prior to a Great Tribulation. This "mix and match" brand of "Bible prophecy" is characteristic of Lindsey's approach and that of dozens of other self-proclaimed prophecy experts. Difficult passages from the book of Revelation are routinely interpreted without any concern for their context in first-century history and theology, as Stephen Sizer observes:

> So, in Lindsey's inspired bible code, John's "locusts" become helicopters, "horses prepared for battle" are heavily armed attack helicopters, "crowns of gold" are the helmets worn by pilots, and the "sound of their wings" are the "thunderous sound of many attack helicopters flying overhead." Just as imaginatively, the "bow" wielded by the Antichrist in Revelation 6:1–2 is apparently, "... a code for long range weapons like ICBM's." The reference to the "colour of fire and of hyacinth and of brimstone" in Revelation 9:17 becomes the "Chinese national flag" ... "emblazoned on the military vehicles." [49]

Lindsey's practice of aligning passages of Scripture—usually without much attention paid to historical context—with modern-day events in the Middle East, Russia, and China is front and center in his work. The best-selling author outlines an eschatology obsessed with detailing future events,

---

[48] Hal Lindsey with C. C. Carlson, *The Late Great Planet Earth* (New York: Bantam Books, 1970), p. 127.

[49] Rev. Stephen R. Sizer, "Hal Lindsey (b. 1929): The Father of Apocalyptic Christian Zionism". Accessed online at www.virginiawater.co.uk/christchurch/articles/hallindsey.htm.

antagonistic toward anyone who dares to differ with it, and often condescending toward a whole host of groups and institutions: Catholics, mainline Protestants, non-dispensationalist Evangelicals, Palestinians, Muslims, Russians, Chinese, and the American government. Lindsey believes he has an inside track on what passages of biblical prophecy *really* mean and sees himself as a sort of prophet who has been chosen by God to warn the world of impending destruction. Commenting about the book of Revelation in *The Apocalypse Code*, a recent work, he remarks, "I believe that the Spirit of God gave me a special insight, not only into how John described what he actually experienced, but also into how this whole phenomenon encoded the prophecies so that they could be fully understood only when their fulfillment drew near.... I prayerfully sought for a confirmation for my apocalypse code theory." [50] In the introduction to his subsequent work, *The Final Battle*, Lindsey makes another bold claim:

> You won't find another book quite like this one. We will examine why and how the world is hurtling toward disaster.... My background as a student of prophecy allows me to place all this information in perspective in a way that is sure to lead many people to the ultimate truth about the coming global holocaust—and, if they are open, to a wonderful way of escaping it. Read this book. Learn from it. Pass it on to your friends. It may be the last chance some of them will ever have to avoid the horrible fate this book describes. [51]

[50] Hal Lindsey, *The Apocalypse Code* (Palos Verdes, Calif.: Western Front, 1997), p. 37.

[51] Hal Lindsey, *The Final Battle* (Palos Verdes, Calif.: Western Front, 1995), p. xxi. Lindsey also writes: "This book describes in more detail and explicitness than any other just what will happen to humanity and to the Earth, not

This appeal to fear is another common feature of Lindsey's books. They are filled with descriptions, often accompanied by charts and maps, of the battles that will take place between Russia, Israel, China, and various Arab nations. He repeatedly insists there will be a worldwide nuclear war that will destroy the vast majority of mankind, and he interprets the various judgments found in the book of the Revelation by correlating them to modern chemical, nuclear, and hi-tech warfare.[52]

The restoration of an Israeli state is central to Lindsey's eschatalogical beliefs and is based on the standard dispensationalist distinction between Israel and the Church. He explains in *The Late Great Planet Earth* that the "distinction between God's dealings with the church and His dealing with another group of believers who are largely gathered around Israel is very important.... For us, as believers, our hope is different from Israel's."[53] In a later book he proclaims, "The center of the entire prophetic forecast is the State of Israel.... The prophets told us that the rebirth of Israel—

---

a thousand years from now, but in our lifetime—indeed in this very generation." He then adds, a bit later, this modest disclaimer: "As always, I have not written this book claiming to be a prophet. Rather I have sought to faithfully interpret the only system of prophecy that has been proven 100 percent in history. It is contained in the Book of Books" (*Final Battle*, pp. xiii, xiv).

[52] See, for example, "The Arsenal from Hell" in *Final Battle*, pp. 169–93. There Lindsey goes into great detail regarding the number of tanks, missiles, men, and aircraft owned by nations like Russia, Libya, Iran, Turkey, Syria, and, of course, Israel. In a later chapter, "The Last War and Final Battle" (pp. 234–57), Lindsey claims that about half the world's population, around three billion people, will be annihilated in a matter of a few months (pp. 250–51). "There will be so much fighting that blood will flow for 200 miles" (p. 251), and there will be a nuclear war "that wipes out every major city in the world" (p. 254).

[53] Lindsey and Carlson, *Late Great Planet Earth*, p. 128.

no other event—would be the sign that the countdown had begun. Since that rebirth [in 1948], the rest of the prophecies have begun to be fulfilled quite rapidly." [54] For Lindsey and those who emulate him, *all* of Jesus' words in Matthew 24 must be interpreted to refer to modern times, especially the reference to the "fig tree":

> From the fig tree learn its lesson: as soon as its branch becomes tender and puts forth its leaves, you know that summer is near. So also, when you see all these things, you know that he is near, at the very gates. Truly, I say to you, this generation will not pass away till all these things take place. (Mt 24:32–34)

Lindsey teaches that the "fig tree" is a metaphor for the rebirth of the nation of Israel and that "this generation" is the one that witnesses this rebirth—it is *our* generation. These premises lead Lindsey to write, "A generation in the Bible is something like forty years. If this is a correct deduction, then within forty years or so of 1948, all these things could take place. Many scholars who have studied Bible prophecy all their lives believe that this is so." [55] This meant that the pretribulation Rapture should have occurred as early as 1981, once the seven years of tribulation were subtracted from 1988. However, as the 1980s approached and passed, Lindsey began to rethink how long a biblical generation might actually be. He has more recently written in *Planet Earth—2000 A.D* that "A biblical generation is somewhere between 40 to 100 years, depending on whether you take the example from

[54] Lindsey, *1980's: Countdown to Armageddon*, pp. 11–12.
[55] Lindsey and Carlson, *Late Great Planet Earth*, p. 58.

Abraham's day or from the discipline of Israel in the Wilderness of Sinai. In either case, you do the arithmetic, folks. No matter how you cut it, there's not much time left." [56] In the same book he also states, "My recent study of Daniel 9:24–27 has convinced me that the capture of Jerusalem in 1967 may be a more prophetically significant event than the rebirth of the nation." [57] So much for the "fig tree" and twenty years of clamoring about 1948!

Not one to be concerned about past errors, Lindsey continues to proclaim his controversial and successful brand of Bible prophecy. Currently he hosts a weekly television program, *International Intelligence Briefing*, on Trinity Broadcasting Network (TBN). (Trinity is the same Pentecostal network that financed and produced *Omega Code* in 1999, an apocalyptic, end-time thriller featuring a very Hal Lindsey–like mixture of dispensationalism and Bible Code pseudo-science. Not surprisingly, it also featured a conspiratorial view of the Catholic Church and the papacy.) [58] Lindsey continues to hold the attention of numerous Christians who believe that he can do little or no wrong when it comes to interpreting Scripture. Although his writings and teachings have been seriously criticized—most often by Evangelical scholars and theologians—Lindsey shows no signs of going away soon.

---

[56] Lindsey, *Planet Earth—2000 A.D.* (Palos Verdes, Calif.: Western Front, 1994), p. 3.

[57] Ibid., p. 144.

[58] *The Omega Code* is one of the most successful Christian films ever made, earning more than $12 million in 1999, the highest-grossing independent film of that year. Its sequel, "Megiddo: Omega Code 2", had a $20 million budget and was released in September 2001 (Marc Peyser, "God, Mammon and 'Bibleman'" *Newsweek* [July 16, 2001], p. 45).

And I Saw a Great Host of End-Time Contenders ...

Although a full accounting of influential contemporary dispensationalist authors is not possible here, some do deserve mention for their important place in popular dispensationalism. As we have seen, although Lindsey takes a popular and non-technical approach to explaining his dispensationalist views, he is theologically very much in the same stream as Darby, Scofield, Chafer, and Ryrie. This is also true of authors such as Jack Van Impe, John Walvoord, John Hagee, Dave Hunt, Grant Jeffrey, and Tim LaHaye. While differing on some issues—some dealing with the Catholic Church— the dispensationalism they teach is rooted in the same major premises and core doctrinal positions.

Although his name never gained the household recognition the famed Southern evangelist Billy Graham enjoyed, during the 1960s and 70s, Jack Van Impe was also a popular Protestant evangelist in America. Nicknamed "The Walking Bible" because he has memorized vast portions of Scripture, Van Impe and his wife, Rexella, host a half-hour weekly television program, *Jack Van Impe Presents*, in which he connects breaking global news to prophetic passages of Scripture. The author of over twenty books, most of them on Bible prophecy, Van Impe does distinguish himself from most other dispensationalists in his high praise for Catholicism in general and Pope John Paul II in particular. He stated a few years ago that "I was deeply moved as Pope John Paul II opened his humble heart of love to all of us. Billy Graham calls him the moral voice of the twentieth century, and I agree." [59] Having read the *Catechism of the Catholic Church*, he remarked,

[59] *Jack Van Impe Presents*, July 23, 1995.

"We [Roman Catholics and he] agree on the great fundamentals of the faith.... I've been reading the *Catholic Catechism*, 2,865 points, backed with 5,000 to 6,000 verses of Scripture. This is the Word of God. Of course there are some things where I don't agree. But I find many of these things in our Protestant churches as well. But this thing blessed my heart. This piece of literature, saturated with the precious Word of God." [60] Van Impe has also revealed that Catholics make up the second largest group of supporters of his program (trailing only Baptists). [61] Aside from occasionally praising Pope John Paul II and the *Catechism*, Van Impe's interest in the Catholic Church centers on his dubious contention that the pope following John Paul II will be apostate. He claims to have received this information from Malachi Martin, a former Jesuit whose comments on the Church and Vatican politics have sometimes stirred up controversy among Catholics. [62]

John F. Walvoord has been associated with Dallas Theological Seminary for his entire adult life and was president of that dispensationalist school from 1952 to 1986. A staunch dispensationalist in the mold of Chafer (who was his mentor), Walvoord has written numerous books on Bible prophecy and the end times, including *The Rapture Question* (1957),

---

[60] *Jack Van Impe Presents*, December 1994 tape.

[61] From a TBN program that aired in 1998, viewed by the author. Requests for written confirmation of this claim were not answered by JVIMI.

[62] In the November 1996 issue of his regular newsletter *Intelligence Briefing*, Van Impe makes the following claims: "In his book, *The Keys to This Blood*, Martin indicates that the current pope believes the world is very close to witnessing unusual latter-day events. Hal Lindsey, best-selling author of *The Late Great Planet Earth* and a close friend of Malachi Martin, reports that Pope John Paul II expects the return of Christ in his lifetime." ("Is John Paul II the Last Pope?", Van Impe's *Intelligence Briefing* [November 1996]; accessed online).

The Millennial Kingdom (1959), *The Church in Prophecy* (1964), and *Major Bible Prophecies* (1991). Although Walvoord is considered to be a scholarly dispensationalist, he has had great success in the popular dispensationalist world. His biggest best seller was *Armageddon, Oil and the Middle East Crisis* (1990), originally written in the early seventies, but revised at the start of the Persian Gulf War. Readers eagerly sought Walvoord's depiction of impending doom, and the book sold over a million and a half copies in the early 1990s. Walvoord has always been staunchly opposed to the Catholic Church and believes that she will be an instrumental part of the coming one-world apostate religion, which will consist of people from all different Christian traditions.[63]

John Hagee is the founder and pastor of Cornerstone Church, a "megachurch" in San Antonio, Texas. He is also president of Global Evangelism Television, which broadcasts his sermons on television and radio. Hagee usually delivers his sermons in front of a huge chart of end-times chronology, his message a constant warning of rapidly approaching apocalyptic destruction. Like Lindsey, Hagee is extremely pro-Israeli and anti-Palestinian, and his books reflect this position. His best-selling titles include *Beginning of the End: The Assassination of Yitzhak Rabin and the Coming Antichrist* (1996), *Day of Deception* (1997), *From Daniel to Doomsday: The Countdown Has Begun* (1999) and *The Battle for Jerusalem* (2001).

---

[63] "Eventually the Babylonian religion found its way to Rome. There it had influence on Christian religion, and traces of Babylonianism can be found in some of the rituals of the Roman Catholic Church.... The fulfillment [of the one world religion], accordingly, will not be specifically by the Roman Catholic Church but rather by the union of the three major branches of the church [Catholic, Orthodox, and Protestant] that exist in the world today" (Walvoord, *Major Bible Prophecies: 37 Crucial Prophecies That Affect You Today* [New York: HarperPaperbacks, 1994], pp. 380, 383).

The latter was quickly revised in the wake of the September 11, 2001, terrorist attacks and renamed *Attack on America: New York, Jerusalem, and the Role of Terrorism in the Last Days* (2001). Recently he has begun writing fiction in the mold of La-Haye and Jenkins; his first novel is *Devil's Island*, subtitled *Book One: The Apocalypse Diaries* (2001), a fictional account of the Apostle John and the writing of the book of Revelation.

Dave Hunt is known by many Catholic apologists as the author of *A Woman Rides the Beast: The Roman Catholic Church and the Last* Days (1994). It is one of the most anti-Catholic, staunchly Fundamentalist books of the 1990s, and it insists that the Catholic Church is the beast of Revelation 17. This belief, Hunt claims, "provides insights into occurrences which have shaped world history in the past and which will profoundly determine human destiny in the future. [The woman] sits, in fact, not only astride the beast, but upon the culmination of centuries of related Bible prophecy." [64] While some dispensationalists have toned down their anti-Catholic rhetoric, Hunt has always taken great pride in upholding the

---

[64] Dave Hunt, *A Woman Rides the Beast: The Roman Catholic Church and the Last Days* (Eugene, Ore.: Harvest House Publishers, 1994), p. 15. The title of Hunt's book is based on Revelation 17:7, which speaks of "the mystery of the woman and of the beast". Hunt writes: "[The] revival of Rome's religion will undoubtedly be a blend of Christianity and paganism, as occurred under Constantine and continued thereafter. That perverted and paganized form of Christianity eventually became known as Roman Catholicism. Claiming to be infallible and unchanging ... the Roman Catholic Church stands poised today to become the vehicle for the final ecumenical union of all religions" (p. 39). Harvest House is one of today's foremost publishers of Fundamentalist, dispensationalist books, having published works by Hunt, Tim LaHaye, Charles Ryrie, Peter and Patti Lalonde, and John Ankerberg. An excellent examination of Hunt and his anti-Catholic beliefs is "A Look at Dave Hunt, Leading Anti-Catholic Fundamentalist: The Whore of Babylon, The Rapture, and the End Times", *New Oxford Review*, January 1999, pp. 30–35, written by W. Robert Aufill, a Benedictine novice.

position of the Protestant Reformers and the Plymouth Brethren in attacking the Catholic Church. Known for his best-selling books about the New Age movement and tele-vangelists, Hunt's "end times" works include *Global Peace and the Rise of Antichrist* (1990), *How Close Are We? Compelling Evidence for the Soon Return of Christ* (1993), and *A Cup of Trembling: Jerusalem and Bible Prophecy* (1995).

Grant Jeffrey is a Canadian (and, like Dave Hunt, a former accountant) whose books have sold over two million copies since the early 1990s. Jeffrey's sensationalistic works are directly from the Hal Lindsey school of biblical prophecy, featuring an obsession with numbers, dates, and statistical proof for the accuracy of Bible prophecy. Titles include *Apocalypse: The Coming Judgment of the Nations* (1992), *Armageddon: Appointment with Destiny* (1989, 1997), *Messiah: War in the Middle East and the Road to Armageddon* (1992), *Prince of Darkness: Antichrist and the New World Order* (1995), *Final Warning: Economic Collapse and the Coming World Government* (1996), and *The Mysterious Bible Codes* (1999). Jeffrey's penchant for number-crunching is notable, as are his descriptions of vast global conspiracies that will soon overwhelm the free world and plunge humanity into the end times. An important player in Jeffrey's apocalyptic vision is the Catholic Church, whose current pope, Jeffrey insists, "is the most traditional pope of this last century and the strongest advocate of worship of Mary as the 'co-redemptrix' along with Jesus Christ".[65] The

[65] Jeffrey, *Prince of Darkness: Antichrist and the New World Order* (New York: Bantam Books, 1995), p. 305. Needless to say, Jeffrey's presentation of Pope John Paul II's beliefs and Catholic teachings about Mary are flawed. This is hardly surprising since Jeffrey appears to garner all of his information about the Catholic Church from very suspect sources.

coming one-world religion, according to Jeffrey, will be a mixture of all religions: "It is called the New Age." [66]

Numerous other end-time "experts" continue to churn out books, write articles, produce audio and video tapes, and host television shows. Others have made their money and retired, while a few have fallen from favor. One expert who managed to do both was Edgar Whisenant, a former NASA engineer who worked on the early Apollo missions, whose meteoric rise and fall reflect the interest in the Rapture held by so many Americans. Whisenant reasoned that although Jesus had said that no one knows the day or hour of his return, this did not mean we could not pinpoint the month or year.[67] Using a complex series of calculations, Whisenant figured out the month and year of Christ's return (September 11–13, 1988) and published it in a book titled *88 Reasons Why the Rapture Will Be in 1988*. It sold 4.5 million copies in a matter of a few months.[68] When 1988 came

---

[66] Ibid., p. 307. The belief that the one-world apostate religion will be "New Age" in character has become the overwhelming favorite for popular dispensationalists.

[67] "Willing to go boldly where no man (or not many) had gone before, Whisenant set his dates without the usual safety net of hedges and qualifications. The fact that Jesus said no man can know the *day* or the *hour* of the Second Coming, he logically pointed out, does not mean we cannot know the month or the year" (Boyer, *When Time Shall Be No More*, p. 130).

[68] "Despite warnings from various church leaders from thoughtful segments of the Christian community, believers nationwide flocked to local bookstores to get Whisenant's books. In fact, Christian booksellers had a hard time keeping his volumes in stock. By the time the predicted date arrived, more than 4.5 million copies of *88 Reasons* had been sold, and 300,000 had been sent out *free* to ministers in America" (Abanes, *End-Time Visions: The Road to Armageddon?* [New York: Four Walls Eight Windows, 1998], pp. 93–94). For a Catholic examination of Whisenant's predictions, see Karl Keating's *The Usual Suspects: Answering Anti-Catholic Fundamentalists* (San Francisco: Ignatius Press, 2000), pp. 95–98.

and went, Whisenant recalculated and admitted that he had missed a year—Christ would actually be returning in 1989. He then began fading in popularity, even as he continued to produce new booklets each year with revised dates. Although Whisenant is a rather extreme example and while most dispensationalists are careful to avoid setting specific dates, some do flirt with this sort of recklessness.

The Evidence of History, the Direction of the Future

Although relatively short, the history of premillennial dispensationalism is filled with numerous personalities, events and theological, cultural shifts. While it is inaccurate and unfair to say that dispensationalism has been or currently is monolithic in character, core features and tendencies have remained consistent to this day.

First, the history and writings of dispensationalism demonstrate that it has always been a reactionary and defensive movement. The same basic fear of apostasy, dislike of liberal methods of biblical interpretation, and conviction of impending doom motivated Darby, Scofield, and Chafer and continue to motivate Lindsey, LaHaye, and other contemporary dispensationalists. Dispensationalism has never been a positive or optimistic movement; its singular claim to a unique teaching—the pretribulational Rapture—is the result of a reactionary method of interpreting Scripture and is based on an equally reactionary judgment of other Christians. There is a palpable element of fear within dispensationalism, both as a theology and as a cultural movement, that cannot be denied. Fear of dying, a chaotic world, suffering, apostasy, the Great Tribulation—all are used by dispensationalist teachers to drive home their message: *We* will be raptured; *we* are the faithful remnant; *we* will not have to suffer or die like others will.[69] The appeal of this message is understandable, especially in a culture where Christianity is so often maligned and attacked.

But fear and the desire to escape the world and its troubles are not the only—or even the primary—reasons that people are dispensationalists. Rather, it is their conviction that dispensationalist teachers are accurately interpreting the Bible and that the Bible itself teaches a pretribulational Rapture, a seven-year Tribulation, and a thousand-year millennial Kingdom on earth.[70] This conviction naturally leads to the divisive and rigid qualities that have characterized dispensationalism from its beginning. Darby's arrogance toward other Christians and his condemnation of those who disagreed with him (often on minor matters) would, unfortunately, be, not the exception, but the rule. Openness to reasonable dialogue has been a rare quality among staunch dispensationalists.

---

[69] Hal Lindsey makes the bold claim "that many of you who are reading this will experience this mystery. You will never know what it is to die physically" (Lindsey, *Rapture*, p. 43). As Abane notes, "The inescapable theme permeating the messages of these prophecy pundits could not be any clearer: we are a special generation. Hence, we as individuals must also be unique in God's eyes. Every person alive has the distinction of being picked to see history's culmination. Such a notion is much more appealing than the thought of having to work a boring job for the next twenty or thirty years, only to die in obscurity as billions of people have previously done. Many cannot resist believing that they stand at the very pinnacle of history" (Abanes, *End-Time Visions*, p. 316).

[70] Timothy Weber writes: "It would be too simplistic to say ... that people become premillennialists primarily out of some kind of psychological need for security and escape. While such factors may be significant, they can hardly be considered determinative for most people. All personal reasons aside, most people accept premillennial doctrine because they believe that the Bible teaches it.... For the vast majority of premillennialists, the religious or doctrinal appeal is more important than the personal one" (*Living in the Shadow of the Second Coming*, p. 178).

For Christians trying to make sense of the world in light of Scripture, popular dispensationalism offers a convenient vision and an air-tight solution. Matching up current events to passages of Scripture fulfills both the desire to understand the Bible better and to make sense of what is happening around the globe. It assures people that the Bible is true and historically accurate without any need to grapple with the complex challenges of the Bible. It also frees the reader from any sense of obligation to improve or change significantly the culture, the arts, the political order, or any other aspect of society. The impending end of the world makes such pursuits trivial, even ridiculous—what matters is saving souls from the approaching tribulation. The ability of popular dispensationalists to frighten people with talk about imminent disaster and to link current events to Scripture is what will determine the longevity of the movement, as Timothy Weber notes: "As long as premillennialists are able to fit current events into their system, there seems little doubt that they will be able to attract significant numbers of adherents."[71]

[71] Ibid., p. 180.

PART TWO

A CATHOLIC CRITIQUE
OF DISPENSATIONALISM

7

THE KINGDOM, THE CHURCH,
AND ISRAEL

The premillennial system of interpretation has especially relied on a proper understanding of the doctrine of the church as a body distinct from Israel and from saints in general.... It is safe to say that pretribulationalism depends on a particular definition of the Church, and any consideration of pretribulationalism that does not take this major factor into consideration will be largely beside the point.

—John F. Walvoord

He planned to assemble in the holy Church all those who would believe in Christ. Already from the beginning of the world the foreshadowing of the Church took place. It was prepared in a remarkable way throughout the history of the people of Israel and by means of the Old Covenant. In the present era of time the Church was constituted and, by the outpouring of the Spirit, was made manifest. At the end of time it will gloriously achieve completion, when, as is read in the Fathers, all the just, from Adam and "from Abel, the just one, to the last of the elect," will be gathered together with the Father in the universal Church.

—Second Vatican Council, Dogmatic Constitution
on the Church, *Lumen Gentium*

What a person believes about the Church (*ecclesiology*) has a profound effect on what he believes about the last things (*eschatology*). As a leading proponent of the pretribulation Rapture correctly notes: "The doctrine of the Church must ... be carefully examined before eschatology can be understood." [1] The differences between Catholic doctrine and dispensationalist beliefs are most pronounced when it comes to the nature and purpose of the Church and to her relationship to the Kingdom and to Old Testament Israel. On one hand, this is not surprising, since dispensationalists—consisting of various Fundamentalists, Evangelicals, and Pentecostals[2]—possess an ecclesiology quite different from that of Catholics. Some of these differences are obvious: a lack of hierarchy or episcopal structure, little or no emphasis on sacraments, low regard for Church history or tradition, and a belief in *sola scriptura*—"Scripture only"—that excludes any substantial Church authority. While local gatherings are considered to be visible manifestations of the universal Body of Christ, the universal Church is understood to be invisible in nature. In addition to these general characteristics, dispensationalists teach several unique beliefs about the nature of the Church. These include:

- God has two distinct people, Israel and the Church, and is pursuing two different programs in history with them.

---

[1] John F. Walvoord, *The Millennial Kingdom* (Grand Rapids, Mich.: Zondervan Publishing House, 1959), p. 221.

[2] Many Pentecostals also adhere to dispensationalism. The Assemblies of God, which has thirty-two million members and is the fastest-growing and largest Pentecostal denomination in the world, is staunchly dispensationalist. Its "Statement of Fundamental Truths" includes the denomination's belief in the "blessed hope" of the pretribulational Rapture and "the visible return of Christ with His saints to reign on earth for one thousand years".

■ There is little or no continuity between the Israel of the Old Testament and the New Testament Church.

■ The Church and the Church age (extending from Pentecost to the Rapture) is a "parenthesis" or "intercalation" into history, the existence of which was not prophesied or foreshadowed in any way in the Old Testament.

■ Christ offered an earthly, political Kingdom to the Jews, but they rejected him and so he formed a new people, the Church, from both Jews and Gentiles.

■ The New Covenant was not for the Church but for Israel, just as the Kingdom is a future, earthly reality meant for the Jews and *not* a spiritual reality inaugurated by Christ and/or located in some way in the Church today.[3]

---

[3] Keith A. Mathison, a former dispensationalist and now a Reformed theologian and critic of dispensationalism, has outlined several key beliefs of dispensational ecclesiology, including the following:

1. God has two distinct programs in history, one for Israel and one for the Church.
2. The Church does not fulfill or take over any of Israel's promises or purposes.
3. The Church age is a "mystery", and thus no Old Testament prophecies foresaw it.
4. The present Church age is a "parenthesis" or "intercalation" during which God has temporarily suspended His primary purpose with Israel.
5. The Church age began at Pentecost and will end at the pretribulation Rapture of the Church before Christ's Second Coming.
6. The Church, or Body of Christ, consists only of those believers saved between Pentecost and the Rapture.
7. The Church as the Body of Christ, therefore, does not include Old Testament believers.

See Mathison, *Dispensationalism: Rightly Dividing the People of God?* (Phillipsburg, N.J.: P and R Publishing, 1995), pp. 17–18. These points parallel the seven points presented by dispensationalist Charles C. Ryrie in *The Basis of the Premillennial Faith* (Neptune, N.J.: Loizeaux Brothers, 1981), pp. 135–38.

Not only are these beliefs contrary to the teachings of the Catholic Church, they are also at odds with the beliefs of the Eastern Orthodox and the majority of Protestants. Rooted in Darby's peculiar views of both Christ and the Church, they are the basis of prominent dispensationalist beliefs about future events such as the pretribulational Rapture and the earthly, millennial Kingdom of Christ. On a practical and immediate level, they result in an anemic ecclesiology that drains the Church of any real significance in today's world.

Dispensationalism: Two Peoples, Two Purposes

As we have seen in detail, the radical dichotomy between Old Testament Israel and the Church is the heart and soul of dispensationalism. It was created by Darby based on a faulty view of the Church[4] and was eventually championed by Scofield in both his *Reference Bible* and his influential booklet *Rightly Dividing the Word of Truth.*[5] Chafer systematized this tenet and further applied it to major areas of theological

---

[4] Craig A. Blaising, a progressive dispensationalist, writes, "The ecclesiological-eschatological synthesis of Darby was his genius and the dominating conceptual center of modern dispensationalism.... In Darby's dispensationalism the distinction between the heavenly people and the earthly people is absolutely essential. It gives meaning to all the other elements of his thought. The postponement of the kingdom, the parenthesis Church, and the pretribulational rapture, for example, all fit with this distinction" (Blaising, "Development of Dispensationalism by Contemporary Dispensationalists", *Bibliotheca Sacra*, July–September 1988, pp. 273–74).

[5] Scofield declared that "just as distinctly as Israel stands connected with temporal and earthly things, so distinctly does the church stand connected with spiritual and heavenly things" (C. I. Scofield, *Rightly Dividing the Word of Truth: Ten Outline Studies of the More Important Divisions of Scripture* [Neptune, N.J.: Loizeaux Brothers, 1896], pp. 5–6).

belief.[6] Two other key dispensationalist theologians, Walvoord and Ryrie, also insisted on the centrality of this thorough split between Israel and the Church. Walvoord contends, "One of the major factors of confusion in eschatology in the history of the church has been to confuse the program of God for Israel with the program of God for the church. The distinction of these two programs is an essential feature of contemporary dispensationalism."[7] Ryrie explains that this

---

[6] Chafer writes, "The distinction between the purpose for Israel and the purpose for the church is about as important as that which exists between the two testaments. Every covenant, promise, and provision for Israel is earthly, and they continue as a nation with the earth when it is created new. Every covenant or promise for the Church is for a heavenly reality, and she continues in heavenly citizenship when the heavens are recreated" (Lewis Sperry Chafer, *Systematic Theology* [Dallas, Tex.: Dallas Seminary Press, 1947], 4:47). Late in the same volume, writing of the relationship between Judaism and Christianity, Chafer states: "Judaism is not the bud which has blossomed into Christianity. These systems do have features which are common to both—God, holiness, Satan, man, sin, redemption, human responsibility, and the issues of eternity—yet they introduce differences so vast that they cannot coalesce. Each sets up its ground of relationship between God and man—the Jew by physical birth, the Christian by spiritual birth; each provides its instructions on the life of its adherents—the law for Israel, the teachings of grace for the Church; each has its sphere of existence—Israel in the earth for all ages to come, the Church in heaven. To the end that the Church might be called out from both Jews and Gentiles, a peculiar, unrelated age has been thrust into the one consistent ongoing of the divine program for the earth. It is in this sense that Judaism, which is the abiding portion of the nation Israel, has ceased. With the completion and departure of the Church from the earth, Judaism will be again the embodiment of all the divine purpose in the world" (pp. 248–49).

[7] John F. Walvoord, *The Rapture Question*, rev. ed. (Grand Rapids, Mich.: Academic Books, 1979), p. 56. In *The Millennial Kingdom* he writes, "The question is whether the main elements of the church in the present age which are revealed as mysteries support the conclusion that the church is the purpose of God separate from Israel. It should be obvious that this is vital to premillennialism. *If the church fulfills the Old Testament promises to Israel of a righteous kingdom on earth, the amillenarians are right. If the church does not fulfill these predictions and in fact is the fulfillment of a purpose of God not revealed until the New Testament, then the premillenarians are right*" (p. 231, emphasis added).

distinction is "probably the most basic theological test of whether or not a person is a dispensationalist, and it is undoubtedly the most practical and conclusive. The one who fails to distinguish Israel and the church will inevitably not hold to dispensational distinctions; and one who does will." [8]

This "dispensational distinction" is also front and center in the movement's popularized manifestations. In *The Late Great Planet Earth*, Lindsey writes:

> There is a great distinction between God's purpose for the nation of Israel and his purpose for the church, which is His main program today. The church is composed of both Gentiles and Jews. We are now living during the church age and the responsibility of evangelizing the world rests upon the church. We should re-emphasize here that we are speaking of the true meaning of the church, which is the body of believers in Jesus Christ.[9]

In a later work, *The Rapture*, he reiterates this stance even more succinctly: "I believe that God's purpose for Israel and His purpose for the church are so distinct and mutually exclusive that they cannot both be on earth at the same during the seven-year Tribulation." [10] LaHaye correctly observes that the pretribulational dispensationalist view is the "only view that distinguishes between Israel and the church". He goes on to remark that "[t]he confusion of Israel and the church is one of the major reasons for confusion in prophecy as a whole.... Pre-Tribulationism is the only position which

---

[8] Charles C. Ryrie, *Dispensationalism* (Chicago: Moody Press, 1965), p. 39.

[9] Hal Lindsey, with C. C. Carlson, *The Late Great Planet Earth* (New York: Bantam Books, 1970), p. 131.

[10] Hal Lindsey, *The Rapture* (New York: Bantam Books, 1983), p. 80.

clearly outlines the program of the church." [11] Van Impe dismisses the idea that the Church might be the fulfillment of promises made to Israel, stating: "This one misconception has caused more damage to the cause of prophecy in our day than any other teaching! The theory started with Augustine in about 190 A.D. [sic!] and has led to endless symbolizing, with many others following his error. That's where the confusion began. One cannot justify it. Israel is Israel—period!" [12]

The distinction between Israel and the Church rests upon the so-called "literal" method of interpretation employed by dispensationalists. This method of interpretation will be examined at length in the next chapter, but it can be generally summarized as a system that claims to look for the "plain" meaning of Scripture, but always does so in light of the distinction between Israel and the Church. This is not surprising, since making divisions and distinctions is at the heart of a dispensationalist reading of the Bible, just as the title of Scofield's *Rightly Dividing the Word of Truth* indicates. Commenting on 2 Timothy 2:15, Scofield writes that "The Word of Truth, then, has right divisions, and it must be evident that . . . any study of that Word which ignores those divisions must be in large measure profitless and confusing." [13] Unfortunately, Scofield bases his entire method of interpretation on a faulty reading of this single verse—the King James Version interpretation of the Greek word *orthotomounta* as "rightly dividing" is either misunderstood or misused by Scofield. Literally translated as "keeping on a straight course",

[11] Tim LaHaye, *Rapture under Attack* (Sisters, Ore.: Multnomah Publishers, 1998), p. 211.

[12] Jack Van Impe, *Everything about Prophecy* (1981; Troy, Mich.: Jack Van Impe Ministries, 1999), p. 14.

[13] Scofield, *Rightly Dividing the Word of Truth*, p. 3.

the term is better understood as "rightly handling"[14] or "accurately handling"[15] "the word of truth". Rather than emphasizing divisions in Scripture, Paul is exhorting Timothy to teach the Christian faith correctly.

While Scofield and subsequent dispensationalists have inserted divisions and distinctions in Scripture, often arbitrary and artificial in nature, the approach of the Catholic Church has been to base all interpretation of Scripture on the continuity found in the person and teaching of Jesus Christ. The need for such a unity and a stronger emphasis on the centrality of Jesus Christ in interpreting all of Scripture is being recognized by a growing number of "progressive dispensationalists".[16] As these newer dispensationalist scholars move away from a radical distinction between Israel and the Church, traditional dispensationalists realize that any recognition of continuity between Israel and the Church spells eventual doom

---

[14] *Revised Standard Version.* The *New American Bible* translates that phrase as "imparting the word of truth without deviation".

[15] *New American Standard Version.*

[16] Darrell L. Bock, a leading progressive dispensationalist, writes: "When progressives speak of a complementary relationship between Old Testament and New Testament texts, they are claiming that a normal, contextually determined reading often brings concepts from the Hebrew Scriptures together in the New Testament in a way that completes and expounds what was already present in the older portion of God's Word. As revelation proceeds, the texts themselves, New and Old Testament, are brought together in a way that links concepts together, so that both old and fresh associations are made (Matt. 13:52). Such fresh associations, canonically determined and defined, have a stable meaning because they emerge from within a normal reading of the text. In sum, if there is a difference between progressives and more traditional dispensational readings, it is that progressives are asking dispensationalists to work more integratively with the biblical text" (Bock, "Hermeneutics of Progressive Dispensationalism", in Herbert W. Bateman IV, ed., *Three Central Issues in Contemporary Dispensationalism: A Comparison of Traditional and Progressive Views* [Grand Rapids, Mich.: Kregel Publications, 1999], p. 89).

for the entire system of dispensationalist interpretation and belief. Stanley D. Toussaint, a retired Dallas Theological Seminary professor, candidly admits that "if the Church and Israel become so blurred in dispensationalism that there is no separation between them, dispensationalism will become as extinct as the pitied dodo bird." [17]

The Nature of Israel

"Israel" can be defined and understood in more than one way, which can lead to serious confusion. Many dispensationalists focus upon the nation of Israel, viewing its reemergence as a prophetic sign. Yet Scripture is not so concerned, in the end, with Israel as a nation as it is with Israel as a people—a people following after God and having his law written on their heart (Jer 31:33). Jesus' challenge to ethnic Israel to be true followers of God and not merely people relying upon their physical ties to Abraham was a central theme of his ministry. Prior to Jesus' ministry this can be seen in John the Baptist's admonition to those who came to be baptized by him: "Bear fruits that befit repentance, and do not begin to say to yourselves, 'We have Abraham as our

[17] Stanley D. Toussaint, "Israel and the Church of a Traditional Dispensationalist", in Bateman, *Three Central Issues*, p. 227. Toussaint continues: "In the original form of Darby's dispensationalism, the line drawn between Israel and the Church was heavy, dark, and broad. According to Darby, the promises to the Church were spiritual and heavenly whereas those to Israel and the nations were earthly. The Tribulation and the Millennium do not concern the Church for those prophecies were earthly.... In brief, in classical dispensationalism the Jews are God's earthly people and the Church is God's heavenly people. This dualism was maintained by dispensationalists for more than a hundred years by men such as ... Scofield, and Chafer" (p. 228).

father'; for I tell you, God is able from these stones to raise up children to Abraham" (Lk 3:8). It is evident in Jesus' reply to those who exclaimed that "Abraham is our father" as an argument for their supposed moral superiority: "If you were Abraham's children, you would do what Abraham did" (Jn 8:39). This point is brought home even more emphatically in another passage from Luke's Gospel, in which Christ's mission to the Gentiles is also revealed:

> There you will weep and gnash your teeth, when you see Abraham and Isaac and Jacob and all the prophets in the kingdom of God and you yourselves thrust out. And men will come from east and west, and from north and south, and sit at table in the kingdom of God. (Lk 13:28–29)

This mission to save and bless all of humanity and not just ethnic Israel is a fulfillment of the Abrahamic Covenant (Gen 12). Jesus spoke of this mission in various ways. In the Gospel of John he speaks of the Gentiles as "other sheep" who will become part of "one flock": "And I have other sheep, that are not of this fold; I must bring them also, and they will heed my voice. So there shall be one flock, one shepherd" (Jn 10:16). Jesus' mission was not to restore Israel as a political, earthly power either in his day or in the future, but to gather together true believers of God into an *ekklesia*—a Church, the New Israel, which would include the "remnant of Israel" referred to by the prophets:

> In that day the remnant of Israel and the survivors of the house of Jacob will no more lean upon him that smote them, but will lean upon the LORD, the Holy One of Israel, in truth. A remnant will return, the remnant of Jacob, to the mighty God. For though your people Israel be as the sand of the sea, only a remnant of them will return. Destruction is decreed, overflowing with righteousness (Is 10:20–22).

Only when the continuity between this believing Israel (as opposed to a national or ethnic Israel) and the New Israel is appreciated can the Gospels be rightly interpreted and the Catholic Church's ecclesiology be correctly understood. Otherwise one may embrace the errors of dispensationalism, believing that God's concern is for an earthly, millennial Kingdom (the very thing Christ rejected), that the Gospels are largely meant for the future Jewish Kingdom and not for the Church, and that the Church was a result of the rejection of Christ instead of part of God's plan from all eternity.

The Catholic Church: One People, One Plan

Dispensationalists often accuse those who disagree with their Israel/Church distinction of replacing Israel with the Church, as though Israel had been shoved aside by God without so much as a second thought.[18] This is, however, an incorrect understanding of how Catholics, the Eastern Orthodox, and many Protestants view the relationship between Israel and the Church. Catholic doctrine emphasizes that the promises given to Old Testament Israel and the covenants made with it are brought to fulfillment in the New Covenant instituted by Christ. The Church and the New Covenant are in continuity with the Old Covenant and fulfill it precisely because Jesus Christ, the founder and head of the Church, fulfilled the Law (Mt 5:17–18) and the prophets

---

[18] "When we, as the church, take these [Bible] prophecies to Israel literally, we see a great prophetic agenda that lies ahead for Israel as a people and a nation. When the church spiritualizes these promises, as it has done too often in history, Israel's prophetic uniqueness is subsumed and merged unrealistically into the church" (Thomas Ice and Timothy Demy, *Fast Facts on Bible Prophecy* [Eugene, Ore.: Harvest House Publishers, 1997], p. 103). Also see Tim LaHaye, *Understanding the Last Days: The Keys to Unlocking Bible Prophecy* (Eugene, Ore.: Harvest House Publishers, 1998), p. 73.

(Lk 24:44) and founded a New Israel (Mt 16:16–19). This has been summarized well by Hans K. LaRondelle, a Seventh-Day Adventist theologian, who writes, "Christ created His Church, not beside Israel, but as the faithful remnant of Israel that inherits the covenant promises and responsibilities. Christ's Church is not separated from the Israel of God, only from the Christ-rejecting Jewish nation." [19] In a similar vein, the *Catechism* teaches that the Church is a rightful heir to the people of the Old Covenant: "By calling itself 'Church,' the first community of Christian believers recognized itself as heir to that assembly. In the Church, God is 'calling together' his people from all the ends of the earth." [20] The Church, the *Catechism* continues, is the family of God formed throughout history and was prepared in the people of Israel. [21] This teaching permeates the writings of Paul and other New Testament authors. In his epistle to the Ephesians, Paul explains to Gentile Christians that they, being part of the Church, are partaking in the promises and covenants of Israel:

> Therefore remember that at one time you Gentiles in the flesh, called the uncircumcision by what is called the circumcision, which is made in the flesh by hands—remember that you were at that time separated from Christ, alienated from the commonwealth of Israel, and strangers to the covenants of promise, having no hope and without God in the world. (Eph 2:11–12)

---

[19] Hans K. LaRondelle, *The Israel of God in Prophecy: Principles of Prophetic Interpretation* (Berrien Springs, Mich.: Andrews University Press, 1983), p. 102. Although not altogether friendly toward the Catholic Church, LaRondelle's book is an excellent work that is quite Catholic in both its arguments and conclusions. It is one of the best critiques of dispensationalism ever written. In fact, its impact can be measured by the silence from the dispensational camp—it is rarely, if ever, referred to or mentioned by dispensationalists.

[20] CCC 751.

[21] See CCC 759.

Romans 9 through 11 contains St. Paul's most lengthy and detailed treatise on this relationship. The Apostle states: "For not all who are descended from Israel belong to Israel, and not all are children of Abraham because they are his descendants" (Rom 9:6–7). The point here—as it is throughout the entire epistle to the Romans—is that it is not one's ethnicity but one's faith in God through Jesus Christ that is the basis for salvation. "For there is no distinction between Jew and Greek" (Rom 10:12), he writes, echoing his words to the Galatians, who struggled with the same Judaizing tendencies as the Jewish Christians in Rome:

> For as many of you as were baptized into Christ have put on Christ. There is neither Jew nor Greek, there is neither slave nor free, there is neither male nor female; for you are all one in Christ Jesus. And if you are Christ's, then you are Abraham's offspring, heirs according to promise. (Gal 3:27–29)

Later in the same letter the Apostle to the Gentiles refers to Christians as the "Israel of God" (Gal 6:16), again identifying the Church as the New Israel.[22] Peter is equally

---

[22] Galatians 6:15–16 states: "For neither is circumcision anything, nor uncircumcision, but a new creation. And those who will walk by this rule, peace and mercy be upon them, and upon the Israel of God" [NASB]. Walvoord contends that this passage does not refer to the Church as "the Israel of God", but "is rather a specific instance where Jewish believers are distinguished from Gentile believers, and this by the very term *Israel of God*" (Walvoord, *Millennial Kingdom*, pp. 169–70). Hoekema takes exception to this interpretation: "Who are meant by 'all who follow this rule'? Obviously, all those who are new creatures in Christ, for whom neither circumcision nor uncircumcision means anything. This would have to include all true believers, both Jews and Gentiles. What follows in the Greek is *kai epi ton Israel tou theou*. John F. Walvoord, a dispensational writer, insists that the word *kai* must be translated *and*, so that 'the Israel of God' refers to believing Jews. The problem with this interpretation is that believing Jews have already been included in the words 'all who follow this rule'—that is, of all true believers, including both Jews and

emphatic about this fact in his first epistle, deliberately appropriating a number of titles used in the Old Testament of Israel and applying them to the Church:

> But you are a *chosen race*, a *royal priesthood*, a *holy nation*, *God's own people*, that you may declare the wonderful deeds of him who called you out of darkness into his marvelous light. Once you were no people but now you are God's people; once you had not received mercy but now you have received mercy. (1 Pet 2:9–10)[23]

Lumen Gentium explains that God's gradual instruction of the "Israelite race ... happened as a preparation and figure of that new and perfect covenant which was to be ratified in Christ, and of the fuller revelation which was to be given through the Word of God made flesh."[24] *Lumen Gentium* further stresses the continuity by remarking, "As Israel according to the flesh which wandered in the desert was already called the Church of God (2 Esd. 13:1; cf. Num. 20:4; Deut. 23:1 ff.), so too, the new Israel, which advances in this present era in search of a future and permanent city (cf. Heb 13:14), is called also the Church of Christ (cf. Mt. 16:18)."[25]

In light of these passages from Scripture and magisterial documents, several problems with the dispensational distinction between Israel and the Church are highlighted:

Gentiles, who constitute the New Testament Church. Here, in other words, Paul clearly identifies the Church as the true Israel" (Anthony A. Hoekema, *The Bible and the Future* [Grand Rapids, Mich.: W. B. Eerdmans, 1979], p. 197).

[23] Emphasis added. On the emphasized phrases, see Is 43:20; 61:6; Ex 19:6; Deut 14:2.

[24] *LG* 9.

[25] Ibid.

1. It rests on a flawed method of interpreting Scripture, which, in turn, relies upon artificial divisions while ignoring the continuity located in the person and teaching of Jesus Christ.

2. It passes over the teachings of Christ and the apostles that show the New Covenant is an establishment of a New Israel, the Church, fulfilling and continuing, in a perfected manner, the Old Testament promises and covenants.

3. It actually undermines the importance of the Church by incorrectly asserting that God's attention will be primarily focused on the nation of Israel in the end times.

4. It overlooks the fact that God has always had just one people throughout history, and that he has worked to build that people through a series of covenants that culminate in the New Covenant, established in and with the Person of Jesus Christ.

The Church of the Mysterious Parenthesis

Dispensationalists believe that among the hundreds of prophecies found in the Old Testament there is none referring, in any shape or form, to the Church and the "Church age". They claim to find complete silence in the Old Testament regarding the Church, a so-called "mystery" unexpectedly inserted into history and revealed at Pentecost. Dispensationalists, Walvoord writes, "have regarded the present age [the Church age] as a parenthesis unexpected and without specific prediction in the Old Testament."[26] Dwight Pentecost, another leading dispensationalist theologian, teaches

[26] Walvoord, *Millennial Kingdom*, p. 227.

the Church is "manifestly an interruption of God's program for Israel".[27] Charles Ryrie states: "The church age is not seen in God's program for Israel. It is an intercalation. The church is a mystery in the sense that it was completely un-revealed in the Old Testament and now revealed in the New Testament."[28] Ryrie further explains the importance of this belief:

> If the church is not a subject of Old Testament prophecy, then the church is not fulfilling Israel's promises, but instead Israel herself must fulfill them and that in the future. In brief, premillennialism with a dispensational view recognizes the church as a distinct entity, distinct from Israel in her begin-ning, in her relation to this age, and in her promises. If the church is not a distinct body, then the door is open wide for amillennialism to enter with its ideas that the church is some sort of full-bloomed development of Judaism and the ful-filler of Israel's promises of blessing (but not of judgment). Thus premillennialism and ecclesiology are inseparably related.[29]

[27] J. Dwight Pentecost, *Things to Come* (Grand Rapids, Mich.: Zondervan Publishing House, 1958), p. 201.

[28] Ryrie, *Basis of the Premillennial Faith*, p. 136.

[29] Ibid., p. 126. Ryrie's comments here are misleading, especially when he states that the amillennial view is that the Church receives all of the blessings but does not have to face any judgment. His assumption is that amillennialism discards Israel, when in reality most amillennialists—especially Catholics—understand that the believing Israel (consisting of Mary, the apostles, the dis-ciples, etc.) was never cast aside, but formed the core of the New Israel. In other words, there is a true and significant continuity between the Old and New Covenants. Secondly, those who are part of the Church do face cov-enantal blessings and curses, as did those in the Old Covenant. Christians who turn away from Christ, who destroy the life of grace through sin, will be removed from covenantal life and—if they do not repent—will die outside of it.

What is the basis for this belief that the Church is a paren-thetical people, or institution, with no direct relationship to the people of Israel in the Old Testament? Ryrie provides three general arguments: A "parenthesis" or "intercalation" between the promises and their fulfillment is predicted in the Old Testament; the Church is described as a "mystery" in the New Testament; and the Church is described as a "dis-tinct body of saints in this age".[30]

The first argument rests heavily on the dispensationalist interpretation of the ninth chapter of Daniel, verses 24–27. This prophetic passage divides seventy "weeks" into periods of seven "weeks", sixty-two "weeks", and one "week". Each "week" refers to a period of seven years, based on the cor-relation between the seventy years spoken of to Jeremiah (Dan 9:2) and the seventy weeks that puzzle Daniel (Dan 9:24). Walvoord writes, "Conservative scholars usually trace the ful-fillment of the first sixty-nine sevens of years as culminating in the crucifixion of Christ", and then insists that, while "the most literal interpretation of the first sixty-nine sevens is thus afforded a literal fulfillment, nothing can be found in history that provides a literal fulfillment of the last seven years of the prophecy to the future preceding the second ad-vent".[31] Two conclusions result from this premise: There is an indefinite break in time between the sixty-ninth and sev-entieth "week", and the final "week", or seven years, will be the future time of tribulation that will begin as soon as the Church is raptured from earth.

The problem with such an interpretation is that Daniel 9 never indicates in any way that there is a parenthesis of un-known length between the sixty-ninth and seventieth "week".

[30] Ibid., pp. 126–38.
[31] Walvoord, *Millennial Kingdom*, p. 227.

Any such break is unwarranted by the passage and reflects a presumption—not sound exegesis. LaRondelle writes,

> The normal, natural, exegetical assumption is that the seventy weeks are an unbreakable unity. They are presented as a unit, just as are the seventy years of Babylonian exile in Daniel 9:2.... Because the other predicted time periods are consecutive, the natural expectation can only be that the seventy weeks of Daniel are also consecutive.... The dispensational break in the unit of the seventy weeks destroys the very point in specifying seventy consecutive weeks.[32]

LaRondelle goes on to make several compelling points, including the intriguing argument that "the middle of the week" (Dan 9:27) refers to the three and a half years from the time of Christ's baptism to his death on the Cross—the very point when "the legitimacy of the temple sacrifices had come to an end."[33]

Also problematic is Ryrie's second argument, based on the premise that since the Church is a "mystery" she cannot be found in the Old Testament. Ryrie defines the word *mystery* as "something that is imparted only to the initiated, some-

---

[32] LaRondelle, *Israel of God in Prophecy*, pp. 172–73.

[33] Ibid., p. 178. LaRondelle continues: "The Jews as a whole did not accept this divine decision and immediately reinstituted their bloody sacrifices. But the Shekinah glory had now departed from their temple; it was therefore no longer the temple of God, and Jerusalem was no longer the holy city. Instead of God's blessing, His curse now rested on their house ('your house,' Matthew 23:38; cf. 1 Thessalonians 2:16). Total destruction by the Roman armies would soon follow. 'They will not leave one stone on another, because you did not recognize the time of God's coming to you' (Luke 19:4; cf. 21:20–24). This fatal consequence of Israel's rejection of the Messiah—the destruction of Jerusalem in A.D. 70—was part and parcel of Daniel's prophecy. Christ explained: 'For this is the time of punishment in fulfillment of all that has been written' (Luke 21:22)" (p. 178).

thing that is unknown until it is revealed".[34] While this definition is compatible with Catholic doctrine, it makes no sense for Ryrie to conclude that since the Church is a mystery she could not have been foreshadowed or prophesied in the Old Testament. If such were the case, could it also be said that there is no relationship between the Yahweh of the Old Testament and the triune God of the New Testament since the Trinity was not revealed until after the coming of Christ? Of course not. But Ryrie errs in not recognizing that what is foreshadowed reveals that which foreshadows; without a New Testament fulfillment, the Old Testament type would not have any meaning.[35] The fact that the New Testament Church was unknown until she was revealed does not mean that she was not foreshadowed or prophesied in the Old Testament. It only means that such foreshadowing could not be seen or understood clearly until the New Testament fulfillment was realized. This is what happened with Christ himself, who had to spend time showing his disciples "in all the scriptures the things concerning himself" (Lk 24:27).

The argument that the Church is a "distinct body of saints in this age" is a conclusion, Ryrie states, based on a number of other "facts". Among these are the claims that the Church is not fulfilling "in any sense the promises to Israel", that the

---

[34] Ryrie, *Basis of the Premillennial Faith*, p. 131.

[35] Protestant scholar J. Barton Payne writes: "The *type* consists of an action—not to be confused with a verbal message–that represents and conveys a teaching of double import: its truth was a reality to its contemporaries, and yet it had accomplishment in the future work of Jesus Christ. The justification for typology derives from the fundamental unity that exists within God's plan of salvation in general and within His redemptive testament in particular (Heb 9:15, 11:40)" (Payne, *Encyclopedia of Biblical Prophecy* [New York: Harper and Row, 1973], pp. 22–23).

use of the term *Church* in the New Testament indicates that she was still in the future, and that the Greek word *ekklesia*—even though used for "Church" in the New Testament and for "assembly" in the Septuagint—offers no proof of a connection between Old Testament Israel and the Church.[36] These points will be addressed in examining Catholic teaching about the nature and purpose of the Church.

Catholicism: The Continuity of the Church

Contrary to the dispensationalist belief that the Church is an abrupt insertion, or "intercalation",[37] into history, the *Catechism of Catholic Church* teaches that "God created the world for the sake of communion with his divine life, a communion brought about by the 'convocation' of men in Christ, and this 'convocation' is the Church. The Church is the goal of all things [cf. St. Epiphanius, *Panarion* 1, 1, 5: PG 41, 181C]." [38] If this is true, then the Church must be in continuity with—and a continuation of—Old Testament Israel, and the Old Testament must have predicted, in some shape or form, the Church.

---

[36] Ryrie, *Basis of the Premillennial Faith*, pp. 136–37.

[37] Chafer writes that "parenthetical" is not strong enough and is "inaccurate" since a "parenthetical portion sustains some direct or indirect relation to that which goes before or that which follows; but the present age-purpose is not thus related and therefore is more properly termed an intercalation. The appropriateness of this word will be seen in the fact that, as an interpolation is formed by inserting a word or phrase into a context, so an intercalation is formed by introducing a day or a period of time into the calendar. The present age of the Church is an intercalation into the revealed calendar or program of God as that program was foreseen by the prophets of old. Such, indeed, is the precise nature of the present age" (Chafer, *Systematic Theology*, 4:41).

[38] CCC 760.

Indications of such predictions can be found in the promises made to Abraham of blessings to Gentiles through him and his offspring: "And by you all the families of the earth shall bless themselves" (Gen 12:3) and "by your descendants shall all the nations of the earth bless themselves, because you have obeyed my voice" (Gen 22:18). Psalm 22, a Messianic psalm, declares "All the ends of the earth shall remember and turn to the LORD; and all the families of the nations shall worship before him" (Ps 22:27). Similar language is found in the prophet Isaiah, through whom the Lord states: "I have given you [Israel] as a covenant to the people, a light to the nations" (Is 42:6). Another Messianic passage from Isaiah referring to God's plan of blessing for all people is found in chapter 60:

Arise, shine; for your light has come,
  and the glory of the LORD has risen upon you.
For behold, darkness shall cover the earth,
  and thick darkness the peoples;
but the LORD will arise upon you,
  and his glory will be seen upon you.
And nations shall come to your light,
  and kings to the brightness of your rising (Is 60:1–3).

A profound prophetic passage with a similar message, cited frequently by many of the early Church Fathers as a reference to the New Covenant and the Eucharist, comes from the prophet Malachi: " 'For from the rising of the sun to its setting my name is great among the nations, and in every place incense is offered to my name, and a pure offering; for my name is great among the nations, says the LORD of hosts' " (Mal 1:11). While these passages do not make overt references to the Church, they show that God's desire has been to draw all men, whether Jews or Gentiles, to himself and to make them one family. This, according to Paul, was a "mystery" revealed to him, the Apostle to the Gentiles:

> When you read this you can perceive my insight into the mystery of Christ, which was not made known to the sons of men in other generations as it has now been revealed to his holy apostles and prophets by the Spirit; that is, how the Gentiles are fellow heirs, members of the same body, and partakers of the promise in Christ Jesus through the gospel.
>
> Of this gospel I was made a minister according to the gift of God's grace which was given me by the working of his power. To me, though I am the very least of all the saints, this grace was given, to preach to the Gentiles the unsearchable riches of Christ, and to make all men see what is the plan of the mystery hidden for ages in God who created all things; that through the church the manifold wisdom of God might now be made known to the principalities and powers in the heavenly places. This was according to the eternal purpose which he has realized in Christ Jesus our Lord. (Eph 3:4–11)

A central passage connecting Old Testament prophecies with the establishment of the Church is Peter's sermon on Pentecost. Quoting the prophet Joel, Peter preaches that "And in the last days it shall be, God declares, that I will pour out my Spirit upon all flesh" (Acts 2:17; see Joel 2:28–32). Ryrie, in the notes of his *Study Bible*, writes: "The fulfillment of this prophecy will be in the last days, immediately preceding the return of Christ." [39] However, this misrepresents both Peter's message and the meaning of the term "last days". Peter's sermon is intended to explain his reference to Joel by showing that "this Jesus Christ raised up again" has fulfilled the words of the prophet *and* his promise of the Holy Spirit being poured out—an event that had taken place that very morning. Far from being a reference to a future event, Peter's

---

[39] *Ryrie Study Bible*, NASB (Chicago: Moody Press, n.d.), pp. 1645–46).

quotation of Joel underscores the immediacy of the fulfillment: "Being therefore exalted at the right hand of God,
and having received from the Father the promise of the Holy
Spirit, he has poured out this *which you see and hear*" (Acts
2:33; emphasis added).

As noted, there are many references to the Church in the
New Testament using language previously reserved for Israel
alone, including the actual name "Israel". There is also the
term *ekklesia*, which, as Hoekema explains, is directly related
to Old Testament references to the assembly of Israel:

> The Hebrew term *qahal*, commonly rendered *ekklesia* in the
> Septuagint (the Greek translation of the Hebrew Bible), is
> applied to Israel in the Old Testament. To give just a few
> examples, we find the word *qahal* used of the assembly or
> congregation of Israel in Exodus 12:6, Numbers 14:5, Deu-
> teronomy 5:22, Joshua 8:35, Ezra 2:64, and Joel 2:16. Since
> the Septuagint was the Bible of the apostles, their use of the
> Greek word *ekklesia*, the Septuagint equivalent of *qahal*, for
> the New Testament Church clearly indicates the continuity
> between the Church and Old Testament Israel.[40]

---

[40] Hoekema, *Bible and the Future*, p. 215. Not surprisingly, many dispensationalists downplay the connection between Israel and the Church created by
the word *ekklesia*. Walvoord argues that use of the word "ecclesia" in the Septuagint means little, if anything, since it "is not specifically religious, and though
used of Israel is also used of an assembly of evil doers (Ps. 26:5) and of an army
(Ezek. 32:22–23). It is clearly not a technical word and must be interpreted by
the context. It is never used in the sense of spiritual presence or relationship"
(*Millennial Kingdom*, p. 225). This ignores the fact that the word *ekklesia*, although not used in a religious sense by the Greeks, was appropriated by Jewish
scholars to refer to a religious assembly: "[*Ekklesia*] was adopted by the LXX
to render the [Hebrew] word *kahal*, which with the [Hebrew] word *edah* signifies in later [Hebrew] the religious assembly of the Israelites.... The earliest
uses of the word in the NT reflect the idea both of ... the religious assembly
of God, and the local assembly. The word is first applied to the *ekklesia* of
Jerusalem, which was itself a local assembly. It was at the same time the assembly
of all those who believed in Jesus Christ, and thus was the legitimate successor

The Church is also understood to be the new and heavenly Jerusalem, another sign of continuity with Old Testament Israel: "But you have come to Mount Zion and to the city of the living God, the heavenly Jerusalem, and to innumerable angels in festal gathering, and to the assembly of the first-born who are enrolled in heaven, and to a judge who is God of all, and to the spirits of just men made perfect" (Heb 12:22–23). This new Jerusalem is the bride of Christ (Rev 21:2; Eph 5).

Just as important are the references to the Church as the "temple of God". The Temple was for the Jews the seat of the divine presence of God and the sign of election for God's covenantal people.[41] It would be difficult, writes historian Henri Daniel-Rops, to overstate the importance and centrality of the Temple for Israel:

> The splendid building stood at the very heart of Israel's most urgent spiritual needs, just as it stood in the heart of the most sacred part of the holy city. In every possible respect, it was one of the essential realities of the life of the People of God. There was but one Temple.[42]

---

of the Israelite assembly of Yahweh" (John L. McKenzie, S.J., *Dictionary of the Bible* [New York: Touchstone, 1995], pp. 133–34).

[41] Dominican scholar Roland de Vaux states: "Solomon's Temple was the religious centre of Israel, and it remained so even after the separation of the two kingdoms" (de Vaux, *Ancient Israel*, vol. 2 [New York: McGraw-Hill, 1965], p. 325). De Vaux also points out that the Temple was the "seat of the divine presence" and "the sign of election" (p. 327).

[42] Henri Daniel-Rops, *Daily Life in the Time of Jesus* (New York: Mentor-Omega, 1962), p. 349. Elsewhere Daniel-Rops writes, "The Temple had its own branch of theology, as the place of the divine presence and the proof of the choosing of God's own people, a branch much worked upon by the rabbis. There was even a symbolism that centered about the Temple, and the apocryphal literature, Josephus and Philo give us the general ideas of it: the Temple was the center of the world; it is also the world's image, and its furnishings represented the attributes of God" (pp. 357–58).

Because of this, Jesus' many words about the Temple are all the more striking, especially his explicit prophecies that the Temple would be thoroughly destroyed:

> And as he came out of the temple, one of his disciples said to him, "Look, Teacher, what wonderful stones and what wonderful buildings!" And Jesus said to him, "Do you see these great buildings? There will not be left here one stone upon another, that will not be thrown down" (Mk 13:1–2; see Mt 24:1–2; Lk 21:5–6).

In casting out the moneychangers, Jesus demonstrated his authority over the Temple and his superiority to it. Moreover, the presence of God in Christ himself is incomparably greater than the presence of God in the Temple, and Christ is present in the Church. The Church, therefore, is the true Temple where God dwells. This is confirmed by Paul, who explains that Christians, united to Christ, make a "holy temple":

> So then you are no longer strangers and sojourners, but you are fellow citizens with the saints and members of the household of God, built upon the foundation of the apostles and prophets, Christ Jesus himself being the cornerstone, in whom the whole structure is joined together and grows into a holy temple in the Lord; in whom you also are built into it for a dwelling place of God in the Spirit. (Eph 2:19–22)

In direct contrast, dispensationalists believe that during the future, earthly millennial reign of Christ, the Temple will be rebuilt on the Temple Mount in Jerusalem and animal sacrifices will take place there in memorial of Christ's death. Many dispensationalists are anticipating work on a new Temple and believe that such activity will be a concrete sign of the "end times".[43] But such anticipation overlooks a central truth found in Christ's words and deeds: He is the new and everlasting Temple—there is no need for another, even if it is built.[44]

No Kingdom for Christians?

Although there have been variations on Darby's teaching regarding the nature, purpose, and current state of the Church, popular dispensationalists have maintained his pessimistic ecclesiology without any major changes. This is most evident in their belief that the Church has little or nothing to do with the promise and reality of the Kingdom. This is due to distinctions made between the "Kingdom of God", "the Kingdom of heaven", and the Church. According to Scofield the "kingdom of God ... includes whatever God rules over, the intelligences in any world or in any sphere who are willingly subject to the rule of God."[45] The "kingdom of heaven", Scofield claims—along with other dispensationalists—is altogether different and distinct, for "it refers

[43] "The most exciting evidence that the Lord's return may be very close at hand is the activity surrounding preparations for the rebuilding of the temple on the Temple Mount in Jerusalem.... Ezekiel 40 to 46 gives detailed instructions for the temple that will stand on the Temple Mount during the millennium. However, Daniel 9:27 states that there will be a temple in Jerusalem during the tribulation period, when the sacrifices will be stopped. Preparations for this temple are already complete! There is evidence that all of the items needed to build and operate a third temple, plus man this worship center for the sacrifices that are to be performed there, are already set in place" (Jimmy DeYoung, "Preparations for the Potente", in *Countdown to Armageddon: The Final Battle and Beyond*, ed. Charles C. Ryrie, Joe Jordan, and Tom Davis [Eugene, Ore.: Harvest House Publishers, 1999], p. 125).

[44] See CCC 1197 and 586.

[45] C. I. Scofield, "The Millennium", in *Brief Outlines of Things to Come*, ed. Theodore H. Epp (Chicago: Moody Press, 1952), p. 84.

to this period which we call the Millennium.... The 'kingdom of heaven' is the establishment, through Christ, of God's righteous reign on the earth. It is always limited to the earth." [46] Finally, the Church "is composed of those who are saved, mostly Gentiles, between the first and second advent of the Lord Jesus Christ".[47] Scofield attempts to explain the relationship between the three in this way: "[The] Church is in the kingdom of God, but the Church is not the kingdom of God, neither is the Church the kingdom of Heaven. The Church is in the kingdom of Heaven, which is in the kingdom of God." [48] This distinction between the kingdoms of heaven and God is another example of Scofield's arbitrary and forced dichotomies. Most Protestant and

---

[46] Ibid.

[47] Ibid. John Walvoord writes: "There is ... a validity to the concept of an eternal kingdom to be identified with God's government of the universe. In contrast, however, to this universal aspect, the millennial kingdom is the culmination of the prophetic program of God relative to the theocratic kingdom or rule of the earth.... Though there is a rule of God in the present age which can properly be described by the word kingdom, it is not the fulfillment of those prophecies that pertain to the millennial reign of Christ upon the earth" (*Millennial Kingdom*, p. 297). Reformed theologian Vern S. Poythress notes that Scofield, in his *Reference Bible* (Mt 6:33), "distinguishes the kingdom of God from the kingdom of heaven in no less than five aspects" (Poythress, *Understanding Dispensationalists* [Phillipsburg, N.J.: P and R Publishing, 1994], p. 27).

[48] Scofield, "Millennium", p. 86. Dispensationalist theologian Stanley D. Toussaint believes that the Church will "[enter] into Israel's millennial promises.... The apostles, who are part and parcel of the church, are going to reign over Israel in the land during the Millennium." He notes that some dispensationalists have differing ideas about how the Church will reign during the millennial period. For example, Walvoord "sees the raptured and resurrected church as inhabiting the New Jerusalem, which may be in orbit around the earth". Toussaint quotes Walvoord's hypothesis that the New Jerusalem will be a "satellite city in relation to the millennial earth" and that Christians "will be able to commute to the earth" (Toussaint, "Israel and the Church", pp. 250–51).

Catholic scholars agree that the term "Kingdom of heaven", which is used only in Matthew's Gospel, is oriented toward Matthew's Jewish audience—taking into consideration that Jews often avoided using the name of God[49]—and is identical in meaning with "Kingdom of God". It was used for at least two reasons: it avoided earthly, political overtones and expectations, and it pointed to the heavenly nature of the Kingdom, which would begin on earth but culminate in heaven.

Although details vary, the generally accepted dispensationalist belief is that Jesus came to offer the Jews an earthly, Davidic kingdom, but when they rejected him this offer was postponed until his Second Coming, at which time it would be offered, accepted, and then fulfilled during the millennial period. During the current Church age Jesus is not actually reigning as King, nor will he until his Second Coming. Ryrie explains:

Gabriel announced to Mary that her Baby would have the throne of David and reign over the house of Jacob (Luke

---

[49] " 'Kingdom of heaven': this expression is identical to 'Kingdom of God'. The former is the one used by St. Matthew, and is more in line with the Jewish turn of phrase. Out of reverence, the Jews avoided pronouncing the name of God and substituted other words for it" (*Navarre Bible. Saint Matthew's Gospel* [Dublin: Four Courts Press, 1988], p. 42, commenting on Matthew 3:1). *The New Dictionary of Theology*, a Protestant reference work, states: "There is no difference in reference between 'the kingdom of God' and 'the kingdom of heaven.' ... [Matthew] almost always used the latter (in distinction from Mk. and Lk. who never do), probably in view of the Jewish background of his audience for whom 'heaven' was a reverent circumlocution for the divine name. Also the Gk. word *basileia*, conventionally translated 'kingdom,' can have the dynamic meaning of 'rule', 'reign', 'kingship', as well as the concrete meaning of 'realm', 'territory governed by a king', 'kingdom'" (Sinclair B. Ferguson, David F. Wright, and J. I. Packer, eds., *New Dictionary of Theology* [Downers Grove, Ill.: InterVarsity Press, 1988], p. 367).

1:32-33). Throughout his earthly ministry Jesus' Davidic kingship was offered to Israel (Matt. 2:2; 27:11; John 12:13), but He was rejected.... Because the King was rejected, the messianic, Davidic kingdom was (from a human viewpoint) postponed. Though He never ceases to be King and, of course, is King today as always, Christ is never designated as King of the Church.... Though Christ is a King today, He does not rule as King. This awaits His second coming. Then the Davidic kingdom will be realized (Matt. 25:31; Rev 19:15; 20).[50]

This reasoning is confused in a number of ways. First, it is incorrect to say or imply that all Jews rejected Jesus. There was always a faithful remnant of Israel.[51] The Mother of Jesus, the Twelve, and many other disciples did not reject Christ, but believed that he was the Messiah, the Son of God.[52] Jesus did not offer a physical, political Davidic kingdom to the Jews—such a earthly kingdom was what they desired, and he refused to give it to them (see Jn 6:15; 18:36). Instead, he offered them the Kingdom of God, which is spiritual communion with God (Jn 3:1-5) and freedom from bondage to sin and death (Col 1:13). Furthermore, Jesus made

[50] Charles C. Ryrie, *Basic Theology* (Wheaton, Ill.: Victor Books, 1986), p. 259.

[51] The belief in a faithful remnant was a key theme of Isaiah and other later prophets: "In that day the remnant of Israel and the survivors of the house of Jacob will no more lean upon him that smote them, but will lean upon the LORD, the Holy One of Israel, in truth. A remnant will return, the remnant of Jacob, to the mighty God. For though your people Israel be as the sand of the sea, only a remnant of them will return. Destruction is decreed, overflowing with righteousness" (Is 10:20-22). For more on the importance of the Old Testament "remnant" and its relation to the Church, see LaRondelle, *Israel of God in Prophecy*, pp. 81-123, and John Bright, *The Kingdom of God, the Biblical Concept and Its Meaning for the Church* (Nashville: Abingdon-Cokesbury Press, 1953), pp. 71-97.

[52] See CCC 437-45.

it clear on many occasions that the Kingdom was "at hand". More than once it is declared, by either Jesus or John the Baptist: "Repent, for the kingdom of heaven is at hand" (Mt 3:2; 4:17; 10:7) and "The time is fulfilled, and the kingdom of God is at hand; repent, and believe in the gospel" (Mk 1:15; Mt 10:7). Jesus states, "But if it is by the Spirit of God that I cast out demons, then the kingdom of God has come upon you" (Mt 12:28) and "Truly, I say to you, there are some standing here who will not taste death before they see the kingdom of God come with power" (Mk 9:1; Lk 9:27). Obviously Jesus believed that the Kingdom of God was at hand and was being realized even as he healed, taught, and performed miracles.[53]

Finally, Scripture is filled with evidence that the Kingdom was and is intimately connected with the Church. This is clear in Peter's famous confession of faith—"Thou art the Christ, the Son of the living God":

> And Jesus answered him, "Blessed are you, Simon Bar-Jona! For flesh and blood has not revealed this to you, but my Father who is in heaven. And I tell you, you are Peter, and on this rock I will build my church, and the powers of death shall not prevail against it. I will give you the keys of the kingdom of heaven, and whatever you bind on earth shall be bound in heaven, and whatever you loose on earth shall be loosed in heaven." (Mt 16:17–19)

If the Church has little or nothing to do with the Kingdom, it would seem odd for Jesus to give the "keys of the kingdom" to the leader of the Church. But, as Jesus subsequently tells the chief priests and scribes, the Kingdom that had been promised to them would be given to others: "Therefore I

---

[53] See CCC 541.

tell you, the kingdom of God will be taken away from you and given to a nation producing the fruits of it" (Mt 21:43). This is why Jesus tells his disciples that "it is your Father's good pleasure to give you the kingdom" (Lk 12:32) and why Peter encourages the Christians of the early Church with these words: "But you are a chosen race, a royal priesthood, a holy nation, God's own people" (1 Pet 2:9).

The initiated Kingdom and Christ's kingship over all things is referred to throughout the New Testament. Jesus commissions the apostles to "make disciples of all nations" since "*All authority* in heaven and *on earth* has been given to me" (Mt 28:18–20; emphasis added). Peter, in his sermon at Pentecost, leaves no doubt that Jesus Christ now rules over all things from heaven, seated at the right hand of the Father:

> "Being therefore exalted at the right hand of God, and having received from the Father the promise of the Holy Spirit, he has poured out this which you see and hear. For David did not ascend into the heavens; but he himself says, 'The Lord said to my Lord, Sit at my right hand, till I make thy enemies a stool for thy feet.' Let all the house of Israel therefore know assuredly that God has made him both Lord and Christ, this Jesus whom you crucified." (Acts 2:33–36)

Later in the Acts of the Apostles, Paul and Silas apparently created a disturbance in Thessalonica by "saying that there is another king, Jesus" (Acts 17:7); although these words are given by their accusers, it is reasonable to think Paul uttered them. In his letter to the Colossians, Paul writes, "He has delivered us from the dominion of darkness and transferred us to the kingdom of his beloved Son" (Col 1:13). If Christ is not currently reigning as a king, how is it that Christians have been transferred into his Kingdom? And in his first letter to Timothy, Paul declares this blessing: "and this will be made manifest at the proper time by the blessed and only Sovereign, the King of kings and Lord of lords, who alone has immortality and dwells in unapproachable light, whom no man has ever seen or can see. To him be honor and eternal dominion. Amen" (1 Tim 6:15–16).

The Church Is the Kingdom!

The Second Vatican Council Fathers taught that the Church is "on earth the seed and beginning of [the] kingdom".[54] The intimate relationship between the Kingdom and the Church is proclaimed within the teachings of Jesus himself (especially in Matthew's Gospel) and throughout the New Testament. The Kingdom is already present, although not completely manifest and realized, in the Church. This teaching of the Catholic Church, reiterated in *Lumen Gentium*, is essential:

> To carry out the will of the Father Christ inaugurated the kingdom of heaven on earth and revealed to us his mystery; by his obedience he brought about our redemption. The Church—that is, the kingdom of Christ—already present in mystery, grows visibly through the power of God in the world.[55]

Unfortunately, this teaching has not always been faithfully conveyed to many Catholics. As Scott Hahn has noted, "Certain [Catholic] biblical scholars resist the Magisterium's teaching that the Catholic Church is the kingdom of God that Christ promised. They contend ... that Jesus came promising the kingdom, but all He left us was the Church." Hahn then writes words that could just as easily be applied to dis-

---

[54] LG 5.
[55] LG 3; see CCC 669.

pensationalists as to wayward Catholic theologians: "They are looking for the kingdom in all the wrong places, and they are looking for the wrong kind of kingdom." [56]

Dispensationalists are puzzled and bothered by the high regard Catholics have for the Church. Antagonistic toward the Catholic Church for any number of reasons, dispensationalists tend to view her as a major piece in the end-times puzzle. As one dispensationalist Baptist pastor matter-of-factly told me in a phone conversation: "I'm interested in the Catholic Church for the simple reason that I believe there will soon emerge a one-world apostate religion, and the Catholic Church is the only Church large enough to fit that description." He then admitted that he was very puzzled by "the Catholic obsession with 'the Church'". This puzzlement is a natural consequence of dispensationalist theology in particular and Fundamentalist premises in general. It can be seen in the insistence that the Church is an invisible reality whose only visible form exists on a local level. Little or no worldwide structure or unity can be found among the many thousands of Fundamentalist and Evangelical denominations that now exist in the world, most of them founded in the United States. [57] Lindsey expresses the Fundamentalist

---

[56] Scott Hahn, "The Church as Kingdom: Davidic and Eucharistic", *Crisis*, July/August 2000, pp. 39–40. Also see Christoph Cardinal Schönborn, *From Death to Life: The Christian Journey* (San Francisco: Ignatius Press, 1995), especially chapter 3, "The Kingdom of God and the Heavenly-Earthly Church: The Church in Transition according to *Lumen Gentium*", pp. 65–98.

[57] George Marsden explains these connections by observing that for traditional dispensationalists "The church is ... a historical 'parenthesis.' The Old Testament hardly intimated its coming, the age having been rather a 'mystery' revealed only with the Jews' rejection of Christ's kingdom. Unlike the postponed kingdom, which has a definite material and institutional structure, the interim church age of grace is a non-institutional age of the Holy Spirit. The true church is not the institutional church, which is worldly and steadily growing in apostasy. It is rather a faithful remnant of the spiritual who are 'separate

view of "Church" when he writes, "It doesn't make any difference what religious 'brand' they're [true believers] under as long as they're in a living union with Christ through a personal faith in Him as their Savior." [58]

Catholics believe the Church is *both* invisible and visible, spiritual and institutional, a spiritual reality that exists within time and space. The Church is historical but also transcends history. [59] She must be visible on earth in order for her unity to be seen, understood, and experienced by humanity. The Church is at one and the same time a pilgrim Church, in exile on earth, and also the holy and unblemished bride of the Bridegroom, Jesus Christ. [60]

Many Christians, including dispensationalists, have such an emaciated view of the Church that she has ceased to exist for them in any concrete and vibrant way. Instead of looking to the Church, they rely on private, subjective interpretations of the Bible, often moving from group to group seeking others who share beliefs similar to their own. Often they become spiritually homeless, without any objective source of authority on earth. Scripture, however, has a very high view of the Church. Paul wrote that the Church is "the household of God" and "the pillar and bulwark of the truth" (1 Tim 3:15). The one, true, catholic, and apostolic Church proclaims the gospel, knowing that Christ has promised that "the powers of death shall not prevail against it" (Mt 16:18).

---

and holy' from the world" (George M. Marsden, *Fundamentalism and American Culture: The Shaping of Twentieth Century Evangelicalism, 1870–1925* [New York: Oxford University Press, 1980], p. 54).

[58] Hal Lindsey with C. C. Carlson, *There's a New World Coming* (Santa Ana, Calif.: Vision House Publishers, 1973), p. 41.

[59] See CCC 770.

[60] See CCC 769 and 796. Also see Rev 22:17; Eph 1:4; 5:27.

8

"BIBLE PROPHECY" AND
INTERPRETING SCRIPTURE

This is no time in history to avoid "the study of future things," which is what prophecy is. If we avoid teaching Christians the basics about prophecy, they will be "tossed to and fro" by false teachers who come to them with cunningly devised fables and interpretations that will deceive them.... Christians need to know more about prophecy, not less, for that is the only way for them to be armed with the truth.

—Tim LaHaye

The method of dispensationalism is a literalism in which great care is taken to arrange passages of Scripture from throughout the whole Bible ... to establish biblical truths, especially truths concerning the end of the world.

—Mark A. Noll

However, since God speaks in sacred Scripture through men in human fashion, the interpreter of sacred Scripture, in order to see clearly what God wanted to communicate to us, should carefully investigate what meaning the sacred writers really intended, and what God wanted to manifest by means of their words.

—Second Vatican Council, Dogmatic Constitution
on Divine Revelation, *Dei Verbum*

242   WILL CATHOLICS BE "LEFT BEHIND"?

An entire book could be devoted to a critique of the dispensationalist method of biblical interpretation. The importance of this complex issue cannot be overstated, especially
since many Christians—whether Catholic or Protestant—do
not spend much time considering *why* and *how* they interpret Scripture. A person's hermeneutics[1]—his method of interpreting and understanding Scripture—is usually taken for
granted, like the air he breathes and the ground he walks on.
But just as clean air and firm footing are necessary for a healthy
life, a proper method of biblical interpretation leads to spiritual life and truth, while a faulty approach results in half-
truths and distorted doctrine.

One of the most attractive features of dispensationalism is
that it is a method of interpreting Scripture that appears to
be logical, tidy, and all-encompassing. It stresses that "[Bible]
prophecy is not so difficult", merely requiring that the Christian "spend a little time comparing Scripture with Scripture" while avoiding "the temptation to spiritualize anything
that at first seems complex".[2] It promises that the Bible, even
its most difficult and bewildering parts, is easy to understand, if only the dispensationalist method is embraced.[3] Mark

---

[1] The word *hermeneutics* comes from the Greek word *ermeneuein*, "to interpret". It is the "theory and practice of understanding and interpreting texts,
biblical or otherwise. Hermeneutics, while seeking to (a) establish the original
meaning of a text in its historical context and (b) express that meaning today,
recognizes that a text can contain and convey meaning that goes beyond the
original author's explicit intention" (Gerald O'Collins, S.J., and Edward G.
Farrugia, S.J., *A Concise Dictionary of Theology* [New York: Paulist Press, 1991],
p. 90).

[2] Tim LaHaye and Jerry B. Jenkins, *Are We Living in the End Times?* (Wheaton, Ill.: Tyndale House Publishers, 1999), pp. 4–5.

[3] Former Evangelical and apologist Mark Shea writes that to understand
Scripture properly, "it is well for the student of Scripture to be forearmed
against the common fallacies that can hinder the study of the Bible. Perhaps

Noll, an Evangelical historian and a critic of dispensational-ism, observes, "The key to dispensationalism's popularity has been an ability to render the prophetic parts of the Bible understandable to ordinary people and applicable to current circumstances."[4] This explains the publishing success of au-thors such as Lindsey and LaHaye, whose approach to Scrip-ture consists mostly of matching passages from the Bible to current events. As Lindsey states in *The Late Great Planet Earth*, "the Bible contains clear and unmistakable prophetic signs. We are able to see right now in this Best Seller [i.e., the Bible] predictions made centuries ago being fulfilled before our eyes."[5] LaHaye echoes this sentiment: "The ability to rightly evaluate the [prophetic] signs in our times is increas-ing almost daily, from Israel being reestablished as a nation, to the hatred of Israel by Russia and her Arab allies, to the emergence of China, and many other events–all part of the end-times prophetic tapestry."[6]

Once the premises of dispensationalism have been ac-cepted, the entire system appears cohesive and air-tight, seem-ingly able to make complete sense of Scripture. But although some Fundamentalists claim that understanding the Bible is simple and requires no specific knowledge or skills, com-mon sense and Scripture itself say otherwise. The thoughtful reader recognizes that the study of languages, cultures, and

---

the most mysterious and widespread of those fallacies is the great, fat, well-swilled nonsensical superstition that Scripture ought always to be 'simple'" (Mark P. Shea, *Making Senses out of Scripture: Reading the Bible as the First Chris-tians Did* [San Diego, Calif.: Basilica Press, 1999], p. 163).

[4] Mark Noll, *The Scandal of the Evangelical Mind* (Grand Rapids, Mich.: W. B. Eerdmans, 1994), p. 119.

[5] Hal Lindsey, with C. C. Carlson, *The Late Great Planet Earth* (New York: Bantam Books, 1970), p. 7.

[6] LaHaye and Jenkins, *Are We Living in the End Times?*, p. xi.

ancient practices and customs sheds invaluable light on the meaning of scriptural texts. Scripture itself warns of the difficulties of interpreting many passages without reliable guidance. Peter tells his first-century readers that many false teachers will misinterpret Scripture (in this case, the writings of Paul), for there are "some things in them hard to understand, which the ignorant and unstable twist to their own destruction, as they do the other scriptures" (2 Pet 3:16). Although dispensationalists in the pew claim that they believe in the pretribulational Rapture or a future, earthly millennial reign "because it's in the Bible", their acceptance of those teachings is based upon the books, study Bibles, tape series, and sermons that they have read and heard. Undoubtedly they have heard and read many times that they must "interpret the Bible literally" in order to "understand its plain meaning".

"I Believe It's True Because It's Literally True!"

Reformed Protestant scholar C. Norman Kraus observes, "If there is any one word which can be used to describe the dispensationalist's approach to the Bible, it is the word literalism. The term is not only used as a criticism by those opposing the movement, but is accepted as a virtue by those within the movement." [7] Ryrie provides a working definition of dispensationalist Scripture interpretation in *Dispensationalism Today*. Written nearly forty years ago, Ryrie's explanation is still accepted today by popular dispensationalists such as Lindsey and LaHaye. "Dispensationalists claim that their principle of hermeneutics is that of literal interpretation", Ryrie states. He continues:

[7] C. Norman Kraus, *Dispensationalism in America.: Its Rise and Development* (Richmond, Va.: John Knox Press, 1958), p. 131.

This means interpretation which gives to every word the same meaning it would have in normal usage, whether employed in writing, speaking, or thinking. This is sometimes called the principle of grammatical-historical interpretation since the meaning of each word is determined by grammatical and historical considerations. The principle might also be called normal interpretation since the literal meaning of words is the normal approach to their understanding of all languages. It might also be designated plain interpretation so that no one receives the mistaken notion that the literal principle rules out figures of speech.[8]

This appears, on the surface, to be logical and acceptable to a wide range of Christians, including Catholics. Ryrie acknowledges this fact, admitting "literal interpretation is not the exclusive property of dispensationalists. Most conservatives would agree with what has just been said." In light of this admission, what makes the dispensationalist approach to "literal" interpretation unique? In response, Ryrie makes a bold claim:

What, then, is the difference between the dispensationalists' use of this hermeneutical principle and nondispensationalists'? The difference lies the dispensationalist's claims to use the normal principle of interpretation *consistently* in *all* his study of the Bible. He further claims that the nondispensationalist does not use the principle everywhere. He admits that the nondispensationalist is a literalist in much of his interpretation of the Scriptures but charges him with allegorizing or spiritualizing when it comes to the interpretation of prophecy. The dispensationalist claims to be consistent in his use of this principle, and he accuses the nondispensationalist of being inconsistent in his use of it.[9]

---

[8] Charles C. Ryrie, *Dispensationalism* (Chicago: Moody Press, 1995), p. 80.
[9] Ibid., p. 82; emphasis in original.

Put simply, dispensationalists claim that they alone interpret Scripture correctly. This is, they insist, based on a simple, common-sense approach to reading the Bible that results, coincidentally, in the reader accepting premillennial dispensationalist beliefs. Anything else would be contrary to both Scripture and sound hermeneutics, as LaHaye asserts in explaining the so-called "golden rule of interpretation":

> When the plain sense of Scripture makes common sense, seek no other sense, but take every word at its primary, literal meaning unless the facts of the immediate context clearly indicate otherwise. Anyone who follows the golden rule of interpretation will become a pre-Millennialist. As a test of the validity of this golden rule, apply it to the readings of Revelation chapters 19 and 20 and draw your own conclusion.[10]

At this point LaHaye quotes Revelation 19:11–16 and 19:19–20:6. Then, without any commentary and without applying his previous comments to the passages quoted, he continues: "The plain sense of these Scriptures equals pre-Millennialism. The study of prophetic passages is not difficult when we take the Bible literally whenever possible."[11] LaHaye's point, apparently, is that the "plain sense" of the passage reveals a future, literal one-thousand-year reign of Christ (Rev 20:4).

However, such an interpretation raises difficult questions. For instance, will Christ actually ride a horse down from heaven? Will his robe really be bloody? Will an actual "sharp sword" come out from his mouth? Will the angel with the

---

[10] Tim LaHaye, *Rapture under Attack* (Sisters, Ore.: Multnomah Publishers, 1998), p. 228. Of course, LaHaye does not provide a biblical source for his golden rule (it actually comes from Dr. David L. Cooper, LaHaye's mentor), or say why his readers should accept it—all of which is clearly at direct odds with his belief in *sola scriptura*.

[11] Ibid., p. 229.

key to the bottomless pit use a real chain in binding Satan? Is it *consistent* to interpret some parts of this passage "literally" and other parts otherwise? Since it appears that the passage is using symbolic language, is it correct to assume that the "plain sense" of the passage reveals a literal one-thousand-year period? Or could it be that the author of the book of Revelation consistently uses a *figurative method* of communicating *literal truths* that LaHaye inconsistently interprets both literally and non-literally? While LaHaye's explanation might initially seem convincing, a closer examination reveals that it is inconsistent and based upon faulty premises and that it results in flawed application.

In Need of Some Correct Definitions

Dispensationalists are frequently confusing in their discussions of other methods of interpretation. A revealing example is given by Reformed theologian and amillennialist William Cox in his book *Amillennialism Today*,[12] a refutation of dispensationalism. Cox, who describes himself as a former follower of "Scofieldism",[13] is particularly concerned that dispensationalists mischaracterize the amillennial approach to interpreting Scripture. He writes that "blanket statements by ardent premillenarians lead many unwary readers to believe that (1) all Scripture is spiritualized by the amillenarian,

---

[12] William E. Cox, *Amillennialism Today* (Phillipsburg, N.J.: P and R Publishing, 1966). Although Cox is quite antagonistic toward the Catholic Church, his books provide solid critiques of dispensationalism and are all the more valuable because Cox was once a dispensationalist himself.

[13] William E. Cox, *Why I Left Scofieldism* (Phillipsburg, N.J.: P and R Publishing, 1978).

while (2) all Scripture is interpreted literally by premillenarians." [14] He refers to John Walvoord's book *The Millennial Kingdom*, in which Walvoord claims that "Premillenarians follow the so-called 'grammatical-historical' literal interpretation while amillenarians use a spiritualizing method." [15] Cox points out that just three pages later Walvoord states, "The amillennial method of interpreting Scripture is correctly defined as the spiritualizing method. It is clear, however, that conservative amillennialists limit the use of this method, and in fact adopt the literal method of interpreting most of the Scriptures." [16] So, within the space of a few pages, Walvoord labels the amillennial method as "spiritualizing", but then admits that amillennialists use "the literal method" when interpreting "most of the Scriptures". As Cox asks in exasperation: "What statement does he really mean to stand by?" [17]

A bit later, Cox observes, Walvoord admits that amillenarians "reject the figurative method of interpreting the Bible as a general method" but insists they use the "figurative method ... extensively not only in the interpretation of prophecy but in other areas of theology as well". [18] Yet in another place Walvoord states, "Amillenarians use two methods of interpretation, the spiritualizing method for prophecy and the literal method for other Scriptures." [19] How can all of these different claims be reconciled? They cannot, as Cox writes in summary:

[14] Cox, *Amillennialism Today*, pp. 14–15.

[15] John F. Walvoord, *The Millennial Kingdom* (Grand Rapids, Mich.: Zondervan Publishing House, 1959), p. 59.

[16] Ibid., p. 62.

[17] Cox, *Amillennialism Today*, p. 15.

[18] Walvoord, *Millennial Kingdom*, p. 15.

[19] Ibid., p. 63.

These contradictory and inflammatory statements by Walvoord lead us to one of two conclusions: either his blind spot keeps him from seeing the true method of interpretation used by amillenarians, or he deliberately sets out to poison his readers' minds by using half-truths.[20]

Similar problems exist in the works of popularizers such as Lindsey and LaHaye. These authors are often quick to label as "liberal" and contrary to the true Word of God any method of biblical interpretation not aligned with theirs. LaHaye, for example, calls into question the humility of postmillennialists and amillennialists:

> Attacks by post-Millennialists are ineffective, and those by amillennialists are all but ignored. Anyone who is obliged to elevate his system of theology over the Word of God in order to "clarify" what God is saying cannot be a match for the humble servant of Christ who receives the Bible as the inerrant Word of God and interprets it literally. To most Bible students, accepting the Bible literally wherever possible is natural, which explains why the other theories are so unpopular; consequently, their attacks are usually ignored, for their real confusion relates to Scripture or interpretation, not to eschatology.[21]

It appears LaHaye equates himself with the "humble servant of Christ" while insinuating that those who disagree with him—even those who are conservative Evangelicals—do not believe the Bible is the inspired Word of God. This attitude is prevalent among grass-roots dispensationalists. I recall as a young boy asking my mother why she believed Lutherans and Catholics were not really Christians. "Because they have

---

[20] Cox, *Amillennialism Today*, p. 16.
[21] LaHaye, *Rapture under Attack*, p. 172.

the Bible, but do not believe in it", she told me. This was, she also said, most obvious in how Lutherans and Catholics avoid the book of Revelation. "They simply don't believe that it's true", she said, faithfully following the dispensationalist view she had heard taught from the pulpit. As far as she and millions of other American Fundamentalists are concerned, their "literal" interpretation of Scripture is the one and only way of truthfully "dividing the Word of God". But what are the actual origins of this approach to understanding the Bible?

The Historical Basis for Dispensationalist Literalism

In *Fundamentalism and American Culture*, his study of the roots of Fundamentalism, Evangelical historian George Marsden explains that early dispensationalists formed their methods of interpreting while combating the Enlightenment-era liberalism that questioned the historicity and accuracy of the Bible.

> Dispensationalists were responding to some of the very same problems in Biblical interpretation that were troubling theological liberals in the nineteenth century. If Biblical statements were taken at face value and subjected to scientific analysis, major anomalies seemed to appear. Among these were that many Old Testament prophecies did not seem to refer precisely to the church, that Jesus and his disciples seemed to expect his return and establishment of the kingdom very shortly, and that much of the teaching of Jesus seemed to conflict with the theology of Paul. Liberals resolved such problems by greatly broadening the standards for interpreting Biblical language. Dispensationalists did the opposite. They held more strictly than ever to a literal interpretation but introduced a new historical scheme whose key was the

interpretation of the church age as a parenthesis. Once the key step was accepted, the rest of Scripture could be fit into the scheme, and aspects that others viewed as inconsistencies could be explained as simply referring to different dispensations.[22]

Just like their twentieth-century heirs, nineteenth-century dispensationalists had the commendable goal of defending and explaining the Bible. But they went about it incorrectly. Their flawed approach included an ignorance of—or a complete disregard for—Church history, a disdain for "organized" or "institutional" Christianity,[23] and an uncritical, even naïve, acceptance and use of nineteenth-century scientific methods.

All of these mistakes—especially the latter—are contained in the remarks of Arthur T. Pierson, a dispensationalist leader who, at a prophecy conference in 1895, stated, "I like Biblical theology that does not start with the superficial Aristotelian method of reason, that does not begin with an hypothesis,

---

[22] George M. Marsden, *Fundamentalism and American Culture: The Shaping of Twentieth Century Evangelicalism, 1870–1925* (New York: Oxford University Press, 1980), p. 54. Clarence Bass notes: "The growth of dispensationalism paralleled the rise of a rationalistic attack upon the authority of the Bible. One great impetus to its growth has been an invariable insistence that the Bible must be taken literally as the Word of God and that its meaning must not be 'spiritualized.' To this day, in the minds of many, a non-literal interpretation is synonymous with liberalizing tendencies which are equated with denying the validity of the Word" (Clarence B. Bass, *Backgrounds to Dispensationalism: Its Historical Genesis and Ecclesiastical Implications* [Grand Rapids, Mich.: Baker Book House, 1977], p. 21).

[23] Noll, *Scandal of the Evangelical Mind*, p. 122. Noll also writes: "In the United States, the doctrine of biblical inerrancy, which was such a critical presupposition for the dispensationalist effort to interpret Scripture literally, received much more learned defense than in Britain. Finally, the dispensational attack on the institutional church was an argument more likely to find a favorable audience in the United States" (p. 122).

and then warp the facts and the philosophy to fit the crook of our dogma, but a Baconian system, which first gathers the teachings of the word of God, and then seeks to deduce some general law upon which the facts can be arranged." [24] Reliance upon the methods of Francis Bacon, the "early seventeenth-century champion of the objective empirical method", [25] was widespread in the formative years of the dispensationalist movement and can still be seen today. The emphasis placed by dispensationalists on "inductive Bible studies" reflects Bacon's own reliance upon an inductive method of scientific methodology, [26] and the rigorous arranging, classifying, and categorizing of biblical phrases and words parallel Bacon's own use of such methods in making "scientific" inquiry: "With the Scriptures at hand as a compendium of facts, there was no need to go further. [Dispensationalists] needed only to classify the facts, and follow wherever they might lead." [27] "Classifying" and "systematizing" are apt descriptions of the dispensationalist approach to Scripture, as this statement by Chafer, the movement's leading systematizer, demonstrates: "[Dispensationalism] has changed the Bible from being a mass of more or less conflicting writings into a classified and easily assimilated revelation of both the earthly and heavenly purposes of God, which purposes reach on into eternity to come." [28]

[24] Quoted in Marsden, *Fundamentalism and American Culture*, p. 55.

[25] Ibid.

[26] "Bacon's methodology also proposed, within an overall framework for the classification of the sciences, a distinctively inductive structure for the study of nature" (Ted Honderich, ed., *The Oxford Companion to Philosophy* [New York: Oxford University Press, 1995], p. 75).

[27] Marsden, *Fundamentalism and American Culture*, p. 56.

[28] L. S. Chafer, "Dispensationalism", *Bibliotheca Sacra*, 93 (October 1936): 446–47.

Noll laments that the embrace of a flawed and limited methodology by dispensationalists introduced serious errors into American Evangelicalism in the late 1800s and early 1900s. He observes that the damage to biblical study was severe and led to an attitude of arrogance and separatism:

> Especially dispensationalism was heavily dependant upon nineteenth-century views of the goals and systematizing purposes of science.... Fundamentalist naiveté concerning science was matched by several other nineteenth-century traits that also undercut the possibility for a responsible intellectual life. These included a weakness for treating the verses of the Bible as pieces in a jigsaw puzzle that needed only to be sorted and then fit together to possess a finished picture of divine truth ... and a self-confidence, bordering on hubris, manifested by an extreme antitraditionalism that casually discounted the possibility of wisdom from earlier generations.[29]

This reference to "the verses of the Bible as pieces in a jigsaw puzzle" brings to mind the writings of today's popular dispensationalist authors. Hal Lindsey often writes about the "prophetic puzzle", stating that "the prophecies [of Scripture] can be pieced together to make a coherent picture, even though the pieces are scattered in small bits throughout the New and Old Testaments."[30] This ill-fated approach,

---

[29] Noll, *Scandal of the Evangelical Mind*, pp. 126–27. Noll also observes that "Fundamentalism—especially as articulated in dispensationalism, the most self-conscious theological system supporting the movement—was important for encouraging several kinds of simple anti-intellectualism, for reinforcing some of the questionable features of the nineteenth-century American evangelical synthesis, and for promoting right conclusions with the wrong kind of thought. The result was a tendency toward a docetism in outlook and a gnosticism in method that together constitute the central intellectual indictment against the fundamentalist past" (pp. 122–23).

[30] Lindsey and Carlson, *Late Great Planet Earth*, p. 33.

Noll notes, has been at the heart of dispensationalist hermeneutics for the entire history of the movement: "The influential popular leaders of dispensationalism, from the time of Cyrus Scofield through the era of Charles Ryrie, spoke with one voice in defending the scientific, objective character of theology and making that defense entirely in the terms of the nineteenth century."[31] But the average dispensationalist today has little or no knowledge of this background and is not concerned about the roots of and first principles of his beliefs—he is more interested in unraveling the mysteries of biblical prophecy, matching Scripture to current events, and seeing the future as the Bible supposedly outlines it.

Defining and Clarifying Key Terms

Dispensationalists claim to interpret the Bible "literally" while avoiding a "spiritual" reading of Scripture. What do they mean by the terms "literal" and "spiritual" in the context of interpreting Scripture? Ryrie admits that the "literal" approach does not exclude "figures of speech"[32] and states the strength of the dispensationalist approach is that it is "consistent".[33] He refers to the "normal usage" of words, or the "normal approach to [the] understanding of all languages", but does not explain what "normal" might mean. How does he define "normal"? Or "spiritual"? These words have a wide range of meaning depending upon one's perspective and the context in which they are used. The terms "literal" and "spiritual" are commonly used by the Catholic Church to describe her method of interpreting Scripture: "According to

---

[31] Noll, *Scandal of the Evangelical Mind*, p. 127.
[32] Ryrie, *Dispensationalism*, pp. 80–81.
[33] Ibid., p. 82.

an ancient tradition, one can distinguish between two *senses* of Scripture: the literal and the spiritual."[34]

Words such as "literal", "spiritual", and "allegorical" can be easily misunderstood and misrepresented because they mean different things to different people.[35] Some people (including many Fundamentalists) have the idea that "spiritual" equals "symbolic", and that "symbolic", in turn, means "nonliteral"—or even nonexistent in some way. Dispensationalists are antagonistic toward a "spiritual" interpretation of text because they believe it is simply a way of removing meaning from a biblical passage, turning it into a poetic, but mostly empty, expression. An example of this can be found in Lindsey's rant against Augustine, a Church Father often maligned by dispensationalists as the popularizer of false "spiritual" interpretations of Scripture:

---

[34] CCC 115.

[35] In writing about the terms "literal", "allegorical", and "spiritual", Dom Celestin Charlier states: "These terms can be very misleading unless we are clear what we mean by them. There is difficulty over the word 'spiritual' because it is nowadays applied to different things. It is used not only for the 'typical' sense properly so called, but also for a host of subjective pious interpretations. On the whole it generally has a 'pious' connotation. A sense is called 'spiritual' if it nourishes spiritual life. It is distinguished from the aridity that is expected of scientific exegesis. The word has taken on a modern flavour, and now denotes the subjective affective life of the spirit, with special reference to religion. It is almost the opposite of 'intellectual'. To say that this word has the authority of the Fathers to support it can only lead to confusion. 'Spiritual' with them does not mean the world of the spirit or of 'religious feeling' as opposed to the world of matter or of reason without religion. To denote the spiritual world they used the term 'psychic'. By 'spiritual' they understood what the Bible understands, namely divine and objectively transcendent. It's opposite is 'carnal', that which is merely human. It signifies the plane of reality and fullness upon which God moves, the world of 'Spirit and Truth', as distinct from the earthly world of phenomena and sensible symbols" (Dom Celestin Charlier, *The Christian Approach to the Bible* [Westminster, Md.: Newman Press, 1965], pp. 255–56).

The influential early Christian leader, Augustine (A.D. 354–430) dealt the doctrine of prophecy the most damaging blow of anyone in history. He plunged the study of prophecy into darkness for almost 1,400 years by systematically teaching that prophecy could not be interpreted literally. Augustine taught that the Church had taken Israel's place, and had been given the promises and covenants which (in this view) Israel had forfeited by rejecting Christ. He taught that the Church is the kingdom of God in an allegorical sense, and that there would be no literal future 1,000 year earthly kingdom over which Christ would reign. (Amillennialism began here).[36]

However, as we have seen, Augustine did not teach that the Church is the Kingdom of God "in an allegorical sense", but in a very literal way: the Church really and actually is the Kingdom of God. Another example of dispensational distortion comes from Grant Jeffrey's *Apocalypse*, a guide to the book of Revelation:

> [Augustine] wrote his pivotal book *The City of God* in the beginning of the fifth century which rejected the literal interpretation of Scripture and the premillennial return of Christ. He proposed an allegorical method of interpretation to escape the clear teaching of premillennialism. This allegorical method refuses to interpret the words of Scripture in the common-sense, literal manner we apply to normal language and writing. The allegorical method interprets the words of Scripture in any manner the interpreter desires. There are no rules.[37]

---

[36] Hal Lindsey, *The Rapture* (New York: Bantam Books, 1983), pp. 199–200.

[37] Grant R. Jeffrey, *Apocalypse: The Coming Judgment of the Nations* (New York: Bantam Books, 1992), pp. 17–18. LaHaye quotes John Walvoord to similar effect: "Nevertheless, in the fourth and fifth centuries, with Augustine, a consolidation was achieved by separating eschatology from other areas of systematic theology. Two principles of interpretation were adopted by Augustine—

It is odd to see the book of Revelation described as consisting of "normal language and writing" when everyone, including dispensationalists, admits that it is a strange and difficult book. But overt simplification and sensationalism are the standard for "prophecy experts" such as Lindsey and Jeffrey. They are rarely hindered or humbled by the difficulties and complexities of the book of Revelation or any other passage of Scripture. Their work is a testament to G. K. Chesterton's observation: "The simplification of anything is always sensational." [38]

A crucial dispensationalist premise is that a literal interpretation of Scripture *must* result in a literal fulfillment. LaRondelle writes that there is "a secret assumption implied [in 'literal interpretation'] which has an axiomatic and fundamental value for the dispensationalist: that literal exegesis of an Old Testament prophecy 'demands' an identical or absolutely literal fulfillment". [39] He cites the dispensationalist belief that a literal fulfillment of the Davidic covenant means that "Christ must reign on David's throne on earth over David's people forever." [40] But there is a key difference between the original meaning of a text and how that text is actually fulfilled and applied: "This distinction between exegesis and application is crucial, because they are not necessarily identical." [41] An example can be found in Matthew 2:14–15 and the flight of the Holy Family to Egypt:

---

a literal, historical and grammatical interpretation of noneschatological passages, and a nonliteral or figurative interpretation of prophetic Scriptures" (LaHaye, *Rapture under Attack*, p. 198).

[38] G. K. Chesterton, *Varied Types* (New York: Dodd, Mead, 1908), p. 126, quoted in *The Quotable Chesterton* (San Francisco: Ignatius Press, 1986), p. 325.

[39] Hans K. LaRondelle, *The Israel of God in Prophecy: Principles of Prophetic Interpretation* (Berrien Springs, Mich.: Andrews University Press, 1983), p. 23.

[40] J. D. Pentecost, quoted in ibid., p. 23.

[41] Ibid., p. 24.

> And he rose and took the child and his mother by night, and
> departed to Egypt, and remained there until the death of
> Herod. This was to fulfil what the Lord had spoken by the
> prophet, "Out of Egypt have I called my son."

The original, literal meaning of the Old Testament text, taken
from Hosea 11:1, refers to God calling the nation of Israel—
his "son" and "first-born" (Ex 4:22)—out of Egypt in the
Exodus. When interpreted in the light of the Incarnation,
this passage takes on a meaning not considered by the prophet
Hosea. So is this prophecy fulfilled "literally" by Jesus Christ?
According to dispensationalist criteria it is not, and yet Matthew interprets Hosea this way (see Mt 2:15), and Christians
believe this prophecy was truly and actually fulfilled. The
problem is that dispensationalists tend to interpret Old Testament prophecy in the light of the Old Covenant, not in
the light of the New Covenant and Jesus Christ.

Do Dispensationalists Consistently Interpret Scripture Literally?

Although dispensationalists claim that their approach to exegesis is consistent, there are significant disagreements among
dispensationalists about specific passages and interpretations
of Scripture. Many dispensationalists in the pew will, on one
hand, personalize each passage they read, but then claim that
certain passages are for the Jews only, others for those who
will inhabit the future earthly Kingdom, and even others for
Christians currently living in the Church age.

The Sermon on the Mount is a case in point. Many dispensationalists apply the Sermon on the Mount to their lives
but admit that it is a set of principles meant for the future
Jewish millennial reign. More "hard-line" dispensationalists

will "carefully separate the parts of the Bible that address the different dispensations" and make *no* application to their own Christian walk.[42] For these dispensationalists the Gospels have little concrete application to their lives, a stance that is contrary to the central place of the Gospels in Catholic doctrine, liturgy, and spirituality.[43]

Popular dispensationalists still rely (even if in a secondhand fashion) upon many of Scofield's interpretations as found in his *Reference Bible* and other writings. Scofield taught that every time the word "Israel" is found in either the Old or New Testaments, it refers to the "literal", earthly Israel:

> [In prophetic Scriptures] we reach the ground of *absolute literalness*. Figures are often found in the prophecies, but the figure invariably has a literal fulfillment. Not one instance exists of a "spiritual" or figurative fulfillment of prophecy.... Jerusalem is always Jerusalem, Israel is always Israel, Zion always Zion.... Prophecies may never be spiritualized, but are always literal.[44]

Of this claim Reformed theologian Vern Poythress observes: "Scofield is not a pure literalist, but a literalist with respect

---

[42] Vern S. Poythress, *Understanding Dispensationalists* (Phillipsburg, N.J.: P and R Publishing, 1994), p. 31. Poythress describes the first group as "applicatory" dispensationalists and the latter group as "hardline" dispensationalists. Scofield's notes on the Sermon on the Mount read: "The Sermon on the Mount has a twofold application: (1) Literally to the kingdom. In this sense it gives the divine constitution for the righteous government of the earth.... The Sermon on the Mount in its primary application gives neither the privilege nor the duty of the Church. These are found in the Epistles.... (2) But there is a beautiful moral application to the Christian" (C. I. Scofield, *The Scofield Reference Bible* [New York: Oxford University Press, 1945], p. 1000).

[43] See CCC 139; also see CCC 127.

[44] From Scofield's *Correspondence Bible School* courses. Quoted in Poythress, *Understanding Dispensationalists*, p. 24.

to what pertains to Israel. The dualism of Israel and the church is, in fact, the deeper dualism determining when and where the hermeneutical dualism of 'literal' and 'spiritual' is applied."[45] Scofield does not approach the text with only a method of interpretation, but with a theology already in place, based on the conviction that Old Testament Israel and the Church are radically separate realities.

Whenever faced with a New Testament passage that indicates that the Church is the New Israel, Scofield resorts to making a "distinction" between the "physical/earthly" and "spiritual/heavenly" subjects of the passage in question. He does this in his notes on Genesis 15, claiming that the Abrahamic covenant is "Fulfilled in a threefold way: (a) natural posterity ... the Hebrew people. (b) In a spiritual posterity ... all men of faith, whether Jew or Gentile. (c) Fulfilled through Ishmael."[46] This artificial distinction is used throughout Scofield's *Reference Bible*; an example of this can be seen in the notes to Romans 9:6–8, where Paul writes:

> But it is not as though the word of God had failed. For not all who are descended from Israel belong to Israel, and not all are children of Abraham because they are his descendants; but "Through Isaac shall your descendants be named." This means that it is not the children of the flesh who are the children of God, but the children of the promise are reckoned as descendants.

Scofield's note states: "The distinction is between Israel after the flesh, the mere natural posterity of Abraham, and the Israelites who, through faith, are also Abraham's spiritual children."[47] But this ignores Paul's explanation that there is

---

[45] Poythress, *Understanding Dispensationalists*, p. 24.
[46] *Scofield Reference Bible*, p. 25.
[47] Ibid., p. 1202.

only one, true Israel, a point also made earlier in his epistle: "For he is not a real Jew who is one outwardly, nor is true circumcision something external and physical. He is a Jew who is one inwardly, and real circumcision is a matter of the heart, spiritual and not literal. His praise is not from men but from God" (Rom 2:28–29). Walvoord takes up Scofield's "threefold way" of interpreting the Abrahamic in commenting on Galatians 3:29, where Paul tells the Christians at Galatia, "And if you are Christ's, then you are Abraham's offspring, heirs according to promise." Walvoord teaches that the Christians addressed are "Abraham's seed in the spiritual sense only",[48] a claim that seriously begs the question of who is "spiritualizing" Scripture and who is interpreting it "literally".

As for Galatians 6:16, where Paul refers to the Church as the "Israel of God", Scofield is completely silent. Walvoord attempts to reinterpret the verse by dividing it into two sections, the first—those who will "walk by this rule"—being Gentile Christians, while the second—"the Israel of God"—are Jewish Christians. This, Walvoord states, is "another indication that Gentile and Jewish believers are on the same level, as *and* is used principally to link co-ordinate parts of a sentence".[49] However, the phrase "those who walk by this rule" would already include Jewish Christians, meaning that the phrase "Israel of God" necessarily "is a further description of ... all true believers, including both Jews and Gentiles, who constitute the New Testament church. Here, in other words, Paul clearly identifies the church as the true Israel." [50]

[48] Walvoord, *Millennial Kingdom*, p. 146.

[49] Ibid., p. 170.

[50] Anthony A. Hoekema, *The Bible and the Future* (Grand Rapids, Mich.: W. B. Eerdmans, 1979), p. 197.

Another Scofieldian distinction is found in his notes for Acts 2 and Peter's sermon at Pentecost. Instead of admitting that Peter's reference to the "last days" (Acts 2:17) means that Joel's prophecy was being fulfilled on Pentecost by the outpouring of the Holy Spirit in the Upper Room, Scofield claims that Peter is pointing to *two* different "last days"—one for Israel and one for the Church:

> A distinction must be observed between "the last days" when the prediction relates to Israel, and the "last days" when the prediction relates to the church.... The "last days" as related to the church began with the advent of Christ (Heb1:2), but have especial reference to the time of declension and apostasy at the end of this age (2 Tim. 3:1; 4:4). The "last days" as related to Israel are the days of Israel's exaltation and blessing, and are synonymous with the kingdom-age (Isa. 2:24; Mic. 4:1–7). They are "last" not with reference to this dispensation, but with reference to the whole of Israel's history.[51]

This forced interpretation is made necessary because the clear literal meaning of Peter's sermon is that the prophet Joel's words have been fulfilled in reference to the Church alone, rendering Scofield's absolute rule of interpretation invalid. So he creates an artificial, unwarranted distinction and forces it on the passage in an attempt to maintain cohesiveness in his hermeneutical system.

A glaring double standard is also found in the common dispensationalist interpretation of Ezekiel 40–48. Most dis-

---

[51] *Scofield Reference Bible*, p. 1151. Of this dispensational distinction, Poythress writes: "Scofield's general principle of 'absolute literalism' with respect to prophetic interpretation would seem to lead us to say that Joel is referring to Israel and not the church. But since Peter is using the passage with reference to the church, Scofield has to make room for it. He does so by splitting the meaning in two" (Poythress, *Understanding Dispensationalists*, p. 27).

pensationalist authors agree that these chapters describe the renewal of animal sacrifices in the Jerusalem Temple during the future millennial reign of Christ.[52] In his commentary *Revelation Unveiled*, LaHaye writes that the prophet Ezekiel

> goes into great detail regarding the matter of worshipping in the Temple, even pointing out that the sacrificial systems will be reestablished. These sacrifices during the millennial Kingdom will be to the nation of Israel what the Lord's Supper is to the Church today: a reminder of what they have been saved from. No meritorious or efficacious work will be accomplished through these sacrifices. Instead, they will remind Israel repeatedly of their crucified Messiah.[53]

Obviously this is at odds with Catholic teaching and Scripture in what it implies about Christ's sacrifice and the Eucharist. This belief in reestablished Temple sacrifices, in fact, is a return to the "shadow" of the Law (Heb 10:1) and a step backward into a system that cannot remove sins (Heb 10:4), all at the expense of Christ's redeeming work. The epistle to the Hebrews states that Christ "abolishes the first in order to establish the second" (Heb 10:9); his perfect offering abolished the entire Old Testament sacrificial system, a system that foreshadowed his perfect sacrifice on the Cross (Heb 9). LaHaye hastens to point out that these Temple sacrifices will

---

[52] "[T]he only [view] which provides any intelligent explanation of this portion of Scripture is that which assigns Ezekiel's temple to the future millennial period. Inasmuch as no fulfillment of this passage has ever taken place in history, if a literal interpretation of prophecy be followed, it would be most reasonable to assume that a future temple would be built in the millennium as the center of worship" (Walvoord, *Millennial Kingdom*, p. 310).

[53] Tim LaHaye, *Revelation Unveiled* (Grand Rapids, Mich.: Zondervan Publishing House, 1999), p. 341.

have no value—they will be mere symbolic "reminders" of Christ's work, just as the Lord's Supper is a simple reminder of the Christian's salvation.[54] Ironically, it is a common Fundamentalist claim that the Mass violates Hebrews 10:12, which states Christ "offered for all time a single sacrifice for sins", not a continually repeated sacrifice. This is based, of course, on a faulty understanding of the Mass and the eucharistic sacrifice. But it is also very strange in light of the belief that an entire sacrificial system once replaced by Christ will be brought back in the future and used to celebrate that which it foreshadowed.

LaHaye's interpretation of Ezekiel 40–48 is selective and inconsistent in nature. First, his *literal* interpretation of the passage is that the physical Temple will be rebuilt and that actual sacrifices will be offered in it—but he insists these offerings are merely *reminders* of Christ's death. Yet no actual reference to "reminders" occurs in Ezekiel 40–48; on the contrary, the passage refers repeatedly to "sin offerings", "burnt offerings", and "peace offerings", all sacrificed in order to restore a right relationship with God. LaHaye never mentions this aspect of Ezekiel's vision, perhaps because it

---

[54] However, some dispensationalists do think that the animal sacrifices will be more than merely commemorative in nature. Dr. Joe Jordan, director of Word of Life Fellowship, writes: "We also observe that the millennial sacrifices will be more than a memorial. In a theocracy (where the government law is God's law—such as Israel had under the Mosaic law), the breaking of the theocratic law brings temporal judgement (Zechariah 14:16–19)—no rain, famine, illness, or disease. In order to escape the temporal judgement, an animal sacrifice is offered to atone for the breaking of the theocratic law. This will be the case during the millennium where the whole world will be under a theocracy" (Joe Jordan, "The Marvelous Millennium", in Charles C. Ryrie, Joe Jordan, and Tom Davis, eds., *Countdown to Armageddon: The Final Battle and Beyond* [Eugene, Ore.: Harvest House Publishers, 1999], p. 233).

cannot be reconciled with his portrayal of millennial Temple worship.[55]

Interpretation-saving distinctions are also introduced by Walvoord in handling Hebrews 8. There Paul writes that Christ "has obtained a ministry which is as much more excellent than the old as the covenant he mediates is better, since it is enacted on better promises" (Heb 8:6). This better covenant is the New Covenant, introduced and established by Christ. This covenant obviously refers to the Church since it is already in place, as seen in the statement: "This makes Jesus the surety of a better covenant" (Heb 7:22). The author of Hebrews quotes at length from Jeremiah 31:31–40, affirming that the "new covenant with the house of Israel" (Heb 8:8; Jer 31:31) has been fulfilled in the New Covenant with the Church. Since dispensationalists believe that Jeremiah 31 refers to a future covenant yet to be made with Israel and resulting in the millennial Kingdom, how do they interpret this passage? Walvoord's solution is to make *two* new covenants, insisting that since the passage speaks of a "better

---

[55] Walvoord makes an attempt to defend this teaching, based on his claim that "opponents of literal sacrifices [i.e., amillennialists] ... have no real exegesis to offer for the Ezekiel passage and other references to millennial sacrifices" (*Millennial Kingdom*, p. 314). Of course, they do have an explanation—it simply is not "literal" enough for him. Amillennialists—including Catholics—believe that Ezekiel's prophetic vision, given in the language and the context of the prophet's time, is a depiction of the eternal state of those who will enter into the presence of God. John's vision of the New Jerusalem (Rev 21–22) depicts the same reality, based squarely on Ezekiel's vision. Regardless, Walvoord insists that "The millennial sacrifices are no more expiatory than were the Mosaic sacrifices which preceded the cross. If it has been fitting for the church in the present age to have a memorial of the death of Christ in the Lord's Supper, it is suggested that it would be suitable also to have a memorial of possibly a different character in the millennium in keeping with the Jewish characteristics of the period" (*Millennial Kingdom*, p. 312).

covenant" but "does not state here or anywhere else that this better covenant is 'the new covenant with the house of Israel,' or that Israel's new covenant has been introduced", it must refer to a future event and covenant.[56] He reasons that the point of the epistle to the Hebrews is that the Mosaic covenant has ended and that the Old Testament "predicts a new covenant for Israel" so that "the new covenant in force in the present age is not claimed to fulfill the new covenant with Israel at all." [57] But this is circular reasoning based on the presupposition that no Old Testament prophecy can be applied to the Church, therefore meaning that any Old Testament prophecy apparently referring to the Church in the New Testament is really about Israel, while somehow— almost incidentally—asserting "the superiority of the Christians [sic] order as superceding the Mosaic covenant." [58] In other words, the New Covenant with the Church is a second-rate covenant compared to the future first-rate covenant with Old Testament Israel.

Although dispensationalists insist that Christ's Church is of great value, their interpretations indicate that Christ and his Church take a back seat to the future millennial Jewish Kingdom on earth. "Dispensational literalism does not allow that Jesus Christ provided a new perspective for interpreting the Old Covenant." LaRondelle observes, "Dispensationalism is therefore basically oriented to the Old Covenant instead of to the Cross." [59] Such an orientation is historically, logically, and theologically untenable for Christians. Yet it remains a basic premise of dispensationalist interpretations of

---

[56] Ibid., p. 217.
[57] Ibid.
[58] Ibid.
[59] LaRondelle, *Israel of God in Prophecy*, p. 26.

Scripture, found in Bible colleges, Fundamentalists groups, and popular literature.

Hal Lindsey: A Study in Popular Dispensationalist Biblical Interpretation

Calling the Bible "the greatest sourcebook of current events in the world"[60] and the book of Revelation "the 'Grand Central Station' of the whole Bible",[61] Lindsey claims modern-day readers are in the privileged position of seeing the final book of the Bible "literally" fulfilled right before their eyes—if only they will let him interpret it for them. The book of Revelation and its puzzling symbolism are only understandable, Lindsey asserts, when readers recognize that the Apostle was describing modern technology and events that he "was at a loss for words to describe nineteen centuries ago! ... After all, how could God transmit the thought of a nuclear catastrophe to someone living in the year A.D. 90!"[62] The book of Revelation "is written in such a way that its meaning becomes clear with the unfolding of current world events".[63]

For Lindsey, interpreting the book of Revelation begins with the premise that John was "transported nineteen centuries into the future"[64] and then continues by systematically aligning "Bible words and Scripture references" with the "help of a good concordance",[65] a form of the popular

---

[60] Hal Lindsey with C. C. Carlson, *There's a New World Coming* (Santa Ana, Calif.: Vision House Publishers, 1973), p. 15.

[61] Ibid., p. 16.

[62] Ibid.

[63] Ibid., p. 21.

[64] Ibid., p. 23.

[65] Ibid., p. 24.

"inductive Bible study" practiced by many Fundamentalists. The result is that modern-day events and elements appear to emerge from the Scriptures. Yet inconsistencies abound. References in Old Testament prophecies to ancient nations and lands, oddly enough, are not interpreted "literally" but as symbols of modern nations and political alliances. So that his readers are never confused about these identities, Lindsey often provides bracketed notes within the biblical texts. For example, he writes of Daniel 11:40–45:

> This will be the sign that immediately precedes the Russian-led Islamic invasion of Israel.... "At the time of the end the King of the South [the Muslim Confederacy] will engage him [the False Prophet of Israel] in battle, and the King of the North [Russia] will storm out against him with chariots and cavalry and a great fleet of ships. He [the Russian Commander] will invade many countries and sweep through them like a flood. He will also invade the Beautiful Land [Israel]. Many countries will fall, but Edom, Moab and leaders of Ammon [Jordan] will be delivered from his hand." [66]

Not only does this passage—and many like it—violate Lindsey's claim to interpret Scripture "literally", it demonstrates his view of the Bible as a futuristic code book waiting to be cracked so that "true believers" can have an inside track on the world's impending demise.

Lindsey's obsession with Bible prophecy has taken him into strange territory. Because he believes that the main purpose of biblical prophecy is to predict the future, he often compares the Bible to people such as Nostradamus, Jeane Dixon, and fortune-tellers, explaining that

---

[66] Hal Lindsey, *Planet Earth: The Final Chapter* (Palos Verdes, Calif.: Western Front, 1998), pp. 182–83.

compared to the speculation of most that is called prophetic today, the Bible contains clear and unmistakable prophetic signs.... The Bible makes fantastic claims; but these claims are no more startling than those of present day astrologers, prophets and seers. Furthermore, the claims of the Bible have a greater basis in historical evidence and fact.[67]

In his later books Lindsey compares the accuracy of Bible prophecy to the druids of Stonehenge,[68] astrologers, and assorted clairvoyants,[69] and chapter headings have included "Polishing the Crystal Ball"[70] and "John's Chain of ESP".[71] It seems that Lindsey wants to be counted among the biblical prophets, for he boasts that "Today, almost before I finish explaining a developing trend—it's already an accomplished fact."[72] Despite such confident assertions, critics allege a pattern of constant revisions in Lindsey's insights over the years,

[67] Lindsey and Carlson, *Late Great Planet Earth*, p. 7.

[68] The back cover of the 1973 edition of *There's a New World Coming* has a photo of Lindsey and his wife, Jan, at Stonehenge. The text beneath reads: "These giant stone monoliths on the Salisbury Plains, two hours from London, stand as a mute tribute to early man's determination to understand and predict his own future. Through these stones, 4000 years ago, priests could site the sun, moon and stars and eclipses of the sun and moon. Their power to predict became their power to control the people. There have been many, throughout the centuries of man's long history, who have sought to predict the course of human events, but none have had the incredible accuracy of the ancient Hebrew prophets. The story of *their* predictions is what this book is all about!"

[69] These range from ancient astrologers to modern-day foretellers of the future like Edgar Cayce and Jeane Dixon (a Lindsey favorite). See Lindsey and Carlson, *Late Great Planet Earth*, pp. 1–8.

[70] Ibid., p. 169.

[71] Lindsey and Carlson, *There's a New World Coming*, p. 20.

[72] Lindsey and Carlson, *Late Great Planet Earth*, rev. ed., p. 3. Quoted by Stephen Sizer, "Hal Lindsey (b. 1929): The Father of Apocalyptic Christian Zionism". Accessed online at www.virginiawater.co.uk/christchurch/articles/hallindsey.htm.

with major chunks of his books either rewritten or removed, the names of nations changed in light of world events,
and technologies updated to reflect the latest advancements
in science and weaponry. Stephen Sizer notes that Lindsey's

> popularity may also in part, however, have to do with his
> tendency to revise [his] predictions in the light of changing
> world events. So for example *The Final Battle* (1994) is es-
> sentially an unacknowledged rewrite of the *Late Great Planet
> Earth* (1970); *Apocalypse Code* (1997) is a rewrite of *There's a
> New World Coming* (1973); and *Planet Earth 2000 A.D.* (1994)
> ... [is a revision] of *The 1980's: Countdown to Armageddon*
> (1980). *Planet Earth: The Final Chapter* (1998) is the latest
> version in the "Planet Earth" series.[73]

Christ Is the Heart and Center of Scripture

The proper approach to understanding and interpreting Scripture is not based, first and foremost, in a method of hermeneutics but in the reality of the incarnate Son of God. Jesus
Christ, states the *Catechism of the Catholic Church*, is "the
unique Word of Sacred Scripture",[74] and the unity of Scripture is located in this one Word of God.[75] This unity of
Scripture exists because God's plan of salvation is a unified
one at the center of which is the incarnate Word, Jesus
Christ.[76] God, who is triune and is Love, has just one plan

[73] Sizer, "Hal Lindsey".

[74] CCC 101.

[75] See CCC 102. This is, of course, recognized and taught by many Protestants. It has been summarized well by LaRondelle, who states "The key to
the Old Testament is not a rationalistic method or principle, be it literalism or
allegorism, but Christ Jesus, the Son of God, as revealed in the New Testament" (*Israel of God in Prophecy*, p. 19).

[76] See CCC 112.

in history, to give us his own divine and blessed life[77] and to make us "partakers of the divine nature".[78] The Bible is oriented in every way toward this communion of humanity with God, made possible through the person of Jesus Christ, as *Dei Verbum*, states: "In the sacred books, the Father who is in heaven comes lovingly to meet his children, and talks with them." [79] There are not two people of God or two plans of God—just one family formed in the One Redeemer through the one plan of the One Triune God. The centrality of Christ in the Catholic interpretation of Scripture has been explained well by the French scholar Dom Celestin Charlier:

> [Christ] is therefore the *logical* focal point of the Scriptures. At whatever stage they are considered, the various doctrinal themes are all centered on the idea of a divine and freely bestowed salvation, realized by an envoy sent by God. . . . His foreshadowing in the Bible is not therefore merely a subjective one; he is prefigured on the objective plane of reality (whether potential or actual). Only rarely were its writers, the Prophets included, even implicitly aware of Christ. It was not important that they should be. His presence in the Bible transcends the consciousness of men. . . . Christ is the focal point of the Scriptures as the *incarnation of the Word*. . . .

---

[77] See CCC 257.

[78] 2 Pet 1:4. See CCC 460, 1692, 1721, 1996.

[79] *DV* 21. Also: "The Church has always venerated the divine Scriptures just as she venerates the body of the Lord, since, especially in the sacred liturgy, she unceasingly receives and offers to the faithful the bread of life from the table both of God's word and of Christ's body. She has always maintained them, and continues to do so, together with sacred tradition, as the supreme rule of faith, since, as inspired by God and committed once and for all to writing, they impart the word of God Himself without change, and make the voice of the Holy Spirit resound in the words of the prophets and Apostles. Therefore, like the Christian religion itself, all the preaching of the Church must be nourished and regulated by Sacred Scripture" (*DV* 21).

The divine Word must be spoken in sounds that the human ear can hear; the divine Light must shine in a way that the human eye can see. The Bible is the Word of God become audible, Christ is the Word of God become visible. Whether its function is to be heard or to enlighten, God has only one Word, and he speaks it only to give it.[80]

This centrality of Christ does not mean, of course, that the place of proper methods of interpretation is ignored. Having Christ at the heart of all interpretation of Scripture is imperative for a truly Catholic hermeneutical method and is in total harmony with such a method. *Dei Verbum* outlines several essential principles of interpretation necessary in the task of interpreting Scripture:

1. *Authors' Intention:* "God speaks in sacred Scripture through men in human fashion", so the reader of Scripture "should carefully investigate what meaning the sacred writers really intended, and what God wanted to manifest by means of their words".[81]

2. *Cultural and Literary Contexts:* The interpreter of Scripture must "have regard for 'literary forms.'" For truth is proposed and expressed in a variety of ways, depending on whether a text is history of one kind or another, or whether its form is that of prophecy, poetry, or some other type of speech. The interpreter must investigate what meaning the sacred writer intended to express and actually expressed in particular circumstances as he used contemporary literary

---

[80] Charlier, *Christian Approach to the Bible*, pp. 204–5; emphasis in original.
[81] *DV* 12 § 1.

forms in accordance with the situation of his own time and culture."[82]

3. *Light of the Spirit:* "Holy Scripture must be read and interpreted according to the same Spirit by whom it was written."[83]

4. *Unity of Scripture:* "No less serious attention must be given to the context and unity of the whole of Scripture, if the meaning of sacred texts is to be correctly brought to light."[84]

5. *Tradition of the Church:* The reality and authority of the Church must be given a proper place in the interpretation of Scripture. "The living tradition of the whole Church must be taken into account along with the harmony which exists between elements of the faith."[85]

Church Authority and Interpretation of Scripture

No discussion of the Catholic approach to Scripture would be complete without considering the issue of Church authority and its relationship to the task of interpreting Scripture. Dispensationalists believe that the Catholic Church adds false teachings to Scripture (e.g., purgatory, veneration of Mary, the papacy, etc.), makes false claims of authority in interpreting Scripture, and wrongly places tradition alongside Scripture in a position of equality. They insist that "Scripture alone" (*sola scriptura*) is all that is necessary for Christian

---

[82] *DV* 12 § 2.
[83] *DV* 12 § 3.
[84] *DV* 12 § 3.
[85] *DV* 12 § 3. Also see CCC 114.

doctrine and living; anything more is a man-made addition that is either a distraction or a form of apostasy. Scofield states: "The student is earnestly exhorted not to receive a single doctrine upon the authority of this book, but, like the noble Bereans (Acts 17:11), to search the *Scriptures* daily whether these things are so. No appeal is made to human authority."[86] While a detailed analysis of *sola scriptura* cannot be given here,[87] some basic observations can be made.

First, the belief in *sola scriptura* is a product of the Protestant Reformation and did not exist in the early Church; nor was it taught by the early Church Fathers or councils. Secondly, *sola scriptura* cannot be found in Scripture itself, which never states that "Scripture is the church's only rule of faith."[88] The common appeal to 2 Timothy 3:16–17 does not prove the point but merely asserts Catholic teaching: "All scripture is inspired by God and profitable for teaching, for reproof, for correction, and for training in righteousness, that the man of God may be complete, equipped for every good work." No mention is made of Scripture being the *exclusive* means of authority and teaching in the life of the Christian. Rather, final authority comes from Christ, who has given it to the teaching office of the Church, "the household of God ... the pillar and bulwark of the truth" (1 Tim 3:15; see Mt 16:16–19). While *sola scriptura* is appealing, especially in our individualistic culture, it is practically flawed and theologically lacking. In actual practice it results in disunion, as evi-

---

[86] C. I. Scofield, *Rightly Dividing the Word of Truth: Ten Outline Studies of the More Important Divisions of Scripture* (Neptune, N.J.: Loizeaux Brothers, 1896), p. 4; emphasis in original.

[87] For a succinct critique of *sola scriptura*, see Patrick Madrid, "Sola Scriptura: A Blueprint for Anarchy", *Catholic Dossier*, March/April 1996.

[88] James McCarthy, *The Gospel according to Rome* (Eugene, Ore.: Harvest House Publishers, 1995), p. 309.

denced by the thousands of Protestant denominations and sects that have emerged since the Reformation.[89] This disunion, in turn, is contrary to the teaching of Scripture itself, which states that the Body of Christ is one and should be unified (cf. Jn 17:23; Eph 4:1–13).

Ironically, Scofield's reference to the ancient Bereans actually proves the Catholic position. The Catholic Church teaches that Christ gave authority to preach the gospel and govern the Church to the apostles, who in turn passed on that authority to their successors.[90] A careful reading shows that the story of the Bereans validates the Catholic belief:

> The brethren immediately sent Paul and Silas away by night to Beroea; and when they arrived they went into the Jewish synagogue. Now these Jews were more noble than those in Thessalonica, for they received the word with all eagerness, examining the scriptures daily to see if these things were so. Many of them therefore believed, with not a few Greek women of high standing as well as men. (Acts 17:10–12)

Scofield focuses on the Bereans' act of examining Scriptures but misses that they *first* "received the word" from the apostles, Paul and Silas, and *then* compared that preaching with the Old Testament (since the New Testament was not yet in existence). This pattern is still followed by the Catholic Church when she authoritatively interprets Scripture or

---

[89] See Madrid, "Sola Scriptura", in *Catholic Dossier*, March/April 1996. In words that are especially applicable to many dispensationalist teachers and "prophecy experts", Madrid writes: "Scripture alone, as the tragic history of Protestantism has shown, becomes the private play toy of any self-styled 'exegete' who wishes to interpret God's Word to suit his own views. The history of Protestantism, laboring under *sola scriptura*, is an unending kaleidoscope of fragmentation and splintering."

[90] See CCC 1087.

defines doctrine, guided by the Holy Spirit, the soul and protector of the Church.[91] The Church's teaching office, the Magisterium,[92] ultimately has the final say in interpreting Scripture—not due to human ability, but because of the authority and guidance given by Jesus Christ.[93] Rather than a form of control and coercion, this is a safeguard and protection against false teaching and a witness to the truthfulness of Scripture, just as Augustine confessed: "For my part I should not believe the Gospel except as moved by the authority of the Catholic Church."[94]

The Senses of Scripture, Allegory, and Typology

The Catholic Church upholds the ancient practice of reading Scripture according to its various "senses". There are the two main senses of Scripture, the literal and the spiritual, with the latter divided into three senses: allegorical, moral, and anagogical.[95] Understanding the differences between these senses assists the reader in appreciating the depths of Scripture. It also refutes the dispensationalist claim that the Catholic Church "spiritualizes" many texts at the expense of their "literal" meaning. In actuality, Catholic doctrine states that *all* of Scripture possesses a literal sense, it being "the mean-

---

[91] "It is clear, therefore, that sacred tradition, sacred scripture, and the teaching authority of the Church, in accord with God's most wise design, are so linked and joined together that one cannot stand without the others, and that all together and each in its own way under the action of the one Holy Spirit contribute effectively to the salvation of souls" (*DV* 10; see also CCC 95).

[92] See CCC 96–100.

[93] See CCC 119.

[94] Augustine of Hippo, *Against the Epistle of Manicheus Called Fundamental*, 5. Quoted by Jaroslav Pelikan, *The Emergence of the Catholic Tradition (100–600)* (Chicago: University of Chicago Press, 1971), p. 303.

[95] See CCC 115.

ing conveyed by the words of Scripture and discovered by exegesis, following the rules of sound interpretation: 'All other senses of Sacred Scripture are based on the literal' [St. Thomas Aquinas, *STh* I, 1, 10, *ad* 1]." [96] Biblical passages as different in character as the creation account in Genesis, the poetry of the Song of Solomon, and the apocalyptic vision of John all have a literal meaning—and it is the primary sense of those texts. As apologist Mark Shea explains, the kind of writing—history, poetry, psalm, myth, or otherwise—

> will not, however, affect one tiny bit whether the text has a literal meaning because—mark this—*every biblical text has a literal meaning*. Many people are stunned to hear this. That is because many people think a "literal meaning" can only be conveyed by literal language. . . . Indeed, more often than not, metaphor is exactly the right vehicle for conveying a literal meaning and is far better than nonfigurative language. The shortest distance between two minds is a figure of speech.[97]

This fact can be observed in our modern use of language, which uses concrete images metaphorically to express literal truth. When full of joy we say, "I'm walking on air", and

[96] CCC 116.

[97] Shea, *Making Senses out of Scripture*, pp. 166–67. Dominican scholar Aidan Nichols writes: "To grasp the literal sense we have to know whether the author was using imagery or literal (that is, nonmetaphorical) forms of linguistic expression, but the choice of linguistic mode or vehicle does not in itself determine whether a passage has or has not a literal sense. Every passage must have a literal sense, simply by virtue of being written at all. . . . [A]s St. Thomas points out, the literal sense must be the primary sense of Scripture in the sense of being the necessary foundation for any other sense that Scripture may carry. Whether or not the literal sense is always the most important sense, it has to be the foundational sense" (*The Shape of Catholic Theology: An Introduction to Its Sources, Principles, and History* [Collegeville, Minn.: Liturgical Press, 1991], pp. 142–43).

when overly busy we exclaim, "I'm completely buried in paperwork!" Both expressions are literally true—but not in a literalist fashion. Scripture overflows with passages where a concrete image is used metaphorically to convey a literal truth. Sometimes this is obvious, as when Jesus states "I am the true vine" (Jn 15:1) or "I am the door" (Jn 10:9), while other instances are more difficult to judge. Many tools aid the reader in identifying the literal meaning,[98] but one of the most important is an understanding of the historical period—"its culture, its politics, its economics, and ... its patterns of social interaction." [99]

The events described in Scripture can be signs pointing to deeper, spiritual realities.[100] Of the three subdivisions that make up the spiritual sense—the allegorical, the moral, and the anagogical—the one of most concern here is the allegorical sense, of which the Catechism says, "We can acquire a more profound understanding of events by recognizing their significance in Christ; thus the crossing of the Red Sea is a sign or type of Christ's victory and also of Christian Baptism [cf. 1 Cor 10:2]." [101] Here the Catechism brings together two

---

[98] These tools include, Nichols writes, "biblical archeology, textual criticism, comparative literature, source criticism, form criticism, redaction criticism, and tradition-history criticism" (Shape of Catholic Theology, pp. 143–44).

[99] Ibid., p. 144. Nichols emphasizes that the historical background will keep a check on the other tools, which can tend to "degenerate into the manipulation of data, divorced from the living culture embedded in a distinctive society" (p. 144). He also insists that Scripture must be interpreted in light of the canon: "Inspiration is ordered to the production of the canon of Scripture; it is the entire Bible as a self-correcting whole which enables us to identify the inerrant aspect of any one text. The ultimate redactor is the Holy Spirit, who brought together this library of books and enabled the Church to recognize them, in their unity, as divine truth. Here we move on to a sense of Scripture which forms a bridge between literal and spiritual interpretation: the canonical sense" (p. 154).

[100] See CCC 117.

[101] CCC 117.

methods of interpretation—allegorical and typological—
that are distinct from one another, at least as they were often
understood and used by the Church Fathers. Confusion between these terms goes back to the earliest days of the Church
when they were sometimes used interchangeably. Traditionally, patristic scholar J. N. D. Kelly writes, "In allegorical exegesis the sacred text is treated as a mere symbol, or allegory,
of spiritual truths. The literal, historical sense, if it is regarded at all, plays a relatively minor role, and the aim of the
exegete is to elicit the moral, theological or mystical meaning
which each passage ... is presumed to contain." [102] In typological exegesis there was much more respect for the literal
sense of the passage:

> It was a technique for bringing out the correspondence be-
> tween the two Testaments, and took as its guiding principle
> the idea that the events and personages of the Old were
> "types" of, i.e. prefigured and anticipated, the events and
> personages of the New. The typologist took history seri-
> ously; it was the scene of the progressive unfolding of God's
> consistent redemptive purpose.[103]

---

[102] J. N. D. Kelly, *Early Christian Doctrines*, 5th ed. (New York: Harper and
Row, 1978), p. 70.

[103] Ibid., p. 71. Nichols writes: "The practice of typological exegesis implies that there are in Scripture discernible patterns, which we can see once
we stand back and take in the Bible as a whole. Christological typology is an
application of this more general typological idea. That idea presupposes two
things. First, there is a providential connection between the persons and events
of biblical history. Second, God is consistent in his communication with us. If
we accept these two postulates of divine providence and divine consistency,
then we shall find that not only can texts speak of the future, as in prophecy;
events can also speak of the future" (*Shape of Catholic Theology*, pp. 157–58).
Here lies one of the problems with dispensationalism: it does not see God's
communication—especially regarding salvation—as consistent, evidenced by
its belief in a discontinuity in salvation history created by the rejection of Jesus
by the majority of Jews.

Therefore, throughout history God's single plan of salvation can be seen, first in shadows and hints within the Old Testament, and then as a fully realized fact in Christ and his Church.

Typology has always played an important role in demonstrating the unity of the Old and New Testaments.[104] Typology is found throughout the New Testament,[105] used by Jesus and the inspired authors to show that the Old Covenant foreshadowed and prefigured the New Covenant. In Matthew's Gospel Jesus is revealed to be the New David (Mt 1:1; 20:30–31; 21:9), the New Moses (Mt 5–7), the New Jonah (Mt 12:39–41; 16:4), the New Solomon (Mt 12:42), the New Temple (Mt 12:6) and the New Covenant personified (Mt 26:28). Paul uses typology extensively, such as in Romans 5, where he teaches that Jesus Christ is the New Adam: "Yet death reigned from Adam to Moses, even over those whose sins were not like the transgression of Adam, who was a type of the one who was to come" (Rom 5:14). Other instances can be found in 1 Corinthians 10:1–11, where the pillar of smoke ("the cloud") and the Red Sea are types of baptism, and in Galatians 4:22–31, where Hagar is a type of the Old Covenant and Sarah is a type of the New Cov-

---

[104] See CCC 128.

[105] An excellent book demonstrating the use of typology in the New Testament and by the Church Fathers is Jean Daniélou's *The Bible and the Liturgy* (1956; Notre Dame, Ind.: University of Notre Dame Press, 1987). Nichols emphasizes: "When we reach the New Testament, this general typological exegesis becomes specifically Christological. The Christian conviction was that, as the Word incarnate, Jesus Christ, the God-man, constituted the center of history. As the fullest expression of God in human terms, Jesus summed up everything that Israel had known of God.... So in principle the whole of Old Testament revelation could be reapplied in a unique way to Christ himself. The central events and images of the Jewish Scriptures were so many types or foreshadowings of the life, death, and resurrection of Christ" (*Shape of Catholic Theology*, pp. 156–57).

enant. The sacraments were also prefigured in various ways in the Old Testament, as in the manna pointing to the Eucharist (Jn 6) and Noah's passage through water pointing to baptism (1 Pet 3:20–21).[106]

While dispensationalists accept some limited typology from the Old Testament, they reject the notion that the Old Covenant is itself a type pointing to its fulfillment, the New Covenant.[107] This explains their antagonism to the spiritual—especially the typological—reading of the Old Testament, for it demonstrates the continuity between the Old and New Covenants, a continuity that traditional and popular dispensationalism can neither allow nor acknowledge. Chafer, for example, cautiously accepts that "when an account is given of the marriage of any man of the Old Testament who is himself a type of Christ, that marriage may have typical signification",[108] but he still insists that the Church "was wholly unforeseen and is wholly unrelated to any divine purpose

---

[106] See CCC 1094.

[107] Scofield, for example, often notes instances of typology that are not obvious or overt, but then largely ignores the typology set forth clearly in many passages of the New Testament. In his note on Genesis 1:4 he writes that the "greater light" is "a type of Christ", the "Sun of righteousness (Mal. 4:2)". He then states that "A type is a divinely appointed illustration of some truth. . . . Types occur most frequently in the Pentateuch, but are found, more sparingly, elsewhere. The antitype, or fulfillment of the type is found, usually, in the Old Testament" (*Scofield Reference Bible*, p. 4). Yet Scofield makes no remarks about 1 Corinthians 10 and brushes off Galatians 4:19–31 by remarking that the allegory has "no application to a sinner seeking justification" (*Scofield Reference Bible*, p. 1246).

[108] Lewis Sperry Chafer, *Systematic Theology* (Dallas, Tex.: Dallas Seminary Press), 4:137. Quoted by LaRondelle, *Israel of God in Prophecy*, p. 48. Chafer continues: "Moses is a type of Christ as Deliverer; thus Zipporah his wife, chosen from the Gentiles while he was away from his brethren, is a suggestion of the calling out of the Church during the period between the two advents of Christ" (quoted by LaRondelle, *Israel of God in Prophecy*, p. 49). Such a statement is difficult to reconcile with Chafer's insistence that the Church was in no way foreshadowed or hinted at in the Old Testament.

which precedes it or which follows it",[109] despite the New Testament's use of types such as Zion and Jerusalem (Heb 12:22), Israel (Gal 6:16), and Bride (Eph 5; see Hos 2:19–20; Is 54:5–8) in reference to the Church. Once again, the solution for the dispensationalist is to create divisions: God will have *two* brides, an "earthly wife" and a "heavenly bride".[110] Such divisions bring up difficult questions: If God has two brides, is he a polygamist? As LaRondelle observes, these "dispensationalist distinctions and dilemmas are the result of unwarranted inferences and a literalism which loses sight of the theological typology between the Israel of God and the Church of Christ in God's single, ongoing plan of salvation for all mankind."[111]

Pedagogy, Prophecy, and Preparation

So how does the Catholic explain the many Old Testament prophecies that seem to predict a future earthly paradise, filled with material wealth and blessing? In a single word: pedagogy. A general comparison between the dispensationalist

---

[109] Chafer, *Systematic Theology*, 4:137, quoted by LaRondelle, *Israel of God in Prophecy*, p. 49.

[110] Commenting on Hosea 2, Scofield writes: "That Israel is the wife of Jehovah ... now disowned but yet to be restored, is the clear teaching of the passages" (*Scofield Reference Bible*, p. 922). Of Revelation 19:7 he writes: "The 'Lamb's wife' here is the bride (Rev 21:9), the Church, identified with the 'heavenly Jerusalem' (Heb 12:22, 23), and to be distinguished from Israel, the adulterous and repudiated 'wife' of Jehovah, yet to be restored (Is 54:1–10; Hos 2:1–17), who is identified with the earth (Hos 2:23)" (*Scofield Reference Bible*, p. 1348).

[111] LaRondelle, *Israel of God in Prophecy*, p. 51. Poythress remarks: "The major weakness of classic dispensationalist interpretive theory, at this point, has been the neglecting of the integration of typological interpretation with grammatical-historical interpretation" (Poythress, *Understanding Dispensationalists*, p. 115).

and Catholic views of salvation history will illustrate and explain this important term.

Dispensationalism understands salvation history as a series of compartmentalized dispensations, or periods of history, that are related to one another in small ways but remain largely isolated one from the other. Catholicism teaches that salvation history is a continuous progression in instruction and understanding, moving toward and culminating in the person of Jesus Christ. This growth in understanding is pedagogy, an education in the salvific work of God. *Dei Verbum* explains,

> The principal purpose to which the plan of the Old Covenant was directed was to prepare for the coming both of Christ, the universal Redeemer, and of the messianic kingdom, to announce this coming prophecy (cf. Lk. 24:44; Jn. 5:39; 1 Pet. 1:10), and to indicate its meaning through various types (cf. 1 Cor. 10:11).... The [Old Testament] books, though they also contain some things which are incomplete and temporary, nevertheless show us true divine pedagogy.[112]

This pedagogical process can be seen in various ways, especially in the ever-growing covenants, which begin with a small family, expand to a nation, then to a kingdom, and then culminate in a worldwide covenant.[113] It is also evident in the developing language of the Old Testament, which moves from a strictly earth-bound view of material blessing to an increasingly spiritual understanding of fulfillment. This slow but sure movement throughout the Old Testament toward the Incarnation is highlighted within the New

---

[112] *DV* 15. See CCC 122 and 53.
[113] See CCC 54–67.

Testament.[114] There is Christ's bold statement in the Sermon on the Mount, "Think not that I have come to abolish the law and the prophets; I have come not to abolish them but to fulfil them" (Mt 5:17), and his strong words to the despairing disciples on the road to Emmaus:

> And he said to them, "O foolish men, and slow of heart to believe all that the prophets have spoken! Was it not necessary that the Christ should suffer these things and enter into his glory?" And beginning with Moses and all the prophets, he interpreted to them in all the scriptures the things concerning himself (Lk 24:25–27).

Many of the promises made by God to Abraham and Moses were fulfilled in the Old Testament, as in the conquering of the Promised Land.[115] Others, being conditional in nature, were cancelled out by the faithlessness of the Israelites.[116] Meanwhile, the glorious visions of the future revealed to the

---

[114] See CCC 1964. Of this progressive movement toward Christ in salvation history, Dom Charlier writes: "Though it is something less than identity, there is more than mere analogy between the Covenant of Sinai and the Covenant ratified in the Spirit by the risen Christ, between the crossing of the Red Sea and Christian baptism, between Abraham's race and the royal race of the elect. Between these realities is a living unity, which progresses but is constant, which is able to effect change without itself changing, which can operate on different levels without losing its irresistible and unifying dynamism.... The Bible is like a reel of film which shows the different forms assumed by a living tradition throughout the ages. To cut this film in order to rearrange the sequence of its frames is to take all meaning out of it and destroy the possibility of it ever being screened. The Bible will have meaning only if its sequence is preserved and its upward movement understood. This cannot be done without the living Spirit which continues to breathe this tradition in the Church" (Charlier, *Christian Approach to the Bible*, pp. 172–73).

[115] See Deut 1:8; Josh 21:43–45.

[116] See, for instance, the conditions placed before Solomon (1 Kings 1:1–4; 9:2–9; 11:9–13; 1 Chron 28:6–9; 2 Chron 7:16–22), all of which were broken by Solomon and later kings.

prophets, couched in images of land and earthly prosperity, are depictions of the fullness of God's salvific love, all of which are fulfilled in Jesus Christ, who is Immanuel, God with us (Mt 1:23). As Paul explains to the Christians at Corinth, "For all the promises of God find their Yes in him [Christ]. That is why we utter the Amen through him, to the glory of God" (2 Cor 1:20). This interpretation of the prophets does not demean or avoid a "literal" fulfillment but recognizes that Jesus Christ is the literal, actual fulfillment of all prophecy. The fact that the prophetic references are realized in Christ, the New Covenant, and the Church (the New Jerusalem) is, according to Louis Bouyer, "but a transposition of the transitory into the eternal, of the passing into the perfected.... It is precisely this transition, in the very act of taking place, from the Old Testament to the New, from the Word which, after having expressed Itself little by little and in different ways by the prophets, is given to us perfectly in the Son." [117]

[117] Louis Bouyer, *Meaning of Sacred Scripture* (Notre Dame, Ind.: University of Notre Dame Press, 1958), p. 50.

9

UNWRAPPING THE RAPTURE

A man and wife asleep in bed
She hears a noise and turns her head, he's gone
I wish we'd all been ready

Two men walking up a hill
One disappears and one's left standing still
I wish we'd all been ready

There's no time to change your mind
The Son has come and you've been left behind

—Larry Norman, "I Wish We'd All Been Ready"

My prophetic studies have convinced me that we Christians living today have more evidence to believe we are the generation of His coming than any generation before us. So I am not surprised by the increase of confusion by deceived attackers of the spiritually inspiring pre-Tribulation position of end time events.

—Tim LaHaye

Like the dispensational hermeneutical methodology in general, the pretribulational rapture doctrine is a gigantic hoax. Because the pretribulational rapture is a pillar of the dispensational system, we should expect to find proof of its existence in clear texts. Even one text would suffice. There is not a single passage that clearly and dogmatically supports a pretribulational rapture.

—Gary DeMar

The most well-known dispensationalist belief is that Christians will be raptured—"taken up"—to meet Christ in the air prior to his Second Coming. For dispensationalists these "are obviously two separate events".[1] LaHaye states that "while some Christians may disagree as to the length of time between the two events, all must concur that they are two distinct experiences."[2] Dispensationalists teach that during the Rapture believers will be "translated" or "snatched up" to heaven, while at the Second Coming there will be no such "translation" since saints who have already been raptured will be returning in triumph to earth with Christ.[3] At the Rapture, Christ will come *for* his own and will meet them in the air, while at the Second Coming he will come *with* his own as he returns to earth. Only those being raptured will see him, while all of mankind will see him at the Second Coming. The Rapture will not be preceded by any signs or warnings but is imminent, any-moment, signless, and secret.[4] The Second Coming will be preceded by definite signs, especially the seven years of the Great Tribulation. At the time of the Rapture the earth will not be judged, but the Tribulation period will begin; at the Second Coming the earth will be judged and "righteousness established" in the millennial

[1] Tim LaHaye, *Rapture under Attack* (Sisters, Ore.: Multnomah Publishers, 1998), p. 37.

[2] Ibid.

[3] A comparison of these two events, complete with charts, can be found in Thomas Ice and Timothy Demys' *Fast Facts on Bible Prophecy* (Eugene, Ore.: Harvest House Publishers, 1997), pp. 186–87. Also see Tim LaHaye, *Revelation Unveiled* (Grand Rapids, Mich.: Zondervan Publishing House, 1999), pp. 99–112.

[4] "Imminency in the New Testament teaches that Christ could return and rapture His church at any moment, without prior signs or warning" (Ice and Demy, *Fast Facts on Bible Prophecy*, p. 101).

kingdom.[5] Each of these distinctions, dispensationalists claim, can be deduced from Scripture.

Catholics believe that the "Rapture"—properly understood—and the Second Coming are part of a single, unified event. Believers in Jesus Christ here on earth will be "caught up together" (1 Thess 4:17) to meet him at the Second Coming—the Parousia—as he returns with all of those saints already with him in glory. The Catholic belief that this "rapture" and the Second Coming are one event is shared by the Eastern Orthodox, the ancient Oriental Churches, Anglicans, and most mainline Protestant denominations, including Lutherans and Reformed Protestants.

Pre-, Mid-, or Posttrib?

Within premillennialism there are three main competing views about the timing of the Rapture in relation to the Tribulation, which all agree will last seven years. *Pretribulationists* believe the Rapture will occur prior to the seven-year Tribulation; *midtribulationists* believe the Rapture will occur at the midpoint of the Tribulation;[6] and *posttribulationists* believe

---

[5] "The coming of Christ in His Glorious Appearing with the heavenly armies will not only bring to consummation the enmity of Satan, his Antichrist, the False Prophet, and the millions they deceive, but will usher in the millennial kingdom—the righteous reign of Christ on earth" (LaHaye, *Revelation Unveiled*, p. 307).

[6] A view similar to the midtribulationalist Rapture, but unique in key areas, is the prewrath Rapture. "The prewrath view is different from the midtribulational view in that it does not have the rapture exactly in the middle of the week [the seven-year Tribulation period]. Midtribulationism places the rapture with the sounding of the seventh trumpet (Rev 11) while prewrath rapturism places it with the sounding of the first trumpet and at the same time as the Second Coming which is before the Day of the Lord begins" (Robert P. Lightner, *The Last Days Handbook* [Nashville: Thomas Nelson, 1990], pp. 67–68).

the Rapture will occur at the end of the Tribulation *and* at the same time as the Second Coming. Posttribulationalism is the most similar to the Catholic belief that a "rapture" and the Second Coming are part of a single event. Of these three positions the pretribulational dispensationalist view is easily the most popular among Fundamentalists and Evangelicals. The midtribulational stance is of recent origin, first developed seriously in 1941 by Norman B. Harrison in his book *The End: Rethinking the Revelation.*[7] The posttribulational stance is the most ancient view, with roots going back to the earliest centuries of the Church. Premillennial proponents of the posttribulational view are usually referred to as "historical premillennialists" and include noted theologians George E. Ladd and Robert Gundry.

The disagreements between these three groups are often harsh and polemical. Marvin Rosenthal, a proponent of the prewrath position, a variation on midtribulationalism, condemns the pretribulational view as satanic in origin. Referring to the claim of some critics that Darby based his pretribulational view on the charismatic utterances of a young Scottish girl, Rosenthal states, "To thwart the Lord's warning to His children, in 1830, Satan, the 'father of lies,' gave to a fifteen-year-old girl named Margaret McDonald a lengthy

---

In other words, the prewrath belief is that the Rapture will occur toward the very end of the seven-year Tribulation period, immediately prior to the unleashing of God's wrathful judgment on the earth.

[7] "[Harrison] believed the Rapture of the church would occur midway through the seven-year period known as Daniel's seventieth week. As a result, the church will not be on earth when God pours out His wrath during the three and one-half years before Christ returns to earth" (Richard R. Reiter, "A History of the Development of the Rapture Positions", in Richard R. Reiter et al., *The Rapture: Pre-, Mid-, or Post-Tribulational?* [Grand Rapids, Mich.: Academie Books, 1984], p. 31).

vision." [8] Posttribulationist Gundry and pretribulationist Wal-voord have engaged in a more civilized but still contentious debate over the years, with Walvoord writing *The Blessed Hope and the Tribulation*[9] in response to *The Church and the Tribulation*,[10] Gundry's critique of pretribulational dispensationalism. As we've already seen, both Lindsey and LaHaye are openly—even harshly—critical of midtribulationists and posttribulationists. While LaHaye admits that the "post-Trib position (in its primitive form) is the oldest point of view", he discounts the position because, he claims, "Doctrine must be provable by Scripture or discarded. . . . History is not sacrosanct; the Bible is." [11] He describes the posttribulational understanding of the Rapture and the Second Coming as "ludicrous".[12] Polemics aside, what scriptural and historical proof actually exists for the pretribulational Rapture?

The Pretribulational Rapture Is Not in the Bible!

Although many biblical references are used to support it, the pretribulational Rapture has no basis in Scripture. In fact, prominent dispensationalists admit that no clear and obvious scriptural support exists for this belief. LaHaye acknowledges

[8] Marvin J. Rosenthal, "Is the Church in Matthew Chapter 24?", *Zion's Fire*, November–December 1994, p. 10. Rosenthal refers here to the alleged influence of McDonald's vision on Darby, a topic former journalist Dave MacPherson has written about extensively. See Dave MacPherson, *The Rapture Plot*, 2d ed. (Simpsonville, S.C.: Millennium III Publishers, 2000).

[9] John F. Walvoord, *The Blessed Hope and the Tribulation: A Historical and Biblical Study of Posttribulationism* (Grand Rapids, Mich.: Zondervan Publishing House, 1976).

[10] Robert H. Gundry, *The Church and the Tribulation: A Biblical Examination of Posttribulationism* (Grand Rapids, Mich.: Zondervan Publishing House, 1973).

[11] LaHaye, *Rapture under Attack*, p. 197.

[12] Ibid., p. 201.

this fact, ironically, at the start of a chapter titled "Who Says It's Obscure?":

> One objection to the pre-Tribulation rapture is that no one passage of Scripture teaches the two aspects of His Second Coming separated by the Tribulation. *This is true.* But then, no passage teaches a post-Tribulation or mid-Tribulation rapture, either.[13]

Walvoord makes the same admission in the first edition of *The Rapture Question*: "Neither pretribulationism nor posttribulationism is an explicit teaching of Scripture."[14] Walvoord removed the statement from later editions of the book. At the end of the same book Walvoord lists "Fifty Arguments for Pretribulationalism". None contains a passage from Scripture explicitly teaching the pretribulational Rapture— for the simple reason that no such passage exists. Walvoord instead appeals to arguments from history, hermeneutics, the nature of the Tribulation, the nature of the Church, and the doctrine of imminency.[15] Considering that the pretribulational Rapture is often referred to as the "Blessed Hope", one would think Scripture would be more clear about its existence. Why is it not?

---

[13] Ibid., p. 75; emphasis added. However, in his first major work about biblical prophecy, *The Beginning of the End* (Wheaton, Ill.: Tyndale House Publishers, 1972), LaHaye wrote: "Some critics of the pretribulation Rapture assert that no one Bible passage teaches both stages of our Lord's Second Coming. Actually, such passages can be found" (p. 24). He then mentions Titus 2:13, 2 Thessalonians 2, and Revelation 2 and 3.

[14] Quoted by David Currie in "The Roots of the Rapture", tape 1 of the three-tape series *The Rapture Revealed* (West Covina, Calif.: St. Joseph Communications, 1999). The first edition of *The Rapture Question* was published in 1957 by Dunham Publishing Company, Findlay, Ohio.

[15] Walvoord, *The Rapture Question* (Grand Rapids, Mich.: Academie Books, 1979), pp. 269–76.

A revealing admission comes from Thomas Ice, LaHaye's colleague and director of the Pre-Trib Research Institute in Washington, D.C. He writes:

> A certain theological climate needed to be created before premillennialism would restore the Biblical doctrine of the pretrib Rapture. Sufficient development did not take place until after the French Revolution. The factor of the Rapture has been clearly known by the church all along; therefore the issue is the timing of the event. Since neither pre nor posttribs have a proof text for the time of the Rapture ... then *it is clear that this issue is the product of a deduction from one's overall system of theology*, both for pre and posttribbers.[16]

In other words, first create the theological system, then build doctrines supporting the system, and then search for texts substantiating the doctrines. It is an obviously problematic and flawed approach resulting in even more difficulties for the dispensationalist.

The True Basis of the Pretribulational Rapture

We return, briefly, to the critical tenet of the dispensationalist system: the radical distinction between Israel and the Church. This distinction and its logical fruits, gathered into an entire theological system by Darby, influence and guide the dispensationalist understanding of Scripture. Evangelical scholar Timothy Weber writes that Darby "claimed that the doctrine [of the secret Rapture] virtually jumped out of the pages of Scripture once he accepted and consistently main-

---

[16] Thomas D. Ice, "The Origin of the PreTrib Rapture: Part II", *Biblical Perspectives*, March/April 1989, p. 5. Quoted by Gary DeMar, *Last Days Madness: Obsession of the Modern Church* (Atlanta: American Vision Press, 1999), p. 222; emphasis added.

tained the distinction between Israel and the church".[17] Darby
minced no words in this regard:

> It is this conviction, that the Church is properly heavenly in
> its calling and relationship with Christ, forming no part of
> the course of events of the earth, which makes its rapture so
> simple and clear; and on the other hand, it shows how the
> denial of its rapture brings down the Church to an earthly
> position, and destroys its whole spiritual character and
> position.[18]

Walvoord is candid on this same point, writing: "It is not too
much to say that the rapture question is determined more by
ecclesiology than eschatology." [19] Ryrie agrees without res-
ervation, stating, "The distinction between Israel and the
Church leads to the belief that the Church will be taken
from the earth before the beginning of the tribulation." [20]
All popular dispensationalists concur, realizing that their entire system of biblical interpretation rests on this premise.
We will now observe this system of interpretation as it attempts to defend the pretribulational Rapture by appealing
to a number of key biblical passages.

1 Thessalonians: Clearly about the Rapture?

Paul's first epistle to the Thessalonians is a favorite text of
dispensationalists. They argue that since Paul teaches that the

---

[17] Timothy P. Weber, *Living in the Shadow of the Second Coming: American Premillennialism 1875–1925* [New York: Oxford University Press, 1979], p. 22.

[18] Darby, *Collected Works*, 11:156. Quoted by Weber, *Living in the Shadow of the Second Coming*, p. 22.

[19] Quoted by Hal Lindsey, *The Rapture* (New York: Bantam Books, 1983), p. 79.

[20] Charles C. Ryrie, *Dispensationalism Today* (Chicago: Moody Press, 1965), p. 159.

return of Christ is an imminent event, but makes no mention of the Great Tribulation, he must be referring to the pretribulational Rapture. Walvoord states that "this book [1 Thessalonians] presents the Rapture uniformly as an imminent event, as if there were no Great Tribulation preceding it." [21] He further claims passages such as 1 Thessalonians 1:10; 2:19; 3:13; 4:13–18; 5:1–11, and 5:23 all refer to the Rapture,[22] and contends 1 Thessalonians "contributes more to the doctrine of the Rapture than any other book of the New Testament".[23]

The signature passage is found in 1 Thessalonians 4. Dispensationalist author Thomas Ice writes, "The teaching of the rapture is most clearly presented in 1 Thessalonians 4:13–18." [24] The word "rapture" is derived from this passage, deriving from the Latin word *rapiemur*, which St. Jerome used in translating the Greek word *harpazo*; in English it is usually translated "caught up". The core of the passage reads:

[21] Walvoord, *Rapture Question*, pp. 197–98.

[22] "The Rapture is mentioned in one way or another in every chapter of this book" (ibid., p. 197).

[23] Ibid. M. R. DeHaan, a popular dispensationalist author of the 1960s and 1970s, writes: "The first two epistles which Paul wrote, First and Second Thessalonians, were written to correct two serious errors, both of them with regard to this very subject, the return of the Lord Jesus. First Thessalonians was inspired and written to correct a misunderstanding concerning the *premillennial* Rapture or the return of the Lord Jesus Christ before the Millennial Kingdom was to be set up. However, Second Thessalonians was written to correct an error concerning the *pre-tribulation* Rapture, and sets forth in no uncertain terms that not only will the Lord return before the Kingdom age, the Millennium, but He will also return for His Church before the Tribulation sets in upon this earth. So let me repeat, First Thessalonians teaches the truth of the *premillennial* Rapture, while Second Thessalonians establishes the truth of the *pre-tribulation* Rapture" (M. R. DeHaan, *Coming Events in Prophecy* [Grand Rapids, Mich.: Zondervan Publishing House, 1973], p. 128).

[24] Ice and Demy, *Fast Facts on Bible Prophecy*, p. 163.

> For the Lord himself will descend from heaven with a cry of command, with the archangel's call, and with the sound of the trumpet of God. And the dead in Christ will rise first; then we who are alive, who are left, shall be caught up together with them in the clouds to meet the Lord in the air; and so we shall always be with the Lord. (1 Thess 4:16–17)

Is this a description of a pretribulational Rapture, as dispensationalists insist? Although Paul refers to believers being "caught up" to "meet the Lord", there is no indication this happens prior to the Tribulation and the Second Coming. Even though dispensationalists teach that the Rapture will be silent and secret, the very opposite is the case here: there is a "shout" uttered by Christ as well as "the voice of an archangel" and "the trumpet of God". A literal interpretation, as defined by dispensationalists, seems to indicate this event will be both visible and vocal. Some dispensationalists argue that only those being raptured will see or hear what is happening, giving the impression they are forcing a theological assumption onto the text. What is most striking about this passage is that it provides no evidence at all for the pretribulational Rapture and even contradicts it. In contrast, Catholics and the vast majority of other Christians believe this passage refers explicitly to the Second Coming, the Parousia, when the dead in Christ will rise again. In answering the question of "When will the dead rise?" the *Catechism* states: "Definitively 'at the last day,' 'at the end of the world' [Jn 6:39–40, 44, 54; 11:24; LG 48§3] Indeed, the resurrection of the dead is closely associated with Christ's Parousia", and then goes on to quote 1 Thessalonians 4:16.[25]

---

[25] CCC 1001.

Dispensationalists combine 1 Thessalonians 4 with other biblical passages in their quest to prove the pretribulational Rapture. LaHaye often refers to 1 Corinthians 15:51–53, a passage that plays a prominent part in his novel, *Left Behind*[26] as well as in his works of nonfiction. The passage states:

> Lo! I tell you a mystery. We shall not all sleep, but we shall all be changed, in a moment, in the twinkling of an eye, at the last trumpet. For the trumpet will sound, and the dead will be raised imperishable, and we shall be changed. For this perishable nature must put on the imperishable, and this mortal nature must put on immortality. (1 Cor 15:51–53)

LaHaye contends that "in order to gain a complete picture of the Rapture, one must consider these two passages [1 Thess 4:13–18 and 1 Cor 15:51–53] together, along with our Lord's promise of rapture in John 14:1–3."[27] Even with the combination of these two passages, there is a striking absence of proof for the pretribulational Rapture. LaHaye equates the change in "the twinkling of an eye" to the Rapture, but the actual point of the passage is that Christians, the Church, will be glorified—not that they will be secretly whisked off the planet prior to the Tribulation. No mention is made of the Rapture being separate from the Second Coming or prior to the Tribulation. The same holds true for John 14:13, in which Christ tells his disciples "And when I go and prepare a place for you, I will come again and will take you to myself, that where I am you may be also." Not only does this passage fail to support the pretribulational Rapture; it makes much more sense as a reference to the Second Coming.

---

[26] See Tim LaHaye and Jerry B. Jenkins, *Left Behind: A Novel of the Earth's Last Days* (Wheaton, Ill.: Tyndale House Publishers, 1995), pp. 208–11.

[27] LaHaye, *Rapture under Attack*, p. 34.

Imminent or Simply Unknown?

Belief in the imminency—the "any moment" possibility—of the Rapture, according to Walvoord, is "the central feature ... [and] heart of pretribulationalism".[28] If the Rapture can occur at any moment, goes the dispensationalist argument, then it follows that nothing has to happen prior to it. Yet prior to the Second Coming there are several events that must occur: a great apostasy, the reign of the Antichrist, and the seven years of Tribulation.[29] One of the passages used to defend the imminent Rapture is found in 1 Thessalonians 5, where Paul writes:

> For you yourselves know well that the day of the Lord will come like a thief in the night. When people say, "There is peace and security," then sudden destruction will come upon them as travail comes upon a woman with child, and there will be no escape. But you are not in darkness, brethren, for that day to surprise you like a thief. (1 Thess 5:2–4)

The image of the "thief in the night" has enjoyed great popularity in dispensationalist circles. In the 1970s a dispensationalist movie about the Rapture, titled *Thief in the Night*, was viewed by hundreds of Fundamentalist groups all across America. But does the phrase refer to the pretribulational Rapture, or does it actually refer to the Second Coming of Christ?

One serious problem for the dispensationalist is the reference in 1 Thessalonians 5 to "the day of the Lord". This

---

[28] Walvoord, *Rapture Question*, pp. 51, 53.

[29] Mark Brumley, "Secret Rapture, Arguments Concerning", from the forthcoming *Catholic Apologetics Encyclopedia* (San Francisco: Ignatius Press, in preparation).

term, also rendered as "the day of judgment",[30] is used in the New Testament to refer to the Second Coming *and* the end of time. Peter, in his second epistle, exhorts his readers to have patience in the face of trials and to recognize that Christ's return will take place at the proper time and is only delayed because of God's mercy toward mankind: "The Lord is not slow about his promise as some count slowness, but is forbearing toward you, not wishing that any should perish, but that all should reach repentance" (2 Pet 3:9). Continuing, Peter employs language similar to that used by Paul in 1 Thessalonians 5:

> But the day of the Lord will come like a thief, and then the heavens will pass away with a loud noise, and the elements will be dissolved with fire, and the earth and the works that are upon it will be burned up.
>
> Since all these things are thus to be dissolved, what sort of persons ought you to be in lives of holiness and godliness, waiting for and hastening the coming of the day of God, because of which the heavens will be kindled and dissolved, and the elements will melt with fire! (2 Pet 3:10–12)

If 1 Thessalonians 5:2–4 pertains to the Rapture, it places that event at the same time as the Second Coming, since the "day of the Lord" refers to the end of time and to judgment. There is no reference to the Tribulation or to a later time of judgment. There is just one event, the day of the Lord, during which several things transpire: the Rapture, the Second Coming, judgment, and the destruction of "the earth and its works".

---

[30] "But by the same word the heavens and earth that now exist have been stored up for fire, being kept until the day of judgment and destruction of ungodly men" (2 Pet 3:7). Also see Mt 10:15; 11:22, 24; 12:36; 2 Pet 2:9, and 1 Jn 4:17.

Walvoord admits the language is a challenge for dispensationalists. However, his answer is unconvincing, a curious claim that the "day of the Lord" is actually symbolic in nature: "References to the day of the Lord, not actually a literal day, have in mind the symbolism of a day beginning at midnight and extending through twenty-four hours to the next midnight."[31] This is an astonishing interpretation from a scholar who claims to interpret Scripture "literally" and in the "plain sense". Walvoord explains that he uses this symbolic interpretation so "the various facts revealed in Scripture relating to the day of the Lord begin to take on meaning and relationship."[32] However, it appears to be an attempt to explain away the fact that the term "the day" in 1 Thessalonians 5 and other passages cannot be accounted for by the dispensationalist system. There are a host of New Testament verses addressing "that day" (2 Thess 1:10; 2 Tim 1:12, 18; 4:8), "the day of (Jesus) Christ" (Phil 1:6, 10; 2:16), "the day of the/our Lord Jesus (Christ)" (1 Cor 1:7–8, 5:4–5; 2 Cor 1:14), and "the day of the Lord" (2 Thess 2:1–3), all describing the same event. Although Walvoord complains that these are wrongly "lump[ed] together", he provides no basis for this complaint except for a vague reference to "the context of each passage".[33] In light of this, another problem arises for dispensationalists. If they believe that the phrase "a

---

[31] Walvoord, *Rapture Question*, p. 215.

[32] Ibid. Of "the day of the Lord", Jack Van Impe writes, "we have to be careful here in defining this one, because the Day of the Lord *begins one minute after the Rapture!* As soon as Christ comes for His bride, the Day of the Lord immediately begins, and it includes the seven-year period of the Tribulation. It also includes the thousand-year millennial period. So the 'Day of the Lord' is actually 1,007 years of time" (Jack Van Impe, *Everything about Prophecy* [Troy, Mich.: Jack Van Impe Ministries, 1999], p. 58; emphasis in original).

[33] Walvoord, *Rapture Question*, p. 214.

thief in the night" means that Christ could return at any moment, while also believing 2 Peter 3:10–12 refers to the Second Coming, will the Second Coming not also be imminent, since Peter writes that "the day of the Lord will come like a thief"? [34]

Another passage used to support the imminence of the "signless", pretribulational Rapture is found in Matthew 24. There, in the Olivet Discourse, Jesus emphasizes that the timing of those events is unknown, even to himself:

> But of that day and hour no one knows, not even the angels of heaven, nor the Son, but the Father only. As were the days of Noah, so will be the coming of the Son of man. For as in those days before the flood they were eating and drinking, marrying and giving in marriage, until the day when Noah entered the ark, and they did not know until the flood came and swept them all away, so will be the coming of the Son of man. Then two men will be in the field; one is taken and one is left. Two women will be grinding at the mill; one is taken and one is left. Watch therefore, for you do not know on what day your Lord is coming. But know this, that if the householder had known in what part of the night the thief was coming, he would have watched and would not have let his house be broken into. Therefore you also must be ready; for the Son of man is coming at an hour you do not expect. (Mt 24:36–44)

Dispensationalists argue that since "no one knows" the "day and hour", the events Jesus describes were imminent for his listeners *and* are equally imminent for us today. No events had to occur before the Rapture could take place. Or did

---

[34] Mark Brumley, "Secret Rapture".

they? In fact, there were events that would take place. For one, the gospel was to be "preached throughout the whole world, as a testimony to all nations; and then the end will come" (Mt 24:14).[35] There was also the death of Peter, which Jesus had predicted would occur when Peter was an old man (Jn 21:17–18). This meant that at least two or three decades would pass before Christ's return could take place. And if two or three decades, why not two or three centuries? Besides, Paul tells the Thessalonians that the day of the Lord will not come "unless the rebellion comes first, and the man of lawlessness is revealed, the son of perdition" (2 Thess 2:3), meaning that at least one biblical prophecy must take place prior to the Rapture. Of course, many dispensationalists believe the Antichrist is alive today and is close to ascending to power, which only goes to show that until the Antichrist comes, the Rapture cannot occur—meaning its "any moment" status is conditional.[36]

Paul's remark about the "thief in the night" and Christ's warning that no one knows "that day or hour" emphasize the need for alertness and watchfulness. This call for awareness is evident in Christ's discourse in Luke 21:

[35] Ibid. See CCC 673.

[36] Most dispensationalists deny they are looking for the Antichrist. LaHaye flatly remarks: "Pre-Tribbers are looking for Christ, not Antichrist" (*Rapture under Attack*, p. 72). Yet dispensationalist literature indicates a substantial interest in the identity of the Antichrist. In 1970 Hal Lindsey wrote that "the dramatic elements which are occurring in the world today are setting the stage for this magnetic, diabolical Future Fuehrer to make his entrance" (Hal Lindsey with C. C. Carlson, *The Late Great Planet Earth* [New York: Bantam Books, 1970], p. 102). A decade later he stated: "As I wrote 10 years ago in *The Late Great Planet Earth*, I believe this man [the Antichrist] is alive today—alive and waiting to come forth" (Hal Lindsey, *The 1980s: Countdown to Armageddon* [New York: Bantam Books, 1980], p. 15).

But take heed to yourselves lest your hearts be weighed down with dissipation and drunkenness and cares of this life, and that day come upon you suddenly like a snare; for it will come upon all who dwell upon the face of the whole earth. But watch at all times, praying that you may have strength to escape all these things that will take place, and to stand before the Son of man. (Lk 21:34–36)

Catholics know (or should know) that Christ will indeed return. The Second Coming could be relatively soon or many centuries in the future. Regardless, all of us will come face to face with our Maker; it is safe to say that each of us will be judged by Christ for our lives and actions. Therefore, more important than when this will happen should be our concern with our state when it does finally occur.

An Escaping Church?

The Church must be raptured, dispensationalists also teach, because Scripture indicates Christians are not destined for wrath (1 Thess 5:9) and will not have to go through the "hour of trial" (Rev 3:10). The essential premise is that "the Tribulation is a special judgment of God" upon the world and the unsaved[37] and is also "a prelude to Israel's restoration and exaltation in the millennial kingdom."[38] Since the Tribulation is not meant for the Church, the Church will not be present on earth during it. Remarking upon this belief, LaHaye quotes Matthew 24:21–22, where Christ speaks of "a great tribulation", and states that "unless those days had been cut short, no life would have been saved; but for

---

[37] LaHaye, *Rapture under Attack*, p. 48.
[38] Walvoord, *Rapture Question*, p. 62.

the sake of the elect those days shall be cut short." LaHaye's use of this passage as a proof text is puzzling. Why would the days of tribulation be shortened for the "sake of the elect" if the elect are in heaven? The answer, Walvoord insists, is that the elect in Matthew 24 does not refer to the Church, but to those who *become* Christian *during* the Tribulation and after the Rapture. He writes: "Pretribulationists concede and uniformly teach that there will be elect, that is, saved people, in the tribulation time. This fact does not in the slightest prove that these mentioned in this way belong to the church, the body of Christ."[39]

This convenient distinction between believers in the "Church age" and those in the Tribulation is based on theological assumption at the expense of the context of Matthew 24. Jesus is speaking to his disciples, the first Christians and the leaders of the early Church. A bit earlier he warned them, "Take heed that no one leads you astray. For many will come in my name, saying, 'I am the Christ,' and they will lead many astray" (Mt 24:4b–5). Clearly he is talking to *them* about *their* situation. Immediately prior to using the term "elect" he states, "Pray that *your* flight may not be in winter or on a sabbath" (Mt 24:20; emphasis added), again indicating the same context: Christians and the Church. In between verses 22 and 24—both of which refer to "the elect"—he tells the disciples: "Then if any one says to you, 'Lo, here is the Christ!' or 'There he is!' do not believe it" (Mt 24:23). Within this context it is unreasonable to believe that the "elect" Jesus refers to are future Christians in the Tribulation—believers, according to dispensationalists, who are not members of the Church. This becomes even more obvious in light of other

[39] Ibid., p. 59.

New Testament passages, such as Romans 8:33–34, where Paul asks the believers in Rome "Who shall bring any charge against God's elect? It is God who justifies; who is to condemn? Is it Christ Jesus, who died, yes, who was raised from the dead, who is at the right hand of God, who indeed intercedes for us?" Once again, the "elect" means "us", that is, Christians who are members of the Church. Within the New Testament, the "elect" are always members of the Church, the Body of Christ.

Dispensationalists also point to Christ's warning in Luke 21 as evidence for the pretribulational Rapture: "But watch at all times, praying that you may have strength to escape all these things that will take place, and to stand before the Son of man" (Lk 21:36). Again, context is vital. Possibly all of Luke 21—or at least a section of the chapter—describes the destruction of Jerusalem in A.D. 70 by the Romans.[40] Luke 21:12–24 refers to events in the first-century, including "Jerusalem surrounded by armies" (v. 20), the complete annihilation and desecration of the Temple ("its desolation", v. 20),[41] and the fact, according to Josephus in *The Jewish*

---

[40] Biblical exegete Luke Timothy Johnson writes that "in the first part of Jesus' discourse [in Luke 21], Luke has shaped the Prophet's words so that they can be perceived by the reader as having been already fulfilled, first in the experience of persecution by the first Christians ... and secondly in the events surrounding the fall of the Temple and the city Jerusalem" (Luke Timothy Johnson, *The Gospel of Luke*, Sacra Pagina Commentary Series [Collegeville, Minn.: Liturgical Press, 1991], pp. 329–30).

[41] "Jerusalem had committed fornication with the heathen nations, but in A.D. 70 they turned against her and destroyed her, making her desolate (the same word used in Matthew 24:15, Mark 13:14, and Luke 21:20, reflecting the Greek version of Daniel 9:26–27: the abomination of desolation)" (David Chilton, *The Days of Vengeance: An Exposition of the Book of Revelation* [Fort Worth, Tex.: Dominion Press, 1987], p. 439).

War, that over one million Jews died in A.D. 70.[42] Apparently no Christians died, having taken seriously Christ's warning to "flee to the mountains" (v. 21). It could be that Luke 21:36 also refers to these events, to "all these things that will take place", a view supported by the remark that "this generation will not pass away till all has taken place" (v. 32). But if Luke 21:25–36 refers to a day still in the future—the "day of the Son of Man"—it still does not validate the pretribulational position, since it would place the Rapture at the same time as the Second Coming. This is established by Christ's warning: "But take heed to yourselves lest your hearts be weighed down with dissipation and drunkenness and cares of this life, and that day come upon you suddenly like a snare" (v. 34). Here "that day" certainly refers to the day of the appearance of the Son of Man (v. 27), also mentioned in verse 36: "praying that you may have strength to escape all these things that will take place, and to stand before the Son of man". Notice that Christ's exhortation is for believers to be aware and on guard so they will have the ability and the strength to escape what is to come—not so they will be raptured. As Catholic apologist Mark Brumley notes, "Unless Pretribulation/Midtribulation advocates want to argue that those whom Jesus addresses here should pray for the capacity to 'rapture' themselves from the scene, the language of 'escape' in the original text doesn't refer to the Rapture." [43]

---

[42] "Flavius Josephus, a contemporary Jewish historian, says that one million, one hundred thousand people died during the siege of Jerusalem in the year 70 (cf. *The Jewish War*, VI, 420)—which gives some idea of the scale of these events. The siege began when the city was full of pilgrims from all over the world, who had come to celebrate the Passover; therefore, Flavius Josephus' figure may not be all that far off the truth" (*Navarre Bible, Saint Matthew's Gospel* [Dublin: Four Courts Press, 1988, 1998], p 204).

[43] Mark Brumley, "Secret Rapture".

Another "escape passage" used by pretribulational advocates is Revelation 3:10–11, where Jesus Christ instructs St. John to write these words to the church at Philadelphia:

> Because you have kept my word of patient endurance, I will keep you from the hour of trial which is coming on the whole world, to try those who dwell upon the earth. I am coming soon; hold fast what you have, so that no one may seize your crown. (Rev 3:10–11)

Like many dispensationalists, LaHaye uses the historicist method of interpreting Revelation 1:19–3:22, claiming each of the seven churches represents a particular era in Church history, from the early Church until the Tribulation.[44] Interpreting Revelation 3:10–11 as a reference to the Rapture, LaHaye conveniently titles Philadelphia "The Church Christ Loved" and dates it from "A.D. 1750 to the Rapture".[45] But the church of Philadelphia is not the final church—the church of Laodicea is. Logically, if the historicist method used is sound, the Rapture would be promised to Laodicea, which LaHaye dates from "A.D. 1900 to the Tribulation".[46] Oddly

---

[44] Gary DeMar points out that in following the historicist interpretation, LaHaye completely contradicts his own belief system: "A glaring inconsistency can be found in Tim LaHaye's defense of an any-moment rapture based on Revelation 4:1. He states that the 'first-century church believed in the imminent return of Christ, possibly during their lifetime.' He means by this that first-century Christians and Christians thereafter believed that Jesus could come at any moment. But later in the same book he writes, 'Chapter 1 is the introduction; chapters 2 and 3 [of Revelation] *cover the church age*, using seven historical churches to describe the entire age....' How could Christians believe that Jesus could come at any moment and also believe that He would not come until the last of the seven representative churches (Laodicea) appeared? This destroys the dispensationalist's doctrine of imminency, the any-moment rapture of the church" (DeMar, *Last Days Madness*, p. 219; emphasis in original).

[45] LaHaye, *Revelation Unveiled*, p. 78.

[46] Ibid., p. 84.

enough, although he does not overlap the first three historical periods, LaHaye overlaps the last four. He offers no explanation except to say "we have Thyatira, Sardis, and
Philadelphia with us at the present time. Thus Laodicea adds
to this church age by arising from the three that preceded
it." [47] Obviously LaHaye has been forced into this arrangement because he believes Revelation 2:25—where Christ tells
the church at Thyatira to "hold fast what you have, until I
come"—is also a reference to the Rapture.[48]

Yet Revelation 3 never mentions the Rapture or being
"taken up" or "translated" to heaven. Rather, Christ assures
the church at Philadelphia by saying, "I will keep you from
the hour of trial" (3:10), a remark quite similar to his request
of the Father, "I do not pray that thou shouldst take them
out of the world, but that thou shouldst keep them from the
evil one" (Jn 17:15), and his statement, "In the world you
have tribulation; but be of good cheer, I have overcome the
world" (Jn 16:33). Christians have been *chosen* "out of the
world" (Jn 15:19), but it does not follow they will be *taken*
out of the world prior to a time of tribulation. While Christians will experience tribulation in the world, their souls will
be safeguarded from evil, the evil one, and the hour of testing. Paul reminds the Galatians that Christ "gave himself for
our sins to deliver us from the present evil age, according to
the will of our God and Father" (Gal 1:4). For the early
Christians, as well as for us today, this deliverance is not

[47] Ibid., p. 85. Hal Lindsey follows a different method and largely avoids
overlapping any time periods. He dates Thyatira A.D. 590–1517, Sardis as 1517–
1750, Philadelphia as 1750–1925, and Laodicea as 1900–Tribulation (Hal Lindsey with C. C. Carlson, *There's a New World Coming* [Santa Ana, Calif.: Vision
House Publishers, 1973], pp. 55–73).

[48] LaHaye, *Revelation Unveiled*, p. 102.

necessarily salvation from physical or emotional distress, but from spiritual death.

Another creative dispensationalist argument is based on the first verses of the fourth chapter of the book of Revelation:

> After this I looked, and lo, in heaven an open door! And the first voice, which I had heard speaking to me like a trumpet, said, "Come up hither, and I will show you what must take place after this." At once I was in the Spirit, and lo, a throne stood in heaven, with one seated on the throne! (Rev 4:1–2)

Many popular dispensationalists teach that this passage describes John, a representative of the Church, being raptured, therefore signifying when the Rapture occurs in the chronology of the book of Revelation. Not surprisingly, this happens immediately prior to the Tribulation. LaHaye comments, "Inasmuch as John was the last remaining apostle and a member of the universal church, his elevation to heaven is a picture of the Rapture of the Church just before the Tribulation begins." [49] He does admit the Rapture is not "explicitly taught in Revelation 4 but definitely appears here chronologically at the end of the Church Age and before the Tribulation".[50] The appearance of convenience is overwhelming. Most puzzling is that a "literalist" like LaHaye has no problem interpreting John and his experience "in the Spirit" as symbolizing the Rapture. The main argument is simply an appeal to chronology: since the church of Laodicea had been promised the Rapture in the previous chapter, and since there is no reference to the Church in chapters six through eighteen in the book of Revelation, it supposedly follows that the Rapture occurs in the opening section of chapter four. But Revela-

---

[49] Ibid., p. 99.
[50] Ibid., p. 100.

tion 4:1–2 does not provide evidence for this argument. John writes that he "was in the Spirit", which points to an ecstatic or visionary state, not a physical removal from earth. Also, John is the only one who experiences this particular vision— and he is nowhere designated as a symbol of the Church.

LaHaye challenges those who disagree with the pretribulational Rapture to "account for the missing church in Revelation chapters 6–18.... The words *church* and *churches* are mentioned seventeen times in just three chapters [Rev 1–3] ... but does not appear once during chapters 6 through 18."[51] This argument is popular, having also been used by Scofield,[52] Walvoord,[53] and Lindsey,[54] among others. This appealing argument is, however, seriously flawed. First, such an approach, applied to other words, leads to odd and untenable conclusions. For example, the word "Jesus" does not occur between Revelation 1:9 and 12:17. Does this mean that Jesus is not the subject of the book of Revelation since his name does not appear for nearly twelve chapters, over half of the book? Because the name "Jesus" is not used, are references to "the Lion of Judah", "the root of David", and "the Lamb" references to someone other than Jesus? Of course not. What about the absence of the words "church" or

---

[51] LaHaye, *Rapture under Attack*, p. 53.

[52] "This call [to John] seems clearly to indicate the fulfillment of 1 Thess. 4:14–17. The word 'church' does not again occur in the Revelation till all is fulfilled" (*Scofield Reference Bible* [New York: Oxford University Press, 1945], p. 1334).

[53] Walvoord remarks that "the main problem with the book of Revelation is that there is no clear mention of the rapture of the church from Revelation 4 through Revelation 18" (Walvoord, *Rapture Question*, p. 260).

[54] "As I said earlier, the Church is mentioned *nineteen times* in the first three chapters of the book of Revelation and isn't mentioned *once* as being on earth from Chapters 4 through 19!" (Lindsey and Carlson, *There's a New World Coming*, p. 78; emphasis in original).

"churches" in "Mark, Luke, John, 2 Timothy, Titus, 1 Peter, 2 Peter, 2 John, or Jude, and not until chapter 16 of Romans"?[55] Do those books have nothing to do with the Church? Hardly. How does the pretribulationist understand the many references to "the saints" in Revelation 6–18 (8:3–4; 11:18; 13:7, 10; 14:12; 16:6; 17:6; 18:20, 24), the "great multitude" (7:9), and the "souls of those who had been slain" (6:9)? Are these not references to the Church? According to the dispensationalist they are not, but instead they refer to those saved *after* the Rapture because, Walvoord contends, "the description of the saved as saints of both Jewish and Gentile backgrounds is quite in contrast to them as combined in one body, the church, in most of the New Testament."[56] This reply makes no sense considering that the words "Jew", "Jewish", and "Gentile" *never* appear in the book of Revelation, while the term "the saints" is used repeatedly throughout the New Testament to describe both local

[55] Gundry, *Church and the Tribulation*, p. 78. Gundry also states: "Unless we are prepared to relegate large chunks of the NT to a limbo of irrelevance to the Church, we cannot make the mention or omission of the term 'church' a criterion for determining the applicability of a passage to saints of the present age" (p. 78). In a later book, *First the Antichrist* (Grand Rapids, Mich.: Baker Books, 1997), Gundry also notes that "if the absence of 'church' from earthly scenes were to imply an absence of the church down here, then the absence of 'church' from heavenly scenes would imply an absence of the church up there." He also points out that within dispensationalism there is "a failure to notice that in the description of Christ's coming after the tribulation ([Rev] 19:11–16), 'church' doesn't appear. Yet in the pretrib scheme, that coming is supposed to be a coming *with* the church as distinct from an earlier coming [the Rapture] *for* the church. If the absence of 'church' from the description of Jesus' return after the tribulation doesn't necessitate the church's absence from that return, neither does the absence of 'church' from descriptions of the tribulation necessitate an absence of the church from the tribulation" (*First the Antichrist*, pp. 83–84).

[56] Walvoord, *Rapture Question*, p. 261.

churches and the universal Church (e.g., Rom 15:25–26, 31; 1 Cor 6:2; 14:33; 2 Cor 1:1; Eph 1:1, 15, 18; 2:9; 3:18; 4:12; Col 1:12; Jude 3). The dispensationalist argument simply begs the question, since it first assumes the Church will not go through a tribulation and then claims any reference to the saints must therefore not refer to the Church but to those saved after the Rapture. A closely related problem is that the words "church" and "churches" do not appear at all after Revelation 3 until the very end of the book, when Christ states "I Jesus have sent my angel to you with this testimony for the churches" (Rev 22:16). A consistent dispensationalist would have to conclude the Church not only does not appear in Revelation 6–18—she disappears completely and forever! It is far more sensible to recognize that "the saints" is a reference to the Church, that there is no pretribulational Rapture, and that the Church will go through a final time of intense tribulation.

This leads to a major flaw in the pretribulational position: If the Church is raptured prior to the Tribulation because Christians are not meant to suffer God's wrath, what about those who become Christian after the Rapture? If they experience God's wrath and are still preserved from destruction, then it is false to claim that Christians are raptured because they cannot experience or endure that wrath. And if they are kept from God's wrath by his divine intervention, it means believers can indeed go through the Tribulation and be protected from harm, therefore making the Rapture unnecessary. This is, Robert Gundry explains, a serious inconsistency:

> Therefore, whatever problems pretribulationists may turn up regarding the presence of the Church in a period of divine wrath are their own problems, too; for whether or not the

tribulational saints belong to the Church or to another group of redeemed people, they also have escaped God's anger by virtue of the blood of Christ, who underwent their judgment for them (Rev 7:14). Will Jewish and Gentile saints suffer God's wrath during the tribulation, according to pretribulationalism? If not, neither would the Church have to suffer God's wrath in the tribulation. If so, arguments against the suffering of wrath by the Church apply equally to tribulational saints of other sorts.[57]

And One Will Be Taken ... Why? Where? Which One?

"Then two men will be in the field; one is taken and one is left. Two women will be grinding at the mill; one is taken and one is left" (Mt 24:40–41). These words from the Olivet Discourse have been used to great effect by dispensationalists, forming the core of Larry Norman's popular 1970s Christian rock tune about the Rapture, *I Wish We'd All Been Ready*, and providing the title for the wildly successful *Left Behind* series. But is this passage really about the pretribulational Rapture? Does Jesus actually talk about a Rapture event and unbelievers being "left behind" to face a time of tribulation?

Once again, the context of the passage cannot be ignored. It is a response to the question of "what will be the sign of your coming and of the close of the age?" (Mt 24:3) and contains intertwining remarks about both the impending destruction of Jerusalem and the Second Coming.[58] In this

---

[57] Gundry, *Church and the Tribulation*, pp. 44–45.

[58] For a Catholic argument that Matthew 24–25 is mostly about "the demise of the Jerusalem Temple", see *The Ignatius Catholic Study Bible* (RSV): *The Gospel of Matthew*, with introduction, commentary, and notes by Scott Hahn and Curtis Mitch (San Francisco: Ignatius Press, 2000), p. 60.

section of the Olivet Discourse Jesus emphasizes that no one knows the time of either event—both will be unexpected, especially for those who are not prepared for them. This unexpected and sudden nature is highlighted in the remarks framing Matthew 24:36–44. At the start of this section Jesus states, "But of that day and hour no one knows, not even the angels of heaven, nor the Son, but the Father only" (Mt 24:36), while at its conclusion he reiterates the same idea: "Watch therefore, for you do not know on what day your Lord is coming.... Therefore you also must be ready; for the Son of man is coming at an hour you do not expect" (Mt 24:42, 44). What lies between these passages further illustrates and illuminates their message. First there is the comparison to the time of Noah:

> For as in those days before the flood they were eating and drinking, marrying and giving in marriage, until the day when Noah entered the ark, and they did not know until the flood came and swept them all away, so will be the coming of the Son of man. (Mt 24:38–39)[59]

Often overlooked is *who* is taken, or swept, away in the days of Noah. Not the righteous, but the unrighteous—eating and drinking and not preparing for judgment—were taken away and condemned.[60] The phrase "took them all away"

---

[59] In Luke's Gospel there is the additional comparison to "the days of Lot" and the destruction of Sodom: "Likewise as it was in the days of Lot—they ate, they drank, they bought, they sold, they planted, they built, but on the day when Lot went out from Sodom fire and brimstone rained from heaven and destroyed them all" (Lk 17:28–29).

[60] The epistle to the Hebrews states: "By faith Noah, being warned by God concerning events as yet unseen, took heed and constructed an ark for the saving of his household; by this he condemned the world and became an heir of the righteousness which comes by faith" (Heb 11:7). The language of "gathering" or "taking up" is used elsewhere to describe judgment at the end of

apparently refers to judgment. This is essential for comprehending verses 40–41, which also speak of those who are taken away. Of course, many dispensationalists insist those who are removed have been raptured, while those who have been "left behind" have been left to endure the Tribulation. Yet the opposite is most likely the case, for the people are not "raptured" or "translated", nor do they "go to meet Christ in the air"—they are "taken".

One problem with the common dispensational interpretation of this passage is that it is so literalistic it overlooks the actual meaning of the text. In thinking the image of the two men and two women is meant primarily to portray people on a hill looking around for the missing person, dispensationalists miss the real point: Christ's return will be swift, unexpected, *and* accompanied by judgment. The image of the two people is a parable-like way of concretely depicting the nature of this event. Jesus repeatedly used parables and similar language in speaking of his return and the Kingdom of heaven, especially within Matthew's Gospel. Even when applied to the destruction of Jerusalem in A.D. 70, the same principle holds: people did not suddenly disappear into thin air; they were "taken" away.

Surprisingly, some leading dispensationalists agree that this passage is not about the Rapture but actually refers to the Second Coming. Walvoord states that Matthew 24:40–51 "is essentially an exhortation to watch".[61] It is partial rapturists—those who believe that only some, holy Christians will be raptured while others are left behind—Walvoord insists, who

---

time: "The Son of man will send his angels, and they will gather out of his kingdom all causes of sin and all evildoers, and throw them into the furnace of fire; there men will weep and gnash their teeth" (Mt 13:41–42).

[61] Walvoord, *Rapture Question*, p. 100.

use this passage to prove the Rapture. But, he writes, a "careful study of the usage here … does not sustain this exegesis.… The *terminus ad quem* is the Second Coming, not the translation of the church." [62] However, there is a qualifier to Walvoord's statement, for he believes that "those who remain enter the blessing of the Millennium." [63] Yet this does not easily fit with the rest of the dispensationalist system, since it stresses that the Rapture will be sudden and unexpected, while the Second Coming will be known to all. Yet Walvoord's explanation means the Second Coming will be unexpected and unforeseen, despite his admission that "the Second Coming is preceded by definite signs." [64]

Straining to Remove the Restrainer

A further contention is that Paul's discussion of "the man of lawlessness" in the second chapter of 2 Thessalonians provides evidence for the pretribulational view:

> And you know what is restraining him now so that he may be revealed in his time. For the mystery of lawlessness is already at work; only he who now restrains it will do so until he is out of the way. And then the lawless one will be revealed, and the Lord Jesus will slay him with the breath of his mouth and destroy him by his appearing and his coming. (2 Thess 2:6–8)

[62] Ibid., p. 101.

[63] Ibid.

[64] Ibid., p. 275. LaHaye writes: "One of the reasons we know Christ is coming before the Tribulation to rapture His Church is because the Rapture is a secret thing. The Glorious Appearing [the Second Coming] will not be secret but well known, for exactly seven years will elapse from the signing of the covenant [between Israel and the Antichrist] to the Glorious Appearing of Christ on the earth" (*Revelation Unveiled*, p. 140).

The "restrainer" is identified by the majority of dispensationalists as the Holy Spirit.[65] Once the restrainer is "out of the way"—once the Church is raptured and the presence of the Holy Spirit is removed from the earth—then the Antichrist can be revealed and the Tribulation will begin. Apparently the Holy Spirit is only removed from the earth in an incomplete way and will still be present in a smaller capacity. This, Lindsey explains, is because the Holy Spirit "cannot be limited to working *only* through the Church in which He personally dwells".[66] He further explains that the Holy Spirit will operate in the Tribulation period just as he did in the Old Testament: "The Holy Spirit will convince men of their need of salvation, bring them to faith and regenerate them as He did from the beginning of man's sin."[67] Walvoord holds a different position: "That the Spirit works in the Tribulation all agree. That the Spirit indwells all believers in the Tribulation is nowhere taught."[68]

Not only is there disagreement among dispensationalists about the role of the Holy Spirit in the Tribulation, dispensationalism has a flawed understanding of the Holy Spirit and his work among mankind. Accepting for argument's sake the basic line of the dispensationalist reasoning, two possibilities exist: (1) the Holy Spirit continues to work in the

---

[65] "Pretribulationists generally hold that if the Holy Spirit is removed from His present position indwelling the church, then the church itself must also be removed, and hence the Rapture must take place at the same time. If this removal of the Holy Spirit in the church takes place before the lawless one can be revealed, it points to an event that must precede the Tribulation. In a word, it is stating that the Rapture precedes the Tribulation" (Walvoord, *Rapture Question*, p. 242). Lindsey dedicates substantial space to this position in *Rapture*, pp. 151–67.

[66] Lindsey, *Rapture*, p. 161.

[67] Ibid., p. 163.

[68] Walvoord, *Rapture Question*, p. 243.

Tribulation just as he did when the Church was on earth—which means he has not really been taken out of the way at all—or (2) people will become Christian during the Tribulation but without being indwelt by the Holy Spirit. The first possibility invalidates the dispensationalist interpretation of 2 Thessalonians 2:6–8, while the second raises disturbing questions about dispensationalist soteriology. If one can be a believer without the Holy Spirit, as Walvoord appears to state, how exactly would salvation be accomplished? After all, the New Testament teaches that salvation involves being baptized in the Holy Spirit (1 Cor 12:13) and sealed by the Holy Spirit (2 Cor 1:22; Eph 1:13; 4:30), for mankind only has access to the Father through the Son and in the Holy Spirit (Eph 2:18).

It is not obvious at all from 2 Thessalonians 2 that the restrainer is the Holy Spirit. Even more tenuous is the dispensationalist belief that the phrase "out of the way" should be attached to the Rapture. A more literal interpretation of the phrase is "coming out of the midst". The concept is "of something or someone standing in the way—in the middle between the present and the revelation of the Antichrist—moving out of the way, not moving off the planet".[69] While this passage is admittedly obscure and difficult to interpret,[70]

[69] Brumley, "Secret Rapture".

[70] *The Catholic Study Bible* (NAB) writes of this passage: "*What is restraining . . . the one who restrains:* neuter and masculine, respectively, of a force and person holding back the lawless one. The Thessalonians know what is meant (6), but the terms, seemingly found only in this passage and in writings dependent on it, have been variously interpreted. Traditionally, v 6 has been applied to the Roman empire and v 7 to the Roman emperor (in Paul's day, Nero) as bulwarks holding back chaos (cf Rom 13, 1–7). A second interpretation suggests that cosmic or angelic powers are binding Satan (9) and so restraining him; some relate this to an anti-Christ figure (1 Jn 2, 18) or to Michael the

it provides no firm foundation for the pretribulational position and, due to its very obscurity, is a poor one upon which to base a major doctrine.

Is the Church Going to Suffer?

Popular dispensationalists have been playing on people's fears and their desire to escape suffering and death for many decades. LaHaye continues this practice, especially in *Rapture under Attack*, subtitled "Will You Escape the Tribulation?" After claiming the pretribulational Rapture "is what the New Testament clearly teaches", he states: "Yet for some reason, this concept, which has brought so much hope and comfort to millions of Christians throughout church history, has been under savage attack during the last sixty years by those who refuse to take prophecy as literally as they do other Scriptures."[71] Farther on, in a chapter titled "The Great Tribulation", readers are given this description of the seven years of Tribulation:

> Take the horror of every war since time began, throw in every natural disaster in recorded history, and cast off all restraints so that the unspeakable cruelty and hatred and injustice of man toward his fellow man can fully mature—then compress it all into a period of seven years. Even if you could

---

archangel (Rv 12, 7–9; 20, 1–3). A more recent view suggests it is the preaching of the Christian gospel that restrains the end, for in God's plan the end cannot come until the gospel is preached to all nations (Mk 13, 10); in that case, Paul as missionary preacher par excellence is 'the one who restrains, whose removal (death) will bring the end (7)" (Donald Senior, ed., *The Catholic Study Bible: New American Bible* [New York: Oxford University Press, 1990], pp. 330–31).

[71] LaHaye, *Rapture under Attack*, pp. 11–12.

imagine such a thing, it wouldn't approach the mind-boggling terror and turmoil of the Tribulation.[72]

One reason LaHaye plays up the unprecedented nature of this Tribulation period is so he can downplay, in comparison, the many "*ordinary* tribulations that plague all men from time to time".[73] He writes, "We often overlook, however, the principle that trials are a standard part of life in a fallen world. By contrast, our Lord specifically informed us that the Tribulation is a special judgment of God",[74] and then quotes from the Olivet Discourse: "For then there will be great tribulation, such as has not been from the beginning of the world until now, no, and never will be. And if those days had not been shortened, no human being would be saved; but for the sake of the elect those days will be shortened" (Mt 24:21–22).

LaHaye's comments demonstrate the failure of Fundamentalism in general and dispensationalism specifically to provide meaningful teaching about suffering and trials. Although he gives passing lip service to "martyrs", it seems clear LaHaye has little appreciation for what Christians, especially Catholics, have endured throughout history. When early Christians watched their children torn apart by lions or burned alive, did they believe these were "ordinary tribulations"? How about the nameless tens of thousands herded into concentration camps by the Nazis, or buried in mass graves by the communists? It is disturbing that future events, of which we have little or no knowledge, are so easily sensationalized by comfortable "Bible prophecy" experts at the expense of

[72] Ibid., p. 56.
[73] Ibid., p. 47; emphasis added.
[74] Ibid., p. 48.

those who have truly suffered for Jesus Christ in the past—
and suffer for him today. It is all the more disturbing that
while Scripture is filled with praise for those who suffered
and died for Christ,[75] LaHaye and others appear more interested in speculating, often irresponsibly, about how horrific
and bloody the future will be. While "God our Savior ...
desires all men to be saved and to come to the knowledge of
the truth" (1 Tim 2:3–4), far too many dispensationalists ob-
sess over the billions who will, they say, be killed in the near
future. Little wonder so many non-Christians are revolted
by the calmness of those who calculate how high the blood
will rise and how far it will flow[76] or who insist that the
Tribulation is God's way of granting humanity a "second
chance".[77] In a disturbing passage, LaHaye writes, "The
Tribulation is a fitting consummation of the grand experiment of the ages from Adam to the Second Coming, giving
individuals an opportunity to worship God voluntarily."[78]
Humanity is an experiment? Tribulation is an "opportunity
to worship"? This is either glib or foolish and reveals a de-
ficient perspective of God, humanity, and salvation history.

When LaHaye and other dispensationalists quote Matthew 24:21–22, they usually ignore its immediate context:
the destruction of the Jerusalem Temple in A.D. 70. This is
made evident by the statement: "Truly, I say to you, *this gen-*

[75] For example, see Mt 10:39; 16:25; Mk 8:35; Lk 9:24; 2 Thess 1:4–10;
Rev 7:14; 12:11; 16:6; 17:6; 18:24; 19:2. Also, see CCC 2473.

[76] One example out of many: "The apostle John predicts that so many people will be slaughtered in the conflict [the battle of Armageddon] that blood
will stand to the horses' bridles for a total distance of 200 miles northward and
southward of Jerusalem (Revelation 14:20)" (Lindsey and Carlson, *Late Great
Planet Earth*, p. 154).

[77] LaHaye, *Rapture under Attack*, p. 64.

[78] Ibid., p. 63.

eration will not pass away till all these things take place" (Mt 24:34; emphasis added).[79] In fact, the destruction of Jerusalem and the Temple forty years after Christ's Ascension was notable for incredible atrocities and bloodshed, with over a million Jews killed in the Roman attack on Jerusalem and mothers resorting to eating their own children in order to survive famine.[80] Also ignored is Christ's promise that "he who endures to the end will be saved" (Mt 24:13). This echoes a consistent theme throughout the New Testament: Endurance and suffering are not just part of the Christian life— they are essential and inevitable. Jesus exhorted his disciples, "Remember the word that I said to you, 'A servant is not greater than his master.' If they persecuted me, they will persecute you; if they kept my word, they will keep yours also" (Jn 15:20). Paul writes, "Therefore I endure *everything* for the sake of the elect, that they also may obtain the salvation which in Christ Jesus goes with eternal glory" (2 Tim 2:10; emphasis added). True life comes through suffering and death, for Christians are called to die with Christ so that they may live with him (2 Tim 2:11–12). When Paul writes that "For God has not destined us for wrath, but to obtain salvation through our Lord Jesus Christ, who died for us so that whether we wake or sleep we might live with him" (1 Thess 5:9–10), he is not saying Christians will escape tribulation or even death. Rather, those who are in Christ and who endure to the end are destined to be saved from "the wrath of God"

---

[79] "The Greek denotes about a forty-year time span. Jesus' words would thus be accomplished within the lifetime of some of his hearers (cf. 10:23; 16:28; 23:36)" (Hahn and Mitch, *Gospel of Matthew*, p. 62. Also see David Chilton, *The Great Tribulation* [Fort Worth, Tex.: Dominion Press, 1987], pp. 2–4).

[80] See Josephus, *The War of the Jews*, bk. 6, chap. 3, sec. 4.

(Rom 1:18). God's wrath does not fall indiscriminately but abides on those who do not obey the Son (Jn 3:36), for "the wrath of God is revealed from heaven against all ungodliness and wickedness of men who by their wickedness suppress the truth" (Rom 1:18).

Dispensationalism can make little sense of life's suffering. Possessing a neo-Gnostic theology and a Manichaean world view, the movement is ill-equipped to provide a sense of purpose in the face of trials and tribulations.[81] Many dispensationalists (and Fundamentalists) believe that since physical suffering is the result of the Fall, it can come to no good—one must simply bear it. The existence of suffering is a reminder of humanity's dire predicament and how rotten the world has become. Compare that attitude to the perspective of Paul, who always sees suffering as an opportunity to experience a deeper and more joyous fellowship with Christ by "becoming like him in his death" (Phil 3:10). While suffering is not part of God's desire for mankind, the death and Resurrection of Jesus Christ have transformed suffering and death into a means of growth and eternal beatitude. Suffering leads to glory (Rom 8:17–18), to comfort (2 Cor 1:5), to favor with God (1 Pet 2:20), rejoicing (Acts 5:41; 1 Pet 4:13), and to union with the Church: "Now I rejoice in my suf-

---

[81] A microcosm of this fact can be seen in the popular Frank Peretti novels *This Present Darkness* (1986) and *Piercing the Darkness* (1989). Noll laments that "they have set the tone for evangelical assessment of cause-and-effect connections in the world. These novels present a nearly Manichaean vision of life where conflicts on earth are paralleled by conflicts between angels and demons in the heavens, and where the line between good and evil runs, not as Solzhenitsyn once wrote, through the heart of every individual, but between the secular forces of darkness on one side and the sanctified forces of light on the other" (Mark A. Noll, *The Scandal of the Evangelical Mind* [Grand Rapids, Mich.: W. B. Eerdmans, 1994], pp. 140–41).

ferings for your sake, and in my flesh I complete what is lacking in Christ's afflictions for the sake of his body, that is, the church" (Col 1:24). In a divine paradox, suffering is a gift, for it is through suffering that we become sacrificial, self-giving lovers of others and of God (Phil 1:29; 2 Tim 2:10–11). Such a perspective is largely absent from dispensationalist and Fundamentalist teaching.

The obsession with escaping the Tribulation speaks volumes about the dispensationalist understanding of the purpose and nature of the Church. Although dispensationalists give lip service to the Church being the "Body of Christ", they do not seem to recognize the significance of this description or how thoroughly it permeates the New Testament. This is readily evident in Ryrie's *Basic Theology*, a 530-page work of systematic theology. Although many pages are devoted to subjects such as demons, the Rapture, and the Millennial Kingdom, only *one* page addresses the topic of "The Relation of the Church to Jesus Christ", even while several pages comment on the relation of the Church to the Kingdom, Israel, and "This Age".[82] There is no examination of the nature of the Body of Christ or the relationship between Christ's sufferings and the sufferings of his Body here on earth. A verse such as Colossians 1:24, containing Paul's challenging claim that his sufferings fill up what is "lacking in Christ's afflictions", cannot be adequately considered by a dispensationalist theologian. Only when the Church is understood in relation to her Head, who "gave himself up for her, that he might sanctify her" (Eph 5:25–26), can such a statement be accepted and acted upon. Since Christians are "Christ-ones", called to intimate communion with their

---

[82] Charles C. Ryrie, *Basic Theology* (Wheaton, Ill.: Victor Books, 1986), pp. 397–402.

Savior, they will endure trials and tribulations up until the end of time and the Parousia. The *Catechism* states:

> "The Church ... will receive its perfection only in the glory of heaven" [*LG* 48], at the time of Christ's glorious return. Until that day, "the Church progresses on her pilgrimage amidst this world's persecutions and God's consolations" [St. Augustine, *De civ. Dei*, 18, 51: PL 41, 614; cf. *LG* 8]. Here below she knows that she is in exile far from the Lord, and longs for the full coming of the Kingdom, when she will "be united in glory with her king" [*LG* 5; cf. 6; 2 Cor 5:6]. The Church, and through her the world, will not be perfected in glory without great trials.[83]

The Catholic Church teaches explicitly that prior to the Second Coming the Church will endure "a final trial" that will cause many to fall away from the Christian faith.[84] Why? Should the Church, the Bride of the risen and victorious Lord, not be exempt from this time of tribulation? On the contrary, the Church follows in the footsteps of her crucified and glorified Lord—it is by sharing in those sufferings that she will also be glorified (Phil 3:8–11; 1 Pet 4:12–13):

> The Church will enter the glory of the kingdom only through this final Passover, when she will follow her Lord in his death and Resurrection [cf. Rev 19:1–9]. The kingdom will be fulfilled, then, not by a historic triumph of the Church through a progressive ascendancy, but only by God's victory over the final unleashing of evil, which will cause his Bride to come down from heaven [cf. Rev 13:8; 20:7–10; 21:2–4]. God's triumph over the revolt of evil will take the form of

---

[83] CCC 769. Also see CCC 672.
[84] CCC 675.

the Last Judgment after the final cosmic upheaval of this passing world [cf. Rev 20:12; 2 Pet 3:12–13].[85]

To Be Deep in History ...

A newcomer on the theological scene, the pretribulational
Rapture is rejected by the vast majority of Christians worldwide. Recognizing that history is not on their side, dispensationalists have resorted to two different approaches: either
denying history has any importance when it comes to "biblical doctrine", or denying that the notion of a pretribulational Rapture is only two hundred years old.

Ryrie attempts the former approach; referring to the "historical attack" on dispensationalism, he writes:

> It seeks to prove that since dispensationalism in its present
> form is apparently recent, it cannot be true; for surely some-
> one would have taught it in the first eighteen centuries of
> the history of the church if it were true. Some who use this
> device to discredit dispensationalism are honest enough to
> admit that history is never the test of truth—the Bible and
> only the Bible is. But they persist in using the approach and
> leave the impression that history is a partly valid test, if not
> the final test.[86]

These are rather astonishing words. Is it logically consistent
for dispensationalist doctrines not to have to answer to history, while Catholic doctrines and practices are often attacked by dispensationalists as late additions in Church history?
Does Ryrie really think the veracity and authenticity of
Scripture can stand without reference to history? Is not

[85] CCC 677.
[86] Ryrie, *Dispensationalism*, p. 14.

Christianity the most historically rooted of faiths, based as it is on the entrance of God into time and space? Ryrie adds, "The fact that the church taught something in the first century does not make it true, and likewise if the church did not teach something until the twentieth century, it is not necessarily false." [87] This raises serious questions. For example, why does Ryrie believe in the Trinity, the two natures of Christ, the hypostatic union, and the canon of the New Testament when all of these were established by Catholic councils and synods not practicing *sola scriptura*? Ryrie's remarks demonstrate why hermeneutics is so significant for dispensationalists. Scripture may be cited as their sole authority, but it is their method of interpretation that most distinguishes them from hundreds of other Protestant groups and movements. It claims to be beyond the reach of history, rendering all tradition and authority powerless—except for what is generated by the individual dispensationalist.

On the other hand, Lindsey, LaHaye, Grant Jeffrey, and others have sought to demonstrate that pretribulational beliefs existed prior to the early 1800s. Since Darby is the undeniable father of the pretribulational dispensational system, these authors claim all of the elements of the system existed long before Darby—he simply put them together "into a cohesive body of thought". [88] LaHaye is adamant that "Darby did not invent the pre-Tribulation rapture, the separation of Israel and the church, dispensationalism, types and symbols, and other distinctives which have made him the most quoted prophecy teacher since the apostle Paul." [89] But if

---

[87] Ibid., pp. 15–16.

[88] LaHaye, *Rapture under Attack*, p. 160.

[89] Ibid. LaHaye's remark is rather odd considering the fact that quotes by Darby are hard to find and reprints of his books are difficult to obtain. Darby's

Darby was not the first to come up with pretribulational Rapture, who was? According to LaHaye, a strong candidate is the late eighteenth-century Baptist minister Morgan Edwards of Pennsylvania, who published two essays on the millennium and the last days in 1788. However, LaHaye admits Edwards "saw only a three and a half year tribulation",[90] meaning Edwards' writings would better support midtribulationalism, a view LaHaye strongly opposes. Even if Edwards did envision some type of Rapture prior to a time of tribulation, his explanation is ambiguous and only gives pretribulationists another fifty years or so of history to claim as their own.[91] In the context of two thousand years, this is hardly persuasive, especially since Edwards' views are not clear or fully formed.

Since the early 1990s, Jeffrey has claimed that a fourth-century writing by a Syrian Christian, St. Ephraem, was found containing "clear evidence of the teaching of the pretribulation Rapture in the early church".[92] The writing, a sermon

---

writing is often so convoluted and obscure it hardly makes for pithy quoting, not to mention bearable reading.

[90] Ibid., p. 43.

[91] Mark Brumley writes, "Edwards' views are contradictory and ambiguous. As a seminarian, he wrote two essays on the Millennium and the Last Days, which were published in 1788. Therein Edwards seems to have proposed the idea that for three-and-a-half years true believers will undergo judgment in heaven to receive their rewards from Christ, while Antichrist and the rest of the wicked are punished on earth. At the end of this time, Jesus will come to defeat Antichrist and to establish his Millennial Kingdom on earth. Yet even if one accepts this scenario as referring to a Pretribulation or Midtribulation Rapture, it provides little basis for seeing the doctrine as anything more than a novelty. At best, Pretribulationists/Midtribulationists can move the origin of their doctrine back 40 years or so, from 1830 to 1788" (Brumley, "Secret Rapture").

[92] Grant R. Jeffrey, *Armageddon: Appointment with Destiny* (Toronto, Ontario: Frontier Research Publications, 1997), p. 173. In 1995 dispensationalists

titled "On the Last Times, the Antichrist and the End of the
World", is pseudonymous and more likely dates somewhere
between the fifth and seventh centuries, although Jeffrey claims
it was written "about A.D. 373".[93] The main passage Jeffrey
cites as proof reads:

> Why therefore do we not reject every care of earthly actions
> and prepare ourselves for the meeting of the Lord Christ, so
> that He may draw us from the confusion, which overwhelms
> the world? Believe you me, dearest brothers, because the com-
> ing of the Lord is nigh, believe you me, because the end of
> the world is at hand, believe me, because it is the very last
> time. Because all saints and the Elect of the Lord are gath-
> ered together before the tribulation which is about to come
> and are taken to the Lord, in order that they may not see at
> any time the confusion which overwhelms the world be-
> cause of our sins.[94]

Posttribulationist Gundry provides a detailed critique of the
Pseudo-Ephraem text in his book *First the Antichrist*, arguing
it does not refer to the pretribulational Rapture at all, but to
a posttribulational Rapture concurrent with the Second Coming. Noting the significant absence of key pretribulational
language in the passages highlighted by dispensationalist scholars, Gundry states that none of them "mentions a coming of
the Lord (as in the classic New Testament description of the
rapture at 1 Thess. 4:16–17), or a resurrection of deceased
Christians and translation of living ones (as in 1 Cor. 15:51–52;

Timothy J. Demy and Thomas D. Ice published a controversial article on the
fragment, "The Rapture and an Early Medieval Citation", *Bibliotheca Sacra*,
July/September 1995, pp. 306–17.

[93] Jeffrey, *Armageddon*, p. 174.

[94] Pseudo-Ephraem, "On the Last Times, the Antichrist and the End of the
World", par. 1, 2. Quoted in Jeffrey, *Armageddon*, pp. 174–76.

see again 1 Thess. 4:16–17 for the resurrection), or a heavenly destination (as in a pretrib understanding of Jn. 14:2–4 and, often, of Rev. 4:1–2)."[95] Another inconsistency is the abundance of references to Christians being persecuted and killed during the Tribulation, with their corpses left lying on the ground. Gundry acknowledges that a "pretrib understanding might posit a distinction between 'all the saints and elect of God'" who make up the church prior to the Rapture and "'Christians' as describing those who become believers after the pretrib rapture of the church".[96] The problem is that Pseudo-Ephraem refers to these Christians as "saints", "elect", "Christian", "righteous ones", and "faithful witnesses of God", terms supposedly reserved only for those who are saved prior to the Rapture.[97] A further wrinkle is that the references to the Rapture and the Second Coming employ similar and overlapping language, indicating the author is referring to the same event, not two separate ones.[98] Gundry interprets the cited passage as a depiction of people being evangelized and "gathered together" in the Church, the people who have been called out of the world and formed into a body in Christ.[99]

Appealing to a single obscure sermon by an unknown writer from the early centuries of Christianity indicates desperation and a lack of consistency. LaHaye, for example, mocks the "pagan" Catholic belief in the Real Presence in the Eucharist and the Church's high regard for tradition, yet these

---

[95] Gundry, *First the Antichrist*, p. 164.

[96] Ibid., p. 168.

[97] Ibid.

[98] See ibid., pp. 167–70.

[99] See ibid., pp. 176–84. Another critique of the dispensational use of the Pseudo-Ephraem text can be found in Dave MacPherson's *Rapture Plot*, pp. 268–73.

and many other distinctively Catholic beliefs are abundantly and unanimously attested by the early Church Fathers. Can his claim of historicity for the pretribulation position, based on a single and inconclusive text, be taken seriously when he either mocks or ignores the unanimous, clear, and consistent testimony of the Fathers about the Eucharist actually and truly being the body and blood of Jesus Christ? Such tactics are desperate attempts to gain some sort of scholarly integrity and to placate adherents in the face of an increasing number of damaging critiques of dispensationalism and its historical roots.

"LaHaying" It on Thick Is Wearing Thin

Since his *Left Behind* books have been so popular, LaHaye's main reasons for believing in the pretribulation Rapture demand comment. His *apologia* for this position, *Rapture under Attack*, has a chapter titled "The Pre-Tribulation Rapture: Believe It", containing fourteen reasons LaHaye finds "satisfying and which convince me [the pre-Trib view] rightly divides and arranges biblical prophecy".[100] Here are some concise responses to the points he raises.

"The pre-Tribulation view is the most logical view of the Second Coming Scriptures when taken for their plain, literal meaning whenever possible."

As we have seen, the "literal" approach is a fabrication inconsistent in practice and misleading in theory. Those scriptural texts used to prove the pretribulational view are hardly

---

[100] LaHaye, *Rapture under Attack*, pp. 207–16.

"plain" and never substantiate the belief in a clear or cogent manner.

"It clearly and logically untangles the contrasting details of Christ's Second Coming."

Hardly. This belief interjects so many distinctions, classifications, separations, and dichotomies that the average person can scarcely follow the logic of the position. By contrast, the Catholic and historically orthodox position is both simple and clear: Christ will return with and for his saints; he will judge all of mankind; time will end; and eternity will begin.

"It allows sufficient time to interject important end-time events."

Here LaHaye refers to the Judgment Seat and the Marriage Supper, arguing that a seven-year interval is needed for these events to take place without being rushed. Why does LaHaye insist on limiting God and the transcendent order to a limited, temporal view of reality? After all, eternity is sufficiently long for just about anything, including both judgment and the Marriage Supper.

"This is the only view that distinguishes between Israel and the church."

Distinguishing between the two is one thing; creating a radical dichotomy between them, as dispensationalism does, is something entirely different. It is an obvious break from centuries of historical teaching, both Catholic *and* Protestant. This radical distinction is based on—and further propagates—an anemic, distorted, and inadequate understanding of the Church and the Old Testament roots of Christianity.

"It is the only view that makes 'the blessed hope' [Tit 2:13] truly a blessed hope."

How so—because it means escaping tribulation? It is actually a mockery of both martyrdom and of Christ's own sufferings. It also misses the fact that the "blessed hope" is, in the end, salvation from sin and communion with God. Enduring some temporal tribulation in exchange for an eternity with the Trinity will only make it sweeter. Which is why St. Paul tells the Romans that "we rejoice in our hope of sharing the glory of God. More than that, we rejoice in our sufferings, knowing that suffering produces endurance" (Rom 5:2–3).

"It is the only view that takes God at His Word and claims His promises literally to save us out of the wrath to come."

As demonstrated above, this is an appeal to passages that have nothing to do with a pretribulational Rapture. In some cases they refer to salvation from eternal damnation; in others they refer to being spared from the destruction of Jerusalem in A.D. 70. Besides, God can save people on earth from his wrath as easily as he can save them in heaven.

"Only the pre-Trib view preserves the motivating power of imminency teaching found in the New Testament that was such a challenge to the early church."

So the main motivation in the Christian life is escaping from a few years of tribulation? What would St. Paul think of such an attitude? He writes: "Indeed I count everything as loss because of the surpassing worth of knowing Christ Jesus my Lord. For his sake I have suffered the loss of all things, and count them as refuse, in order that I may gain Christ" (Phil 3:8).

"Pre-Trib Christians are looking for the coming of the Lord."

As are all Christians who know and live the Christian faith. Catholics confess their belief in the Second Coming each Sunday in their recitation of the Nicene Creed. LaHaye also remarks, "Other views have them awaiting Tribulation, Antichrist, and suffering." Yes, and Christians have already experienced tribulations, antichrists, and suffering, to differing degrees, for two thousand years (cf. Rom 5:3; 8:35; 1 Thess 1:6; 2 Thess 1:5; 1 Jn 2:18, 22; 2 Jn 7). Being aware of these potential difficulties is obedience to Christ's exhortation to be prepared for his return.

"It makes a major event out of the Rapture."

It sure does, which is exactly what LaHaye and other dispensationalists want to do. Yet the Second Coming and the end of time are major events for all Christians, even as the end of their earthly existence is a serious, major event. In reality, the dispensationalist system lessens the meaning of the Second Coming by subverting it to issues such as the supposed Rapture, the Tribulation, and the earthly millennial Kingdom.

"This view most clearly fits the flow of the book of Revelation."

Not at all. While claiming to interpret the book of Revelation "literally", LaHaye ignores vital contextual elements within it, such as the hundreds of references to Old Testament figures and types, as well as its primary historical context: the first century.

"The pre-Trib view explains why the church is not mentioned in Revelation 4:3 through chapter 18."

It may offer an explanation, but it is incorrect, since the Church is mentioned several times (e.g., Rev 5:8; 6:9–11; 8:3–4; 11:18; 13:7, 10; 14:12; 16:6; 17:6; 18:20, 24). This is just another case of trying to force Scripture into pretribulational dispensationalist assumptions.

"It preserves the credibility of Christ's word that Christians will be kept from the Tribulation."

Here LaHaye quotes Revelation 3:10, which says nothing about "the Tribulation" or the Rapture, but states "I also will keep you from the hour of testing." However, John does tell his readers that he "share[s] with you in Jesus the tribulation and the kingdom and the patient endurance" (Rev 1:9). Being kept from the hour of testing cannot be equated with the Rapture, just as being "not of the world" is not equivalent to not being "in the world" (Jn 15:19; 17:11–16).

"The pre-Trib view maintains 1 Thessalonians 4:13–18 as a comfort passage and explains why the young Christians at Thessalonica were so upset about the death of their loved ones."

Yes, the passage is meant to give comfort, but this hardly proves the pretribulational dispensationalist view. The message is simple: Christ will return, and those Christians who have already died will rise again. This confirms nothing about the truthfulness of LaHaye's viewpoint.

"It explains why there is no Bible instruction on preparation for the Tribulation."

Perhaps LaHaye should reread passages such as John 13–17 and verses such as Revelation 1:17–18, where John is encouraged in the face of trials and suffering: "But he laid his right hand upon me, saying, 'Fear not, I am the first and the last, and the living one; I died, and behold I am alive for evermore, and I have the keys of Death and Hades.' " Going through any sort of tribulation calls for reliance upon the power of the Holy Spirit and the desire to endure so that we might reign with Christ (cf. 2 Tim 2:12).

The Great Escape: What's Not to Like?

The appeal of the pretribulational Rapture cannot be denied. The belief that those living today are "the generation" who will see Christ's return is attractive and intoxicating. Once accepted as fact, it is difficult to walk away from it. Both Lindsey and LaHaye, the two best-selling dispensationalists of the past three decades, believe and teach that the Rapture will occur very soon. LaHaye declares, "My prophetic studies have convinced me that we Christians living today have more evidence to believe we are the generation of His coming than any generation before us." [101] No doubt there are many people who want to be told they will not have to suffer much longer, will not have to die, and will see God's wrath poured out on this "terminal generation".

This natural desire to escape suffering and death plays a large part in the success of what Reformed theologian Gary North aptly calls "dispensensationalism". [102] Lindsey proclaims that the Rapture "means no death", and "we Christians are

---

[101] Ibid., p. 27.

[102] Gary North, *Rapture Fever: Why Dispensationalism Is Paralyzed* (Tyler, Tex.: Institute for Christian Economics, 1993), p. 20.

not all going *to die!*"[103] He also states that the "truly elec-
trifying fact is that many of you who are reading this will
experience this mystery. You will never know what it is to
die physically."[104] LaHaye asks a series of melodramatic questions: "Are you able to look at your children playing in the
sunlight and believe firmly in your heart that they will not
have to endure the monstrous horrors of the Tribulation?
Are you able to sit at the deathbed of a believing loved one
and cling to the hope that before your own life has ended—in
an instant of time—you may meet again in the clouds?"[105]
Compare those sentiments with the example of the early martyrs who watched their children die for Christ before they
themselves were killed, their parents torn to pieces by lions,
or their siblings burned alive. Appealing to fear is appealing
to base human nature, but it does not encourage Christians
who are suffering and facing death today. Some Christians
become disillusioned when the Rapture does not come as
expected. Others, however, eagerly buy into the next work
of "Bible prophecy" that comes along, apparently willing to
take yet another chance.[106]

---

[103] Lindsey, *Rapture*, p. 42; emphasis in original.

[104] Ibid., p. 43.

[105] LaHaye, *Rapture under Attack*, p. 20.

[106] The acerbic Gary North writes: "Rapture fever is a deliberately induced
psychological condition. The number of its victims has escalated rapidly since
1970. Millions of readers repeatedly inject themselves with what can best be
described as a psychologically addicting drug: the expectation of the imminent
return of Jesus Christ, which will remove them from their troubles by removing them from history. The results of this addiction are predictable: an initial
'high,' followed by a debilitating letdown, followed by painful withdrawal symptoms (mentally recentering the hum-drum world), followed by another in-
jection. Again and again, millions of emotionally vulnerable Christians return
to their 'pushers' for another 'fix'" (North, *Rapture Fever*, p. 2). Although
North's assessment sounds harsh, I can vouch from personal experience that
his basic point is accurate—an obsession with the pretribulational Rapture is
often a ticket to an emotional and spiritual roller-coaster ride.

Equally disturbing in its implications is the emphasis in dispensationalism on the escape of "believers", while "unbelievers" will undergo the wrath of God, experiencing the "most gruesome period the world has ever known",[107] courtesy of a God who apparently cannot wait to destroy most of humanity. The Tribulation, LaHaye contends, "will become such a holocaust because it combines the wrath of God, the fury of Satan, and the evil nature of man run wild".[108] In an online defense of the *Left Behind* books, one fan openly admits that the main point of the Rapture is to escape the Tribulation:

> These novels were inspired by God—to give a realistic look at the horrible ordeal that those who've been left behind will endure during the tribulation. The point is ... you don't have to be. Left behind that is. This series has given enough truth that those who haven't yet made a decision to follow Jesus Christ, have been given a chance to see what they'll endure if they refuse to acknowledge him as Lord. That's the whole point of these novels. I'm thankful that I won't have to endure it, but I am concerned for those who will.[109]

Is it any wonder many non-Christians are repulsed by this depiction of God? Yes, God hates evil; he will judge humanity; and he will be victorious over evil and death.[110] But this must be balanced by the realization that God desires the salvation of mankind (1 Tim 2:3–4). God's judgment is righteous and based in his love, which is life to those who receive it and wrath to those who reject it.[111] While we can and must make judgments about the moral value of peoples'

---

[107] LaHaye, *Rapture under Attack*, p. 20.
[108] Ibid., p. 56.
[109] Online review taken from www.amazon.com, June 13, 2000.
[110] See CCC 677.
[111] See CCC 1022.

actions and words, we cannot judge their souls: "Therefore do not pronounce judgment before the time, before the Lord comes, who will bring to light the things now hidden in darkness and will disclose the purposes of the heart. Then every man will receive his commendation from God" (1 Cor 4:5).

Yet popular dispensationalists do have a low view of humanity and are convinced they, as God's faithful, are able to render judgment on men's souls—not just on their actions. There exists a self-feeding cycle in dispensationalism: pessimism about humanity and the future feeds the belief that the end of the world is just around the corner, while the belief in the rapidly approaching Tribulation makes such pessimism logical and necessary.[112] Those not embracing this pessimistic perspective are often viewed with suspicion, and if they claim to be Christian, they run the risk of being labeled "liberal" or identified as someone lacking "true knowledge of the Word". Fundamentalism and dispensationalism share in a potent neo-Gnosticism, the conviction that "true believers" possess secret knowledge (*gnosis*) attainable only through their system of interpreting Scripture and rightly discerning "the signs of the times". Related elements include the dualistic nature of the radical distinction made between Old Testament Israel and the Church, as well as a

---

[112] David Chilton asks: "How common it is to hear Christians say, when confronted with a problem: 'I sure hope the Rapture comes soon!'—rather than: 'Let's get to work on the solution right now!' Even worse is the response that is also too common: 'Who cares? We don't have to do anything about it, because the Rapture is coming soon anyway!' And worst of all is the attitude held by some that all work to make this a better world is absolutely wrong, because 'improving the situation will only delay the Second Coming!' A good deal of modern Rapturism should be recognized for what it really is: a dangerous error that is teaching God's people to expect defeat instead of victory" (David Chilton, *Paradise Restored: A Biblical Theology of Dominion* [Tyler, Tex.: Dominion Press, 1994], p. 53).

suspicious (and even hostile) attitude toward the material world. It logically follows that since The End is so near and this world is passing away, there is no need to invest time and effort into social, cultural, or political institutions and efforts.[113] The Christian life, according to this perspective, should be oriented toward heaven and eternity, free from the impediments found in a fallen and depraved world. Of this belief, Noll writes:

> Dispensational writing on eschatology consistently spelled out how the study of biblical prophecy would benefit the believer.... Conspicuous by its absence from such advertisements for the virtues of studying prophetic literature is any sense of how such study might help the believer find a biblical understanding of the world in which the believer lived. Chafer even went so far as to say that such an effort was

[113] Paul Boyer quotes David Wilkerson, a popular dispensationalist author in the 1970s, as stating in 1974: "Let depression or recession come.... Let pollution and inflation come. Let there be wars and rumors of wars. Let the fabric of society disintegrate. Let mankind go to the drunken brink of disaster.... The future is ... under His control so we need not fear. God has it all preprogrammed. He knows the exact moment Christ will return. The final tribulation, the judgment, and the battle of Armageddon are all on His calendar" (Paul Boyer, *When Time Shall Be No More: Prophecy Belief in Modern American Culture* [Cambridge, Mass.: Harvard University Press, 1998], p. 297). Boyer writes that "from John Darby's day on, a vast body of premillennialist writing warned against the lure of social activism. 'The true mission of the church is not the reformation of society,' declared Cyrus Scofield at the height of the Progressive Era. 'What Christ did not do, the Apostles did not do. Not one of them was a reformer.' Through the Depression and World War II, prophecy writers emphasized the uselessness of human efforts at social betterment: regardless of what governments and uplift organizations might do, war, suffering, and conflict were bound to grow worse.... 'One who honestly feels Christ may come at any moment is not involved with this world,' declared Jack Van Impe.... 'God did not send me to clean the fishbowl,' observed Hal Lindsey; 'he sent me to fish.' Others compared social reform to polishing the brass fixtures on a sinking ocean liner" (pp. 298–99).

beside the point: "The divine program of events so faithfully set forth in the Scriptures of truth and as faithfully revealed to the attentive heart by the Spirit of truth is little concerned with an ever shifting and transitory now." [114]

Despite its pessimistic spirit, discredited history, and unbiblical premises, dispensationalism's unique mixture of Christian fatalism, apocalypticism, and neo-Gnosticism continues to mesmerize millions of Americans. As the *Left Behind* books demonstrate, the power of the dispensationalist system rests in its offer of escape from suffering and tribulation, its claim to make sense of Scripture and history, and its invitation to be part of a chosen, knowledgeable few—true believers whom God will soon vindicate with wrath and power. As long as people want to know the future but not live in it, the Rapture will live on—a supernatural escape from an unbelieving world for those who long for a new and better world.[115]

---

[114] Noll, *Scandal of the Evangelical Mind*, p. 136. Noll quotes from Chafer's *Systematic Theology*, 1: xxxiii–xxxiv.

[115] Writing of dispensationalists of the early 1900s, Presbyterian pastor Philip J. Lee observes: "Among those who had no hope in the present cosmos and denied any hint of fulfillment within world history, the idea of a new cosmos under a new dispensation was quite appealing" (Philip J. Lee, *Against the Protestant Gnostics* [New York: Oxford University Press, 1987], p. 96).

10

CONCLUSION:
THE CATHOLIC VISION

The visible universe, then, is itself destined to be transformed, "so that the world itself, restored to its original state, facing no further obstacles, should be at the service of the just," sharing their glorification in the risen Jesus Christ [St. Irenaeus, *Adv. haeres.* 5, 32, 1: PG 7/2, 210].

—CCC 1047

From first to last, and not merely in the epilogue, Christianity is eschatology, is hope, forward looking and forward moving, and therefore also revolutionizing and transforming the present. The eschatological is not one element of Christianity, but it is the medium of Christian faith as such, the key in which everything is set, the glow that suffuses everything here in the dawn of an expected new day.

—Jurgen Moltmann, Lutheran theologian

In my end is my beginning.

—T. S. Eliot

In comparing dispensationalism and Catholic doctrine, there is a striking contrast between the disunity of the former and the unity of the latter. As shown throughout this book, the dispensationalist system rests on the radical disunity its proponents make between the Old Testament and the New Testament, between Israel and the Church, and between the Church and the Kingdom. This disunity is not just a by-product of the system but is the very basis for it—without disunity dispensationalism does not exist. For dispensationalists, history is a series of epochs in which man is offered salvation, is tested, and then fails. Therefore history will end with dramatic violence and calamity. Salvation, in this perspective, is a pessimistic story. Although Christ brought salvation, he was rejected by his people and had to form a new people, the Church, who had no relation or connection to God's first people, the Jews. The end of time is a series of prophetic puzzles, simplified to some degree by a myriad of charts, graphs, and end-time novels, but still largely a mystery for the ordinary person. For many who accept these beliefs, it is enough to know that they will be raptured while the rest of the world will undergo devastating tribulation and trial.

In contrast, Catholic eschatology is marked by unity and continuity. A brief examination of the Catholic doctrine of the "last things" is a fitting conclusion for this book, for not only is eschatology concerned with the end of time, it focuses just as intently upon *all* of time and history. And since eschatology involves the summation of time, history, redemption, salvation, and judgment, it requires some knowledge of what these realities are about and how they relate to one another. What will happen at the end of time? And what does it mean for us today? Other than desiring to escape judgment and make it to heaven, do we seriously consider and contemplate the big picture of salvation history?

The unified nature of God's plan for mankind to share in God's divine life flows from the unity of God himself, who is One. But it also reflects the fact that this unity is not a monolithic (although it is monotheistic) or pantheistic oneness, but a unity of communion and familial relationship. Humanity was created to share in the divine life, to be "partakers of the divine nature" (2 Pet 1:4): "In his Son and through him, [God] invites men to become, in the Holy Spirit, his adopted children and thus heirs of his blessed life."[1] But mankind rejected this life and instead sought a life that was individualistic, self-absorbed, and the bearer of death. Ever since the Fall, God has worked to restore the original plan of unity, but always doing so while respecting man's free will and recognizing his fallen state. He condescends to our situation, coming to us in ways that our weakened minds and darkened hearts can at least partially understand.

What Is the Point of History?

On one hand, history can be understood (as it usually is) as a series of social and political events involving people in different places and cultures. Ambrose Bierce acidly remarked that history is "an account, mostly false, of events mostly unimportant."[2] But from the perspective of eternity all events are important, for they involve acts of free will committed by unique persons making serious moral and spiritual choices. Without an eternal, external reference point, history would be meaningless. Yet such a point does exist, and since that point—the Lord of History, the Alpha and Omega—does exist, history has meaning. Aidan Nichols observes, "History

---

[1] CCC 1. Also see CCC 1877–78.
[2] Ambrose Bierce, *The Enlarged Devil's Dictionary* (New York: Doubleday, 1967), p. 134.

is time in the process of acquiring meaning." [3] That meaning of time is not transitory, as time itself is, but immortal—just as human souls are immortal. The actions and deeds committed by each person will someday be weighed and considered outside of time, both at the individual judgment and at the Last Judgment. The *Catechism* states:

> The Last Judgment will come when Christ returns in glory. Only the Father knows the day and the hour; only he determines the moment of its coming. Then through his Son Jesus Christ he will pronounce the final word on all history. We shall know the ultimate meaning of the whole work of creation and of the entire economy of salvation and understand the marvellous ways by which his Providence led everything towards its final end. [4]

Through the Word made flesh God will pronounce the final word on human history. This judgment has already begun, for the incarnate Word has already been spoken. Today that Word is being spoken to every man. Just as God first spoke creation into being in the book of Genesis, he is now speaking a New Creation into being through the incarnate Word, the Son. [5] The first creation continues, yearning for the transformation promised by the Incarnation and Christ's Resurrection. Growing in time and space, the fullness of the new creation will be revealed on the last day when the presence of God—the Parousia—will consume the veil of temporality and reveal the new heaven and new earth. [6] Mankind will see Christ face-to-face and know him—as both Savior and Judge.

---

[3] Aidan Nichols, *Christendom Awake: On Re-energising the Church in Culture* (Edinburgh: T and T Clark, 1999), p. 221.

[4] CCC 1040.

[5] See CCC 315, 349, 374.

[6] See CCC 1043.

This is the truest sense of the "apocalypse"—the revealing of Christ to man, who in turn "fully reveals man to man himself and makes his supreme calling clear".[7] "The time of history, on the Christian view, is apocalyptic", Nichols writes. "History is a creative movement toward an incalculably great but by no means unknown issue."[8]

History, at its deepest level, involves the battle for the human soul, torn between good and evil. It is where the cosmic conflict of "principalities" and "powers" (Rom 8:38–39) intersects with creatures of mere flesh and blood created in the image of God—creatures who must choose between communion with God or damnation apart from him. Here is the essence of the conflict between the spirit of the Antichrist and Christ: self-love against self-sacrifice, man against God, and man's arrogant desire to be a god against God's loving choice to become man.[9] The test Adam and Eve failed is the same test each person undergoes in temporal history. But creation is not a testing ground that will simply be destroyed at the end of time. Creation also yearns for completeness, for it was also damaged and corrupted by the Fall:

> For the creation waits with eager longing for the revealing of the sons of God; for the creation was subjected to futility, not of its own will but by the will of him who subjected it in hope; because the creation itself will be set free from its bondage to decay and obtain the glorious liberty of the children

---

[7] GS 22. Also: "For now we see in a mirror dimly, but then face to face. Now I know in part; then I shall understand fully, even as I have been fully understood" (1 Cor 13:12) and "Beloved, we are God's children now; it does not yet appear what we shall be, but we know that, when he appears we shall be like him, for we shall see him as he is" (1 Jn 3:2).

[8] Nichols, *Christendom Awake*, p. 219.

[9] See CCC 675; 2 Thess 2:4–12; 1 Thess 5:2–3; 2 Jn 7; 1 Jn 2:1 8, 22.

of God. We know that the whole creation has been groaning in travail together until now. (Rom 8:19–22)

The Parousia—the fully realized presence of God at the conclusion of time—cannot be understood apart from the presence of God in time and space. God entered time and history to become man, not just to save humanity, but to bring about a new creation. He remains in time and space in the Eucharist, giving himself to those who are part of his divine family. Man, as a created being, has an eternal and binding relationship with creation, a relationship that the Son, being Creator and incarnate, possesses in the most perfect and complete way. Therefore, history and creation, suffused with the eternal, will also be fulfilled and transformed on the last day.

The Center of History

The Incarnation is the climactic centerpiece of human history: "The Redeemer of man, Jesus Christ, is the center of the universe and of history." [10] The end times were "ushered in by the Son's redeeming Incarnation",[11] and we now live in the last days, a time of trial but also of hope. This state of tension and testing exists between the first, silent entrance into time and history by the suffering Son and the public, glorious return of the conquering King:

> The death and resurrection of Christ already marks the beginning of the end of the world. By those saving acts Christ introduced into this world and into human history the final order of things. The new creation has begun. We already have eternal life. We enjoy already the life of the world to

---

[10] John Paul II, encyclical letter *Redemptor Hominis* (March 4, 1979), I, I.
[11] CCC 686.

come. We live in the last days. No wonder the first Christians were impatient for everything to be settled quickly. But the ascension of Christ and the promise of his return made it clear that the end of the world would only come about in two stages. The present order is the first stage. The order of things now exists, fully in Christ himself but only in a hidden, incomplete way in the rest of creation. This is an intermediate period. The reason for it is to give men the opportunity of associating themselves freely with the new creation and of co-operating with its gradual penetration into the old. When all is ready, at a time known only to God, Christ will come again. His return will mark the second and ultimate stage.[12]

Again, the continuity is clear. Jesus Christ did not fail in his first coming, nor did he have to change his plan because some of the Jews rejected him. It was always the Father's plan to form the Church, to provide humanity with the means to become a new creation in the new and definitive covenant.[13] All that came before Christ was "'a preparation for and figure of that new and perfect covenant which was to be ratified in Christ ... the New Covenant in his blood; he called together a race made up of Jews and Gentiles which would be one, not according to the flesh, but in the Spirit.' [LG 9; cf. Acts 10:35; 1 Cor 11:25]".[14]

This New Covenant exists in and through the work, death, and Resurrection of Christ. Apart from his Resurrection no one will be resurrected, and apart from his glorification no one will be glorified. The Apostle Paul declares that "if Christ

[12] Charles Davis, *Theology for Today* (New York: Sheed and Ward, 1962), p. 295.
[13] See CCC 759–60 and CCC 778.
[14] CCC 781.

has not been raised, then our preaching is in vain and your faith is in vain" (1 Cor 15:14), for, "If for this life only we have hoped in Christ, we are of all men most to be pitied" (1 Cor 15:19).[15] Without the Resurrection there is no meaning to the term "eternal life", no reason to have hope about what lies beyond the grave, and no lasting significance to our moral choices. Eschatology, properly understood, directs our choices today by focusing our minds and hearts on the future—not one of doom and tribulation, although great trials do exist for Christians in this world, but a future of eternal communion with the triune God.

Not just a matter of "coming back to life", the future resurrection will be an entrance into true and everlasting life.[16] Those who are joined to Christ in baptism and who partake of the Savior in the Eucharist already have a share in that future resurrection: "He who eats my flesh and drinks my blood has eternal life, and I will raise him up at the last day" (Jn 6:54). The redemptive effects of Christ's Resurrection already permeate the universe and creation, silently and secretly transforming all that exists. "For the creation waits with eager longing for the revealing of the sons of God", Paul observes, and on that day of revelation "the creation itself will be set free from its bondage to decay and obtain the glorious liberty of the children of God" (Rom 8:19, 21). Of this final glorification of all things Aidan Nichols re-

---

[15] See CCC 638, 648.

[16] John Paul II writes: "In the resurrection the body will return to perfect unity and harmony with the spirit. Man will no longer experience the opposition between what is spiritual and what is physical in him. Spiritualization means not only that the spirit will dominate the body, but, I would say, that it will fully permeate the body, and that the forces of the spirit will permeate the energies of the body" (*The Theology of the Body: Human Love in the Divine Plan* [Boston: Pauline Books and Media, 1997], p. 241).

marks: "The resurrection of the human body of God's Son is in principle the glorification of the entire visible universe, the regeneration of the cosmos. The sacramental economy of the Church depends on this truth." [17]

The Realization of the Kingdom

Again we see why the study of ecclesiology is so central to eschatology. The Incarnation is the beginning of the new creation living in the Mystical Body of Christ, the Church. And the Church is the "seed" of the Kingdom, for the Kingdom is not a thing, but a Person: "'It may even be ... that the Kingdom of God means Christ himself, whom we daily desire to come, and whose coming we wish to be manifested quickly to us. For as he is our resurrection, since in him we rise, so he can also be understood as the Kingdom of God, for in him we shall reign' [St. Cyprian, *De Dom. orat.* 13: PL 4, 528A]." [18] The continuity and communion between Christ, the Church, and the Kingdom cannot be overstated—it is the heart of God's plan for the unity of mankind:

> The Church is ultimately *one, holy, catholic, and apostolic* in her deepest and ultimate identity, because it is in her that "the Kingdom of heaven," the "Reign of God" [Rev 19:6], already exists and will be fulfilled at the end of time. The kingdom has come in the person of Christ and grows mysteriously in the hearts of those incorporated into him, until its full eschatological manifestation. [19]

[17] Aidan Nichols, O.P., *Epiphany: A Theological Introduction to Catholicism* (Collegeville, Minn.: Liturgical Press, 1996), p. 203.

[18] CCC 2816.

[19] CCC 865. Also see CCC 1186.

The goal of this eschatological manifestation is unity, "to bring under a single head 'all things in [Christ], things in heaven and things on earth' [Eph 1:10]".[20] Within this new cosmos, "the heavenly Jerusalem", God will dwell with mankind—humanity will be united once again, just as at the very beginning. This unity is being brought about through the "sacrament" of the Church, whose very existence and heart speak of her Head, Jesus Christ.[21]

Some Christians focus so much on the future and end-time events they lose sight of how their eternal destination relates to their temporal situation. The old saying is that such folks are "so heavenly minded they are of no earthly good". In fact, those who are *truly* heavenly minded are of the most earthly good. The future hope of heaven provides meaning and purpose for today, spurring us on to seek the Kingdom of God, working to change lives and society, beginning with ourselves and our neighbors.[22] When Christians view the future with fear and a desire to escape, they cannot effectively witness to the truth of the gospel and the Kingdom of God. Looking for an escape from suffering and death is contrary to the way of the Cross and to him who endured suffering and death in order to save us. Paul, an apostle who endured incredible trials, told the saints at Rome: "I consider that the sufferings of this present time are not worth comparing with the glory that is to be revealed to us" (Rom 8:18). Far too many Christians lack such an attitude. Many seem to believe future sufferings will be too great for them or that such sufferings are beneath them! Yet Peter gives this paradoxical exhortation to the early Christians: "But rejoice

---

[20] CCC 1043.
[21] See CCC 775.
[22] See CCC 1049.

in so far as you share Christ's sufferings, that you may also rejoice and be glad when his glory is revealed" (1 Pet 4:13). The witness of the early Christian martyrs demonstrate the reality and power of the resurrection, for they show that this life, for all of its goodness and glory, cannot be compared to the life that awaits those who are children of God.[23]

The Present and Future Judgment

We tend to think of judgment as a future event on the other side of the grave. After all, the epistle to the Hebrews indicates "it is appointed for men to die once, and after that comes judgment" (Heb 9:27). But judgment is more than just a future reality. It takes place each time man commits evil and rejects God: "And this is the judgment, that the light has come into the world, and men loved darkness rather than light, because their deeds were evil" (Jn 3:19). Judgment is an eschatological event, and it occurs every moment of every day. As Jean Daniélou has written, "Between the inauguration of Judgement at the time of Christ's first coming, and its fulfilment at his coming again, Christian life in its entirety is thus a continual judgement." [24] Far from being the action of an angry and vengeful God, judgment is an act of love, an act of transcendent and objective justice whose existence is meant to cause mankind to convert:

---

[23] See CCC 1050.

[24] Jean Daniélou, *The Lord of History* (London: Longmans, Green, 1958), p. 272. Romano Guardini explains that "history is its own judgment, since it tends to push events to their conclusion. Each action has consequences which again produce further consequences, and so a chain of cause and effect is set in motion which, little by little, brings the hidden into the open and separates the good from the bad" (Romano Guardini, *Eternal Life* [1954; Manchester, N.H.: Sophia Institute Press, 1998], p. 96).

The message of the Last Judgment calls men to conversion while God is still giving them "the acceptable time, ... the day of salvation" [2 Cor 6:2].... It proclaims the "blessed hope" of the Lord's return, when he will come "to be glorified in his saints, and to be marvelled at in all who have believed" [Titus 2:13; 2 Thess 1:10].[25]

Judgment is an integral part of the Parousia, for in judgment things will appear as they really are, stripped of secrecy. When God reveals himself to man at the end of time, the heart of every man will be fully exposed to God. "Men and things will appear in their true light, as they are, and every deception will vanish", writes Romano Guardini. "The inner and most hidden nature, both good and evil, will appear plainly, with all trappings stripped away. Every being will attain to what it is in truth." [26] This final judgment is not primarily concerned with revenge, but with holiness and truth, for they are at the heart of each man's relationship with the Righteous One. "The Last Judgment is the fulfillment of redemption." [27] Catholic teaching emphasizes individual eschatology because our lives are the one part of reality and history that we control and for which we are accountable. Since Jesus is the Savior, he is also the Judge; to ignore this is to make a serious mistake, as Clement pointed out nearly two thousand years ago: "Brethren, we ought to think of Jesus Christ just as we do of God, as the Judge of the living and the dead; nor ought we to belittle our salvation. For when we think little of him, we also hope to receive but little." [28]

---

[25] CCC 1041.
[26] Guardini, *Eternal Life*, p. 95.
[27] Ibid., p. 109.
[28] 2 Clement 1:1–2.

A Time of Trial and the Antichrist

As I pointed out in earlier chapters, the Catholic Church teaches that before the final day of judgment there will be a time of severe testing and tribulation. The Church says relatively little about this time; nothing is said about how long it will last or when it might transpire. However, Catholic doctrine explicitly states that the Church will go through this great trial at the end of time.[29]

This time of trial at the end of history will reveal the fullness of the Antichrist, "a pseudo-messianism by which man glorifies himself in place of God and of his Messiah come in the flesh [cf. 2 Thess 2:4–12; 1 Thess 5:2–3; 2 Jn 7; 1 Jn 2:18, 22]."[30] There has been much speculation down through time about the identity of the Antichrist, including writings by the Church Fathers about the Antichrist's ethnicity, his education, and his methods of destruction.[31] What is worth noting here is that Christ taught that the sheep and the goats, the wheat and the tares, and the saved and the damned will grow and live together throughout history (Mt 13:24–30, 36–43; 25:31–46). It should be no surprise that when history draws to a close, Satan and his followers will furiously and desperately attempt to destroy as many souls as possible, unleashing intense evil and causing widespread apostasy. Are we living in that time of trial today? We do not know, nor

---

[29] See CCC 675. Also see CCC 2642.

[30] CCC 675. Also see CCC 676.

[31] An excellent, popular Catholic treatment of the topic of the Antichrist can be found in former Evangelical Protestant Dr. Paul Thigpen's *The Rapture Trap: A Catholic Response to "End Times" Fever* (West Chester, Pa.: Ascension Press, 2001), pp. 208–13. A thorough—and occasionally melodramatic—treatment is Vincent P. Miceli's *The Antichrist* (West Hanover, Mass.: Christopher Publishing House, 1981).

can we really know until the end does come. What we should recognize is that the spirit of the Antichrist is within the world, just as it has been for two thousand years: "Children, it is the last hour; and as you have heard that antichrist is coming, so now many antichrists have come; therefore we know that it is the last hour" (1 Jn 2:18). There is deception and apostasy; there are many who mock Christ and many "Christians" who deny who he really is (see 1 Jn 2:22; 4:3; 2 Jn 7). These will be judged, even though they may speak freely at the moment. For their part, Catholics are called to proclaim the gospel, to work for the Kingdom here on earth, and to grow as children of God, especially through the Eucharist, which is the source and summit of the Catholic faith.

The Eucharist: The Eschatological Sacrament

All of the sacraments have an eschatological character and purpose, oriented as they are to our eternal communion with God. This is most true of the Eucharist, for it is the "pledge of glory" [32] and "an anticipation of the heavenly glory". [33] The Fathers of the Second Vatican Council taught that the Eucharist is "a meal of brotherly solidarity and a foretaste of the heavenly banquet". [34] As James O'Connor points out, through the Eucharist "the present creation breaks into the old, the future into the present", for the Blessed Sacrament is like "a window on the invisible dimensions of the universe". [35] The Eucharist is a covenantal oath, given not just

---

[32] CCC 1419.
[33] CCC 1402.
[34] GS 38.
[35] James O'Connor, *The Hidden Manna* (San Francisco: Ignatius Press, 1988), p. 289.

in words or promises, but in glorified flesh and blood—just as those who become a part of Christ's Body will be glorified. It is the actual body and blood of the risen Lord who transforms humanity through the Most Holy Sacrament, preparing man for the beatific life and the Marriage Supper of the Lamb.[36]

The *Catechism* states, "The Kingdom of God has been coming since the Last Supper and, in the Eucharist, it is in our midst. The kingdom will come in glory when Christ hands it over to his Father." [37] Just as Jesus handed over his life and body to the Father on the Cross, at the end of time he will hand over the Kingdom to the Father: "When all things are subjected to him, then the Son himself will also be subjected to him who put all things under him, that God may be everything to every one" (1 Cor 15:28).[38] This final unity and communion is already being brought about—although not completely realized until the Parousia—through the Eucharist and in the liturgy, for "by the Eucharistic celebration we already unite ourselves with the heavenly liturgy and anticipate eternal life, when God will be all in all [cf. 1 Cor 15:28]." [39]

---

[36] "'Let us rejoice and exult and give him the glory, for the marriage of the Lamb has come, and his Bride has made herself ready; it was granted her to be clothed with fine linen, bright and pure'—for the fine linen is the righteous deeds of the saints. And the angel said to me, 'Write this: Blessed are those who are invited to the marriage supper of the Lamb.' And he said to me, 'These are true words of God'" (Rev 19:7–9).

[37] CCC 2816. Also see CCC 1405, 1682, 2861.

[38] See CCC 1050, 1060, GS 39.

[39] CCC 1326. It has been pointed out by various authors that perhaps Catholics do not focus on the Second Coming as intently as some Christians do because of the eucharistic presence of Christ—the King is already among us, even though the Kingdom has yet to be fully realized and revealed.

The Time Is Near ... And Has Been for a While

Speculation about the exact time of the Second Coming has been rampant among some Christians for many decades, with self-proclaimed "Bible prophecy teachers" eagerly setting or indicating fast-approaching dates. Happily, Catholics have, for the most part, avoided these excesses. Unfortunately, many Catholics have spurned almost all talk of the Second Coming, so focused on achieving justice and social good that their identity as citizens of heaven has nearly faded away. When Jesus stated, "But of that day and hour no one knows, not even the angels of heaven, nor the Son, but the Father only" (Mt 24:36), he did not mean for his disciples to cease anticipating his return, for he also remarks: "Watch therefore, for you do not know on what day your Lord is coming" (Mt 24:42).

Anticipation and readiness need not turn into the error of date setting, no matter how tempting it can be—such attempts at date setting are contrary to Christ's command and lead to a false anticipation. It is true that calculating when Jesus may return can be far more emotionally stimulating and financially rewarding than the steady, silent work of growing in grace and truth, but it means nothing in the end if we have not become children of God. "The doctrine of the Second Coming has failed, so far as we are concerned", wrote C. S. Lewis, "if it does not make us realize that at every moment of every year in our lives Donne's question 'What if this present were the world's last night?' is equally relevant." [40] This life will end one way or another, followed by

---

[40] C. S. Lewis, *The World's Last Night and Other Essays* (New York: Harcourt Brace, 1987), p. 109.

judgment and the revelation of who we have become and who we really are.

At some point in time and history Christ will return in glory. For those of us who are alive, "the time is near" (Rev 1:3; 22:10), just a heartbeat and a single breath away. The end could be centuries away, but the time is always near. Which is why John exhorts his flock to "abide in him, so that when he appears we may have confidence and not shrink from him in shame at his coming" (1 Jn 2:28). For those who abide, there is perfect communion, everlasting joy, and glorification, as Dante wrote so many years ago:

> When our flesh, made glorious at the Judgment Seat,
> Dresses us once again, then shall our persons
> Become more pleasing in being more complete.
>
> Thereby shall we have increase of the light
> Supreme Love grants, unearned, to make us fit
> To hold His glory ever in our sight.[41]

---

[41] Dante Alighieri, *The Paradiso*, trans. John Ciardi (New York: Mentor, 1970), canto 14:43–48.

GLOSSARY OF KEY TERMS

allegorical interpretation: Interpreting Scripture in order to find meanings that go beyond the literal interpretation and beneath the surface narrative, making a deeper connection with the reality of Christ. Examples include seeing the crossing of the Red Sea as a prefigurement of baptism (see CCC 117) or understanding Haggar and Sarah as representatives of the Old and New Covenants (see Gal 4:21–31).

amillennialism: The belief that the millennium of Revelation 20:1–7 refers to a time of fullness such as the current Church age and not to a literal one-thousand-year period of time. While amillennialists disagree about what the millennium is or will be, they do agree it will not be a future, earthly reign of Christ.

Antichrist: In the Bible (1 Jn 2:18, 22; 4:3; 2 Jn 7), a reference to both an anti-Christian religion and a particular individual who will embody that belief at the end of time. The Antichrist will lead a one-world, apostate religion seeking to glorify man while denouncing God (see CCC 675–76).

apocalypse: From the Greek word meaning "unveiling" or "revelation". In Christian doctrine it refers to the unveiling of Jesus Christ as King and Lord that will occur at the end of time at the Parousia, the Second Coming.

apostasy: A rejection of the Christian faith and removal of oneself from the Church (cf. CCC 2089). Today it specifically refers to the abandonment of the Christian faith by a baptized Christian. Many Christians also refer to "the Apostasy", a great and final rejection of the Christian faith toward the end of the world. Dispensationalists and Fundamentalists often teach that the Catholic Church is an apostate institution.

dispensation: An era of history with a distinct beginning and end. The two major dispensations are the Old and New Covenants (see CCC 1076). Dispensationalists commonly believe there are seven dispensations in history, each beginning with a test from God and ending with man failing the test.

dispensationalism: The theological system formed in the 1830s by Plymouth Brethren leader John Nelson Darby and based upon the belief that God is pursuing two different works in history, one involving the Jews, and the other the Church. More accurately known as premillennial dispensationalism, this movement is a largely American phenomenon. Since the early 1900s and the publication of the *Scofield Reference Bible*, dispensationalism has enjoyed tremendous popularity among Fundamentalist and Evangelical Protestant groups.

ecclesiology: Literally, the "study of the church". It is the systematic theological study of the origins, purpose, and nature of the Church.

eschatology: Study of "the last things", especially death, judgment, heaven, and hell (*individual* eschatology). This branch of theology also examines the nature of the Kingdom of God, especially as it relates to history, the Parousia, the end of time, and the Last Judgment (*general* eschatology).

eschaton: The "last things" or "last days", referring to the Parousia, or Second Coming, and the judgment of mankind.

It will be the culmination of salvation history, when the Kingdom of God will be fully revealed and realized.

Evangelicalism: A branch of conservative Protestantism characterized by a belief in the centrality and infallibility of the Bible, the need for a personal conversion to Jesus Christ, a strong missionary focus, academic study, and, increasingly, an ecumenical approach to Catholics and Orthodox.

exegesis: From the Greek, meaning "bringing out the sense". It involves interpreting texts, especially Scripture, and seeking to establish what the authors meant to say and what the texts mean for Christians today.

Fundamentalism: Conservative Protestantism originally formed in the early 1900s in reaction to theological liberalism in mainline Protestant denominations. It is marked by a focus on individual conversion, the sufficiency of Scripture in all aspects of living, a suspicious attitude toward modernity and science, and a negative attitude regarding the Catholic Church.

futurism: The belief that all or most of the book of Revelation describes future events and provides readers with a detailed explanation of those approaching events. Premillennial dispensationalists are futurists, but not all futurists are premillennial dispensationalists.

Gnosticism: An ancient heretical movement characterized by a dualism between the material and spiritual realm, with the material realm being evil and the spiritual realm being good. There were many forms of Gnosticism (some claiming to be Christian), but all taught that *gnosis*, or secret knowledge, was the sole means of salvation—not the loving and merciful action of God. Salvation was understood to be the liberation of a person's spiritual essence from the material realm.

hermeneutics: The science of interpreting and understanding Scripture.

historic premillennialism: An ancient form of premillennialism that teaches that at his Second Coming Jesus Christ will set up an earthly, one-thousand-year reign on earth. Historic premillennialism differs from dispensational premillennialism in its denial of a rapture event separate from the Second Coming and its rejection of a radical distinction between Old Testament Israel and the Church.

historicism: The belief that the book of Revelation provides a prophetic and chronological outline of Christian history. Historicism was embraced by Martin Luther and John Calvin, and a rigid form of it is taught today by groups such as the Seventh-Day Adventists. There are valid elements and insights contained in historicism, and Catholics can benefit from them when they are studied with care and in the light of Church teaching.

idealism: The belief that the book of Revelation is not concerned with either past or current events, but depicts spiritual realities, especially the cosmic struggle between God and Satan. Sometimes called the "spiritual" interpretation of the book of Revelation.

Kingdom of God/Kingdom of heaven: The final and climactic reign of God, ushered in by the Incarnation, growing in the Church, which is the "seed" of the Kingdom (CCC 567), and to be fully realized at the Parousia. The Kingdom is communion with the triune God, entered through Christ in the power of the Holy Spirit.

Last Judgment: The belief that Christ, at his Second Coming, will "judge the living and the dead" (CCC 682). Jesus spoke of this future event in various ways, using images of wheat and chaff being separated (Mt 13:24–40, 36–43), the sorting of the good and bad fish (Mt 13:47–50), and the separation of the sheep and the goats (Mt 25:31–46).

literal interpretation: The "meaning conveyed by the words of Scripture and discovered by exegesis, following the rules of sound interpretation" (CCC 116). This literal meaning is the basis for all other understanding of Scripture.

mark of the beast: The infamous number "666", referred to in the book of Revelation (Rev 13:16–17; 16:2; 19:20).

midtribulationism: The belief of some dispensationalists that the Rapture—the removal of Christians from the earth—will occur at the midpoint of the seven-year-long Tribulation period.

millenarianism: In general, any belief in a future time of earthly utopia. Within Christianity it refers to the belief that Jesus will return and establish a thousand-year-long Kingdom on earth.

millennium: Literally, "a thousand years". Based on Revelation 20:1–10, the meaning of the millennium has been disputed among Christians for many centuries. Dispensationalists believe it refers to a future, earthly reign of Christ, while most other Christians, including Catholics, Orthodox, and many Protestants, believe it represents the current Church age.

Parousia: Literally, "presence". It refers to the Second Coming of Jesus Christ, the end of time, and the surrounding events.

postmillennialism: The belief that Jesus Christ will return after a millennial period, which will be a time of unknown length during which the majority of the world is christianized. Most postmillennialists today are Reformed Protestants.

posttribulationism: The Second Coming and Last Judgment will not occur until after a time of tribulation has been endured by the Church on earth. This belief is held by most Protestant denominations, the Eastern Orthodox churches, and the Catholic Church.

premillennialism: The return of Jesus will occur prior to the millennium, which is envisioned to be an earthly, utopian period, usually a thousand years in length.

preterism: The belief that the events depicted in the prophetic texts of the New Testament—especially the book of Revelation and Matthew 24—have already transpired. Partial preterists believe most, but not all, of those prophecies have been fulfilled. Preterists regard the destruction of the Jerusalem Temple in A.D. 70 as a key event in New Testament prophecy.

pretribulationism: The dispensationalist belief that the Rapture, the secret removal of Christians from earth, will occur prior to the start of the final Tribulation period.

prewrath rapture: A variation on the midtribulationism belief. Prewrath proponents believe Christians will be raptured out of the Tribulation immediately prior to the outpouring of the "great wrath" of God, sometime in the latter half of the Tribulation period.

progressive dispensationalism: A recent version of dispensationalism that seeks to reconcile traditional dispensationalist beliefs with more mainstream Protestant eschatology.

Progressive dispensationalists have revised older dispensationalist ideas about the relationship between the Church, Old Testament Israel, and the Kingdom, and have also advocated methods of biblical exegesis that recognize the unity between the Old and New Testaments.

Rapture: From the Latin (Vulgate) word meaning "taken up" or "caught up", used in 1 Thessalonians 4:17. Generally it refers to the Second Coming of Christ. However, dispensationalists believe it refers to the sudden, secret, and silent removal of Christians from earth prior to (or in the middle of) the final Tribulation.

reconstructionism: A Reformed Protestant postmillennial movement—also known as dominion theology—that teaches there will be a progressive growth in Christ's Kingdom on earth, eventually resulting in a christianized world.

Reformed: Refers to the branches of Protestantism formed and shaped by Calvin, Zwingli, and the Church of England, over against Lutheranism and other forms of Protestantism.

Scofieldism: The form of dispensationalism taught by Cyrus I. Scofield (1843–1921), especially in his influential *Scofield Reference Bible* (1909). Major features include a radical distinction between the Church and Israel, a very literal interpretation of Scripture, and strong distinctions between the Kingdom of God and the Kingdom of heaven.

senses of Scripture: The different meanings that a biblical passage conveys. The two major senses of Scripture are the literal and the spiritual, with "latter being subdivided into the allegorical, moral, and anagogical senses" (CCC 115).

theonomy: A recent Reformed Protestant postmillennial theology that emphasizes the need for "rule by the law of

God" in every aspect of society and culture in order for the Kingdom of God to be realized.

the Tribulation: A future period of trial and testing signaling the end of the world, the final conflict between Satan and God, and the triumphant return of Jesus Christ (cf. CCC 675–77).

whore of Babylon: A title, taken from the book of Revelation (Rev 17:5), that has been applied to various entities throughout history. The early Church Fathers and many contemporary theologians believe it refers to ancient Rome and/or any institution that defies God. The Protestant Reformers and many Fundamentalists today identify the whore of Babylon as the Catholic Church.

LIST OF KEY PERSONS

Augustine of Hippo (354–430): Church Father, Doctor of the Church, and bishop of Hippo, North Africa. His famous *City of God* established the belief that the millennium period of Revelation 20 is the current Church age. Augustine opposed the premillennialists of his time and warned against the dangers of interpreting the book of Revelation in a literalist fashion.

William Blackstone (1841–1935): A prominent Chicago businessman and avid dispensationalist whose 1878 book *Jesus Is Coming* influenced an entire generation of Evangelical Protestants and garnered support for Zionism in America.

John Calvin (1509–1564): Along with Martin Luther the greatest of the Protestant Reformers. Calvin said and wrote very little about eschatology or the book of Revelation, but he did believe the Catholic Church was the whore of Babylon (Rev 17:5) and the papacy the Antichrist. Like most early Protestants he was a postmillennialist.

Lewis Sperry Chafer (1871–1952): A Presbyterian pastor who succeeded C. I. Scofield as leader of American dispensationalism. Chafer systematized dispensationalism in his *Systematic Theology* (1947) and formed Dallas Theological Seminary (in 1924), the most important dispensationalist school in America.

John Nelson Darby (1800–1882): Ex-Anglican priest, leader in the Plymouth Brethren movement, and father of the premillennial dispensationalist movement. In addition to the secret pretribulation Rapture, Darby taught a radical separation between Christians, the "heavenly people" of God, and Jews, the "earthly people" of God.

Edward Irving (1792–1834): A Scottish Protestant minister and millenarian who formed the Catholic Apostolic Church and was instrumental in forming early British millenarian beliefs by initiating Bible prophecy conferences.

Joachim of Fiore (ca. 1135–1202): Catholic biblical scholar, mystic, and monk. Fascinated by the book of Revelation, Joachim developed a trinitarian concept of history in which the Father was aligned with the Old Testament, the Son with the current age, and the Holy Spirit with a rapidly approaching age of utopia. Many of Joachim's views were not accepted by the Church, and his trinitarian doctrine was formally condemned by the Fourth Lateran Council (A.D. 1215).

Manuel Lacunza: A nineteenth-century renegade Jesuit who wrote the strange eschatological work *The Coming of Messiah in Glory and Majesty* (ca. 1791) under the alias of Juan Ben-Ezra. The work strongly influenced Edward Irving and may have shaped certain dispensationalist beliefs, particularly the pretribulation Rapture.

Tim LaHaye: Fundamentalist author, pastor, and activist. One of the most influential Fundamentalist leaders of the past thirty years, LaHaye is the creator and co-author of the *Left Behind* books, author of numerous books explaining and defending dispensationalism, and founder of the Pre-Trib Research Center.

Hal Lindsey (1929–): A former youth pastor and the best-selling dispensationalist author of all time. His *Late Great Planet Earth* (1970) sold over forty million copies worldwide and introduced many non-Fundamentalists to a popular, sensationalized form of dispensationalism.

Martin Luther (1483–1546): A German monk who became the most famous of the Protestant Reformers. Initially reluctant to write about the book of Revelation, Luther eventually taught that the papacy was the Antichrist and the Apocalypse was best interpreted in a historicist fashion.

Marcion (d. ca. 160): An early heretic who taught that the God of the Christians was not the same as the God of the Old Testament—a form of Gnosticism. He created a canon of Scripture that included ten of Paul's epistles and an edited version of Luke's Gospel.

William Miller (1782–1849): A Baptist farmer and the best-known American millenarian of the nineteenth century. Miller predicted Christ would return in 1844, and he gained a large following in the Midwest. Although he retired from public life after his predictions failed, Miller's beliefs were influential in the formation of the Seventh-Day Adventists and, indirectly, the Watchtower Society.

Dwight L. Moody (1837–1899): The greatest American evangelist of his time, Moody founded Moody Bible College (now called Moody Bible Institute) in Chicago, a Fundamentalist and dispensationalist academic center. Although never an overt dispensationalist, Moody's support of the movement played a key role in its success in America in the late 1800s.

Origen (ca. 185–ca. 254): Alexandrian biblical scholar and theologian who wrote hundreds of books and championed an allegorical reading of Scripture. Origen was critical of those who interpreted the book of Revelation literally, and his allegorical interpretations of the Apocalypse proved very influential on subsequent theologians.

Charles C. Ryrie (1925–): Major dispensationalist theologian and author who was a long-time professor of theology at Dallas Theological Seminary. His 1965 apologetic, *Dispensationalism Today*, is considered one of the key works of the movement.

Cyrus I. Scofield (1843–1921): A former lawyer who became a disciple of John Darby and eventually systematized Darby's teachings in the *Scofield Reference Bible* (1909). It was the most influential work among conservative American Protestants in the first half of the twentieth century, selling millions of copies and introducing dispensationalist ideas into mainstream American Christianity.

Jack Van Impe (1931–): A leading popular dispensationalist nicknamed "The Walking Bible" because he has memorized large sections of Scripture. Van Impe has authored numerous books on Bible prophecy, hosts a weekly television show dedicated to outlining end-times events, and has produced countless tapes and videos about the same topic.

John F. Walvoord (1915–): A key dispensationalist theologian and apologist. Walvoord has been associated with Dallas Theological Seminary for his entire adult life and was president of DTS from 1952 to 1986. A staunch dispensationalist in the mold of Chafer (who was his mentor), Walvoord has written numerous books on Bible prophecy and the end times.

Ellen G. White (1827–1915): A central figure in Seventh-Day Adventism whose visions and writings shaped that group's theological beliefs. White's writings, like SDA doctrine, are anti-Catholic and are based on the belief that the Catholic Church is apostate and that worship on Sunday is the "mark of the beast" referred to in Revelation 13.

SELECTED BIBLIOGRAPHY

Book of Revelation

Beale, G. K. *John's Use of the Old Testament in Revelation*. Sheffield, England: Sheffield Academic Press, 1998.

Chilton, David. *The Days of Vengeance: An Exposition of the Book of Revelation*. Fort Worth, Tex.: Dominion Press, 1987.

_____. *The Great Tribulation*. Fort Worth, Tex.: Dominion Press, 1987.

_____. *Paradise Restored: A Biblical Theology of Dominion*. Tyler, Tex.: Dominion Press, 1994.

Collins, Adela Yarbro. *The Apocalypse*. Wilmington, Del.: Michael Glazier, 1979.

Crehan, Joseph, S.J. *The Theology of St. John*. New York: Sheed and Ward, 1965.

Féret, H. M., O.P. *The Apocalypse Explained*. Fort Collins, Colo.: Roman Catholic Books, 1958.

Gentry, Kenneth L. *The Beast of Revelation*. Tyler, Tex.: Institute for Christian Economics, 1994.

Gregg, Steve, ed. *Revelation, Four Views: A Parallel Commentary*. Nashville: Thomas Nelson Publishers, 1997.

Guimond, John. *The Silencing of Babylon: A Spiritual Commentary on the Book of Revelation*. New York: Paulist Press, 1991.

Hahn, Scott. *The Lamb's Supper: The Mass as Heaven on Earth*. New York: Doubleday, 1999.

Harrington, Daniel. *Revelation: The Book of the Risen Christ*. Hyde Park, N.Y.: New City Press, 1999.

Hendriksen, William. *More than Conquerers: An Interpretation of the Book of Revelation.* 1939; Grand Rapids, Mich.: Baker, 1967.

Miceli, Vincent P., S.J. *The Antichrist.* West Hanover, Mass.: Christopher Publishing House, 1981.

Montague, George T., S.M. *The Apocalypse and the Third Millennium: Today's Guide to the Book of Revelation.* Ann Arbor, Mich.: Charis, 1998.

Navarre Bible. Revelation: Texts and Commenaries. Dublin: Four Courts Press, 1992.

Onstad, Esther. *Courage for Today—Hope for Tomorrow: A Study of the Revelation.* Minneapolis, Minn.: Augsburg Publishing House, 1975.

Seiss, J. A. *The Apocalypse: Lectures on the Book of Revelation.* Grand Rapids, Mich.: Zondervan Publishing House, n.d.

Spilsbury, Paul. *The Throne, the Lamb, and the Dragon.* Downers Grove, Ill.: InterVarsity Press, 2002.

Interpreting and Reading Scripture

Bouyer, Louis. *The Meaning of Sacred Scripture.* Notre Dame, Ind.: University of Notre Dame Press, 1958.

Brown, Raymond E. *Biblical Exegesis and Church Doctrine.* New York: Paulist Press, 1985.

Brown, Raymond E., Joseph A. Fitzmyer, and Roland E. Murphy, eds. *The New Jerome Biblical Commentary.* Englewood Cliffs, N.J.: Prentice-Hall, 1990.

Charlier, Dom Celestin. *The Christian Approach to the Bible.* Westminster Press, Md.: Newman Press, 1965.

Daniel-Rops, Henri. *What Is the Bible?* New York: Hawthorn Books, 1958.

Daniélou, Jean. *The Bible and the Liturgy.* Notre Dame, Ind.: University of Notre Dame Press, 1987.

Fitzmyer, Joseph A., S.J. *Scripture, The Soul of Theology*. New York: Paulist Press, 1994.

Freedman, David Noel, ed. *Eerdmans Dictionary of the Bible*. Grand Rapids, Mich.: W. B. Eerdmans, 2000.

Guenter, Ken. *The Prophets in Israel: A Biblical Anthology*. Caronport, Saskatchewan: Briercrest Bible College, 1990.

Guillet, Jacques. *Themes of the Bible*. Notre Dame, Ind.: Fides Publishers, 1964.

Hahn, Scott. *A Father Who Keeps His Promises: God's Covenant Love in Scripture*. Ann Arbor, Mich.: Charis, 1998.

LaRondelle, Hans K. *The Israel of God in Prophecy: Principles of Prophetic Interpretation*. Berrien Springs, Mich.: Andrews University Press, 1983.

Latourelle, René, S.J. *Theology of Revelation*. Staten Island, N.Y.: Alba House, 1966.

McKenzie, John L., S.J. *Dictionary of the Bible*. New York: Touchstone Press, 1995.

Pontifical Biblical Commission. "The Interpretation of the Bible in the Church." April 23, 1993.

Ryan, Sister M. Rosalie, C.S.J., ed. *Contemporary New Testament Studies*. Collegeville, Minn.: Liturgical Press, 1965.

Senior, Donald, ed. *The Catholic Study Bible* (New American Bible). New York: Oxford University Press, 1990.

Shea, Mark P. *Making Senses out of Scripture: Reading the Bible as the First Christians Did*. San Diego, Calif.: Basilica Press, 1999.

_____. *By What Authority? An Evangelical Discovers Catholic Tradition*. Huntington, Ind.: Our Sunday Visitor, 1996.

Vatican Council II. Dogmatic Constitution on Divine Revelation, *Dei Verbum*, 1965.

Von Balthasar, Hans Urs. *Word and Revelation*. New York: Herder and Herder, 1964. Incorporated into *The Word Made*

Flesh, Explorations in Theology, vol. 1 (San Francisco: Ignatius Press, 1989).

Von Rad, Gerhard. *The Message of the Prophets*. New York: Harper and Row, 1962, 1965.

Woods, Ralph L., ed. *The Catholic Companion to the Bible*. New York: J. B. Lippincott, 1956.

Ecclesiology: The Church and the Kingdom

Adam, Karl. *The Spirit of Catholicism*. New York: Doubleday, 1954.

Bouyer, Louis. *The Church of God*. Chicago: Franciscan Herald Press, 1982.

Bright, John. *The Kingdom of God, the Biblical Concept and Its Meaning for the Church*. Nashville: Abingdon-Cokesbury Press, 1953.

Congar, Yves. *This Church That I Love*. Denville, N.J.: Dimension Books, 1969.

De Lubac, Henri, S.J. *The Splendour of the Church*. Glen Rock, N.J.: Deus Books/Paulist Press, 1963.

———. *The Church: Paradox and Mystery*. Staten Island, N.Y.: Alba House, 1969.

———. *Catholicism: Christ and the Common Destiny of Man*. 1950; San Francisco: Ignatius Press, 1988.

Guardini, Romano. *The Church of the Lord*. Chicago: Henry Regnery, 1965.

Hahn, Scott. "The Church as Kingdom: Davidic and Eucharistic". *Crisis*, July/August 2000.

Martin, Ralph. *The Catholic Church at the End of an Age*. San Francisco: Ignatius Press, 1994.

Mersch, Emile, S.J. *The Theology of the Mystical Body*. St. Louis, Mo.: B. Herder, 1952.

Nichols, Aidan, O.P. *Christendom Awake: On Re-energising the Church in Culture*. Edinburgh: T and T Clark, 1999.

Pope John Paul II. *Redemptoris Missio*, "Mission of the Redeemer". 1990.

Pope Paul VI. *Ecclesiam Suam*, "On the Church". 1964.

Ratzinger, Joseph Cardinal. *Called to Communion—Understanding the Church Today*. San Francisco: Ignatius Press, 1996.

———. *Many Religions—One Covenant: Israel, the Church and the World*. San Francisco: Ignatius Press, 1999.

Saucy, Mark. *The Kingdom of God in the Teaching of Jesus in 20ᵗʰ Century Theology*. Dallas, Tex.: Word Publishing, 1997.

Schnackenburg, Rudolf. *God's Rule and Kingdom*. New York: Herder and Herder, 1963.

Vatican Council II. Pastoral Constitution on the Church in the Modern World, *Gaudium et Spes*. 1965.

Vatican Council II. Dogmatic Constitution on the Church, *Lumen Gentium*. 1964.

Von Balthasar, Hans Urs. *The Office of Peter and the Structure of the Church*. San Francisco: Ignatius Press, 1986.

Dispensationalist Works

Ankerberg, John and John Weldon. *One World: Biblical Prophecy and the New World Order*. Chicago: Moody Press, 1991.

Bateman, Herbert W. IV, ed. *Three Central Issues in Contemporary Dispensationalism: A Comparison of Traditional and Progressive Views*. Grand Rapids, Mich.: Kregel Publications, 1999.

Blaising, Craig A. and Darrell L. Bock, eds. *Dispensationalism, Israel and the Church: The Search for Definition*. Grand Rapids, Mich.: Zondervan Publishing House, 1992.

Blaising, Craig A., and Darrell L. Bock, *Progressive Dispensationalism*. Wheaton, Ill.: Victor Books, 1993.

Campbell, Donald K., ed. *Walvoord: A Tribute*. Chicago: Moody Press, 1982.

Chafer, Lewis Sperry. *Systematic Theology*. 8 vols. Dallas, Tex.: Dallas Seminary Press, 1947–1948.

———. *Dispensationalism*. Dallas, Tex.: Dallas Seminary Press, 1936.

———. *Grace: The Glorious Theme*. 1922; Grand Rapids, Mich.: Academie Books, 1950.

DeHaan, M. R. *Coming Events in Prophecy*. 1962; Grand Rapids, Mich.: Zondervan Publishing House, 1973.

Epp, Theodore H., ed. *Brief Outline of Things to Come*. Chicago: Moody Press, 1952.

Hagee, John. *Beginning of the End: The Assassination of Yitzhak Rabin and the Coming Antichrist*. Nashville: Thomas Nelson Publishers, 1996.

———. *From Daniel to Doomsday: The Countdown Has Begun*. Nashville: T. Nelson Publishers, 1999.

Hindson, Ed. *Final Signs: Amazing Prophecies of the End Times*. Eugene, Ore.: Harvest House Publishers, 1996.

Hunt, Dave. *Global Peace and the Rise of Antichrist*. Eugene, Ore.: Harvest House Publishers, 1990.

———. *How Close Are We? Compelling Evidence for the Soon Return of Christ*. Eugene, Ore.: Harvest House Publishers, 1993.

———. *Peace, Prosperity and the Coming Holocaust: The New Age Movement in Prophecy*. Eugene, Ore.: Harvest House Publishers, 1983.

———. *A Woman Rides the Beast: The Roman Catholic Church and the Last Days*. Eugene, Ore.: Harvest House Publishers, 1994.

Ice, Thomas and Timothy Demy. *Fast Facts on Bible Prophecy*. Eugene, Ore.: Harvest House Publishers, 1997.

———. *Prophecy Watch: What to Expect in the Days to Come*. Eugene, Ore.: Harvest House Publishers, 1998.

James, William T., ed. *Foreshadows of Wrath and Redemption.* Eugene, Ore.: Harvest House Publishers, 1999.

Jeffrey, Grant R. *Apocalypse: The Coming Judgment of the Nations.* New York: Bantam Books, 1992.

———. *Prince of Darkness: Antichrist and the New World Order.* New York: Bantam Books, 1995.

———. *Armageddon: Appointment with Destiny.* 1989; Toronto: Frontier Research Publications, 1997.

Kirban, Salem. *666.* Wheaton, Ill.: Tyndale House Publishers, 1970.

———. *Satan's Mark Exposed: 666.* Chattanooga, Tenn.: AMG Publishers, 1978.

———. *The New Age Secret Plan for World Conquest.* 1988; Chattanooga, Tenn.: AMG Publishers, 1992.

LaHaye, Tim and Jerry B. Jenkins. *Left Behind: A Novel of the Earth's Last Days.* Wheaton, Ill.: Tyndale House Publishers, 1995.

———. *Left Behind* series. Wheaton, Ill.: Tyndale House Publishers, 1995–.

    1. *Left Behind: A Novel of the Earth's Last Days* (1995)

    2. *Tribulation Force: The Continuing Drama of Those Left Behind* (1996)

    3. *Nicolae: The Rise of the Antichrist* (1997)

    4. *Soul Harvest: The World Takes Sides* (1998)

    5. *Apollyon: The Destroyer Is Unleashed* (1999)

    6. *Assassins: Assignment—Jerusalem, Target—Antichrist* (1999)

    7. *The Indwelling: The Beast Takes Possession* (2000)

    8. *The Mark: The Beast Rules the World* (2000)

    9. *Desecration: Antichrist Takes the Throne* (2001)

    10. *The Remnant: On the Brink of Armageddon* (2002)

———. *Are We Living in the End Times?* Wheaton, Ill.: Tyndale House Publishers, 1999.

LaHaye, Tim. *The Beginning of the End.* 1972; Wheaton, Ill.: Tyndale House Publishers, 1991.

_____. *Rapture under Attack.* Sisters, Ore.: Multnomah Publishers, 1998.

_____. *Revelation Unveiled.* Grand Rapids, Mich.: Zondervan Publishing House, 1999.

_____. *Understanding the Last Days: The Keys to Unlocking Bible Prophecy.* Eugene, Ore.: Harvest House Publishers, 1998.

LaHaye, Tim, Texe Marrs, David Breese, William T. James, and David A. Lewis. *Storming toward Armageddon: Essays in Apocalypse.* Green Forest, Ariz.: New Leaf Press, 1992.

Lalonde, Peter and Patti. *Left Behind.* Eugene, Ore.: Harvest House Publishers, 1995.

Lalonde, Peter and Paul. *The Mark of the Beast: Your Money, Computers, and the End of the World.* Eugene, Ore.: Harvest House Publishers, 1994.

Lightner, Robert P., Th.D. *The Last Days Handbook.* Nashville: Thomas Nelson, 1990.

Lindsey, Hal, with C. C. Carlson, *The Late Great Planet Earth.* New York: Bantam Books, 1970.

_____. *Satan Is Alive and Well on Planet Earth.* New York: Bantam Books, 1972.

_____. *There's a New World Coming.* Santa Ana, Calif.: Vision House Publishers, 1973.

Lindsey, Hal. *The 1980's: Countdown to Armageddon.* New York: Bantam Books, 1980.

_____. *The Rapture.* New York: Bantam Books, 1983.

_____. *Planet Earth—2000 A.D.* Palos Verdes, Calif.: Western Front, 1994.

_____. *The Apocalypse Code.* Palos Verdes, Calif.: Western Front, 1997.

_____. *The Final Battle.* Palos Verdes, Calif.: Western Front, 1997.

_____. *Planet Earth: The Final Chapter*. Palos Verdes, Calif.: Western Front, 1998.

McQuaid, Elwood. *The Zion Connection*. Eugene, Ore.: Harvest House Publishers, 1996.

Reiter, Richard R., et al. *The Rapture: Pre-, Mid-, or Post-Tribulational?* Grand Rapids, Mich.: Academie Books, 1984.

Richards, Jeffrey J. *The Promise of Dawn: The Eschatology of Lewis Sperry Chafer*. Lanham, Md.: University Press of America, 1991.

Ryrie, Charles C. *The Basis of the Premillennial Faith*. 1953; Neptune, N.J.: Loizeaux Brothers, 1981.

_____. *Dispensationalism*. Chicago: Moody Press, 1965, 1995.

_____. *Basic Theology*. Wheaton, Ill.: Victor Books, 1986.

_____. *The Best Is Yet to Come*. Chicago: Moody Press, 1981.

Ryrie, Charles C., Joe Jordan, and Tom Davis, eds. *Countdown to Armageddon: The Final Battle and Beyond*. Eugene, Ore.: Harvest House Publishers, 1999.

Scofield, C. I. *Rightly Dividing the Word of Truth: Ten Outline Studies of the More Important Divisions of Scripture*. Neptune, N.J.: Loizeaux Brothers, 1896.

_____. *The Scofield Reference Bible* (KJV). 1909; New York: Oxford University Press, 1945.

Showers, Renald E. *There Really Is a Difference! A Comparison of Covenant and Dispensational Theology*. Bellmawr, N.J.: Friends of Israel Gospel Ministry, 1990.

Van Impe, Jack. *Everything about Prophecy*. 1981. Troy, Mich.: Jack Van Impe Ministries, 1999.

Van Kampen, Robert. *The Sign*. Wheaton, Ill.: Crossway Books, 1992.

Walvoord, John F. *The Return of the Lord*. Findlay, Ohio: Dunham Publishing, 1955.

_____. *The Millennial Kingdom*. Grand Rapids, Mich.: Zondervan Publishing House, 1959.

_____. *Armageddon, Oil and the Middle East Crisis*. Grand Rapids, Mich.: Zondervan Publishing House, 1974, 1990.

_____. *The Rapture Question*. Rev. ed. Grand Rapids, Mich.: Academie Books, 1979.

_____. *Major Bible Prophecies: 37 Crucial Prophecies That Affect You Today*. New York: HarperCollins, 1991.

_____. *The Blessed Hope and the Tribulation: A Historical and Biblical Study of Posttribulationism*. Grand Rapids, Mich.: Zondervan Publishing House, 1976.

_____. *The Church in Prophecy*. 1964; Grand Rapids, Mich.: Zondervan Publishing House, 1980.

_____. *Israel in Prophecy*. Grand Rapids, Mich.: Zondervan Publishing House, 1962.

_____. *The Nations in Prophecy*. Grand Rapids, Mich.: Zondervan Publishing House, 1967.

Critiques of Dispensationalism

Allis, Oswald T. *Prophecy and the Church*. Nutley, N.J.: Presbyterian and Reformed Publishing, 1974.

Aufill, W. Robert. "A Look at Dave Hunt, Leading Anti-Catholic Fundamentalist: The Whore of Babylon, the Rapture, and the End Times". *New Oxford Review*. January 1999.

Barr, James. *Fundamentalism*. Philadelphia: Westminster Press, 1978.

Bahnsen, Greg L., and Kenneth L. Gentry, Jr. *House Divided: The Break-up of Dispensational Theology*. Tyler, Tex.: Institute for Christian Economics, 1989.

Cox, William E. *Why I Left Scofieldism*. Phillipsburg, N.J.: Presbyterian and Reformed Publishing, 1978.

Crenshaw, Curtis I., and Grover E. Gunn III. *Dispensationalism: Today, Yesterday, and Tomorrow*. Memphis, Tenn.: Footstool, 1995.

Currie, David B. *Born Fundamentalist, Born Again Catholic*. San Francisco: Ignatius Press, 1996.

DeMar, Gary. *Last Days Madness: Obsession of the Modern Church*. Atlanta: American Vision Press, 1999.

Gerstner, John H. *A Primer on Dispensationalism*. Phillipsburg, N.J.: Presbyterian and Reformed Publishing, 1982.

––––––. *Wrongly Dividing the Word of Truth: A Critique of Dispensationalism*. Brentwood, Tenn.: Wolgemuth and Hyatt Publishers, 1991.

Gorenberg, Gershom. *The End of Days: Fundamentalism and the Struggle for the Temple Mount*. New York: Free Press, 2000.

MacPherson, Dave. *The Incredible Cover-Up: Exposing the Origins of Rapture Theories*. 1975; Medford, Ore.: Omega Publications, 1999.

––––––. *The Rapture Plot*. 2d ed. Simpsonville, S.C.: Millennium III Publishers, 2000.

Mathison, Keith A. *Dispensationalism: Rightly Dividing the People of God?* Phillipsburg, N.J.: P and R Publishing, 1995.

Mauro, Philip. *The Gospel of the Kingdom: With an Examination of Modern Dispensationalism*. Swengel, Pa.: Reiner Publications, 1966.

Noe, John. *The Apocalypse Conspiracy*. Brentwood, Tenn.: Wolgemuth and Hyatt Publishers, 1991.

Noll, Mark A. *The Scandal of the Evangelical Mind*. Grand Rapids, Mich.: W. B. Eerdmans, 1994.

North, Gary. *Rapture Fever: Why Dispensationalism Is Paralyzed*. Tyler, Tex.: Institute for Christian Economics, 1993.

_____. *Shattering The "Left Behind" Delusion*. Bradford, Pa.: International Preterist Association, 2000.

Olson, Carl E. "Are We Living in the Last Days?" *The Catholic Faith*. September/October 2001.

_____. "The Time Is Near: Five Common Misinterpretations of the Book of Revelation". *This Rock*. September 2002.

_____. "Recycled Rapture". *This Rock*. September 2001.

_____. "LaHaying the Rapture on Thick". *Envoy*. September/October 2001.

_____. "No Rapture for Rome: The Anti-Catholics behind the Best-Selling *Left Behind* Books". *This Rock*. November 2000.

_____. "Waiting for the Rapture In America". *This Rock*. April 1999.

Poythress, Vern S. *Understanding Dispensationalists*. 1987; Phillipsburg, N.J.: P and R Publishing, 1994.

Provan, Charles D. *The Church Is Israel Now: The Transfer of Conditional Privilege*. Vallecito, Calif.: Ross House Books, 1987.

Reese, Alexander. *The Approaching Advent of Christ*. Grand Rapids, Mich.: Grand Rapids International, 1975.

Schlissel, Steve, and David Brown. *Hal Lindsey and the Restoration of the Jews*. Edmonton, Alberta: Still Waters Revival Books, 1990.

Thigpen, Paul. *The Rapture Trap: A Catholic Response to "End Times" Fever*. West Chester, Pa.: Ascension Press, 2001.

Wilson, Dwight. *Armageddon Now! The Premillenarian Response to Russia and Israel since 1917*. Tyler, Tex.: Institute for Christian Economics, 1991.

Historical Works

Abanes, Richard. *End-Time Visions: The Road to Armageddon?* New York: Four Walls Eight Windows, 1998.

Bass, Clarence B. *Backgrounds to Dispensationalism: Its Historical Genesis and Ecclesiastical Implications*. 1960; Grand Rapids, Mich.: Baker Book House, 1977.

Baumgartner, Frederic J. *Longing for the End: A History of Millennialism in Western Civilization*. New York: St. Martin's Press, 1999.

Boyer, Paul. *When Time Shall Be No More: Prophecy Belief in Modern American Culture*. 1992; Cambridge, Mass.: Harvard University Press, 1998.

Clouse, Robert G., Robert N. Hosack, and Richard V. Pierard. *The New Millennium Manual: A Once and Future Guide*. Grand Rapids, Mich.: Baker Books, 1999.

Clouse, Robert G., ed. *The Meaning of the Millennium: Four Views*. Downers Grove, Ill.: InterVarsity Press, 1977.

Cohn, Norman. *The Pursuit of the Millennium*. New York: Harper Torchbooks, 1961.

Daley, Brian E., S.J. *The Hope of the Early Church: A Handbook of Patristic Eschatology*. Cambridge: Cambridge University Press, 1991.

Daniel-Rops, Henri. *Daily Life in the Time of Jesus*. New York: Mentor-Omega, 1962.

Daniélou, Jean. *The Theology of Jewish Christianity*. The Development of Christian Doctrine before the Council of Nicaea, vol. 1. London: Darton, Longman and Todd, 1964.

Emmerson, Richard K., and Bernard McGinn, eds. *The Apocalypse in the Middle Ages*. Ithaca, N.Y.: Cornell University Press, 1992.

Firth, Katharine R. *The Apocalyptic Tradition In Reformation Britain, 1530–1645*. Oxford: Oxford University Press, 1979.

Friedrich, Otto. *The End of the World: A History*. New York: Fromm International Publishing, 1986.

Griffen, William, ed. *Endtime: The Doomsday Catalog*. New York: Collier Books, 1979.

Kleinhenz, Christopher and Fannie J. LeMoine, eds. *Fearful Hope: Approaching the New Millennium*. Madison, Wis.: University of Wisconsin Press, 1999.

Knox, Ronald A. *Enthusiasm: A Chapter in the History of Religion*. 1950; Notre Dame, Ind.: University of Notre Dame Press, 1994.

Kraus, C. Norman. *Dispensationalism in America: Its Rise and Development*. Richmond, Va.: John Knox Press, 1958.

Kyle, Richard. *The Last Days Are Here Again: A History of the End Times*. Grand Rapids, Mich.: Baker Books, 1998.

_____. *The Religious Fringe: A History of Alternative Religions in America*. Downers Grove, Ill.: InterVarsity Press, 1993.

Marsden, George M. *Fundamentalism and American Culture: The Shaping of Twentieth Century Evangelicalism, 1870–1925*. New York: Oxford University Press, 1980.

_____. *Understanding Fundamentalism and Evangelicalism*. Grand Rapids, Mich.: W. B. Eerdmans, 1991.

Newcombe, Jerry. *Coming Again: But When?* Colorado Springs, Colo.: Chariot Victor Publishing, 1999.

Noll, Mark A. *A History of Christianity in the United States and Canada*. Grand Rapids, Mich.: W. B. Eerdmans, 1992.

Pelikan, Jaroslav. *The Emergence of the Catholic Tradition (100–600)*. Chicago: University of Chicago Press, 1971.

Reeves, Marjorie. *Joachim of Fiore and the Prophetic Future: A Medieval Study in Historical Thinking*, New rev. ed. Stroud: Sutton Publishing, 1999.

Robbins, Thomas, and Susan J. Palmer, eds. *Millennium, Messiahs, and Mayhem: Contemporary Apocalyptic Movements*. New York: Routledge, 1997.

Sandeen, Ernest R. *The Roots of Fundamentalism: British and American Millenarianism, 1800–1930*. Chicago: University of Chicago Press, 1970.

Thompson, Damian. *The End of Time: Faith and Fear in the Shadow of the Millennium*. Hanover, N.H.: University Press of New England, 1996.

Weber, Timothy P. *Living in the Shadow of the Second Coming: American Premillennialism 1875–1925*. New York: Oxford University Press, 1979.

Non-dispensationalist Eschatology

Boettner, Loraine. *The Millennium*. Philadelphia: Presbyterian and Reformed Publishing, 1957.

Cox, William E. *Amillennialism Today*. Phillipsburg, N.J.: Presbyterian and Reformed Publishing, 1966.

_____. *Biblical Studies in Final Things*. Phillipsburg, N.J.: Presbyterian and Reformed Publishing, 1966.

Daniélou, Jean. *The Lord of History*. London: Longmans, Green, 1958.

Erickson, Millard J. *A Basic Guide To Eschatology: Making Sense of the Millennium*. 1977; Grand Rapids, Mich.: Baker Book House, 1998.

Gundry, Robert H. *First the Antichrist*. Grand Rapids, Mich.: Baker Books, 1997.

Gundry, Robert H. *The Church and the Tribulation: A Biblical Examination of Posttribulationalism*. Grand Rapids, Mich.: Zondervan Publishing House, 1973.

Haggith, David. *End-Time Prophecies of the Bible*. New York: G. P. Putnam's Sons, 1999.

Hoekema, Anthony A. *The Bible and the Future*. Grand Rapids, Mich.: W. B. Eerdmans, 1979.

Ladd, George Eldon. *Jesus and The Kingdom: The Eschatology of Biblical Realism*. Waco, Tex.: Word Books, 1964.

_____. *The Presence of the Future*. Grand Rapids, Mich.: W. B. Eerdmans Publishing, 1974.

Lewis, Daniel J. *3 Crucial Questions about the Last Days*. Grand Rapids, Mich.: Baker Books, 1998.

Lewis, C. S. *The World's Last Night and Other Essays*. 1952; New York: Harcourt, Brace, 1987.

Martin, Ralph. *Is Jesus Coming Soon? A Catholic Perspective on the Second Coming*. San Francisco: Ignatius Press. 1997.

Mussner, Franz. *Christ and the End of the World: A Biblical Study in Eschatology*. Notre Dame, Ind.: University of Notre Dame Press, 1965.

Nash, Ronald H. *Great Divides: Understanding the Controversies That Come between Christians*. Colorado Springs, Colo.: NavPress, 1993.

Pieper, Josef. *The End of Time: A Meditation on the Philosophy of History*. 1954; San Francisco: Ignatius Press, 1999.

———. *Hope and History*. New York. Herder and Herder, 1969.

Ratzinger, Joseph. *Eschatology, Death and Eternal Life*. Washington, D.C.: Catholic University of America Press, 1988.

Schonborn, Christoph Cardinal. *From Death to Life: The Christian Journey*. San Francisco: Ignatius Press, 1995.

Sproul, R. C. *The Last Days according to Jesus: When Did Jesus Say He Would Return?* Grand Rapids, Mich.: Baker Books, 1998.

Von Balthasar, Hans Urs. *A Theology of History*. New York: Sheed and Ward, 1963.

Wright, N. T. *The Millennium Myth: Hope for a Postmodern World*. Louisville, Ky.: Westminster John Knox Press, 1999.

General Works

Abbott, Walter M., S.J., ed. *The Documents of Vatican II*. New York: Guild Press, 1966.

Catechism of the Catholic Church, 2d ed. Libreria Editrice Vaticana. 1997.

Cross, F. L., and E. A. Livingstone, eds. *The Oxford Dictionary of the Christian Church*. 3d ed. Oxford: Oxford University Press. 1997.

Davis, Charles. *Theology for Today*. New York: Sheed and Ward, 1962.

Dupuis, Jacques, S.J., ed. *The Christian Faith in the Doctrinal Documents of the Catholic Church*. 6th ed. Staten Island, N.Y.: Alba House, 1996.

Ferguson, Sinclair B., David F. Wright, and J. I. Packer, eds. *New Dictionary of Theology*. Downers Grove, Ill.: InterVarsity Press, 1988.

Keating, Karl. *Catholicism and Fundamentalism*. San Francisco: Ignatius Press, 1988.

———. *The Usual Suspects: Answering Anti-Catholic Fundamentalists*. San Francisco: Ignatius Press, 2000.

Kelly, J. N. D. *Early Christian Doctrines*. 5th ed. New York: Harper and Row, 1978.

Kreeft, Peter. *Catholic Christianity: A Complete Catechism of Catholic Beliefs Based on the Catechism of the Catholic Church*. San Francisco: Ignatius Press, 2001.

McBrien, Richard P., ed. *Encyclopedia of Catholicism*. San Francisco: HarperCollins, 1995.

Newman, John Henry Cardinal. *The Development of Christian Doctrine*. New York: Longmans, Green, 1949.

Nichols, Aidan. *The Shape of Catholic Theology: An Introduction to Its Sources, Principles, and History*. Collegeville, Minn.: Liturgical Press, 1991.

———. *Epiphany: A Theological Introduction to Catholicism*. Collegeville, Minn.: Liturgical Press, 1996.

O'Collins, Gerald, S.J., and Edward G. Farrugia, S.J. *A Concise Dictionary of Theology*. New York: Paulist Press, 1991.

Ott, Ludwig. *Fundamentals of Catholic Dogma.* Rockford, Ill.: Tan Books, 1974.

Payne, J. Barton. *Encyclopedia of Biblical Prophecy.* New York: Harper and Row, 1973.

Rahner, Karl, and Herbert Vorgrimler. *Theological Dictionary.* 3d ed. New York: Herder and Herder, 1968.

Ratzinger, Joseph. *Introduction to Christianity.* San Francisco: Ignatius Press, 1990.

———. *Principles of Catholic Theology: Building Stones for a Fundamental Theology.* San Francisco: Ignatius Press, 1987.

Stravinskas, Peter M. J., ed. *Our Sunday Visitor's Catholic Encyclopedia.* Huntington, Ind.: Our Sunday Visitor, 1991.

ABBREVIATIONS

ANF   *Ante-Nicene Fathers*, ed. Alexander Roberts and James Donaldson. Peabody, Mass.: Hendrickson Publishers, 1994.

CCC   *Catechism of the Catholic Church*, 2d ed. Vatican City: Libreria Editrice Vaticana, 1997.

DV   Vatican Council II, Dogmatic Constitution on Divine Revelation, *Dei Verbum*, November 18, 1965.

GS   Vatican Council II, Pastoral Constitution on the Church in the Modern World, *Gaudium et Spes*, December 7, 1965.

LG   Vatican Council II, Dogmatic Constitution on the Church, *Lumen Gentium*, November 21, 1964.

NPNF1   *Nicene and Post-Nicene Fathers*, 1st series, ed. Philip Schaff. Peabody, Mass.: Hendrickson Publishers, 1994.

ACKNOWLEDGMENT
OF SOURCES CITED

The author expresses his appreciation for the following permissions.

Quotes from *Are We Living in the End Times?* by Tim LaHaye and Jerry B. Jenkins, copyright © 1999, used by permission of the publisher, Tyndale House Press, Wheaton, Ill.

Quotes from *Fundamentalism and American Culture: The Shaping of Twentieth-Century Evangelicalism*, by George M. Marsden, copyright © 1980, used by permission of the publisher, Oxford University Press, Oxford, England.

Quotes from *Dispensationalism*, by Charles C. Ryrie, copyright © 1995, used by permission of the publisher, Moody Press, Chicago.

Quotes from *The Study of Catholic Theology: An Introduction to Its Sources, Principles, and History*, by Aidan Nichols, copyright © 1991, used by permission of the publisher, Liturgical Press, Collegeville, Minn.

Quotes from *The Last Days Are Here Again: A History of the End Times*, by Richard Kyle, copyright © 1998, used by permission of the publisher, Baker Book House, Grand Rapids, Mich.

Quotes from *Backgrounds to Dispensationalism: Its Historical Genesis and Ecclesiastical Implications,* by Clarence Bass, copyright © 1977, used by permission of the publisher, Baker Book House, Grand Rapids, Mich.